church-sponsored
higher education
in the united states

CHURCH-SPONSORED HIGHER EDUCATION IN THE UNITED STATES

Report of the Danforth Commission

MANNING M. PATTILLO, JR./DONALD M. MACKENZIE

AMERICAN COUNCIL ON EDUCATION, WASHINGTON, D.C.

Preface

In June, 1962, the Board of Trustees of the Danforth Foundation authorized a systematic assessment of church-related higher education in the United States. This segment of the educational system, more than one-third of all the colleges and universities in America with more than one-sixth of the students, had never been studied on a comprehensive basis. Moreover, these institutions have had persistent problems in defining their role and obtaining adequate financial support. The existing scholarly literature on the subject was too limited to provide much help.

It seemed logical that the Danforth Foundation should sponsor such a project. The Foundation has always been primarily interested in the improvement of liberal education, and the church-affiliated institutions constitute a majority of the liberal arts colleges of the country. It was the hope of the Trustees that the recommendations resulting from the study would have a constructive effect on the future planning of institutions of this type.

The inquiry was to deal with the basic problems of colleges and universities associated with both Christian and Jewish religious bodies. The conclusions were to be published in readable form. The principal questions to which the study was to be addressed were:

1. What have been the most influential forces and ideas, academic and religious, that have shaped the church-sponsored institutions of higher education in the United States?

2. What are the essential facts concerning their students, graduates, faculties, curricula, facilities, government (including the forms of relationship with churches), financing, and educational results?

3. What are their major points of strength and weakness and their most important contributions to American education?

4. What should be their distinctive roles as academic and religious institutions in our predominantly secular culture and educational system?

5. What courses of action can be recommended for their sound development in the years ahead?

The study employed a variety of methods of investigation. Questionnaires, legal and historical documents, interviews, statistical analyses, testing of students, group discussions, and personal inspection (for example, of physical facilities) were used, where appropriate, as means of gathering facts and interpreting them. Heavy emphasis was placed on detailed case studies of 50 representative colleges and universities in 29 states and the District of Columbia. We also visited 116 other institutions in the course of the project. We interviewed hundreds of administrators, trustees, faculty members, students, and church officials. About 30 technical consultants were employed from time to time as needed.

Early in the project the Danforth Commission on Church Colleges and Universities, a group of distinguished educators and churchmen, was appointed to provide expert guidance. We express our deep appreciation to the members of the Commission for their invaluable contributions. The Commission was composed of the following persons (with their titles at the time of appointment):

Virgil M. Hancher, President, University of Iowa (Chairman)[1]

Ernest C. Colwell, President, School of Theology at Claremont (Acting Chairman)

Oliver C. Carmichael, Consultant, Fund for the Advancement of Education and the Ford Foundation

Merrimon Cuninggim, Executive Director, Danforth Foundation

Theodore A. Distler, President, Association of American Colleges

James M. Godard, President, Council of Protestant Colleges and Universities

Arthur C. Lichtenberger, Presiding Bishop of the Episcopal Church

Howard F. Lowry, President, College of Wooster, and Trustee, Danforth Foundation

Paul C. Reinert, S.J., President, St. Louis University.

Much of the last year of the project was devoted to efforts to disseminate the findings and recommendations and to discuss them with interested groups. To this end, the Commission sponsored regional conferences in eleven major cities across the country in the spring of 1965, which were attended by more than 1,400 representatives of 600 institutions. In attendance were trustees, presidents, other administrative officers, faculty members, church officials, and

[1] Deceased January 30, 1965.

officials of various educational organizations. A preliminary report, prepared in advance of these conferences, was used intensively in discussions of the tentative recommendations that had been drafted. In addition, members of the Commission and the authors spoke to dozens of local, regional, national, and international groups responsible for policy determination in colleges and universities. We also served as consultants to many institutions and several church boards of higher education. All of this provided excellent opportunities to test the ideas and conclusions advanced before the publication of this report.

It will become clear, we believe, that the most basic problem of church-sponsored higher education is, in a very real sense, theological. The shifting sands of religious faith today provide an uncertain foundation for religiously oriented educational programs. Our proposals for action do not—indeed, cannot—solve this central problem. There is no way to manufacture agreement on fundamental questions. What we have tried to do is to present, as distinctly as possible, the theological dilemma the church-affiliated institutions of higher education face today. In this, every effort has been made to avoid partisanship or sectarianism throughout all phases of the study. This, we trust, is the best that anyone can do to illuminate a problem which appears insoluble in the immediate future.

We are grateful to the trustees of the Foundation for their generous support of the project. We acknowledge the part played by Merrimon Cuninggim in bringing the need for such an inquiry to the attention of the trustees initially and in interesting us in undertaking it.

It is impossible to acknowledge properly the contributions of information, thought, and time made by all of the individuals who assisted in this study. About 5,200 people—college administrators, trustees, faculty members, students, church officials, and others—have helped in one way or another. Administrative officers in all 1,189 private colleges and universities kindly answered a questionnaire about the relationships, if any, of their institutions with religious bodies. Hundreds of staff members in the 50 colleges and universities selected for case studies gave generously of their time during our visits. The following are some of the persons to whom we are especially indebted:[2]

[2] Titles shown are those held at the time of assistance to the study.

A. K. Adlington, Vice President, Finance, University of Waterloo, Waterloo, Ontario, Canada

Arthur M. Ahlschwede, Executive Secretary, Board for Higher Education, Lutheran Church-Missouri Synod

Wallace M. Alston, President, Agnes Scott College

Chester M. Alter, Chancellor, University of Denver

David K. Andrews, President, Principia College

George H. Armacost, President, University of Redlands

Sanford S. Atwood, President, Emory University

Mary Aurelia, President, Rosary College

E. Theodore Bachmann, Executive Secretary, Board of Higher Education, Lutheran Church in America

Henry G. Badger, retired, United States Office of Education

James O. Baird, President, Oklahoma Christian College

Samuel Belkin, President, Yeshiva University

Howard C. Bennett, President, East Texas Baptist College

Daniel Bernian, F.S.C., President, LaSalle College

Lloyd M. Bertholf, President, Illinois Wesleyan University

Robert W. Bertram, Associate Professor of Historical and Systematic Theology, Concordia Seminary

Gordon W. Blackwell, President, Furman University

Hunter B. Blakely, Secretary, Division of Higher Education, Board of Christian Education, Presbyterian Church in the United States

Landrum R. Bolling, President, Earlham College

Hugh Borton, President, Haverford College

Rabun L. Brantley, Executive Secretary, Education Commission, Southern Baptist Convention

J. Lawrence Burkholder, Victor S. Thomas Professor of Divinity, Harvard Divinity School

Norman Burns, Executive Secretary, North Central Association of Colleges and Secondary Schools

Daniel Callahan, Associate Editor, *The Commonweal*

Tollie L. Caution, Associate Secretary, Home Department, National Council, Protestant Episcopal Church

John B. Cobb, Jr., Ingraham Memorial Professor of Theology, School of Theology at Claremont

William G. Cole, President, Lake Forest College

William H. Conley, Director, Study of Catholic Education, University of Notre Dame; President, Sacred Heart University

C. Eugene Conover, Dean of the Chapel and Chairman, Department of Philosophy and Religion, Lindenwood College

Bernard J. Cooke, S.J., Chairman, Department of Theology, Marquette University

Arthur G. Coons, President, Occidental College

Donald A. Cowan, President, University of Dallas

John Crocker, Headmaster, Groton School

Frank Cunningham, President, Morris Brown College

John L. Davis, President, Chapman College

Paul L. Dressel, Director, Office of Institutional Research, Michigan State University

Edward J. Drummond, S.J., Vice President for the Medical Center, St. Louis University

Frank E. Duddy, Jr., President, Westminster College, Salt Lake City, Utah

William J. Dunne, S.J., Associate Secretary, College and University Department, National Catholic Educational Association

Ruth E. Eckert, Professor of Higher Education, University of Minnesota

V. Raymond Edman, President, Wheaton College, Wheaton, Illinois

A. Randle Elliott, President, Hood College

E. D. Farwell, President, Luther College

Brother Fidelian of Mary, F.S.C., Vice-President, Academic Affairs, LaSalle College

Norman Fintell, Assistant Director, Board of College Education, American Lutheran Church

James Forrester, President, Gordon College

Luther A. Foster, President, Hannibal-LaGrange College

Thomas M. Freeman, Office of Institutional Research, Michigan State University

Francis C. Gamelin, Secretary of College Education, Lutheran Church in America

Hallie G. Gantz, President, Phillips University

Edward D. Gates, President, Beaver College

Wayne F. Geisert, President, Bridgewater College

Paul H. Giddens, President, Hamline University

Brother Gregory, F.S.C., President, Manhattan College

John O. Gross, General Secretary, Division of Higher Education, Board of Education, The Methodist Church

James M. Gustafson, Professor of Christian Ethics, Yale Divinity School

Arno Gustin, O.S.B., President, St. John's University, Collegeville, Minnesota

Richard Hammill, Associate Secretary, Department of Education, General Conference of Seventh-day Adventists; President, Andrews University

Kyle E. Haselden, Editor, *The Christian Century*

Harold A. Haswell, Director, Higher Education Programs Branch, United States Office of Education

A. A. Heckman, Secretary and Executive Director, Louis W. and Maud Hill Family Foundation

Eileen Marie Heckman, S.L., President, Loretto Heights College

David K. Heenan, Office of Evaluation Services, Michigan State University

Fred Helsabeck, President, Culver-Stockton College

John W. Henderson, President, Iowa Wesleyan College

Carl F. H. Henry, Editor, *Christianity Today*

Weimer K. Hicks, President, Kalamazoo College

Frederick G. Hochwalt, Executive Secretary, National Catholic Educational Association

John E. Horner, President, Hanover College

Alfred F. Horrigan, President, Bellarmine College

Wesley A. Hotchkiss, General Secretary, Division of Higher Education and the American Missionary Association, United Church Board for Homeland Ministries, United Church of Christ

John R. Howard, President, Lewis and Clark College

Mary Ann Ida, B.V.M., President, Mundelein College

Albert C. Jacobs, President, Trinity College, Hartford, Connecticut

W. Theophil Janzow, President, Concordia Teachers College, Seward, Nebraska

Helen James John, S.M.D., Associate Professor of Philosophy, Trinity College, Washington, D.C.

Esther L. Johnson, Associate Professor of Philosophy and Religion, Lindenwood College

Bob Jones, Jr., President, Bob Jones University

Thomas E. Jones, President Emeritus, Earlham College; Administrative Consultant, Association of American Colleges

Marvin C. Josephson, Director, American Church Institute for Negroes, National Council, Protestant Episcopal Church

William F. Kelley, S.J., President, Marquette University

Perry F. Kendig, President, Roanoke College

Reamer Kline, President, Bard College

Warren B. Knox, President, College of Idaho

Clarence Laplante, O.F.M., President, St. Francis College, Biddeford, Maine

James W. Laurie, President, Trinity University

William S. Litterick, President, Keuka College

Jerome J. Marchetti, S.J., Executive Vice President, St. Louis University

Benjamin E. Mays, President, Morehouse College; Trustee, The Danforth Foundation

Paul M. McCain, President, Arkansas College

Abner V. McCall, President, Baylor University

Agnes Geraldine McCann, S.C.N., President, Nazareth College

William J. McDonald, Rector, Catholic University of America

James J. McGinley, S.J., President, Canisius College

James F. Meara, S.J., Director, Department of Religion, St. Louis University

James C. Messersmith, Specialist, State and Regional Organization, Division of Higher Education, United States Office of Education

Allen O. Miller, Professor of Systematic Theology, Eden Theological Seminary

Elmer G. Million, Director, Department of Schools and Colleges, Board of Education and Publication, American Baptist Convention

Clyde A. Milner, President, Guilford College

Paul Mininger, President, Goshen College

Ansley C. Moore, President, St. Andrews Presbyterian College

Robert A. L. Mortvedt, President, Pacific Lutheran University

John D. Moseley, President, Austin College

John W. Nason, President, Carleton College; Trustee, The Danforth Foundation

Martin J. Neeb, President, Concordia Senior College

Vernon Neufeld, President, Bethel College, North Newton, Kansas

Eleanor M. O'Byrne, R.S.C.J., President, Manhattanville College of the Sacred Heart

Raymond M. Olson, President, California Lutheran College

Robert H. Parker, President, Wesley College

Mary Patrick, O.P., President, Dominican College of San Rafael

Allan O. Pfnister, Dean of the College, Wittenberg University

Fred O. Pinkham, President, Ripon College

John L. Plyler, President, Furman University

William A. Poehler, President, Concordia College, St. Paul, Minnesota

Stafford Poole, C.M., Dean, St. Mary's Seminary, Perryville, Missouri

Earl V. Pullias, Professor of Higher Education, University of Southern California

Royal M. Puryear, President, Florida Memorial College

Sidney A. Rand, Executive Director, Board of College Education, American Lutheran Church; President, St. Olaf College

Robert Rankin, Associate Director, The Danforth Foundation

Robert G. Rayburn, President, Covenant College

Harvey M. Rice, President, Macalester College

Miller A. F. Ritchie, President, Pacific University

Millard G. Roberts, President, Parsons College

Edward B. Rooney, S.J., President, Jesuit Educational Association

John H. Russel, Specialist, College and University Organization, Division of Higher Education, United States Office of Education

William G. Ryan, President, Seton Hill College

M. E. Sadler, Chancellor, Texas Christian University

Rose Maureen Sanders, President and Dean, Loretto Junior College

Samuel Sandmel, Provost, Hebrew Union College

William H. Schecter, President, Tarkio College

Bruno P. Schlesinger, Chairman, Program for Christian Culture, St. Mary's College, Notre Dame, Indiana

M. Viatora Schuller, O.S.F., President, College of St. Joseph on the Rio Grande

William K. Selden, Executive Director, National Commission on Accrediting

Andrew C. Smith, S.J., President, Loyola University, New Orleans, Louisiana

G. Herbert Smith, President, Willamette University

Harlie L. Smith, President, Board of Higher Education, Disciples of Christ

Tilman R. Smith, President, Hesston College

Edward V. Stanford, O.S.A., Administrative Consultant, Association of American Colleges

Guy E. Snavely, Chancellor, Birmingham-Southern College; formerly Executive Director, Association of American Colleges

John N. Stauffer, President, Wittenberg University

Gordon W. Sweet, Executive Secretary, Commission on Colleges, Southern Association of Colleges and Schools

James W. Swift, Assistant Director, The Danforth Foundation

Raymond J. Swords, S.J., President, College of the Holy Cross

William W. Thomas, Assistant Professor of Philosophy and Religion, Lindenwood College

Donald M. Typer, President, Doane College

Kenneth Underwood, Director, Danforth Study of Campus Ministries

Mother Ursula, M.S.C., President, Cabrini College

Harold H. Viehman, Secretary, General Division of Higher Education, Board of Christian Education, United Presbyterian Church in the U.S.A.

Paul E. Waldschmidt, C.S.C., President, University of Portland

Michael P. Walsh, S.J., President, Boston College

Ann Patrick Ware, S.L., Chairman, Department of Theology, Webster College

Lionel A. Whiston, Jr., Professor of Old Testament, Eden Theological Seminary

Goodrich C. White, Chancellor, Emory University; Administrative Consultant, Association of American Colleges

Myron F. Wicke, Associate General Secretary, Division of Higher Education, Board of Education, The Methodist Church

Gould Wickey, Executive Director, National Lutheran Educational Conference

Terry Wickham, President, Heidelberg College

Philip M. Widenhouse, President, Rocky Mountain College

Ernest L. Wilkinson, President, Brigham Young University

Daniel Day Williams, Roosevelt Professor of Systematic Theology, Union Theological Seminary

John Page Williams, Dean of Church Schools, Episcopal Diocese of Virginia

Gordon Duncan Wimpress, President, Monmouth College

Stephen J. Wright, President, Fisk University

Louis C. Zahner, Retired Master, Groton School

We wish to pay special tribute to three other persons without whose assistance the study could not have been completed: Marjorie Stauss, who served as secretary to the staff and Commission for the entire period of three and one-half years; Horace G. Rountree, who so expertly edited the manuscripts of the preliminary and final reports; and Evelyn Chambers, who did most of the typing.

We are greatly indebted to Jane P. Newman, of the American Council on Education, for her remarkable patience and expert guidance during the process of publication.

Manning M. Pattillo, Jr.
Donald M. Mackenzie

September 1, 1966

Contents

Preface   v

List of Tables   xvii

1. The Church Institution in the History of American Higher Education   1

2. Dimensions of Church-Sponsored Higher Education   18

3. Relationships with Religious Bodies   30

4. What Makes a Good College?   54

5. Freedom, Responsibility, and Institutional Purpose   70

6. An Academic Evaluation of the Institutions   76

7. Studies of College Graduates   102

8. Religion in America: Background of Church-Sponsored Higher Education   124

9. A Religious Evaluation of the Institutions   137

10. Faculty Evaluations of Church-Sponsored Colleges and Universities   155

11. Significant Innovation and Experimentation   177

12. Patterns of Institutional Character   191

13. Conclusions and Recommendations   198

Appendices

A. Questionnaire on Relationships with Religious Bodies   215

B. List of Fifty Case-Study Institutions   217

C. Procedure for Institutional Self-Study   219

D. American Colleges and Universities Associated with Religious Bodies   230

E. National Church Agencies for Higher Education   249

Bibliography   279

Index   297

List of Tables

1. Religious Bodies Represented among the 817 Institutions 21

2. Distribution by Type of Student Body 22

3. Distribution by Accrediting Association Membership 23

4. Distribution by Type of Program 24

5. Distribution of Five Groups by Type of Student Body 25

6. Distribution of Five Groups by Accrediting Association Membership 25

7. Distribution of Five Groups by Type of Program 26

8. Number of Different Elements of Relationships to Religious Bodies Reported by Individual Institutions 32

9. Number of Different Elements of Relationships to Religious Bodies Reported by Individual Institutions in Seven Groups . . . 33

10. Number of Institutions Reporting Each Element of Relationship 34

11. Number of Institutions in Seven Groups Reporting Each Kind of Relationship to Religious Body 35

12. Church Membership as a Requirement for Election to Board . . . 36

13. Church Membership as a Requirement for Election to Board (by Seven Groups of Institutions) 37

14. Church Nomination or Election of Board Members 38

15. Church Nomination or Election of Board Members (by Seven Groups of Institutions) 39

16. Church Nomination or Election of Board Members in Absence of Church Membership Requirement 40

17. Church Nomination or Election of Board Members in Absence of Church Membership Requirement (by Seven Groups of Institutions) 41

18. Percentage of Educational and General Income Received from Church Sources 43

19. Percentage of Educational and General Income Received from Church Sources (by Seven Groups of Institutions) 44

20. Percentage of Educational and General Income of Roman Catholic Institutions Received in Contributed Services 45

21. Extent to Which "Substantial" Capital Funds Are Received from Official Church Sources 46

22. Current and Capital Income of Representative Institutions 82

23. Indebtedness of Representative Institutions 83

24. Plant Expenditures of Representative Institutions 83

25. Faculty Data for Representative Institutions 86

26. Estimates of Student Academic Ability in Representative Institutions 89

27. Composition of Student Bodies in Representative Institutions .. 91

28. Class Size in Representative Institutions 95

29. Library Data for Representative Institutions 96

30. Highest Ranking Institutions in Production of Younger Scholars, 1946-51 103

31. Undergraduate Colleges with the Highest Percentage of Male Graduates Receiving M.D. Degrees, 1950-59 105

32. Highest Ranking Institutions in Production of College Teachers, as of 1955 109

33. Colleges and Universities with 100 or More Graduates Attending Theological Schools, Fall 1962 111

34. Colleges and Universities with Highest Indices of Graduates Attending Theological Schools, 1960-61 113

35. Colleges and Universities with Five or More Graduates Elected Danforth Fellows, 1952-62 115

36. Colleges and Universities with Ten or More Graduates Appointed Woodrow Wilson Fellows, 1945-60 117

37. Course Requirements in Religion in 196 Church-Sponsored Institutions 141

38. Freshman and Senior Performance on Test of Religious Knowledge According to Groups of Institutions.................... 145

39. Number of Courses in Religion Completed by Students Taking Test According to Groups of Institutions.................... 145

40. Performance of Freshmen with Public and Private School Backgrounds on Portion of Test Common to Roman Catholic and Protestant Versions.. 146

41. Performance of Men and Women on Portion of Test Common to Roman Catholic and Protestant Versions................ 146

42. Performance on Common Portion of Test and Number of Courses in Religion Completed by Seniors According to Major Field 146

43. Performance of Seniors and Freshmen on Common Portion of Test According to Religious Preference.................... 147

1

The Church Institution
in the History
of American
Higher Education

One of the most illuminating ways to assess the status of the church-affiliated college and university today is to review the evolution of American higher education over the last three hundred years, taking special note of those influences which have affected its purposes and philosophy. How did we reach our present position? What have been the events and the ideas that have shaped academic institutions in the United States?

Although, as we shall see, colleges and universities associated with churches differ in many respects (they do, in fact, give American higher education much of its cherished diversity), they have certain characteristics in common. Most of them are colleges of the liberal arts and sciences or have liberal education as their core. They have a churchly or religious dimension. They are private in control and basically private in support. We shall see that developments in higher education, in general, have had an impact on the church-affiliated institutions affecting all three of these aspects.

In 1619, when Sir Edwin Sandys and his associates in the Virginia Company made a grant of 10,000 acres of land for the establishment of America's first university, at Henrico, Virginia, they brought to the task a concept of education which, in its essentials, had stood the test of some fifteen centuries.[1] Theirs was a tradition of liberal education which had come down from the fifth century through the palace

[1] Christopher Dawson, *The Crisis of Western Education* (New York: Sheed and Ward, 1961), pp. 9-12.

1

schools and the monastic and cathedral schools to the medieval universities, on to the seventeenth-century colleges at Oxford and Cambridge and the Scottish universities.[2] It combined classical learning and the Christian religion, the aim being to cultivate the humane person. It was a broad and general education emphasizing the arts of thought and communication and the principles which should govern personal and public affairs. Little did our forefathers in Virginia realize that this time-honored concept would be transformed by the powerful educational solvents of the next three centuries.

The ambitious plans at Henrico, interrupted by malaria and an Indian massacre in 1622, came to nought until 1693 when the College of William and Mary was founded as an Anglican institution at Williamsburg.[3] Puritan efforts, meanwhile, had resulted in the establishment of Harvard College in 1636, patterned after Emmanuel College, Cambridge University. The Harvard mottoes were "Christo et Ecclesiae" and "In Christi Gloriam." [4] The well-known statement of the purposes of America's first college reflects the religious motivation of all of the colonial institutions:

After God had carried us safe to *New England,* and we had builded our houses, provided necessaries for our livelihood, rear'd convenient places for Gods worship, and setled the Civill Government: One of the next things we longed for, and looked after was to advance *Learning,* and perpetuate it to Posterity, dreading to leave an illiterate ministry to the Churches, when our present Ministers shall lie in the Dust.[5]

It is important to observe that, although the founders of Harvard had in mind education for the ministry, the curriculum was broadly conceived along the lines of the ancient tradition of liberal education and was intended for leaders in other fields as well.[6]

In the 134 years following the establishment of Harvard, eight

[2] An informative treatment of the medieval curriculum may be found in Charles Homer Haskins, *The Rise of Universities* (Ithaca: Cornell University Press, 1957). The author discusses the seven liberal arts (grammar, rhetoric, logic, arithmetic, geometry, astronomy, and music) on pages 27-34.

[3] Herbert B. Adams, *The College of William and Mary.* Circulars of Information of the Bureau of Education, No. 1 (Washington: Government Printing Office, 1887), pp. 14-15.

[4] Samuel Eliot Morison, *The Founding of Harvard College* (Cambridge: Harvard University Press, 1935), pp. 250, 330.

[5] *New England's First Fruits.* Old South Leaflets, Vol. III, No. 51 (Boston: Directors of the Old South Work, n.d.), p. 1.

[6] John S. Brubacher and Willis Rudy, *Higher Education in Transition, An American History: 1636-1956* (New York: Harper & Brothers, 1958), p. 6.

other colleges, in addition to William and Mary, were organized—
Yale, Princeton, Pennsylvania, Washington and Lee, Columbia,
Brown, Rutgers, and Dartmouth. All of these institutions were
strongly religious in tone and curriculum, although not all were
sponsored by individual denominations. They followed a fairly uni-
form pattern of classical learning—a curriculum largely prescribed including Greek and Latin languages and literature, philosophy, religion, mathematics, and some science.[7]

The University of Pennsylvania is generally considered to be the
first American college not directly connected with a church. However,
at least two of the colonial colleges were ecumenical in their control.
King's College, now Columbia University, though initiated by Anglicans at Trinity Church, had a board whose membership included not
only Anglicans but also laymen and ministers of the Dutch, Presbyterian, and Lutheran churches.[8] Likewise the original charter of
Brown University provided for Baptist, Friends, Congregational, and
Episcopal trustees. It was required that the President be a Baptist,
but the professors could be members of other churches.[9] The royal
charter of William and Mary had certain interesting provisions with
respect to governmental relationships. The faculty of the College
was authorized to elect two members of the Virginia House of Bur-
gesses, and, in accordance with a medieval-university custom, the
faculty was exempt from taxation.[10] The Rutgers board included the
Governor, three other state officials of the Province of New Jersey,
13 ministers and 24 laymen.[11] As Frederick Rudolph has pointed out,
several other colonial colleges had definite ties with state government,
so that "whether they should be thought of as state colleges or as
church colleges is a problem in semantics that is perhaps best re-
solved by calling them state-church colleges."[12] It is surprising that
the small and simply organized colleges of the colonial period ex-

[7] *Ibid.*, p. 14.
[8] *A History of Columbia University, 1754-1904.* Prepared by a committee under the
chairmanship of Brander Matthews (New York: Columbia University Press, 1904),
pp. 7-8.
[9] Walter C. Bronson, *The History of Brown University, 1764-1914* (Providence:
Brown University, 1914), pp. 502-3.
[10] Brubacher and Rudy, *op. cit.*, p. 33.
[11] William H. S. Demarest, *A History of Rutgers College, 1766-1924* (New Brunswick, New Jersey: Rutgers College, 1924), pp. 58, 61-62.
[12] Frederick Rudolph, *The American College and University, A History* (New
York: Alfred A. Knopf, 1962), p. 13.

hibited such a variety of board membership and relationships with church and state. However, in every case the strongly religious character of collegiate education was apparent, and in general the traditional curriculum was maintained. It was the most stable period in the history of American higher education.

What of the early state universities that were established in the late eighteenth century and the first half of the nineteenth century? What kind of education programs did they offer? Walton E. Bean, historian of the state university, describes their character as follows:

The early "state universities" differed very little from the many private denominational institutions that were also founded on the pattern of the colonial colleges. The early American college curriculum, with its core in the classics of Greek, Latin, and Hebrew literature, had been designed for the training of ministers and gentlemen in an aristocratic society. The early state universities simply imitated this "literary" and "classical" college pattern, which remained almost static until after the middle of the nineteenth century.[13]

Many of these early state universities had ministers as presidents and required their students to attend chapel and take courses in religion. Several of the state universities, especially in the South and Middle West, had been started through church efforts. For example, the University of Michigan was organized as a result of the initiative of a judge and two clergymen.[14] The commonly accepted point of view of the times was well expressed in a famous paragraph from the Ordinance of 1787, which created the Northwest Territory and was often quoted in justification of public higher education.

Religion, morality, and knowledge being necessary to good government and the happiness of mankind, schools and the means of education shall forever be encouraged.[15]

In 1789 Georgetown University, the first Roman Catholic institution of higher education in the United States, was established, followed in 1808 by Mt. St. Mary's College, Emmitsburg, Maryland,

[13] Walton E. Bean, "What is the State University?" in *Religion and the State University*, ed. by Erich A. Walter (Ann Arbor, Michigan: University of Michigan Press, 1958), pp. 60-61. (©1958 by University of Michigan Press. Permission to quote granted.)

[14] Christian Gauss (ed.), *The Teaching of Religion in American Higher Education* (New York: Ronald Press Company, 1951), pp. 4-7.

[15] Algo D. Henderson, *Policies and Practices in Higher Education* (New York: Harper & Brothers, 1960), p. 85.

and in 1818 by St. Louis University, the first university west of the Mississippi River. This was the beginning of a new group of church institutions which was not, however, to expand greatly until the last half of the nineteenth century. Roman Catholic higher education for women, which began with the establishment of the College of Notre Dame of Maryland in 1896, is largely a product of the twentieth century.[16]

The decision of the Supreme Court in the Dartmouth College case in 1819, which assured private institutions of freedom from state interference, gave impetus to the establishment of many new liberal arts colleges. By the time of the Civil War, 516 colleges had been founded in 16 of the 34 states, most of them under church sponsorship.[17] Many of these institutions, especially in the South, did not survive the difficult times of the Civil War.

In our day of large, well-equipped institutions of higher education we are inclined to regard the simple colleges of the pre-Civil War period as weak and educationally limited. In some respects they were, but it is well to remind ourselves that they had their virtues, too. The historians Richard Hofstadter and Walter Metzger, writing of the old-fashioned college, have this to say:

Men of considerable intellectual distinction came in reasonable numbers from its halls. It tried seriously to cultivate both the minds and the characters of its students. Its classical curriculum exposed them to great writers, great ideas, and fine expression. It encouraged articulate writing and thinking, and indicated that these abilities were to be put to work in civic as well as private affairs. It introduced its students to the problems of philosophy and theology. By inculcating serious application to mental, if not always intellectual, work, it does seem to have bred in its students a capacity for persistence and effort that modern education frequently fails to produce.[18]

Two other eminent American historians, Samuel Eliot Morison and Henry Steele Commager, praising the work of the colleges of the period 1825-1850, make the following statement, which, though

[16] Edward J. Power, A History of Catholic Higher Education in the United States (Milwaukee: Bruce Publishing Company, 1958), pp. 28-48.

[17] Donald G. Tewksbury, The Founding of American Colleges and Universities Before the Civil War (New York: Bureau of Publications, Teachers College, Columbia University, 1932), p. 90.

[18] Richard Hofstadter and Walter P. Metzger, The Development of Academic Freedom in the United States (New York: Columbia University Press, 1955), p. 227.

probably somewhat romanticized, suggests the points of strength in these institutions:

For an integrated education, one that cultivates manliness and makes gentlemen as well as scholars, one that disciplines the social affections and trains young men to faith in God, consideration for his fellow men, and respect for learning, America has never had the equal of her little hill-top colleges.[19]

In this manner the ancient tradition of humanistic education, combining classical learning and the Christian religion, was firmly rooted in American private and public institutions alike from the very earliest times.

Meanwhile, in England, where inroads of secular thought were already being felt in the universities, a controversial churchman and educator was writing a definitive statement on liberal education. In superb English prose, John Henry Newman delivered, in 1852, the lectures which were later published under the title *The Idea of a University*. Basing his work on the Oxford he had known as a student a quarter of a century earlier, Newman argued for a liberal education in which the cultivation of the intellect would be the primary purpose; a knowledge of first principles and relations rather than mere facts would be the aim. Religious studies were to occupy a prominent place in the curriculum. Newman spoke of "Liberal or Philosophical Knowledge," by which he meant an understanding of "the great outlines of knowledge, the principles on which it rests, the scale of its parts, its lights and its shades, its great points and its little . . ." [20] In a time of skepticism, Newman was advocating a kind of education that placed an emphasis on precise thought, in the philosophical sense, and on the aggressive defense of traditional Christianity in intellectual terms. Though the church college he had been called to establish—the Catholic University in Dublin—never materialized, his lectures stand as perhaps the most convincing argument for such an institution. *The Idea of a University* has had an extraordinary

[19] Samuel Eliot Morison and Henry Steele Commager, *The Growth of the American Republic* (New York: Oxford University Press, 1950), p. 514.

[20] John Henry Cardinal Newman, *The Idea of a University* (New York: Doubleday & Company, Inc., 1959), p. 129.
It may be observed that, in its secular dimension, Newman's definition of liberal education has striking similarities to some of the ideas developed in the "general education movement" of the mid-twentieth century in American colleges. For a valuable history of this movement see Russell Thomas, *The Search for a Common Learning: General Education 1800-1960* (New York: McGraw-Hill Book Company, 1962).

influence on American liberal arts colleges, and even today, when undergraduate education has lost much of the substance of what Newman was advocating, some of his concepts are often appealed to in educational discourse. The verbal justification of liberal education in the United States still reflects, in large measure, his analysis and that of his British contemporaries.

In this connection, Thomas Arnold, Headmaster of Rugby from 1828 to 1842, should be mentioned. Arnold is generally credited with having transformed the English public schools through the influence of his work at Rugby. Primarily a priest, teacher, and administrator, not a theoretician, Arnold made few changes in the formal curriculum but, rather, used the existing structure of liberal education at the secondary-school level as a medium for inculcating a new sense of moral responsibility based on religious conviction. The impact of his ideas on British public life is probably unparalleled. Arnold's contribution has significance to American education because the public school in England plays, in some respects, a role similar to that of the liberal arts college in the United States.

One of the classic statements on liberal education came from the pen of John Stuart Mill, English philosopher and economist, writing a few years after Newman's lectures. The following passage has often been cited for its essential fidelity to the liberal arts ideal:

> Men are men before they are lawyers, or physicians, or merchants, or manufacturers; and if you make them capable and sensible men, they will make themselves capable and sensible lawyers or physicians. What professional men should carry away with them from a university is not professional knowledge, but that which should direct the use of professional knowledge, and bring the light of general culture to illuminate the technicalities of a special pursuit. Men may be competent lawyers without general education, but it depends on general education to make them philosophic lawyers.[21]

Newman's pronouncements on university education were intended to combat the growth of secularism and religious "liberalism" (as he called it) in Great Britain. The seventeenth and eighteenth centuries had been a period of questioning and controversy in theological, political, and economic thought, and the new ideas which had

[21] From "Inaugural Address" delivered at the University of St. Andrews, February 1, 1867.

been gaining ascendancy were soon to produce quite basic modifications in higher education.

The curriculum of the American college changed little from 1636 to the Civil War. Although, on a limited scale, new subjects had been introduced into the liberal arts curriculum, and a few specialized schools of engineering, theology, agriculture, medicine, and law had been organized, these developments had not influenced the main stream of collegiate education. By the end of the eighteenth century, however, the dominant beliefs and values of the early colonial period were being seriously challenged. The crosscurrents of thought that had swept over Western Europe were affecting America. Orthodox Christianity was struggling to hold its own against secular doctrines and interests. The philosophies of the Enlightenment (rationalism, deism, naturalism, empiricism, humanitarianism, and others) were being strongly felt in intellectual circles. The scientific investigations which had begun in the fifteenth century were raising insistent questions in philosophy and theology. Proponents of the scientific approach to knowledge were attacking the deductive methods of classical philosophy. The ideas of Descartes, Bacon, Hobbes, Locke, Rousseau, and Adam Smith were very much in the air. A new industrial and mercantile outlook was developing rapidly. All of these influences were placing an unbearable strain on the curriculum of the traditional college of liberal arts.[22]

The passage of the Morrill Act in 1862, by which Congress endowed colleges of agriculture and mechanical arts in the various states, was a landmark in the history of American education (though uncelebrated at the time). The significance of the land-grant college thus established was two-fold. It broke radically with the historic pattern of liberal education. It gave a new impetus to public higher education. The curriculum emphasized the "practical" branches of knowledge. The University of Pennsylvania and Brown University had paid modest attention to vocational studies at an earlier time, but it was the founding of Cornell University in 1865 which really marked the beginning of the revolutionary changes that were to take place in

[22] An excellent account of the intellectual tensions of this period is provided in R. Freeman Butts and Laurence A. Cremin, A History of Education in American Culture (New York: Holt, Rinehart and Winston, 1953), pp. 43-63. See also, for an analysis of secularism, Howard Lowry, The Mind's Adventure (Philadelphia: Westminster Press, 1950), pp. 20-33.

the years ahead. Cornell was to be the prototype of the frankly secular university geared to the emerging industrial society. It was to produce men and women technically trained to take their places in the agricultural and industrial life of the country, without benefit of liberal education. "I would found an institution," said Ezra Cornell, "in which any person can find instruction in any study." [23] The acceptance of this conception of higher education across the United States, especially by public institutions, has had far-reaching effects on our whole educational system. Undoubtedly it has made possible a rapidity of industrial progress which never could have been sustained by liberal arts colleges or by private education. And, in their field, the land-grant institutions have been the models for the world.

Another influence, which has been even more pervasive, was the importation of the German university idea in the last quarter of the nineteenth century, dramatized by the founding, in 1876, of Johns Hopkins University. Until this time, American universities had been undergraduate colleges with modest graduate and professional programs appended. But, consciously modelled on the great universities of Heidelberg, Göttingen, Leipzig, and Berlin, the new Johns Hopkins gave priority to graduate study leading to the Ph.D. degree and to faculty research. From the very beginning the teaching of undergraduates was a distinctly secondary function. (As a matter of fact, the organization of an undergraduate program was not undertaken immediately; it came almost as an afterthought.) The Ph.D. requirements reflected the scientific, technical, and specialized notion of scholarship which had made the German universities the greatest in the world.

Other universities soon followed the Johns Hopkins model. Hopkins graduates and faculty members were aggressively sought by universities throughout the country. A revolutionary change was under way in American higher education. Clark, Chicago, and Stanford were established in much the same way as Hopkins and with a similar philosophy. Harvard, Columbia, Yale, Pennsylvania, Michigan, Wisconsin, and other major universities joined the movement by superimposing strong graduate schools on undergraduate colleges.

[23] Richard Hofstadter and C. DeWitt Hardy, *The Development and Scope of Higher Education in the United States* (New York: Columbia University Press, 1952), p. 37.

Thus two traditions—the British collegiate heritage and the German university idea—were conjoined in the new American university. This marriage was to have far-reaching results. There can be no question that the research emphasis imported from Germany, and now thoroughly embedded in the American university, has engendered a scholarly rigor and an objectivity that were lacking in classical education. A critical spirit of inquiry has been nurtured. Nothing is immune from investigation. There is to be no orthodoxy except the doctrine of the right to pursue the truth. Implicit in the research tradition is a commitment to freedom as a necessary condition of scholarship, and, by and large, our better universities have a good record of protecting their faculties from improper invasions of teaching and research. The priority given to investigation has resulted in an amazing increase of knowledge, particularly in the sciences. These are important contributions directly attributable to the modern university. They are cultural and educational innovations of the first order.

They have not been unmixed blessings, however. The German university tradition of the nineteenth century carried with it certain assumptions about scholarship which have played havoc in American education. Scholarship was conceived in technical, almost pedantic, terms. The emphasis was on factual knowledge rather than on broader meaning. It must be granted by the most charitable observer of the academic scene that this notion of research has led to an enormous amount of pretentious busy work in our universities. As Oliver Carmichael pointed out, the different varieties of graduate degrees, especially professional degrees, have multiplied almost to the point of absurdity. No less than 150 different master's degrees and 68 doctorates are being conferred by American universities! How can one defend the degrees of Master of Science in Public Health Engineering (M.S.P.H.E.) and Master of Science in Ornamental Horticulture (M.S. Orn. Hort.)? And what about the awarding of the Ph.D. degree for a dissertation on "A Study of Some Factors in the Written Language of a Group of Texas Land-Grant College Freshmen to Show How the Nature of the Language Reflects the Socio-Economic Backgrounds of These Students" or "Instrumentation for Locating and Identifying Noises in Mechanical Equipment"? [24] If these were iso-

[24] Oliver C. Carmichael, *Graduate Education: A Critique and a Program* (New York: Harper & Brothers, 1961), pp. 51-57.

lated cases we could smile and let them pass, but every informed observer knows that this sort of thing is all too prevalent, even in the best universities, and that it has been going on for many years.[25] The seriousness of examples such as these is not so much that they are evidence of a waste of student and faculty time (which they certainly are) but that they reflect deeper weaknesses in graduate education—confusion of purpose, laxity of administration, and distorted notions of what is important.

From the point of view of our analysis of higher education, the tragedy of this graduate-school approach is primarily its effect on liberal education. This influence is brought to bear through the opinions of university faculty who have a hand in the shaping of undergraduate curricula and through the graduates of universities who go out to teaching posts in colleges.

In the last century the liberal arts curriculum has evolved into something quite different from that of the pre-Civil War college. The graduate-school view of education has been apparent in some of the most basic changes. The attention of the graduate school is, of course, focused primarily on knowledge, not on students as persons. This attitude has, in large measure, carried over into undergraduate education. A preoccupation with factual knowledge has tended to undermine the humane values which could give unity and purpose to the educational program. In the latter part of the nineteenth century and the early decades of the twentieth century, the adoption of the elective system, or variations of it, by most colleges destroyed all semblance of a pattern of education, a rational scheme which assigned priorities to objectives and fields of study. The number of courses, each concerned with some small segment of knowledge, was permitted to multiply almost indiscriminately. All kinds of knowledge tended to become equal. Notwithstanding the retreat from the curricular anarchism of the elective system and the return by most institutions to some measure of prescription, higher education as a whole lacks a theoretical basis for a unified program of liberal education.

Some of our wisest academic commentators have spoken on this point. After visiting classes at several colleges, Paul Klapper, a former

[25] See, for example, the earlier criticisms of Abraham Flexner in *Universities: American, English, German* (New York: Oxford University Press, 1930).

college president and a careful student of higher education, reported in 1949:

Aimlessness is the most important single cause of ineffectiveness in teaching and of frustration of educational effort. Again and again one looks in vain for evidence of purpose in classroom, lecture hall, and laboratory. The only apparent purpose that the observer can discover in these visits is to fill the interval from bell to bell with another segment of the subject matter of the course which the student—being literate—can and should acquire for himself. In the wake of this purposeless procedure come habits of mind and of work decidedly deleterious to both student and teacher, for neither is exerting his best creative effort.[26]

Paul Dressel, an experienced consultant on college curricular problems and evaluation, has reported similar conclusions and attributes the lack of purpose to the graduate training of faculty members.[27] Earl J. McGrath, in a carefully documented study of the influence of graduate education on the liberal arts college, commented:

Except through accident or personal recalcitrance, the programs of studies pursued by the majority of college students exhibit no common body of knowledge, intellectual procedures, or philosophical wholeness. Yet many of these students whose education is composed of infinite permutations of elements united by no transcending purpose other than a vocational goal receive the ancient Bachelor of Arts degree signifying to the world that they possess the qualities of mind and character associated with a liberal education.[28]

An analysis of the plight of liberal education, against the background of historical development as it has been outlined, suggests that the fundamental difficulty is the impossibility of blending two quite different conceptions of higher education. The British notion of the residential college, based on the centuries-old tradition of broad, humane education, and the modern university idea, stressing specialized scholarship, simply cannot be combined because their purposes are too different. In trying to combine two incompatible types of education, we may have produced a hybrid institution which lacks the brilliance of the university at its best and the philosophical

[26] Paul Klapper, "The Professional Preparation of the College Teacher," *Journal of General Education*, XXIV (1949), pp. 228-44.
[27] Paul Dressel, "The Current Status of Research on College and University Teaching," in *The Appraisal of Teaching* (Ann Arbor, Michigan: University of Michigan Press, 1959), p. 7.
[28] Earl J. McGrath, *The Graduate School and the Decline of Liberal Education* (New York: Teachers College Press, 1959), p. 8.

breadth and depth of the strong liberal college. Paul Farmer, a historian of European education, has made the distinction nicely:

The university in continental Europe was held responsible as an agent of the nation-state for husbanding the store of knowledge. But neither the university as a whole nor its members—students and professors—were held responsible for education understood as the formation of personality and character, or as adjustment—at the highest level and on a personal basis—between the individual and his environment. In this respect the European universities stood in marked contrast to the English universities of Oxford and Cambridge and to the American colleges of the nineteenth century.[20]

Was there in the German university idea some basic flaw which could account for so many ill effects? We seem almost to be gathering up all the weaknesses that have developed in undergraduate education and heaping them at the door of the German university. This would, of course, be too simple an explanation of our difficulties. Yet the German university does seem to have had a serious defect which, because it was philosophical, affected scholarship and teaching in a very fundamental and pervasive way. Built into much of German scholarship of the late nineteenth century, almost as a part of the system, were certain presuppositions about the nature of truth and the means of arriving at it. Research in the physical sciences had yielded spectacular results. The inductive method of science had achieved unprecedented prestige as a research technique. It was a method that depended more on observation, on facts, than had the linguistic and logical methods of the older speculative disciplines. Scholars looked to this exciting and productive new approach to solve an ever-wider range of problems.

Hoping to secure the same remarkable results in their fields that the scientists had achieved in theirs, scholars in the humanistic and social disciplines seized upon the methods and the concepts of the natural sciences and tried to make their fields scientific, too. This was to be the means of acquiring surer, less speculative, more objective knowledge. Thus—*positivism* came to be the dominant climate of the academic world of the nineteenth century and especially of the German university. The language and the attitudes of German scholars reflected this mental outlook, and positivistic assumptions became

[20] Paul Farmer, "Nineteenth Century Ideas of the University: Continental Europe," in Margaret Clapp (ed.), *The Modern University* (Ithaca: Cornell University Press, 1950), pp. 19-20.

part of the fabric of modern scholarship. This was the very time at which the influence of the German university on American education was greatest, and the prevailing climate of German scholarship was thus incorporated into the new American university. Positivism was built right into the apparatus of graduate education in this country.

In retrospect we can see that this imitating of the physical sciences has done grave damage to many disciplines, especially those concerned with values, since the critical study of values, except in the descriptive sense, is not best advanced by being "scientific." There is now an impressive body of literature on this subject. It may well be, as Lilge and Hallowell have suggested, that the rapid destruction of the German university itself in the days of Hitler was the direct result of the undermining of liberal social principles by positivism within the universities.[30] Positivism tends toward a preoccupation with facts as distinct from values and principles. It encourages technical scholarship and discourages broadly philosophical studies. Carried to the extreme, it seems to weaken commitment to large purposes. In the words of Oswald Spengler, who followed the doctrine to its logical conclusion, "in the historical world there are no ideals, but only facts—no truths, but only facts. There is no reason, no equity, no final aim, but only facts." [31]

Professor Hocking gives a perceptive analysis of the relationship of science to values in his fascinating book, *What Man Can Make of Man*.[32] In his chapter entitled "Science and the Dismissal of Value," he delineates the effects of scholarship too narrow in its presuppositions. Hocking's point is that science is a good thing in itself but values are indispensable:

If we are required to choose between science and value, we defy the requirement—we choose both. If we are told we must choose between modern psychology and the soul, we ask the pretending authority to present his papers—we choose both. We are informed that a concrete interest in social good has displaced the antiquated conception of a natural right with a metaphysical root, we reply that the alleged displacement is an illusion due to a non-existent contradiction—we choose both.

[30] Frederic Lilge, *The Abuse of Learning* (New York: Macmillan Company, 1948); John H. Hallowell, *Main Currents in Modern Political Thought* (New York: Henry Holt and Company, 1950), pp. 289-327.
[31] Quoted by Hallowell, *op. cit.*, p. 323.
[32] William Ernest Hocking, *What Man Can Make of Man* (New York: Harper & Brothers, 1942).

We cannot have both in any of these cases without some hard thinking, for the supposed antitheses are plausible. They are none-the-less false and it is they that have cracked and are cracking human nature asunder.[33]

This has been a long discussion of theoretical questions that seems to have taken us far afield from the church college and university; these matters do have a crucial bearing, however, on the present and future health of liberal education, of religion in education, and of private sponsorship of higher education. We shall return to them after commenting briefly on the growth of higher education during the last century.

The years between the Civil War and World War I were a period of widespread establishment of new institutions of higher education in the United States. Many hundreds of colleges, perhaps as many as two thousand, were organized during that time. Exact statistics are not available, because many of the institutions did not survive, and their records have been scattered or lost. The mortality rate among colleges founded prior to the Civil War is reported at 80 percent.[34]

Over eight hundred colleges and universities now in operation were founded between the Civil War and World War I. A substantial portion of these were established under religious auspices. The Methodists, Baptists, Roman Catholics, Presbyterians, and Lutherans were especially active. The "Great Awakening" of the mid-nineteenth century, the need for ministers, the fear of rising secularism, the expansion of missionary efforts in the South and the West, the desire to provide educational opportunity, the ambitions of frontier towns— all these factors contributed to the founding of new institutions. In most areas and most churches, this development went forward without national or local planning. It was not uncommon for a denomination to establish several colleges in a single state without recognizing a responsibility to provide continuing financial support. A nineteenth-century observer in Illinois made the comment that "a settler could hardly encamp on the prairies but a college would spring up beside his wagon." [35]

By World War I this frenzied activity had come to an end. The organization of regional accrediting agencies had brought some order

---

[33] *Ibid.*, pp. 56-57.
[34] Brubacher and Rudy, *op. cit.*, p. 71.
[35] *Ibid.*

into higher education and a greater awareness of educational standards. However, many new colleges have been established since that time, especially by religious orders and congregations of the Roman Catholic Church. Some of the newer religious groups, such as the Churches of Christ, the Assemblies of God, the Church of the Nazarene, the Church of God, and various Baptist and Pentecostal sects have entered the field of higher education. About 250 Bible colleges and institutes have begun operation in the United States and Canada, half of them since World War II. The latter institutions do not come within the purview of our study, but they deserve to be mentioned as a growing segment of education at the collegiate level. Some of them are competing for students and funds with liberal arts colleges, and a few are evolving into liberal arts colleges themselves.

Although church-related colleges and universities have increased in enrollment in recent years, their percentage of the total enrollment in American higher education is declining. About twenty years ago public institutions began to outstrip private institutions in number of students, and that trend has accelerated in recent years. In the fall of 1965, there were 5,967,411 students in 2,238 institutions; 3,999,940 in public and 1,967,471 in private institutions. The enrollment in 788 church institutions was 1,032,312, 17.3 percent of the total.[36]

On the basis of this brief historical review, we can make several preliminary observations on the position of church institutions in the context of American higher education.

First, something serious has happened to teaching and learning in the liberal arts. Critics have been saying this for a long time—perhaps it has been said so often that it is no longer heard. Under the influence of ideas inimical to the humanistic tradition, liberal education has lost a clear sense of purpose and therefore of unity. It would be reasonable to expect that the colleges sponsored by churches, being primarily liberal arts institutions, would be affected by the plight of liberal education in general. There is no reason to suppose that they have been immune to the erosion in humane values and the conflicts of purpose resulting from the blending of the British college and the German university. Their faculties are, after all, the products of

---

[36] Enrollment figures are from A. M. Wood, *Opening (Fall) Enrollment in Higher Education, 1965.* Office of Education Circular No. 796 (Washington: U.S. Department of Health, Education, and Welfare, 1966).

graduate schools oriented toward technical scholarship. In subsequent chapters we shall inquire further into the question of whether the church colleges do, in fact, suffer from the same uncertainty and the same lack of compelling purpose or ordering principle for the undergraduate curriculum, which students of higher education believe they see in the total enterprise of liberal education as it has developed over the last century.

Second, religiously the church colleges are in a difficult position. The academic world today is essentially a secular world. Religion has been under attack or suspect by intellectuals for several generations. Probably no contemporary institution, however strong its religious foundation, can wholly escape the inroads of secular thought. These subtle influences might be expected to weaken the religious convictions of faculty and students and thus undermine the very principles that could unify church institutions. Is it true of these institutions, as the Harvard Report suggested, that "religion is not now for most colleges a practicable source of intellectual unity"? [37]

Third, as institutions which are private in control and basically private in support, the colleges and universities affiliated with churches are confronted with the fact that private higher education now plays a minority role in the United States. The public sector in higher education has become much larger than the private; the gap is increasing yearly. This does not preclude the possibility of significant, perhaps crucial, service for private institutions, but it has important consequences of various kinds.

These, then, are some of the historical influences to which we should be sensitive as we examine the programs and problems of church-affiliated colleges and universities today.

[37] *General Education in a Free Society*. Report of the Harvard Committee. (Cambridge, Massachusetts: Harvard University Press, 1946), p. 39.

2

Dimensions of Church-Sponsored Higher Education

This study is concerned with colleges and universities related to Christian and Jewish religious bodies in the United States. It includes junior colleges, liberal arts colleges, teachers colleges and other separately-organized professional schools (except theological schools), and universities (that is, institutions of complex organization offering extensive graduate and professional programs). Schools engaged exclusively in the preparation of ministers, priests, or other church workers are omitted, although institutions which offer theological programs but have other major functions, such as general education or teacher training, are included.

The Protestant institutions constitute the largest single group, followed by the colleges and universities associated with the Roman Catholic Church and its religious orders and communities. Next are the institutions representing Christian bodies which do not consider themselves properly classified as either "Protestant" or "Roman Catholic," such as the Church of Christ, Scientist; the Church of Jesus Christ of Latter-day Saints; the Churches of Christ; and the Orthodox Church. Finally, there are the Jewish institutions.

Much has been said and written about the definition of a church college or university and the criteria for determining whether a given institution should be called "church controlled," "church related," "church sponsored," "church affiliated," "Christian," "sectarian," "denominational," "religiously oriented," or described in other terms indicative of church association of some sort. These expressions are often used quite loosely, almost interchangeably, by writers and speakers on the subject. In first considering the matter, we found it im-

18

possible to arrive at a simple definition of a church institution of higher education which fits all institutions, so varied are they in character and in their relationships with religious bodies. To identify the institutions to be included in this study a questionnaire was sent to every non-publicly controlled institution, except theological seminaries, included in the 1962-63 *Education Directory* with the request that the president provide us with specific information on any existing church association.[1] Responses were received from all of the 1,189 institutions to which these inquiries were addressed. On the basis of the replies, 817 colleges and universities were identified as having relationships of sufficient significance to be considered church-sponsored institutions. (The criteria used, and an analysis of the data obtained through these inquiries, are discussed in Chapter 3. The initial questionnaire is reprinted in Appendix A. A complete list of the 817 institutions and their church relationships appears as Appendix D.) In the majority of cases the data supplied by the institutions left no doubt as to whether they should be listed as church related. In some cases, however, further inquiry was necessary to arrive at a decision.

In addition to this basic list of 817 church-related colleges and universities, we compiled a supplementary list of 18 institutions that cannot be classified technically as church related but do have a definite religious orientation. (These 18 are included in the list of institutions appearing as Appendix D.) For example, Wheaton College, Illinois, although it is not connected with an individual church, describes itself as interdenominational, and its statement of purpose reflects a pervasive interest in religion:

The central purpose of Wheaton College is expressed in the motto engraved on the cornerstone of the main building: *For Christ and His Kingdom.* Since the foundation of the institution, this purpose has produced an enthusiastic concern for truth, righteousness and beauty, and has thereby given meaning to the ideal of a Christian liberal arts college that seeks to understand human culture from a Biblical and theistic viewpoint, and to encourage responsible Christian participation in contemporary society.[2]

The College of Jewish Studies is a somewhat different type of institution. Founded by the Board of Jewish Education, it is not as-

[1] *Education Directory, Part 3, Higher Education* (Washington: U.S. Department of Health, Education, and Welfare, Office of Education, 1963).
[2] *Bulletin of Wheaton College, Catalogue Number, 1962-1963*, p. 4.

sociated with a particular branch of Judaism, but its religious orientation is clear. Its purpose is defined as follows:

The College of Jewish Studies provides study opportunities for young men and women who wish to prepare themselves for the profession of Hebrew and Sunday School teaching and Cantorate, for pre-Rabbinical training, and for leadership in communal activities. It also offers opportunities for systematic study to adults and young people interested in the religion, history, literature, languages and creative arts and thinking of the Jewish people. The College accepts students regardless of race, creed, or nationality. It is the only Jewish institution of its kind in the Middle West whose faculty and student body include persons of all groupings of Judaism.[3]

Wellesley College illustrates further the character of the supplementary list. Wellesley is not connected with a church, yet, on the basis of Article I of its By-Laws, the College has clear religious purposes:

The College was founded for the glory of God and the service of the Lord Jesus Christ by the education and culture of women. To realize this design it is required that the Trustees shall be in manifest sympathy with the traditional religious purpose of the College, that members of the faculty shall be selected with a view to maintaining the Christian purpose of the College; and that every undergraduate shall study the Sacred Scriptures through the second year of the course, with opportunity for election of further study during later years.[4]

In summary, on the basis of the information received from the 1,189 private institutions in the United States to which we directed our inquiry, 817 were classified as having definite present-day connections with religious bodies, 18 as having a clear religious orientation but no relationship to a particular church, and 354 as being independent of religious bodies. It is interesting to note that the lists of affiliated institutions published by denominations includes some colleges that do not themselves claim to be church related.

THE CHURCH-SPONSORED INSTITUTIONS

Sixty-four religious bodies are represented among the 817 institutions. The breakdown described in Table 1 shows that fourteen

---

[3] *The College of Jewish Studies, Schedule of Courses, 1963-1964,* p. 4.
[4] Quoted and commented upon in a letter from Margaret Clapp, President, Wellesley College, dated March 12, 1963.

denominations have more than ten institutions associated with each of them. These together account for 706 institutions, about 86 percent of the total. Fifty denominations are represented among the 111 institutions that make up the remaining 14 percent. About two-fifths (41.5 percent) of the institutions are related to the Roman Catholic Church. The Protestant denomination associated with the largest number of colleges and universities is the Methodist Church, with 102 institutions, 12.5 percent of the total. Twenty-eight religious bodies

Table 1: Religious Bodies Represented among the 817 Institutions

RELIGIOUS BODY	N[a]	%[a]
Roman Catholic Church	339	41.5
Methodist Church	102	12.5
Southern Baptist Convention	52	6.4
United Presbyterian Church in U.S.A.	51	6.2
United Church of Christ	24	2.9
American Baptist Convention	22	2.7
Presbyterian Church in the U.S.	20	2.5
Lutheran Church in America	19	2.3
Disciples of Christ	18	2.2
American Lutheran Church	13	1.6
Lutheran Church-Missouri Synod	12	1.5
Seventh-day Adventist Church	12	1.5
Episcopal Church	11	1.3
Society of Friends	11	1.3
Other (50 religious bodies)	111	13.6
Total	817	100.0

[a] N=Number of institutions; %=Percentage of institutions.

are identified with one institution of higher education, and another ten have two each. Eight of the institutions, or about 1 percent of the total, are interdenominational.

On the basis of enrollment data for fall, 1965, the institutions ranged in size from 19 to 22,382 students. The average enrollment was 1,297. On the average Roman Catholic institutions were somewhat smaller than Protestant ones.

Table 2 shows that the 817 colleges and universities clearly reflect the diversity so characteristic of American higher education. More than one-half of the institutions are coeducational, about one-fourth are women's colleges, and approximately one-sixth admit men only. Only 16, 2 percent, have co-ordinate student bodies. As will be noted from the table, colleges admitting only men or women are predomi-

Table 2: Distribution by Type of Student Body

TYPE OF STUDENT BODY	ROMAN CATHOLIC		NON-CATHOLIC		ALL INSTITUTIONS	
	N	%	N	%	N	%
Coeducational.........	51	15.0	422	88.3	473	57.9
Men.................	112	33.0	18	3.8	130	15.9
Women..............	167	49.3	31	6.5	198	24.2
Co-ordinate..........	9	2.7	7	1.4	16	2.0
Total..............	339	100.0	478	100.0	817	100.0

nant among Roman Catholic institutions, while this is true of only 10.3 percent of the non-Catholic institutions. Co-ordinate colleges are not a common form of organization in church-affiliated higher education.

There are other significant differences with respect to type of student body among the colleges when grouped by denominational affiliation. With few exceptions, notably those institutions associated with Jewish groups and the Greek Orthodox Church, those colleges under the auspices of denominations having fewer than ten institutions are coeducational. More than 91 percent of the colleges related to Methodist bodies are coeducational. However, 35 percent of the Presbyterian (U.S.) colleges admit only men or only women—evidence of a common pattern of higher education in the South, where this church is strongest.

Although the 817 institutions are scattered from coast to coast, about 90 percent of them are located east of the 100th meridian; namely, east of a north-south line bisecting the states from North Dakota to Texas. Nevada and Wyoming have none. On the other hand, there are concentrations of institutions around the larger urban centers. This pattern of a heavy concentration in the eastern half of the country and a thinning out in the western half reflects the relative scarcity of population from the western half of the Great Plains to the Pacific Coast and the pattern of the westward movement of the frontier in the nineteenth century. As the pioneers moved westward, they brought with them their churches and a missionary spirit with respect to the establishment of colleges. However, the growth of publicly supported institutions of higher learning, stimulated by the Morrill Act of 1862, provided for most of the higher-educational needs of the newly settled areas, and this tended to limit the establishment of church colleges.

Table 3 shows the distribution of institutions according to membership in regional accrediting associations. One-half of the institutions (53.3 percent) are accredited by either the North Central Association of Colleges and Secondary Schools or the Southern Association of Colleges and Schools. Less than 10 percent are members of the Western Association of Schools and Colleges and the Northwest Association of Secondary and Higher Schools. About one-fifth of the institutions are not accredited by a regional agency.

Table 3: Distribution by Accrediting Association Membership

ACCREDITING ASSOCIATION MEMBERSHIP	ROMAN CATHOLIC		NON-CATHOLIC		ALL INSTITUTIONS	
	N	%	N	%	N	%
New England..........	22	6.5	7	1.5	29	3.5
Middle States..........	76	22.4	44	9.2	120	14.7
Southern..............	28	8.3	167	35.0	195	23.9
North Central..........	88	26.0	152	31.8	240	29.4
Western..............	18	5.3	18	3.7	36	4.4
Northwest.............	11	3.2	19	4.0	30	3.7
None................	96	28.3	71	14.8	167	20.4
Total..............	339	100.0	478	100.0	817	100.0

There are notable differences between the Roman Catholic and non-Catholic institutions with respect to their distribution among the regions. Almost one-half (48.4 percent) of the Catholic institutions are members of either the Middle States Association or the North Central Association. About two-thirds of the non-Catholic institutions are members of either the Southern Association or North Central Association. The New England Association includes only 6.5 percent of the Catholic institutions and 1.5 percent of others. About twice as many Catholic institutions are unaccredited as non-Catholic (28.3 percent as compared with 14.8 percent).

The 817 institutions further illustrate the diversity of American higher education in terms of the types of programs offered. As can be seen in Table 4, they are predominantly undergraduate institutions. More than one-half (60.2 percent) offer instruction leading to the bachelor's degree only, and almost one-fifth (18.5 percent) are junior colleges. The master's degree is the highest degree conferred by one-sixth (16.8 percent) of the institutions. Only 4.4 percent offer grad-

Table 4: Distribution by Type of Program

TYPE OF PROGRAM	ROMAN CATHOLIC		NON-CATHOLIC		ALL INSTITUTIONS	
	N	%	N	%	N	%
Junior college..........	60	17.7	91	19.0	151	18.5
Bachelor's degree......	195	57.5	297	62.2	492	60.2
Master's degree........	68	20.1	69	14.4	137	16.8
Doctor's degree........	15	4.4	21	4.4	36	4.4
Other...............	1	0.3	0	0.0	1	0.1
Total...............	339	100.0	478	100.0	817	100.0

uate programs at the doctoral level. Clearly, graduate education is not a major function of institutions affiliated with religious bodies.

The differences between Roman Catholic and non-Catholic institutions are not marked with respect to the types of program offered. The bachelor's degree is the highest degree offered in a slightly greater proportion of the non-Catholic institutions (62.2 percent compared with 57.5 percent of the Catholic institutions). On the other hand, a greater proportion of the Catholic colleges (20.1 percent compared with 14.4 percent of the non-Catholic institutions) offer master's degree programs. Both have the same percentage of institutions offering doctoral programs.

There are some differences among the principal Protestant groupings with respect to the types of program characterizing their colleges. To delineate these differences, we set up four major denominational groups by bringing together all denominations that have a common title. For example, a group called simply "Presbyterians" includes those institutions related to the Presbyterian Church in the U.S., the United Presbyterian Church in the U.S.A., the Associate Reformed Presbyterian Church, the Cumberland Presbyterian Church, the Evangelical Presbyterian Church, and the Reformed Presbyterian Church of North America. In similar manner, Baptist, Lutheran, and Methodist groups are listed. Seven denominations or sects, selected as representative of the newer religious bodies, form a fifth category. These seven are the Churches of Christ, the Assemblies of God, the Church of God (Indiana), the Church of God (Tennessee), the Church of God in Christ, the Churches of God in North America, and the Pentecostal Holiness Church, which have 17 colleges associated with them.

The five groups of colleges thus formed account for 333 of the 478 non-Catholic institutions included in this study. While we recognize, of course, that there are many differences, theological and otherwise, within each of these large groups, the form of government is similar and a common heritage provides some commonality of character. The 145 non-Catholic colleges not included are sufficiently diverse not to lend themselves to such grouping.

Comparisons among the five groups suggest important differences as shown in Tables 5, 6, and 7. About one-third of the church-affiliated institutions offering doctoral programs are associated with the Methodist Church. Almost three-fourths of the Presbyterian colleges are four-year undergraduate institutions; about one-eighth are junior colleges. About two-fifths of the colleges associated with the newer religious groups offer bachelor's degree programs, while more than one-third are junior colleges. In considering the predominant type of student body we see that all of the colleges of the newer religious

Table 5: Distribution of Five Groups by Type of Student Body

TYPE OF STUDENT BODY	BAPTIST		LUTHERAN		METHODIST		PRESBYTERIAN		SELECTED NEWER RELIGIOUS GROUPS	
	N	%	N	%	N	%	N	%	N	%
Coeducational..	66	84.6	40	90.9	114	91.2	58	84.1	17	100.0
Men..........	1	1.3	2	4.5	2	1.6	4	5.8	0	0.0
Women.......	9	11.5	1	2.3	7	5.6	7	10.1	0	0.0
Co-ordinate...	2	2.6	1	2.3	2	1.6	0	0.0	0	0.0
Total.......	78	100.0	44	100.0	125	100.0	69	100.0	17	100.0

Table 6: Distribution of Five Groups by Accrediting Association Membership

ACCREDITING ASSOCIATION MEMBERSHIP	BAPTIST		LUTHERAN		METHODIST		PRESBYTERIAN		SELECTED NEWER RELIGIOUS GROUPS	
	N	%	N	%	N	%	N	%	N	%
New England..	1	1.3	0	0.0	3	2.4	0	0.0	0	0.0
Middle States..	2	2.6	8	18.2	10	8.0	7	10.2	0	0.0
Southern......	48	61.5	4	9.1	53	42.4	28	40.6	5	29.4
North Central..	14	17.9	22	50.0	33	26.4	26	37.7	3	17.6
Western......	2	2.6	1	2.3	3	2.4	1	1.4	0	0.0
Northwest.....	1	1.3	1	2.3	3	2.4	3	4.3	2	11.8
None.........	10	12.8	8	18.1	20	16.0	4	5.8	7	41.2
Total.......	78	100.0	44	100.0	125	100.0	69	100.0	17	100.0

Table 7: Distribution of Five Groups by Type of Program

TYPE OF PROGRAM	BAPTIST		LUTHERAN		METHODIST		PRESBYTERIAN		SELECTED NEWER RELIGIOUS GROUPS	
	N	%	N	%	N	%	N	%	N	%
Junior college..	21	26.9	13	29.5	26	20.8	9	13.0	6	35.3
Bachelor's degree.....	43	55.1	27	61.4	71	56.8	49	71.0	7	41.2
Master's degree.....	12	15.4	4	9.1	17	13.6	10	14.5	4	23.5
Doctor's degree.....	2	2.6	0	0.0	11	8.8	1	1.5	0	0.0
Other........	0	0.0	0	0.0	0	0.0	0	0.0	0	0.0
Total.....	78	100.0	44	100.0	125	100.0	69	100.0	17	100.0

bodies are coeducational, while it is the Presbyterians that have the largest percentage of institutions admitting only men or women. Widespread variations exist between these groups in terms of membership in regional accrediting associations. Lutheran institutions are predominantly located in the North Central Association area, while the Baptist institutions are found chiefly in the area of the Southern Association. Two-fifths of the colleges associated with the newer religious groups lack regional accreditation.

The 817 church-affiliated institutions, varied in character as these comparisons show, offer the student in search of higher education under church auspices a wide choice in terms of location, type of program, type of student body, size, and religious environment.

COMPARISONS WITH OTHER SEGMENTS

It is of interest to know how the church-sponsored institutions, as a group, compare quantitatively with the other two segments of American higher education. It was reported above that in the fall of 1965 there were slightly less than six million students enrolled in 2,238 institutions in the United States. Of these slightly less than four million were attending public institutions. Of the somewhat less than two million in private institutions, slightly more than one million were enrolled in 788 church-sponsored institutions, thus representing 17.3 percent of the total 1965 enrollment.[5] More detailed comparisons

[5] For a more detailed analysis of enrollment see A. M. Wood, *op. cit.*

among the three segments further define the dimensions of church-sponsored higher education. The analysis brings to light several general observations.

The enrollment in church-sponsored institutions exceeds somewhat that in independent institutions, but the two groups together serve a little less than half as many students as the public institutions. The private sector, in other words, constitutes about one-third of American higher education.

In numbers of degrees conferred, however, church-sponsored higher education runs appreciably ahead of independent higher education, and the two together account for more than 42 percent of all degrees conferred. In the academic year, 1963-64, for example, the church-sponsored institutions awarded 128,565 bachelor's and first professional degrees whereas the independent private institutions conferred 82,783. Of the total of 502,104 degrees conferred by all surveyed institutions in that year, the church-sponsored institutions awarded 25.6 percent, the independent 16.5 percent. The public institutions conferred 56.1 percent of all such degrees.[6]

Of the 204,561 full-time faculty in all institutions of higher education in 1963-64 a little over a fifth (22.4 percent) were in church-related institutions and only a slightly lower percentage (19.2) were in the independent institutions. Thus, although the privately controlled institutions enroll about a third of the students in higher education, they employ about 42 percent of the full-time faculty. On the other hand, the publicly controlled institutions enroll about 67 percent of the students but employ about 56 percent of the full-time faculty.[7] One may conclude, of course, that in 1965-66 a somewhat more favorable student-faculty ratio prevailed in both the church-sponsored and independent institutions as compared with the public institutions.

In 1963-64 about 32 percent of the 25,513 general administrative staff personnel in all institutions of higher education were in church-

---

[6] A detailed analysis of these figures is given in Patricia S. Wright, *Earned Degrees Conferred, 1963-64*. U.S. Office of Education, Miscellaneous No. 54 (Washington: Government Printing Office, 1966).

[7] Detailed statistics on faculty and staff are given in Ralph E. Dunham and Patricia S. Wright, *Faculty and Other Professional Staff in Institutions of Higher Education, First Term, 1963-64*. U.S. Office of Education Circular No. 794 (Washington: Government Printing Office, 1966).

related institutions. Although public institutions enrolled almost four times as many students as church-related institutions, the percentage of general administrative staff members found in public institutions was not proportionately greater (40.7 percent).

Similarly, total library holdings and expenditures tend to be higher in relation to enrollment in church-sponsored and especially in independent institutions than in public institutions. In 1961-62 church-sponsored institutions held 23.7 percent of the total number of volumes in the libraries of all colleges and universities; independent institutions held 29.1 percent. Expenditures for books in church-related institutions represented about the same proportion of the total spent for books for all higher education in 1961-62 as their share of enrollment (20.5 and 19.7 percent, respectively). Expenditures for books in independent institutions, however, represented 32.7 percent of the total even though these institutions enrolled 13.3 percent of the total enrollment in all institutions.[8] The library data for the independent institutions reflect the heavy emphasis on research and graduate study in about a dozen of the larger private universities.

The comparatively weak position of the church-sponsored college with respect to current income for educational and general purposes is evident from the fact that in 1961-62 these institutions received only 14.5 percent of the total of over six billion dollars received by all institutions that year. The independent institutions represent a much stronger position—their share was 27.3 percent of the total received by all institutions. The data on expenditures tell the same story. It must be remembered, however, that the church institutions are almost all undergraduate colleges. Furthermore, it should be noted that expenditures for organized research in church institutions are quite modest. Of the more than 232 million dollars of income from endowment received by all institutions in 1961-62 for educational and general purposes, 62.2 percent went to the independent institutions, 22.2 percent to the church-sponsored colleges, and only 9.7 percent to the public institutions. The figure for the independent institutions reflects, of course, the rather sizable endowments held by private universities.

The amount of financial aid available to students in church-spon-

[8] Theodore Samore and Doris C. Holladay, *Library Statistics of Colleges and Universities, 1961-62.* U.S. Office of Education Circular No. 699 (Washington: Government Printing Office, 1963).

sored institutions is generous in comparison with that provided by the other two segments. These institutions accounted for well over one-third (37.2 percent) of all scholarships and over one-fourth of all N.D.S.L. loans (27.3 percent) awarded to college and university students in 1959-60 in public and private institutions. Church-related institutions distributed 35.3 percent of all the scholarship dollars awarded that year. Independent institutions awarded 18.4 percent of the scholarships and 33.9 percent of the total scholarship dollars.[9] Data for public institutions were not readily available but in a sense, of course, all students in public institutions have scholarships because of the substantial subsidy from tax funds.

[9] Richard C. Mattingly, *Financial Assistance for College Students: Undergraduate.* U.S. Office of Education Bulletin No. 11. (Washington: Government Printing Office, 1962).

3

Relationships
with
Religious Bodies

In the preceding chapter we remarked that the definition of a church institution has been the subject of extended discussion and that numerous terms have been used in this connection, none of which satisfactorily describes all of the institutions of this type. No single descriptive term can do justice to the wide range of relationships that exist between colleges and the religious bodies with which they are associated. Quite obviously, for example, use of the word "church" is inappropriate in the case of Jewish institutions.

It has often been said that these relationships may best be described in terms of a continuum. A college which is under close ecclesiastical control falls at one end of the continuum, while an institution that has only a vague historical association with a church is placed at the opposite end. Other institutions will fall somewhere between these two extremes, depending on the degree to which they possess whatever it is that establishes the relationship. This attempt at definition, however, assumes that relationship is unitary—that a single criterion may be used to identify the church institution. Though perhaps helpful in describing conditions in three or four of the larger Protestant denominations, this way of viewing the question is a gross over-simplification when applied to all institutions of this type. It leads to easy generalizations which sometimes obscure more than they illuminate.

The relationships between colleges and universities and religious organizations are much too complex to be shown adequately on a one-dimensional graph. It would be closer to the truth to say that no two institutions have exactly the same relationships with religious bodies. Institutional history, church polity, financial considerations, the influence of strong personalities—all these and other factors enter, in varying degrees, into individual cases. Thus there is no concise definition that does justice to the complexity of relationships that exist. In actual practice, each institution needs its own appropriate vocabulary to describe its unique church association.

ELEMENTS IN THE DEFINITION

As we see it, there are several discrete elements involved in church relationship, the possession of any one of which in significant degree, stamps an institution as a church-sponsored college or university. While judgment must enter into the decision as to whether or not a given college possesses a particular type of relationship in *significant* degree, this approach does at least provide a rational basis for classification. It was this type of approach we used in compiling the list of church institutions which appears in Appendix D.

It should be noted that, for the purposes of this study, we have considered a relationship with a religious order or congregation of the Roman Catholic Church to be a "church relationship," though we recognize that there is an important distinction to be made here. Only fourteen Roman Catholic institutions are direct agencies of the Church itself in the United States. Thirteen of these are diocesan colleges and universities, while the Catholic University of America is controlled by the hierarchy of the whole American Church.

In our analysis we have considered six elements in defining college-church relationships. The elements are board composition, ownership, financial support, acceptance of denominational standards or use of denominational name, educational aims, and selection of faculty and administrative personnel. In succeeding paragraphs we shall discuss these six elements of church relationship, describing each and analyzing the extent to which it is found among the 817 institutions. Some readers may feel that our treatment of this subject is unnecessarily technical. The details of church relationship are hardly central to our consideration of the role of these institutions in American life. We believe, however, that a fairly full presentation of data is justified because not only is there serious interest in this subject at the present time, particularly in view of its pertinence to the question of Federal and state assistance to church-affiliated institutions, but the existing literature on the subject is inadequate.

It may be of interest to examine first the frequency with which the six specific elements of relationship occur in the whole group of institutions.[1] The responses from the 817 institutions show that, generally speaking, the relationship between a college and a church rests on a combination of the elements, not on a single factor. In about two-fifths of the cases all six are involved. (See Table 8.) In almost

Table 8: Number of Different Elements of Relationship
to Religious Bodies Reported by Individual Institutions

NUMBER OF ELEMENTS OF RELATIONSHIP	FREQUENCY N	%
1	9	1.1
2	25	3.1
3	76	9.3
4	131	16.0
5	253	31.0
6	323	39.5
Total	817	100.0

one-third of the institutions the relationship rests on five of the factors. In other words, in more than two-thirds of the colleges there are at least five respects in which the institution can be identified as church affiliated. In very few of the institutions (4.2 percent) is the relationship limited to only one or two of the factors.

Using the same general classifications of Baptist, Lutheran, Methodist, Presbyterian, and "Newer Groups" as outlined in Chapter 2 in addition to a general division of Catholic and non-Catholic, a comparison of the data uncovers some interesting differences not only between Catholic and non-Catholic institutions but among the non-Catholic colleges. As shown in Table 9, the relationship between church and college tends to involve a larger number of elements in the

[1] For the actual I.B.M. analysis of these data, we are indebted to Richard A. Conger, Programmer, Yalem Computing Center, St. Louis University. The information summarized in this chapter was obtained from a questionnaire (See Appendix A) which was sent to the presidents of all 1,189 private institutions of higher learning listed in the *Education Directory, 1962-1963* (except theological schools, Bible colleges, and other institutions devoted exclusively to the preparation of persons for church vocations). As has been explained, 817 of these institutions were found to have relationships, in significant degree, with religious bodies.

Table 9: Number of Different Elements of Relationship to Religious Bodies Reported by Individual Institutions in Seven Groups

FREQUENCY BY CHURCH GROUP

NUMBER OF ELEMENTS OF RELATIONSHIP	Roman Catholic		Non-Catholic		Baptist		Lutheran		Methodist		Presbyterian		Newer Groups	
	N	%	N	%	N	%	N	%	N	%	N	%	N	%
1	1	0.3	8	1.7	2	2.6	0	0.0	2	1.6	0	0.0	0	0.0
2	3	0.9	22	4.6	1	1.3	0	0.0	2	1.6	3	4.3	0	0.0
3	22	6.5	54	11.3	6	7.7	3	6.8	11	8.8	8	11.6	9	52.9
4	56	16.5	75	15.7	5	6.4	1	2.3	18	14.4	12	17.4	2	11.8
5	103	30.4	150	31.4	24	30.8	13	29.5	51	40.8	26	37.7	1	5.9
6	154	45.4	169	35.4	40	51.3	27	61.4	41	32.8	20	29.0	5	29.4
Total	339	100.0	478	100.0	78	100.0	44	100.0	125	100.0	69	100.0	17	100.0

case of Roman Catholic institutions than in the case of non-Catholic ones. Among the Protestant groups, the Baptist and Lutheran church bodies report more elements of relationship per institution than the others; 61.4 percent of the Lutheran institutions and 51.3 percent of the Baptist institutions reported that all six applied to them. In no case did a Lutheran institution report fewer than three. Among the institutions affiliated with Presbyterian churches and with the newer religious groups only 29 percent of the colleges reported all six forms of relationship. The frequency with which each of the six factors appears among the 817 colleges and universities is shown in Tables 10 and 11.

Table 10: Number of Institutions Reporting Each Element of Relationship

ELEMENT OF RELATIONSHIP	FREQUENCY	
	N	%
1. Composition of board of control	687	84.1
a. Church membership required	574	70.3
b. Board members nominated/elected by church	438	53.6
2. Institution owned by church (or religious order or congregation)	573	70.1
3. Institution receives financial support from official church sources	766	93.7
a. For educational and general budget	602	73.7
b. In form of contributed services (Roman Catholic)	242	29.6
c. For capital purposes	364	44.6
4. Institution affiliated with church college organization/subscribes to set of standards	631	77.2
a. Institution affiliated with denominational organization of colleges	529	64.7
b. Institution subscribes to standards or policy set by church for colleges.	393	48.1
5. Institutional statement of purpose reflects religious orientation	782	95.7
6. Preference given church members in faculty and staff selection	575	70.4

Each of these types of relationship will be discussed separately, and its prevalence among the institutions noted. Suffice it to say here that the frequency with which any one is found ranges from 70 percent to 95 percent of the cases and that the pattern of relationships varies considerably among the institutions related to the several church groups.

Board Composition

The composition of the board of control of a college has been a common criterion of church relationship. Some denominations, for example the Presbyterian Church in the United States, have made

Table 11: Number of Institutions in Seven Groups Reporting Each Kind of Relationship to Religious Body

FREQUENCY BY CHURCH GROUP

KIND OF RELATIONSHIP	Catholic		Non-Catholic		Baptist		Lutheran		Methodist		Presbyterian		Newer Groups	
	N	%	N	%	N	%	N	%	N	%	N	%	N	%
1. Composition of board of control	276	81.4	411	86.0	70	89.7	43	97.7	111	88.8	58	84.1	17	100.0
a. Church membership required	269	79.4	305	63.8	59	75.6	38	86.4	71	56.8	34	49.3	16	94.1
b. Board members nominated/elected by church	115	33.9	323	67.6	55	70.5	35	79.5	95	76.0	48	69.6	7	41.2
2. Institution owned by church (or religious order or congregation)	321	94.7	252	52.7	49	62.8	35	79.5	71	56.8	29	42.0	7	41.2
3. Institution receives financial support from official church sources	329	97.0	437	91.4	75	96.2	43	97.7	123	98.4	66	95.7	8	47.1
a. Support for educational and general budget	181	53.4	421	88.1	73	93.6	41	93.2	120	96.0	64	92.8	8	47.1
b. Support in form of contributed services	242	71.4	0	0.0	0	0.0	0	0.0	0	0.0	0	0.0	0	0.0
c. Support for capital purposes	59	17.4	305	63.8	55	70.5	33	75.0	85	68.0	36	52.2	7	41.2
4. Institution affiliated with church college organization/subscribes to set of standards	233	68.7	398	83.3	67	85.9	38	86.4	112	89.6	62	89.8	7	41.2
a. Institution affiliated with denominational organization of colleges	191	56.3	338	70.7	63	79.5	23	52.3	101	80.8	53	76.8	2	11.8
b. Institution subscribes to standards or policy set by church for colleges	143	42.2	250	52.3	35	44.9	27	61.4	64	51.2	55	79.7	5	29.4
5. Institutional statement of purpose reflects religious orientation	325	95.9	457	95.6	76	97.4	43	97.7	118	94.4	68	98.6	17	100.0
6. Preference given church members in faculty and staff selection	252	74.3	323	67.6	65	83.3	38	86.4	77	61.6	45	65.2	14	82.4

it an important factor in defining church colleges for financial and other purposes. The relationship between the college and the church through the composition of the board may be effected in two ways: through the requirement that all or a portion of the members of the board be members of the church and through the provision that members of the board be nominated or elected by an official church body.

Considering these two as a single factor, board composition, we found that one or the other or both applied to 84.1 percent of the 817 institutions included in the study. (See Table 10.) As Table 11 shows, it is somewhat less prevalent in Roman Catholic institutions than in non-Catholic ones (81.4 percent and 86.0 percent, respectively). In all the 17 colleges associated with the newer religious groups and in all but one of the 44 institutions affiliated with the Lutheran churches, it was a factor. Among the Protestant groupings, it was found least often in Presbyterian institutions.

The provision that a certain fraction of trustees must be members of a given church is common in American colleges, as may be seen from Table 12. In about 60 percent of the institutions included in

Table 12: Church Membership as a Requirement for Election to Board

PERCENTAGE OF BOARD REQUIRED TO BE MEMBERS OF PARTICULAR CHURCH	INSTITUTIONS REQUIRING CHURCH MEMBERSHIP	
	N	%
0	243	29.7
1 – 25	12	1.5
26 – 50	27	3.3
51 – 75	124	15.2
76 – 100	360	44.0
Majority	16	2.0
Membership required but no percentage indicated	35	4.3
Total	817	100.0

our study more than one-half of the board must be members of a given church, and in about 45 percent of the cases three-fourths or more must be church members. Among the several large groupings this requirement is most commonly found in colleges affiliated with the newer religious groups, the Lutherans, the Baptists, and the Roman Catholics. (See Table 13.)

Table 13: Church Membership as a Requirement for Election to Board (by Seven Groups of Institutions)

| | | | | | | | INSTITUTIONS REQUIRING CHURCH MEMBERSHIP | | | | | | | |
| PERCENTAGE OF BOARD REQUIRED TO BE MEMBERS OF PARTICULAR CHURCH | Roman Catholic | | Non-Catholic | | Baptist | | Lutheran | | Methodist | | Presbyterian | | Newer Groups | |
	N	%	N	%	N	%	N	%	N	%	N	%	N	%
0	70	20.6	173	36.2	19	24.4	6	13.6	54	43.2	35	50.7	1	5.9
1–25	4	1.2	8	1.7	1	1.3	0	0.0	3	2.4	0	0.0	0	0.0
26–50	5	1.5	22	4.6	4	5.1	0	0.0	10	8.0	2	2.9	0	0.0
51–75	21	6.2	103	21.6	12	15.4	12	27.3	39	31.2	16	23.2	1	5.9
76–100	205	60.5	155	32.4	42	53.8	26	59.1	16	12.8	9	13.0	15	88.2
Majority	2	0.6	14	2.9	0	0.0	0	0.0	2	1.6	7	10.2	0	0.0
Membership required but no percentage indicated	32	9.4	3	0.6	0	0.0	0	0.0	1	0.8	0	0.0	0	0.0
Total	339	100.0	478	100.0	78	100.0	44	100.0	125	100.0	69	100.0	17	100.0

The boards of Roman Catholic institutions, it should be noted, are often composed entirely or largely of clergy or members of a particular religious order or community. For example, Georgetown University, being under the control and direction of the Society of Jesus, has a Board of Directors of thirteen, all of whom are Jesuit Fathers.[2] This is fairly typical. It may also be noted that all of the directors are administrative officers and teachers in the University. The government of the Catholic University of America, the one national institution of the Roman Catholic Church, is of interest as an illustration of control by the Church itself, as distinct from religious orders and communities.

The constitutions provide that the University shall forever remain under the Bishops of the United States who have plenary authority in all that pertains to discipline, courses of study, and methods of instruction. This authority is delegated to a Board of Trustees constituted of all the Archbishops of the nation, presiding over metropolitan areas, the remainder to be constituted of bishops, priests, and laymen in such numbers as not to exceed a total of fifty members for the entire Board.[3]

Provisions for nomination or election of college trustees by church bodies—synods, conferences, state conventions, dioceses, and other divisions—are also widespread. (See Table 14.) In over one-half of

Table 14: Church Nomination or Election of Board Members

PERCENTAGE OF BOARD NOMINATED/ELECTED BY CHURCH	INSTITUTIONS REQUIRING CHURCH NOMINATION/ELECTION	
	N	%
0	379	46.4
1 – 25	24	2.9
26 – 50	30	3.7
51 – 75	51	6.3
76 – 100	295	36.1
Percentage not indicated	38	4.6
Total	817	100.0

the institutions included in our study some or all of the board membership is nominated or elected by an official church body.

As reported in Table 15, this provision is most common among

[2] *Georgetown University, General Bulletin, 1962-1963*, p. 6.
[3] *The Catholic University of America Announcements, General Information, 1961-1962*, p. 33.

Table 15: Church Nomination or Election of Board Members (by Seven Groups of Institutions)

INSTITUTIONS REQUIRING CHURCH NOMINATION/ELECTION

PERCENTAGE OF BOARD NOMINATED/ ELECTED BY CHURCH	Roman Catholic		Non-Catholic		Baptist		Lutheran		Methodist		Presbyterian		Newer Groups	
	N	%	N	%	N	%	N	%	N	%	N	%	N	%
0	223	65.8	156	32.6	23	29.5	9	20.5	30	24.0	21	30.4	10	58.8
1 – 25	4	1.2	20	4.3	2	2.5	2	4.5	6	4.8	2	2.9	0	0.0
26 – 50	3	0.9	27	5.6	3	3.9	0	0.0	14	11.2	0	0.0	0	0.0
51 – 75	4	1.2	47	9.8	1	1.3	8	19.2	13	10.4	6	8.7	1	5.9
76 – 100	74	21.8	221	46.2	48	61.5	25	56.8	60	48.0	39	56.5	6	35.3
Percentage not indicated	31	9.1	7	1.5	1	1.3	0	0.0	2	1.6	1	1.5	0	0.0
Total	339	100.0	478	100.0	78	100.0	44	100.0	125	100.0	69	100.0	17	100.0

39

the Lutheran bodies where, it will be recalled, the board member is usually required to be a church member. Among the newer religious groups, nomination or election by a church body is less common even though church membership is usually required for election to a board. An interesting illustration of this kind of relationship is that of Evansville College, which is described as follows:

Under the terms of the charter granted by the Indiana State Legislature, Evansville College is controlled by a board of 48 trustees. Twenty-four trustees are named by the Methodist Church (eighteen by the Indiana Conference and three each by the Northwest and the North Indiana Conferences), nine are named by the Evansville Chamber of Commerce, three by the Alumni Association and twelve by the other trustees.[4]

If a substantial fraction of the trustees of a college is elected by a church body, that body *can* have a large measure of control over the affairs of the institution, including its religious character. Such a relationship may, of course, become perfunctory. Northwestern University is sometimes cited as such a case. Eight members of the 58-member board at Northwestern are elected by four conferences of the Methodist Church in Illinois and Michigan.[5]

Among the 817 institutions under consideration about one-third do not require church affiliation as a basis for board membership. Of these over one-half do not require nomination or election by a church body. (See Table 16.) Thus it is seen, about one-fifth of

Table 16: Church Nomination or Election of Board
Members in Absence of Church Membership Requirement

PERCENTAGE NOMINATED/ELECTED BY CHURCH	INSTITUTIONS REQUIRING CHURCH NOMINATION/ELECTION	
	N	%
0	130	53.5
1 – 25	9	3.3
26 – 50	8	3.0
51 – 75	16	5.9
76 – 100	74	30.5
Percentage not indicated	6	2.2
Total	243	100.0

[4] *Evansville College Bulletin, Catalog Number, 1962-1964*, p. 9.
[5] Allan M. Cartter (ed.), *American Universities and Colleges*. 9th ed. (Washington: American Council on Education, 1964), p. 381.

Table 17: Church Nomination or Election of Board Members by Church in Absence of Church Membership Requirement (by Seven Groups of Institutions)

INSTITUTIONS REQUIRING CHURCH NOMINATION/ELECTION

PERCENTAGE OF BOARD NOMINATED/ ELECTED BY CHURCH	Roman Catholic		Non-Catholic		Baptist		Lutheran		Methodist		Presbyterian		Newer Groups	
	N	%	N	%	N	%	N	%	N	%	N	%	N	%
0	63	90.0	67	38.7	8	42.1	1	16.7	14	25.9	11	31.4	0	0.0
1 – 25	0	0.0	9	5.2	0	0.0	1	16.7	2	3.7	1	2.9	0	0.0
26 – 50	0	0.0	8	4.6	1	5.3	0	0.0	5	9.3	0	0.0	0	0.0
51 – 75	0	0.0	16	9.3	1	5.3	3	50.0	5	9.3	2	5.7	0	0.0
76 – 100	7	10.0	67	38.7	8	42.1	1	16.7	26	48.1	20	57.1	1	100.0
Percentage not indicated	0	0.0	6	3.5	1	5.3	0	0.0	2	3.7	1	2.9	0	0.0
Total	70	100.0	173	100.0	19	100.0	6	100.0	54	100.0	35	100.0	1	100.0

41

the total group, specifically 130 institutions, make no claim of church affiliation on the basis of board composition.

As shown in Table 17, the tendency not to require church nomination or election in the absence of a provision requiring church membership of board members is markedly more pronounced among Roman Catholic institutions than it is among the non-Catholic ones. Where such a provision does exist it is most commonly found among the Lutheran and Methodist church groupings.

It is clear that the composition of the board is an important form of relationship between the colleges included in this study and their sponsoring churches. Because the board has full legal responsibility for the institution, this is potentially one of the most influential means of determining the character of a college or university as a church-affiliated institution.

Ownership

The second element which may constitute a relationship between a college and a church is that of ownership. (Ownership of an institution is, of course, a tangible legal relationship.) Many institutions of higher education are owned outright by a church or a division or an agency of a church. The University of the South, for example, is owned by 21 Southern dioceses of the Episcopal Church.[6] Likewise, the University of Notre Dame is owned by the Indiana Province of the Congregation of the Holy Cross.[7] Baylor University describes itself as the "property of the Baptist General Convention of Texas." [8] Specifically 70 percent of the institutions included in the study indicate that they are owned by a church or religious order or congregation. (See Table 10.)

Ownership of colleges by churches varies considerably, however, among the denominational groupings selected for special study. As Table 11 shows, almost all Roman Catholic institutions are owned by a community, order, or diocese, while only 52.7 percent of the non-Catholic institutions are owned by churches. Among the selected groupings, ownership is most frequent among the Lutherans (79.5

---

[6] *Bulletin of the University of the South, Annual Catalogue,* 1961-62, p. 7.

[7] Cartter, *op. cit.,* p. 424.

[8] *Ibid.,* p. 1096.

percent) and least frequent among the Presbyterians (42 percent) and the newer religious bodies (41.2 percent.)

Financial Support

Another common form of association between a church and its colleges is financial support. Table 10 shows that 93.7 percent of the colleges receive financial support in one form or another (for current or capital purposes) from official church sources.

College administrators usually feel that the amount of financial support is a dependable index of the seriousness of the church's interest in a college. The level of support varies widely. The degree to which the 817 colleges included in our study receive financial support from the churches with which they are associated may be seen from an examination of Table 18.

Table 18: Percentage of Educational and General Income Received from Church Sources

PERCENTAGE OF EDUCATIONAL AND GENERAL INCOME	INSTITUTIONS RECEIVING SUPPORT	
	N	%
0	214	26.2
1 – 5	159	19.5
6 – 10	100	12.3
11 – 25	126	15.4
26 – 50	87	10.6
Over 50	41	5.0
Percentage not indicated	90	11.0
Total	817	100.0

Somewhat less than one-half of the colleges and universities (47.2 percent) receive from one to 25 percent of their educational and general income from official church sources, while only 5 percent receive more than one-half from those sources. One-fourth of the institutions receive no church financial support at all. Where support of this kind is received, the average is 12.8 percent of the total educational and general income.

Table 19 shows that the amount of church support varies considerably among the several large groupings of institutions. One of the points of greatest weakness of Roman Catholic institutions is

Table 19: Percentage of Educational and General Income Received from Church Sources (by Seven Groups of Institutions)

INSTITUTIONS RECEIVING SUPPORT

PERCENTAGE OF EDUCATIONAL AND GENERAL INCOME	Roman Catholic		Non-Catholic		Baptist		Lutheran		Methodist		Presbyterian		Newer Groups	
	N	%	N	%	N	%	N	%	N	%	N	%	N	%
0	159	46.9	55	11.5	5	6.4	3	6.8	5	4.0	5	7.2	9	52.9
1 – 5	29	8.6	130	27.2	15	19.2	5	11.4	42	33.6	30	43.5	0	0.0
6 – 10	13	3.8	87	18.2	18	23.1	9	20.5	26	20.8	12	17.4	0	0.0
11 – 25	23	6.8	103	21.6	23	29.5	11	25.0	30	24.0	11	15.9	6	35.3
26 – 50	17	5.0	70	14.6	14	17.9	10	22.7	17	13.6	5	7.2	1	5.9
Over 50	23	6.8	18	3.8	1	1.3	6	13.6	1	0.8	3	4.4	1	5.9
Percentage not indicated	75	22.1	15	3.1	2	2.6	0	0.0	4	3.2	3	4.4	0	0.0
Total	339	100.0	478	100.0	78	100.0	44	100.0	125	100.0	69	100.0	17	100.0

44

the quite limited financial assistance provided by the Church and its religious orders and communities. About 46.9 percent of the Roman Catholic colleges receive no educational and general income from church sources, while about 12 percent of these institutions receive 10 percent or less of their income from this source. Only about 7 percent obtain more than one-half of their income from the Church or from religious organizations.

At the other end of the scale is the Lutheran Church-Missouri Synod—a notable example of generosity in the financing of colleges. One of the Synod's institutions, Concordia Senior College, describes its support as follows:

The College is financed by the Lutheran Church-Missouri Synod, which underwrites all operating expenses and defrays the original cost of the physical plant, fixtures, and equipment.[a]

Many Roman Catholic colleges receive support for current operation through the services contributed by members of the faculty and staff. Members of the sponsoring religious community are often assigned to a college, teaching or performing administrative tasks as their service to the Church. As is clear from Table 20, these

Table 20: Percentage of Educational and General Income of Roman Catholic Institutions Received in Contributed Services

PERCENTAGE OF INCOME	N	%
0	9	2.6
1 – 5	13	3.8
6 – 10	25	7.4
11 – 25	94	27.7
26 – 50	94	27.7
51 – 75	17	5.0
Over 75	5	1.5
Percentage not indicated	82	24.2
Total	339	100.0

services constitute a significant portion of the resources of Roman Catholic institutions. About 60 percent of the Roman Catholic colleges and universities reported that over 10 percent of their edu-

[a] *Concordia Senior College, Announcements for 1962-1963*, p. 14.

cational and general income was attributable to this type of subsidy.[10]

Among the large Protestant groupings there are marked differences in financial support. Returning to Table 19, we see that the Lutheran churches usually contribute to the educational and general incomes of their colleges; in about 60 percent of the cases they contribute over 10 percent. On the other hand, the Presbyterian churches and the newer religious groups contribute 10 percent or less of the current income in over one-half of their colleges. In only about 5 percent of the cases do either of these two groups contribute over 50 percent of the educational and general income. Approximately three-fourths of the Baptist and Methodist colleges receive up to one-fourth of their educational and general income from their churches.

In addition to funds received for current operating purposes, many institutions receive capital funds from the churches with which they are affiliated. We asked institutions whether they received "substantial" capital funds from their churches—"substantial" being left to each institution to define for itself. Table 21 shows that less than

Table 21: Extent to Which "Substantial" Capital
Funds Are Received from Official Church Sources

INSTITUTIONAL GROUP	INSTITUTIONS RECEIVING CAPITAL FUNDS	
	N	%
Baptist	55	70.5
Lutheran	33	75.0
Methodist	85	68.0
Presbyterian	36	52.2
Selected Newer Groups	7	41.2
Roman Catholic	59	17.4
Non-Catholic	305	63.8
All Institutions	364	44.6

one-half of the institutions (44.6 percent) reported this kind of support. Roman Catholic institutions reported such assistance much less frequently than non-Catholic colleges (17.4 percent and 63.8

[10] A note must be added here concerning the accuracy of the financial data for Roman Catholic institutions. Methods of accounting for contributed services vary from order to order and community to community and are often quite complex. Despite the relatively simple instructions accompanying our request for information on this point, a number of institutions found it difficult to provide the information we were seeking. No information was available from about one-fourth of the institutions. The writers believe, however, that the data presented here are reasonably representative of the whole group of Roman Catholic institutions.

percent, respectively). Among the non-Catholic institutions the colleges associated with Lutheran bodies most often benefit from such support. On the other hand, less than one-half of the colleges affiliated with the newer religious groups receive such funds.

Acceptance of Denominational Standards or Name

Some churches have established minimal standards, subscription to which is the chief basis for recognition as a church college. The United Presbyterian Church in the U.S.A. has such a statement, and Hanover College is an example of an institution that defines its Presbyterian relationship primarily in these terms:

> By its charter, the Trustees of Hanover College are independent of ecclesiastical control, but they have formally adopted for the institution the standards established for Presbyterian colleges . . . Hanover is a member of the Presbyterian College Union.[11]

A good illustration of an institution which, in intangible respects, has always maintained an aura of churchliness is Trinity College, Hartford, but it has a "non-sectarian" charter and no structural or financial connection with a church. By virtue of its membership in the Association of Episcopal Colleges, Trinity identifies itself with the Episcopal Church, and the Church, in turn, endorses the College. Thus it seems appropriate to regard the institution as a church-affiliated college, even though its relationship is informal.[12]

In some cases denominational relationships are reflected in the names of colleges and universities. Catholic University of America, Eastern Mennonite College, Hebrew Union College-Jewish Institute of Religion, Oklahoma Baptist University, Olivet Nazarene College, Pacific Lutheran University, St. Andrews Presbyterian College, and Southern Methodist University are examples. Also, though it is not clearly indicative of church association, a number of institutions bear names having ecclesiastical connotations, as Aquinas College (Roman Catholic), Calvin College (Christian Reformed), Illinois Wesleyan University (Methodist), Loyola University of Los Angeles (Roman Catholic), Luther College (American Lutheran), St.

[11] *1962-1963 Bulletin of Hanover College*, p. 8.
[12] The form of this relationship is defined in *Trinity College Bulletin, Catalogue Issue for 1962-1963*, p. 61.

Augustine's College (Episcopal), and William Penn College (Friends). However, Wesleyan University, Middletown, and St. John's College, Annapolis, are cases in which the names are vestiges of earlier affiliations and have no religious significance today.

The extent to which the acceptance of denominational standards or the use of a denominational name occurs among the 817 institutions is set forth under Item 4 in Table 10. Approximately three-fourths (77.2 percent) of all the colleges in the study reported such relationships. Affiliation with a denominational organization of colleges was claimed by 64.7 percent, while 48.1 percent subscribed to a set of standards adopted by a church for its colleges. On both of these points, the percentages were higher for the non-Catholic than for the Catholic institutions.

Among the several Protestant groups, the Methodist, Baptist, and Presbyterian colleges most frequently belonged to an organization of colleges related to their parent churches. (See Table 11.) The low percentage (11.8) for the colleges connected with the newer church groups derives from the fact that many of these groups sponsor only one college. Subscription to a set of standards as a basis for church relationship is most frequently reported by Presbyterian institutions.

Thus far, we have been talking about types of relationship which may or may not have an influence on the educational process itself. The remaining two elements of church relationship to be discussed are more directly concerned with teaching and scholarship.

Educational Aims

What does a college intend to do? Does it have a strongly religious orientation in its statement of purpose even though such an orientation may not be couched in the terms of a single denomination?[13] Two pronouncements of institutions whose churchly character lies in the kind of education they purport to offer rather than in organizational or financial arrangements follow.

Yeshiva University takes great pride in its "uniqueness" as an institution of higher learning. This singular quality stems from its very origins, which are

---

[13] We recognize that statements of purpose are not always fully realized through the curriculum and teaching of an institution. This is, however, a separate question with which we shall deal later in some detail.

rooted in two different systems of higher education. One is the *Yeshiva*, a school of traditional Jewish learning where the Torah, Talmud, and other original sources of Hebraic culture are studied, and from which the University inherits its essential character as well as its spiritual, moral, and ethical core. The second is the *University*, after which it has patterned its dynamic complex of schools and divisions, each resting on a deep-set foundation of liberal arts and sciences. This partnership of *Yeshiva* and *University* is a pioneering venture, with no precedent in the history of the Jewish community, or in the past traditions of American higher education.[14]

The institution's aim is:

To fuse the teaching of Judaism with the knowledge of the ages, for the development of the complete personality, the enrichment of the life of the Jewish community, and the advancement of our beloved country.[15]

A second institution whose churchly character is expressed through its approach to education is Swarthmore College:

Swarthmore College was founded by members of the Religious Society of Friends, and it seeks to illuminate the life of its students with the spiritual principles of that Society. Although it has been non-sectarian in control since the beginning of the present century, and although the children of Friends compose a minority of the student body, the College seeks to preserve the religious traditions out of which it sprang. The essence of Quakerism is the individual's responsibility for seeking truth and for applying whatever truth he believes he has found. As a way of life, it emphasizes hard work, simple living, and generous giving; personal integrity, social justice, and the peaceful settlement of disputes. The College does not seek to impose on its students this Quaker view of life, or any other specific set of convictions about the nature of things and the duty of man. It does, however, have the two-fold aim of encouraging conscious concern about such questions and unceasing re-examination of any view which may be held regarding them. That is the kind of ethical and religious character which Swarthmore seeks to develop.[16]

As our inquiry into church relationships proceeded, it became clear that the criterion "institutional statement of purpose reflects religious orientation" was too broad to be used properly as an indication of church affiliation. The statistical data reported on this item are not, therefore, particularly helpful for our present purpose. Where this criterion was important to the decision as to whether or not a particular institution was to be included on the list of church institutions

[14] *Yeshiva University Bulletin of General Information,* 1961-62, p. 6.
[15] *Ibid.,* p. 21.
[16] *Swarthmore College Bulletin, Catalogue Issue,* 1962-1963, p. 27.

we found it necessary to reinterpret the criterion to "institutional statement of purpose linked to a particular denomination." Put in these words, the criterion becomes, we believe, a valid indicator of church affiliation for the purposes of our study.

Selection of Faculty and Administrative Personnel

The last of the six elements selected as a means of identifying a college or university as church affiliated is whether church member-ship is a consideration in the selection of faculty and administrative personnel. Does a given college prefer to appoint to its staff persons who are members of a particular church? One of the surest means of influencing the religious character of an institution is through the appointment of staff members who share a common faith. Two noteworthy examples are the Principia College and Florida Christian College.

The Principia is not an activity of the Mother Church, The First Church of Christ, Scientist, in Boston, Massachusetts, or of any branch church, but is a privately owned, non-profit school and college for the sons and daughters of Christian Scientists. All faculty and staff members are Christian Scientists.[17]

In the case of Florida Christian College:

A charter was drafted which provided that all board and faculty personnel would be active members in good standing of some local Church of Christ, but that the College would be independent. No finances are accepted from any church, and there is no organizational tie between the College and any church. The Board nominates and elects its own members and is in every way independent of any church.[18]

While legally these two colleges and others like them have no organizational connection with religious bodies, their insistence on personnel who are members of particular denominations should, in our judgment, bring them within the purview of a comprehensive study of church institutions of higher education. The nine colleges staffed by members of the Churches of Christ are a particularly dramatic illustration of the impact of the outlook and polity (or, in this instance, lack of polity) of a religious group on educational

[17] The Principia College Announcements, 1962-63, p. 9.
[18] Bulletin, Florida Christian College . . . Annual Announcement for the Academic Year 1962-63, p. 17.

institutions. Any college operated by members of the Churches of Christ *must* be independent of church in the technical sense, since it is a matter of fundamental conviction that there cannot properly be any church structure or cooperative activity under church auspices above the level of the local congregation. Thus the only possibility of a Church of Christ college in the organizational sense would be an institution operated by a single congregation without relationships with other congregations.

Other illustrations of selection of personnel as means of maintaining a distinctive character in a church institution are Rosary College, in which 91 members of a total faculty and administrative staff of 125 persons are Sisters of the Order of Saint Dominic of the Congregation of the Most Holy Rosary,[19] and Bethel College, in which 47 of the 52 members of the administrative staff and faculty are Mennonites.[20]

Among the colleges and universities included in our study, 70.4 percent reported that preference was given to members of a particular church in the selection of faculty and administrative personnel. Roman Catholic institutions follow this policy somewhat more frequently than do non-Catholic colleges (74.3 percent and 67.6 percent, respectively). This policy is a factor in about four-fifths of the institutions related to Baptist, Lutheran, and the newer religious groups, and in about three-fifths of those affiliated with Methodist and Presbyterian bodies.

It should be emphasized, however, that relatively few colleges restrict appointments *only* to members of their own churches. It was interesting to find that on many of the forms returned by institutions checking this particular item, a notation was added emphasizing that academic qualifications took precedence over church membership in faculty and staff appointments. The following comments are illustrative: "Other things considered more important, however"; "if they are as well qualified as non-church candidates"; "depending on academic qualifications, etc."; "academic competence is chief consideration"; "emphasis is placed first of all upon educational qualifi-

[19] *Bulletin of Rosary College, 1962-1963*, pp. 11-21.
[20] Letter from Vernon H. Neufeld, President, Bethel College, dated January 4, 1963.

cations and character, after this, preference is given to a person who is actively Christian and to members of our own denomination."

SOME COMMENTS ON RELATIONSHIPS

In summary, the relationships between colleges and religious bodies are varied and often complex. Some institutions are church affiliated by virtue of only one or two specific types of relationship, while others have five or six distinct ties. Roman Catholic colleges tend to have more types of relationship than do Protestant institutions. Among the latter those associated with the Lutheran bodies have, as a group, the most extensive relationships with their churches. Board composition and financial support are the most frequent elements of church affiliation for these 817 institutions. Both elements are potentially significant means of shaping the character of an institution. Although about three-fourths of the colleges receive church funds for current operation, the average amount is only about 10 percent of the current income. Capital fund support from the churches is infrequent, especially in Roman Catholic institutions.

In some cases of institutions that are thought of as being closely held by churches, legal relationships with the churches are entirely or almost entirely absent. Conversely, ownership by a church does not automatically mean that an institution has other strong bonds of relationship. A fair proportion of the colleges give attention to church membership in selecting faculty and staff, but in most instances the colleges state emphatically that this factor is secondary to academic competence.

Almost all of the institutions reported that their statements of purpose reflected a definite religious orientation. Yet it is interesting that there were some whose formal educational purposes do not have a religious flavor, although the institutions are clearly church related. In this phase of our study, of course, we made no effort to ascertain the actual religious influence of the institutions on their students.

The analysis of relationships between colleges and religious bodies underscores clearly why it is so difficult to formulate a satisfactory definition of these institutions. Each one is unique in its relationship, and a rather intimate knowledge of a complex of factors is required to understand its status as a church-affiliated institution.

The correlation between college administration and church polity is a fascinating and complicated area of inquiry. The sociology and psychology of religious bodies are also influential forces in church-affiliated higher education. The distinctive flavor or ethos of a sponsoring group often affects a college in subtle ways of which it is unaware. These are some of the factors that make for wide diversity in American education and culture.

4

What
Makes a
Good College?

If we are to assess the present position of church-affiliated higher education and suggest guidelines for its improvement, we must formulate a reasonably explicit set of criteria—bench marks by which to judge educational quality. These should be criteria that are appropriate to the whole range of colleges and universities with which we are concerned, regardless of their size, location, or church affiliation. In the nature of things, the criteria will be general and will not be susceptible to precise mathematical application. The history of institutional evaluation suggests, however, that there are certain definable characteristics which are generally accepted by the academic world as clues to quality.

In this country the systematic evaluation of colleges goes back about fifty years, when accrediting agencies began to wrestle with the problem of how to bring order out of the chaos that then existed in higher education. Initially the major task was to define a collegiate institution in order to separate colleges from academies. The Carnegie Foundation for the Advancement of Teaching and the United States Bureau of Education, as well as accrediting agencies, were active in this movement. The early "standards," as they were called, were really efforts to describe the level of instruction and the organization of educational institutions which might properly be regarded as colleges. These descriptions were formulated in what we would consider to be mechanical terms, specifying the number of departments, the number of credits to be required for degrees, definitions of subject-matter units for admission, and similar matters. The accrediting bodies were known as "standardizing agencies." Later the require-

54

ments for accreditation were elaborated into more comprehensive standards specifying the minima that were acceptable with respect to faculty training, library holdings, amount of endowment, etc. Heavy reliance was placed on "objective" (that is, quantitative) measures of institutional excellence. For example, a certain number or percentage of Ph.D.'s on the faculty and a certain number of books in the library were regarded as essential. Most of the leadership in the accrediting movement at that time came from the stronger institutions and the better-known college and university presidents of the day.[1]

Meanwhile, a group of pioneers in the survey method, as applied to higher education, were developing more refined techniques. Floyd W. Reeves, Frederick J. Kelly, Arthur J. Klein, John Dale Russell, and George A. Works were perhaps the most prominent men in this effort. They were commissioned to make systematic surveys of individual institutions and also groups of colleges and universities such as those of the Disciples of Christ and of the Methodist Church. Statistical methods were applied ingeniously to almost every aspect of college operation. This type of evaluation reached its high point in two monumental events: the adoption by the North Central Association of Colleges and Secondary Schools of a revised procedure for accrediting—the result of a large-scale study begun in 1929 and financed by the General Education Board; and the completion of the University of Chicago Survey in 1933, under the direction of Floyd W. Reeves. The results of this survey were summarized in 12 volumes containing hundreds of statistical tables. Sixty-four tables appeared in Volume I alone!

The North Central Association procedure became the model for most other accrediting agencies and continues to influence accrediting activities even today. Its study introduced two new principles into institutional evaluation. The first of these was that a college should be judged on the basis of its stated purposes rather than on standards applied uniformly to all institutions regardless of purpose. Second, the notion of minimum standards was abandoned, and in its place a ranking system was employed. Thus the college being appraised was ranked

[1] For a useful history of college accrediting see William K. Selden, *Accreditation: A Struggle Over Standards in Higher Education* (New York: Harper & Brothers, 1960).

on many criteria, and the final judgment about its quality was arrived at by reviewing the total profile. The older idea had been that an institution was unacceptable if it failed to come up to the minimum on any *one* of many standards. The term "standard" was given up and in its place "criterion" was adopted as being a more descriptive term. In the hands of skillful examiners the new methods of evaluating institutions were a marked improvement over the earlier procedures.

Several points are worth noting here. First, over the years there has been a trend in institutional evaluation toward giving a larger place to the personal judgment of competent observers and a smaller place to measurement in the statistical sense. In discussions of the subject, a distinction has often been made between the "qualitative" and "quantitative" approaches, although these terms are not quite accurate, since the "qualitative" approach takes account of quantitative data whenever appropriate. What is really intended by the distinction is that quantitative criteria should not be routinely applied as though they were automatic indices of quality. Second, the criteria of institutional excellence used by accrediting agencies and other appraising bodies have generally reflected the conception of quality held by college and university administrators. Accrediting agencies are governed by administrators, and most of the examiners are themselves administrators. Third, the appraisal of institutions has been based primarily on an examination of the *means* of education. Educators have not yet discovered feasible ways of evaluating different types of institutions by measuring educational *outcomes*. Fourth, reliance is placed not on one or two criteria but on a wide range of institutional characteristics. Fifth, careful analysis of the way in which such criteria are derived shows that there is an unavoidable circularity in the logic. In other words, the criteria are identified from an examination of conditions and practices in the better institutions, but the original judgment as to which are the better institutions depends in turn on the use of criteria, whether stated or not. This circularity was especially apparent in the North Central Association revision of standards.

It should be emphasized that accrediting committees are not the only persons engaged in the appraisal of institutions of higher learning. Educational consultants, foundations, governmental agencies, learned societies, management-consultant firms, and the administrators of individual institutions are all involved in this process in one way or another. Self-surveys of colleges and universities by committees of administrators and faculty members employ many of the same methods. One of the most elaborate of these projects was the survey of the University of Pennsylvania, conducted in the 1950's. More recently, studies of specialized aspects of higher education by psychologists and sociologists have contributed to the refinement of institutional study techniques, though the slowness and expense of these methods have limited their usefulness. The investigation of student values is an area in which social scientists have been especially active.

MEANS OF APPRAISAL

Though methods of appraisal have changed, and though in some respects higher education itself has been modified through the introduction of new teaching and administrative techniques, we are probably safe in saying that the essentials of good collegiate education have remained relatively stable. In the remainder of this chapter we shall suggest eight general criteria which seem to us to embody the best of what has been developed by accrediting agencies and to include certain additional values derived from the nature of the educational process, which accrediting agencies, because of their quasi-public character, are not able to insist upon in their procedures. In fairness to accrediting agencies it should be recognized that they are forced by the circumstances in which they operate to rely more heavily than would be desirable on "objective" means of appraisal. What we propose using in our appraisal here is a rationale which takes into account both objective analysis, as far as that will carry us, and the personal judgments of observers. Although these principles are broad enough for appraisal of any institution of higher learning, we are thinking primarily of the undergraduate college of arts and sciences. Some adaptation and elaboration of the principles are necessary if they are to be used in the assessment of universities containing graduate and professional schools. We shall give further attention to this matter elsewhere. Also, we shall not deal here with the more technical problems involved in applying the criteria. Our interest at this point is in the general question, "What makes a good college?"

ANTECEDENTS TO BUILDING A SOUND PROGRAM

Before discussing the eight criteria, we must mention three antecedents to the building of a sound educational program—leadership, money, and plant and equipment. The role of the president of a college is, of course, crucial. Without an able educator as its chief executive officer, an institution is seriously handicapped in creating or maintaining a quality program. It is normally the president who must provide vision and perspective; he is in the best position to view the institution as a whole and to understand its needs in comprehensive terms. It is he who must unify the college, serve as a link between the trustees and the faculty, and correlate the interests of the various groups that provide funds and exercise influence on the institution. The selection and continuing effectiveness of the president depend, in turn, on a wise and dedicated board of trustees. The leadership of the president and the board cannot, of course, stand alone. Deans and senior faculty members ultimately determine in large part what happens in the classroom. Able faculty leadership is essential. The president and the board, working together, must obtain the necessary financial resources and facilities for the undergirding of the educational program. On them rests the primary responsibility for careful planning of the future of the institution. Adequate funds and facilities are necessary for a strong college. Though not themselves educative, they affect the work of the faculty and students at many points. Given these three elements—leadership, money, and facilities—what are the best indicators of quality as perceived more directly in the process of teaching and learning?

ATTRIBUTES OF A GOOD COLLEGE

Seriousness of Purpose

Perhaps the first attribute of a good college is its seriousness of purpose. The students came for the purpose of learning; the faculty is determined that the students shall succeed in this. The main business is education, and the amenities of campus life are not permitted to interfere. It may seem that this is platitudinous, but the truth is that colleges and universities differ widely in the seriousness of their purposes. Some institutions have a much more tolerant attitude than others toward the casual student—the fellow who came to be with his friends and just to get a degree. As one visits campuses and talks with faculty and students, he can see marked differences in this respect. Seriousness of purpose in a college can overcome many handicaps of other kinds; without it, not much else matters—the institution is destined to mediocrity.

Teaching and learning are not ends in themselves. The goal of the college must have roots in deeper values. A college ought to know what it stands for, and these values should be perceivable in the daily lives of the faculty and students. An important part of the assessment of an institution or group of institutions is the effort to apprehend the convictions or presuppositions having the greatest influence on what is thought and done.

Awareness of Distinctive Role

The second ingredient of quality institutions is a clear awareness of their distinctive roles within the total enterprise of higher education. A good college works hard to define its educational goals and to design its curriculum specifically for the type of student it admits. It has a definite sense of direction. It is to be distinguished from the nondescript institution that does whatever other people are doing, often trying to be all things to all men. A quality institution is not afraid to be different when to be different means to be better.

While the character of a liberal arts college is circumscribed by its primary function of promoting the intellectual, moral, and artistic development of individual students, a wide variety of more specific aims and patterns of education is possible within this broad purpose. The imaginative development, within the general principles of quality, of a distinctive educational idea, a distinctive teaching method, a distinctive location, a distinctive constituency—these are often the means of building strength in a college. The diversity which already exists among some of the better liberal arts colleges of the country is indicative of the possibilities for distinctive character.

The educational purposes of many colleges are infused with religious motivation. This can be an important ingredient of institutional distinctiveness. Where such is the case, the role played by religion in the institution should be carefully defined so that prospective students and faculty members will be properly informed and the statement of purposes can provide a clear guide for the development of the educational program.

Selection and Retention of Faculty

The third ingredient of a first-class college, as we see it, is the care with which it selects and retains faculty members. Each appointment is regarded as a strategic decision. Even in appointments to the lower ranks, the institution acts on the assumption that the young teacher will stay until retirement, to affect the lives of the students for almost half a century. Moreover, the responsible undergraduate college will reject the overriding claims of any one of the broad qualifications for an educational post—sound scholarship, teaching ability, and personal integrity. It will insist on all three.

This point is worth pursuing. There has been some sentiment in academic circles for a separation of the three main qualifications for a teaching scholar. For example, it has been fashionable to elevate scholarly competence and to play down teaching ability and personal integrity. Often, in the name of academic freedom, scholarship and character have been contrasted, as though there were little relationship between the two and the second were an improper criterion. We see no reason for this. Is it too much to expect that the faculty member be a competent scholar, a skillful teacher, and a good person? Surely a responsible institution is interested in academic accomplishment within a context of moral principles, and these principles are most likely to influence students when they are exemplified in the faculty itself.

In the evaluation of faculty competence the question of degrees always arises. The doctorate (particularly the Ph.D. degree) is highly esteemed by college administrators, accrediting agencies, and faculty members themselves as representing the desirable preparation for undergraduate teaching in most fields. Though the Ph.D. is a research degree and is not awarded in recognition of teaching ability, there is certainly much to be said for the Ph.D. program as the highest level of conventional training offered by American universities. However, the persistent and informed criticism of the advanced work in graduate schools as being narrow and poorly organized cannot be ignored. As the supply of persons with this training becomes less and less adequate to meet the demand for college teachers, some better form of preparation may be developed, or it may be found that the doctorate is not so important for undergraduate teaching as many institutions have supposed. Further questions can properly be raised about the uniformity of the doctorate as an index of scholarly attainment. Not only do universities vary greatly in their expectations of graduate students, but there are also differences among departments in a single university. It may well be that a master's degree from some universities indicates a higher level of competence than a doctorate from others. By the same token, a top-ranking student from one of the lesser graduate schools may have greater scholarly potential than a person who barely met the requirements for a doctorate in a more distinguished university. Thus it is seen that the Ph.D. degree (not to mention the sixty-seven other doctor's degrees conferred by American universities) is far from being a well-defined yardstick of scholarship.

In making appointments, some institutions look upon a doctorate from a reputable university as a minimal requirement and then give careful attention to additional qualifications. While this policy can eliminate much of the lack of uniformity represented by the degree itself, it does not deal with the problem of the narrowness of doctoral training. For some men a period of several years may be required to overcome the lack of perspective inherent in advanced graduate study. Some, alas, never overcome it! A strong case can be made for a broader type of preparation for college teaching, such, perhaps, as that represented by a divisional master's degree. Until graduate schools become better organized and their programs of study are more carefully worked out, it will be difficult to defend the emphasis which has been placed upon the doctorate in the selection of faculty members.[2] Interpreted cautiously, however, the doctor's degree remains *one* useful indicator of scholarly maturity. What could we put in its place?

There are several factors which may be deserving of greater attention in the evaluation of college faculties than they are normally given. One is the breadth of backgrounds of faculty members. For example, it is desirable that a faculty, as a group, have a reasonably wide geographical and institutional background. Often a faculty is

---

[2] For documentation of these criticisms the reader is referred to Oliver C. Carmichael, *Graduate Education: A Critique and a Program* (New York: Harper & Brothers, 1961).

weakened by inbreeding or too heavy reliance upon a few neighboring graduate schools.

Some examination of scholarly interests, not just the possession of degrees, is highly desirable in faculty appraisal. This is difficult to accomplish, but it can be done reasonably well in the evaluation of a small college. However, the kind of data obtained by some accrediting agencies on numbers of articles and books written and on amount of faculty participation in learned-society activities is open to so many objections, when gathered routinely, as virtually to undermine all confidence in the findings. A more useful index is a consideration of the provisions made by an institution for faculty growth, such as financial assistance for attendance at professional meetings and for additional graduate study.

Another factor that is deserving of greater attention than it usually receives in the appraisal of faculties is the matter of balance in point of view, especially within departments. If a particular philosophical orientation is implicit in the purposes of an institution, that fact should be taken into account in determining qualifications for appointments. Faculty appointments, however, often reflect bias of one sort or another which is not fully recognized by the appointing authorities. In many fields there are schools of thought vying for academic ascendency and for the allegiance of students. In general, it seems best that administrators understand these biases and arrange faculty appointments in such a way as to assure an opportunity for the student to be exposed to all major schools of thought in a given field. In the social sciences, for example, there are often differences in methodology or values between "behaviorists" and "theoreticians," "liberals" and "conservatives," and so forth. If an educational institution defends its right to permit and even to encourage diversity in the scholarly conclusions of its faculty—and that is indispensable to the whole process of sound teaching and learning—it can hardly allow individual departments to "stack the cards," so to speak, through the appointive procedure.

Where the purposes of an institution require special faculty qualifications beyond the requirement of impartial scholarship, this should be made clear in advance to candidates for teaching positions and to prospective students. The religious commitments of institutions are a case in point. If, for example, a college intends to be a

Christian community and to conduct its work within a Christian context, the appointment of faculty members who are sympathetic with this purpose and can make a contribution to such a community is an important factor in selection. From the point of view of academic integrity, it is essential to make the additional qualification explicit to everyone concerned. The selection of personnel is, of course, the indispensable means by which an institution carries out its purposes. Thus purpose and staffing are intimately associated in a well-administered institution.

Where the purposes of a college necessitate religious or other special qualifications for the faculty, is it wise to expect all members of the teaching staff to meet the qualifications? Should provision be made for what has been called "ventilation"? In a matter so basic as religion, is the student entitled to some teachers who hold other convictions? Would the appointment of a few such persons promote or obstruct the accomplishment of institutional purposes? These are difficult questions to answer with any degree of certitude, but the importance of freedom in an academic institution would seem to argue for some diversity of faculty outlook even at the risk of reducing the religious impact. How "ventilation" is to be provided is a question for which there can be no general answer applicable to all institutions. It will depend upon the particular conditions in the individual college.

It goes almost without saying that a major factor in the retention of able teachers is the maintenance of satisfactory conditions of service, including adequate salaries, provision for tenure, proper teaching loads, opportunity for research and scholarly refreshment, a retirement plan, and other conventional fringe benefits. High faculty turnover in a college is often a symptom of failure to provide conditions of service comparable to those of other institutions.

Selection of Students

The fourth characteristic of a good college is careful selection of students in the light of institutional purposes. As more and more colleges reach the position of having to select their students from a substantially larger number of applicants than can be accepted, it becomes clear that this is a more complex problem than has been generally assumed. An increasing awareness of the human waste involved in the high rate of student attrition in many institutions is also focusing attention on admission policies.

Reliance on a single criterion, such as high school record or College Entrance Examination Board test scores, does not usually serve to match students and institutional objectives. In a thoughtful treatment of this subject President Miller Upton, of Beloit College, recently suggested that a college should try to have a student body that is homogeneous in intellectual ability and diversified in terms of geographic origin, national and cultural background, and socioeconomic status. He stressed these two points: that intellectual homogeneity in the student body is a good thing because it makes for effective teaching; that, while careful selection of students is implicit in educational quality, selection of superior students *only* is not a pre-condition of quality. In his terms a college that admitted only students in the third quarter of their high school classes would be a quality institution if it stimulated them to the highest academic achievement of which they were capable.[3] President Upton's first point runs counter to that expressed some years ago by former President Frank Aydelotte, of Swarthmore College, who, at a time when Swarthmore was beginning to limit its student body to very able young people, emphasized that a college serving primarily high-ability students needs "the humanizing influence of the average student." It is difficult to reconcile these two principles. What we can conclude, however, is that each institution ought to have a well-defined admission policy specifically related to its educational purposes.

Recent research on creativity is useful in this connection. Investigations at the University of California, the University of Minnesota, and elsewhere show that creativity and high intellectual ability, as conventionally measured, are not the same thing.[4] The creative student, the one who is destined to make a major contribution to our scholarly and cultural life, is not always the "good" student. In the circumstances of present-day education, the creative student may graduate from secondary school with a poor academic record. The distinctions between the creative, the bright, the conscientious, and

[3] Miller Upton, "Quality in Higher Education," *North Central Association Quarterly*, XXXVII, 4 (Spring, 1963), pp. 307-314.
[4] E. Paul Torrance, *Guiding Creative Talent* (Englewood Cliffs, New Jersey: Prentice-Hall, Inc., 1962), pp. 16-23.

the highly motivated student are likely to receive greater attention in the future.

Curricular Design

Another aspect of quality in higher education is rational curricular design. A well-planned undergraduate curriculum will assure proper treatment of the various kinds of human experience. The general education of the individual student will give adequate attention to the broad fields of knowledge—the humanities (including religion), the fine or creative arts, the social studies, and the natural sciences. No one can say with any precision what fraction of the student's time should be allocated to each field, but at least the faculty can see to it that the graduating senior has some understanding and appreciation of each.

Rational curricular design also requires a clear formulation by the faculty of the common body of knowledge, intellectual skills, and other learning considered essential to the liberally educated person. This common body of learning is the heart of liberal education. It is the basis of the general requirements for graduation. It is the *raison d'etre*, the indispensable element, of liberal education, and without it the liberal arts college loses its strategic place in higher education.

Atmosphere of Intellectual Ferment

The sixth characteristic of a good college is an atmosphere of intellectual ferment. This quality is manifested in the encouragement of independent study and thought, in the involvement of the faculty and students in the intellectual issues of the day, in freedom of discussion, in student preoccupations, in the centrality of the library in the academic economy, in the educational aspirations of graduates, and in other ways. Though it is a quality that is difficult to measure with precision, it usually strikes the perceptive visitor dramatically as he interviews students and faculty members on the campus. Its importance in liberal education is one of the chief justifications for systematic visits as the proper procedure by which to appraise colleges. Without intellectual excitement liberal education becomes a barren affair.

Many colleges have found that the encouragement of independent work on the part of the student is one of the surest means of creating intellectual ferment. There is reason to believe that the assumption by the student of more responsibility for his education increases the likelihood that he will continue his education on his own after graduation. The notion that learning can take place only in formal courses has plagued American education. A common way of conducting a college course has been to use a textbook and assign a few pages of reading in it for each class session, the class time being devoted to lectures or recitations covering much the same material as that contained in the book. Not only does this make learning dull, but it is also a waste of valuable time. No useful purpose is served by merely repeating in class what the student is supposed to have studied outside. Moreover, this pattern of teaching usually leads to an emphasis on acquiring *information* to the neglect of clarifying *ideas*. There is ample evidence that ideas, once thoroughly understood, become a permanent part of the student, whereas information, unrelated to ideas in the mind of the student, is forgotten to a considerable extent in a few months.[5] This is now being overcome. Spoonfeeding is more and more being viewed as bad education. Both information and ideas —and, it might be added, skills—are important in education. The use of independent study-plans, in which the student is expected to dig out knowledge for himself, preferably from original sources, instead of relying on lectures or textbooks, enhances the quality of higher education.

In this connection, something should be said about informality in relation to learning. It appears that informality and ease of communication exist at some of the institutions that have exhibited unusual intellectual vitality—colleges and universities that have produced far more than their share of the educated leadership of the United States. To be sure, this relationship is more difficult to achieve in a large university than in a small college, and this may in part account for the remarkable productivity of certain small, high-quality colleges. There may well be other educational outcomes to be derived from informality. The use of seminars and other small-group teaching procedures, as distinguished from the large lecture-hall technique, is good preparation for many roles that college graduates play in later

[5] Luella Cole, *The Background for College Teaching* (New York: Farrar & Rinehart, Inc., 1940), pp. 280-90.

life. More and more of the business of the world is being transacted by small groups of people around tables. Almost everywhere today, important decisions are made by committees, boards, commissions, and similar bodies. How better can students learn to take their places in these organizations than by practicing the techniques of discussion, debate, and persuasion in college?

The residential college, which is in a better position than the commuter's institution to give the student a full collegiate experience, has distinct advantages from the point of view of interpersonal relationships. This is one of the reasons that residential life has been so much stressed in the British collegiate tradition, the tradition of which the liberal arts college is the heir in the United States. Residential life is an area of education in which we are likely to see a good deal of significant experimentation in the future. The religiously oriented college, in view of its concern for personal relationships as vested with religious significance, should be in the forefront of this movement.

We mentioned that the involvement of the faculty and students in discussion of the issues of the day is one of the marks of intellectual ferment in a college. You may be saying to yourself that this is all well and good but that it is quite possible for faculty and students to fritter away their time on peripheral causes to the detriment of solid liberal education. Some of the earlier excesses of progressive education, with its emphasis upon the contemporaneous, stand as lamentable examples of superficiality in this respect. Yet the fact remains that grappling with important current issues is a habit that the intelligent student needs to form, and it can contribute greatly to the purposes of liberal education if it is done in the light of enduring principles. This exercise brings home to the student the fact that liberal education, of all types of education, is most concerned with the stuff of real life.

We could say much about the necessity of freedom in a college or university. Freedom is important in a Christian institution, which has not only academic but also theological reasons for insisting on as large a measure of freedom for the individual as is consonant with the freedom of others. As William Temple said, "Freedom is the first presupposition of the Gospel. . . . For it is in and through his freedom that a man makes fully real his personality—the quality of one made in the image of God." [6] As we have already suggested, it is perfectly proper for an institution of higher learning to appoint to its faculty only persons who seem most likely to contribute to its purposes (including whatever religious purposes it has); but, once appointed, faculty members must have intellectual freedom if they are to discharge their educational responsibilities. This is such an important principle that colleges and universities should be prepared to withstand pressures from all quarters and to endure criticism and loss of favor in order to uphold it. And the faculty, in turn, should allow similar freedom to the students.

Another evidence of intellectual ferment in an undergraduate college is the status of the library. Where faculty and students are engaged in serious academic work, the library inevitably becomes an important resource. Heavy demands will be placed upon it for the acquisition of additional materials, and it will be well patronized by faculty and students.

We mentioned the educational aspirations of the graduates of an institution as a sign of intellectual vitality. If a college is serving an academically able group of students and has an alert faculty, a substantial fraction of the students will be stimulated to undertake more advanced study in graduate and professional schools. The record of an institution in this respect will depend in part on the type of student admitted (as well as on the quality of the program), and direct comparisons of institutions without taking that factor into account would be improper. However, the academic record of graduates is one useful index of institutional vitality.

Self-Criticism

The seventh characteristic of a quality institution is self-criticism. A good college is constantly striving to improve its program. It uses the best techniques that have been developed for appraising educational results—techniques far superior to the earlier methods of testing. It gathers systematic evidence regarding the impact of its program on its students. Closely allied with its critical attitude is a willingness to experiment with promising new approaches to the art of teaching and the organization of courses. The possibilities of

---

[6] William Temple, *Christianity and the Social Order* (Harmondsworth, Middlesex, England: Penguin Books, 1956), pp. 61-62.

the discussion and case-study methods of instruction, audio-visual aids, professional librarianship, modern student-personnel services, off-campus educational experiences, and other opportunities for improvement of curriculum and teaching are fully exploited.

Ultimate Effect on Students

The last of our points concerns the ultimate effect of a college on its students. What is the most valuable contribution an institution can hope to make to the lives of its students? Our answer is a reasoned framework of belief that gives meaning to human existence. It should be a faith that has something to say about the inescapable realities of life—good and evil, joy and suffering, death, history, God —a faith that will stand the test of time. It should be the student's own in the sense that it is a part of him—he has thought it through —though probably not his own in the sense that he invented it.

Higher education cannot, even if it would, "give" the student a faith. An adequate faith is a product of many influences. (This is in itself a subtle and complicated matter.) But a college can at least inform the student about the principal alternatives and help him acquire the intellectual tools and a disposition to consider maturely fundamental questions. Through curricular means it can encourage him to organize and unify his knowledge and strive for depth of understanding. It can hold up wisdom and commitment as goals to be sought.

These, then, are eight ingredients of quality in a liberal arts college. Considered in relation to educational leadership, financial support, and plant and equipment, they provide criteria for assessing the present condition of undergraduate education and guidelines for its improvement. In subsequent chapters these will serve as the basis on which we shall try to make judgments about the position of church-sponsored higher education in the United States.

5

Freedom, Responsibility, and Institutional Purpose

One of the criticisms most often made of colleges and universities associated with churches is that they restrict the freedom of their faculties and students and that this weakness is inherent in their reason for being. If their aim is not to indoctrinate, why, ask the critics, do they exist? This is such an important question that we felt it appropriate to devote a separate chapter to the subject. It will not be our purpose here to evaluate the status of freedom in the 817 church-affiliated institutions—we shall attempt that later. Rather, our purpose here is to consider the interrelationships of three conditions we consider necessary to the welfare of collegiate education.

We believe that much of the uneasiness about discussions of academic freedom is caused by simplistic assumptions—that is, by the tendency of each interested group to concentrate on a single aspect of the problem (usually faculty rights or the expectations of the constituency) to the exclusion of other essential factors. It is our thesis that a defensible policy for higher education requires that three elements —freedom, responsibility, and institutional purpose—be considered as an indissoluble cluster of desiderata, no one of which can properly be pursued without reference to the other two. Thus the college administrator is placed in the difficult position of the circus juggler who must do justice to three balls at the same time. How much simpler and tidier it would be to manage one ball and ignore the others! But the sound management of higher education is not simple and tidy, and it can be made so only at the expense of neglecting something essential.

In the preceding chapter we stressed the principle that a college should define its purposes carefully and plan its program in accordance with its announced purposes. This is axiomatic in all social organization.[1] In higher education this principle means that institutional purposes will determine the qualifications for faculty appointments, the policies governing the admission of students, the kind of persons who should be asked to serve as administrative officers and trustees, the curricular requirements to be met by students, the selection of materials for the library, and many other matters. One need only observe the differences in all of these respects between, for example, a medical college and a junior college for women to see how far-reaching are the consequences of differences in purpose.

No one quarrels with this general principle. It is so obviously necessary if education is to be a rational enterprise. Who would suggest that the professor in an engineering college should have the same training and interests as a teacher in a conservatory of music? Nor should we expect to find the same books in the libraries of the two institutions. The competencies required of students for graduation should also differ.

We might say that careful definition of purpose and the organization of the educational program in terms of a clear purpose are the hallmarks of a well-administered institution of higher learning. Unless a college makes every effort to accomplish what it purports to accomplish, it cannot be regarded as an effective institution. Definition of purpose is the first step toward systematic evaluation.[2] However, the point to be noted here is that a carefully-defined institutional purpose is, in the very nature of things, a restriction on freedom. It molds the institution. In effect it precludes some courses of action. As we have seen, it demands that certain things be done. At least, this is true if the institution is to be rationally managed, and a college, of all organizations, should be rational.

As long as institutional purposes prescribe certain kinds of *academic* behavior, academic people tend to accept these demands as "cricket." But when institutional purposes entail behavior in what Huston Smith

---

[1] A classical treatment of the centrality of purpose in the theory of organization is found in Chester I. Barnard, *The Functions of the Executive* (Cambridge: Harvard University Press, 1958), especially pp. 82-95.
[2] Paul L. Dressel and Associates, *Evaluation in Higher Education* (Boston: Houghton Mifflin Company, 1961), pp. 3-53.

has called the area of "human virtues" (as distinct from "intellectual virtues"), the question of freedom is immediately raised.[3] The "intellectual virtues," as identified by Smith, are intellectual honesty, scope of knowledge, dialectical agility, and aesthetic sensitivity. The broader "human virtues," though proclaimed by institutions in their public statements and expected of colleges by the general public, are considered by many college teachers to be "subjective" and not the proper business of higher education—at least when dealt with explicitly. The "human virtues," as Smith uses the term, include those having to do with moral character, citizenship, and religion.

Higher education has been much criticized, directly and indirectly, for not doing what it purports to do with respect to the broader values. The sensitivity of the academic world to these criticisms has been dramatically exhibited in its reaction (amounting almost to an obsession) to such diverse works as William F. Buckley's *God and Man at Yale: The Superstitions of "Academic Freedom"*, C. S. Lewis' *The Abolition of Man*, and Phillip E. Jacob's *Changing Values in College: An Exploratory Study of the Impact of College Teaching*. The last book has probably been more widely discussed by college administrators than any other on higher education written since World War II.

The contemporary educator is torn between the time-honored social responsibility of education for transmitting religious, social, and moral values to the oncoming generation—a responsibility which has been acknowledged throughout history—and inhibitions resulting from the Enlightenment view of man, logical positivism, fear of indoctrination, and a narrowly academic conception of education. These inhibitions are especially strong in the case of religion, but the issues involved are similar in the other disciplines of the humanities and in the social sciences. Certainly, American college teachers have been less reticent about the espousal of liberal secular values than of religious values during the twentieth century.[4] This perhaps reflects

[3] This discussion draws heavily on Huston Smith's illuminating analysis, "Values: Academic and Human", in Marjorie Carpenter, ed., *The Larger Learning* (Dubuque, Iowa: Wm. C. Brown Company Publishers, 1960), pp. 1-22.
[4] Richard Hofstadter, *Anti-Intellectualism in American Life* (New York: Alfred A. Knopf, 1963), pp. 38-40.
Religion, as a field of knowledge, poses more obvious epistemological problems than most other disciplines in colleges and universities. The acknowledgment of revelation as an avenue to truth clashes with the more restricted epistemological con-

the high degree of religious pluralism in our country. In part it may be attributable to the larger measure of consensus among intellectuals in behalf of liberal secular values than has been the case with religious values. Questions about freedom and indoctrination are less likely to be raised by academic people when the values with which they are dealing are implicitly accepted by them. As Sir Richard Livingstone has pointed out in *Education for a World Adrift*, every age has assumptions that are exempted from scrutiny. These are probably the values that are most effectively inculcated by schools and colleges and without misgivings about indoctrination.

"Indoctrination" is a word that calls for comment. The teacher who presents, in a reasoned way, beliefs which he considers to be true and important for the well-being of the student is not likely to describe this process as "indoctrination." He thinks of it, rather, as the proper work of a conscientious teacher. Yet another person, who does not share these beliefs, may feel that the teacher has taken improper advantage of the teacher-student relationship. What is or is not indoctrination in an offensive sense seems, then, to depend largely on the value convictions of the observer and the methods of teaching employed. Perhaps the true criterion is the teacher's motive. If the teacher is trying to help the student *elevate* and *clarify* his values, that is legitimate teaching. If, on the other hand, the student is *being used for a purpose other than his own welfare*, we have indoctrination. Legitimate teaching strives for active understanding, indoctrination for passive acceptance.

How are we to reconcile freedom and commitment, or freedom, responsibility, and institutional purpose? Let it be agreed that the purposes of every educational institution carry within them, unavoid-

---

viction of many present-day scholars. It can be argued that the study of religion gives the student a broader view of truth and thus helps him overcome the logical-positivist provincialism of our age. Viewed in this way, religion may contribute significantly to the liberating process of liberal education.

As for social values, they are in turmoil today. The development of a strong conservative movement has, on some campuses, made controversial liberal economic and political values which have been accepted without serious question by most faculty people. What effect this will have remains to be seen. It may result in greater pluralism with respect to social values. At any rate, the struggle between liberal and conservative or modernist and traditionalist values—no terminology is entirely satisfactory—is a pervasive phenomenon of the middle of the twentieth century, and higher education is deeply involved. For a conservative interpretation of the struggle, as it affects American colleges, see M. Stanton Evans, *Revolt on the Campus* (Chicago: Henry Regnery Company, 1961).

ably, certain values. These values ordinarily represent not only the convictions of the present staff as to what is good, true, and beautiful but at least a residue of the convictions of previous generations who have contributed time, thought, and money to the development of the institution. The purposes, whatever they may be, should be carefully defined and should then become the basis for selection of teachers, development of curriculum, and other major decisions affecting the whole character of the institution. In particular, faculty members should be appointed who can contribute effectively to the achievement of the purposes, including the reasoned and persuasive presentation of the underlying philosophy of the institution. The faculty qualifications which stem from this philosophy should be made explicit to everyone concerned. As was emphasized in the last chapter, the selection of personnel is the principal means by which an institution carries out its purposes. The faculty and administration are then equipped to create a climate of learning in which the purposes can be achieved. In this way they discharge their responsibility to the college and through it to society.

What does this do to freedom? Are the individual teacher and student to be only robots employed to effect the goals of a rigidly organized institution? Is the expression of all opinion which is at variance with the underlying philosophy of the institution to be prohibited on the ground that it interferes with the accomplishment of institutional purposes?, No, this is where the principle of dedication to all three elements—freedom, responsibility, and institutional purpose—becomes important. Institutional purpose and the responsibility of trustees and staff to accomplish it, though essential, must not be permitted to crowd out freedom. Once the faculty member is appointed, he should enjoy a large measure of freedom in teaching, research, and private life. He, in turn, should respect the student's right to freedom. The principle of faculty and student freedom must be made unmistakably clear. It is the duty of the administration and the trustees to safeguard it. They must insist upon as much freedom for the individual as is consonant with the freedom of others. They must be willing to tolerate heresy. If a college develops a strongly affirmative climate in support of the philosophy implicit in its educational purposes, it can afford to have some members of the faculty who hold conflicting views. Unanimity is neither necessary nor desirable. Freedom is so basic to the process of teaching and learning that colleges and universities must protect it at all costs. Moreover, as we have already emphasized, a Christian institution has theological as well as educational reasons for insisting on freedom.

Is it possible, *as a practical matter*, for a college or university to have a definite philosophical or religious position and still maintain a high degree of intellectual freedom for the individual teacher and student in the way that we are suggesting? The chief obstacle to accomplishing this, as we see it, is the tendency of many people to make absolute commitment or freedom so that they become mutually exclusive in an educational setting. No doubt this rigid approach to the problem has historical roots in the abuses of the past and today often seems to be a by-product of the struggle between defensive traditionalism in religion (stressing commitment) and militant anti-traditionalism (stressing freedom). Our point is that neither kind of rigidity is a necessary reaction to the problem and, in fact, we have visited several colleges where commitment and freedom have been happily reconciled. A definite institutional philosophy does not preclude a genuine exposure of the student to alternative views nor prevent free inquiry and expression on the part of the faculty. It is the mark of a good teacher that he can guide the student's judgment and still leave him free to reach his own conclusions. Every administrator is confronted daily with the necessity of balancing corporate policy and individual freedom in many areas of institutional affairs. There are enough examples of success in these respects to establish the feasibility of doing what we are suggesting and to encourage all church-sponsored institutions of higher education to make the effort.

In a world in which both freedom and humane values are gravely threatened, we cannot afford to fail in this task.

An Academic
Evaluation
of the
Institutions

What is the quality of church-sponsored higher education in the United States, appraised in terms of the criteria outlined in Chapter 4? The evaluation that follows is based primarily on detailed case studies of 50 institutions which we selected as being representative of the whole group. A list of these is given in Appendix B.

All 817 colleges and universities participated, in an important manner, in the study, but a considerable part of the time and energy of the project went into the case studies of the representative institutions. These studies were useful in several ways. They provided a substantial body of factual data, obtained by means of the detailed questionnaire reprinted in Appendix C. The case studies also provided a broad body of observations of many different types of colleges and universities. Hundreds of administrators, teachers, students, and trustees were interviewed. A firsthand and up-to-date acquaintance with a cross-section of institutions safeguarded the study from glib generalizations, since we had in mind a large number of concrete situations. When necessary for sound judgment, we made special analyses of selected aspects of the institutions under consideration. In addition to the 50 case-study institutions, visits were made to 116 other colleges and universities for more limited observations.

The case-study institutions were selected on the basis of geographical location, size, church affiliation, and type of program. Under "type of program" proper attention was given to level of program (for example, junior college or doctoral level), character of student body (men, women, coeducational, and so forth), and general strength as indicated by accredited status. On the average two days were spent at an institution.

We must remind ourselves constantly that every college or university has its own unique characteristics. No two institutions are exactly alike. However, if we exercise reasonable caution and avoid unsubstantiated generalizations, there are a number of important conclusions that can be reached about church institutions as a whole. Officials of individual colleges and universities will know best how to discount the general statements for their own institutions.

The evaluative rationale outlined in Chapter 4 listed three antecedents to the building of a sound educational program—leadership, money, plant and equipment—and then eight indicators of quality. In this chapter we shall summarize the more important factual data obtained from the case studies and report the judgments made on the basis of each criterion. The tables used in this analysis were compiled from statistics supplied by the case-study institutions. However, adequate data on all 50 were not available on each item included so that the figures for median, mean, and range are based on between 40 and 50 institutions throughout except as noted. In these tables we have included both the median and the mean as well as the range because of the uneven distribution that often occurs.

ANTECEDENTS OF QUALITY

Leadership

Conclusions on the all-important matter of leadership are mixed. In this group of colleges there are some presidents who are among the ablest educational leaders in the United States, but too many, especially men brought in directly from the ministry, lack strong academic training and experience. We estimate that about one-third of the presidents of church institutions come to their responsibilities well-prepared academically, although there is nothing inherent in church-sponsored higher education which precludes the appointment of such persons.

The boards of trustees of church institutions tend to be heavily weighted with businessmen and clergy. The trustees of Roman Catholic colleges and universities are usually senior members of a religious order or congregation, and the board typically overlaps with the administrative staff. This is now changing as more Catholic institutions develop lay boards with actual governing authority. In the past, the lay boards of Catholic colleges have usually played restricted roles in the areas of public relations and fund-raising; this is becoming less true today.

Our observation is that, in general, college trustees are able and dedicated men. Their contribution to higher education is not sufficiently honored. Much of the secret of developing strong boards lies in the selection process and in the efforts of presidents to give trustees a proper understanding of educational problems. Presidential leadership is critical. The weakness of boards is frequently traceable to a failure to inform trustees on the matters for which they are responsible. The election of trustees by church bodies without sufficient consultation with institutional officials in advance can and sometimes does result in the selection of weak trustees. The heavy concentration of ministers on the boards of trustees of colleges connected with some of the churches is, in our judgment, questionable. Ministers, who are often over-burdened with meetings and committee memberships, usually cannot give the time to their board responsibilities that is necessary for effectiveness. Some of the strongest trustees and presidents we have encountered are devout laymen.

One of the most valuable assets of church colleges is their responsiveness to leadership. This is not so much the result of church sponsorship as it is of the size of the typical church institution. Most church colleges are small, and the small college has a flexibility and a manageability which allow for remarkable change and improvement in a relatively short time. We could cite case after case of small colleges that, in a ten-year period, have been transformed by able leadership, usually presidential. For example, a Middle Western college whose board of trustees almost closed the institution ten years ago is now moving forward aggressively under a new president. Another church-affiliated college has been transformed in nine years from a small and weak local college to a prosperous institution of national reputation. Again, the factor that accounts for the rapid progress is a president of uncommon ability.

By contrast, the large, complex university is much less responsive to leadership. The recent book by President Clark Kerr, of the University of California, describing the "multiversity" is pertinent documentation of this point.[1] Large organizations develop a tremendous amount of bureaucratic inertia. The conflicting interests within the university and the cumbersome machinery to be manipulated in order to get anything done make the role of the university president very different from that which is possible in a small institution. By the same token, of course, authority and responsibility in a small college are often too much concentrated in the president. Thus many church-sponsored colleges are almost proprietary. This difficulty is often accentuated by infrequent meetings of the board and by the habits of mind of both businessman-trustees and minister-presidents who are accustomed to individual action.

The college presidency today is an extraordinarily demanding post. The toll is heavy both from administrative failure and physical breakdown. The average tenure of presidents is only about eight years. A multiplicity of publics and pressures and the stultifying effect of constant fund-raising place an unreasonable burden on the occupants of the office. The modern college president often longs for the simple life of the old-time administrator, as described in this account of Philander Chase, the colorful founder of Kenyon College:

> The King, the Queen, the lords, the earls,
> They gave their crowns, they gave their pearls
> Until Philander had enough
> And hurried homeward with the stuff.
>
> He built the college, built the dam,
> He milked the cow, he smoked the ham,
> He taught the classes, rang the bell,
> And spanked the naughty freshmen well.[2]

We have been speaking primarily of presidential and board leadership. This leadership, of course, cannot stand alone. Deans and senior faculty members ultimately determine in large part what happens in the classroom. Able faculty leadership is indispensable. We observed over and over again in our case studies that many faculty members do not seem to have a broad appreciation of the objectives of the institutions they serve. The typical faculty member works con-

[1] Clark Kerr, *The Uses of the University* (Cambridge: Harvard University Press, 1964).
[2] *Kenyon College Bulletin*, 1963, p. 25.

scientiously to improve his own courses and often his own department, but the professor who contributes to the overall improvement of his institution is rare. No doubt the specialized graduate training of college teachers is largely responsible for this failure.

A major administrative problem in Roman Catholic institutions is the dominant position often held by members of a sponsoring religious order or congregation. This is coming to be an acute issue in many Catholic institutions as the number of lay faculty members increases rapidly. Faculty members frequently complain that they are treated as "employees," not as responsible participants in the life and government of institutions. The proper relationship between the authority of the religious and of the laity in a Catholic institution sponsored by a religious community is by no means a simple matter. An answer would seem to lie in maintaining a proper balance, rather than in going to one extreme or another. And it is likely that there will be significant shifts in the control of Roman Catholic colleges and universities as the increase in the percentage of lay faculty members and administrators continues.

Administrative Skill

As in the case of academic qualifications, the presidents of church institutions differ greatly in administrative skill. Faculties tend to be critical of presidents in this respect. This reflects in part presidential weakness and in part the occupational mind-set of the faculty. It has been traditional for professors to feel that they could manage colleges better than administrators, probably an indication that college teachers do not understand the full complexity of the task. Faculty-administration relationships are strained on many campuses. Probably the most prevalent weakness of college presidents is an inability to delegate responsibility and commensurate authority to other officers. In the small college, in particular, there is a strong temptation for the president to try to keep his hand directly on all decisions.

Financial Resources

Most church institutions have had financial problems, and for many years we have been hearing dire predictions about their survival. While it is unmistakably true that they have not enjoyed the same prosperity as have most public institutions and the richer private colleges and universities, our study indicates that most church institutions are appreciably better off today than they were ten years ago. Of the colleges and universities of which we have made case studies, only two or three are not clearly in a stronger position financially than they were a decade ago.

To administrators who are struggling day in and day out to obtain the resources needed to operate colleges and who know the heart attacks and exhaustion that often accompany this process, it may seem that our comments are too optimistic. The point is that church college presidents have, on the whole, done well in the area of fundraising. In this group there is a tremendous amount of promotional talent. It would be hard to find anywhere in education, business, or government men with a greater flair for enlisting support in good causes.

Granted that the church institutions are stronger financially than they were and that the presidents do a capable and even an heroic job of raising money to meet rising costs, how does the present financial position of this group of institutions compare with that of others? Is the present support adequate?

One of the simplest and best indicators of financial adequacy is the level of faculty salaries. A study made by the American Association of University Professors of faculty salaries for 1963-64 showed that the church-related universities ranked somewhat below public universities and substantially below private independent universities. The average salaries for nine months were: private independent, $10,886; public, $9,367; and church related, $8,652. The salaries for liberal arts colleges, although lower, showed a similar pattern among the three groups of institutions. The averages were $8,455 for private independent; $8,371 for public; and $7,437 for church related. The salaries of church-related institutions were lower than those of the other two groups at each of the four faculty ranks— professor, associate professor, assistant professor, and instructor. However, an encouraging fact revealed by the study was that the *rate of increase* in salaries for the two-year period from 1961-62 to 1963-64 for church-related institutions was well above that for public institutions (both universities and colleges) and was higher for church-related universities than for private independent universities.[3]

[3] "The Economic Status of the Profession, 1963-64: Report on the Self-Grading Compensation Survey," *AAUP Bulletin*, Vol. 50, No. 2 (June, 1964), p. 142.

This tends to corroborate the point made earlier, that the financial position of many church institutions has been improving. Some individual church colleges and universities are able to pay excellent salaries, but the simple fact remains that the present condition of the church institutions as a group is less favorable than that of the other large segments in higher education.

The most urgent financial need of the church institutions is for an increase in current income—that is, funds for general support of the educational program. The growing shortage of qualified college teachers in the United States and the increasing competition for staff make it imperative that these institutions raise their salary levels if they are to attract and retain competent teachers. As we saw in Chapter 3, in most cases official church support is entirely inadequate—the average contribution of churches *where support is received* is only 12.8 percent of college operating budgets. Noteworthy exceptions are the Lutheran Church-Missouri Synod and the Church of Jesus Christ of Latter-day Saints (Mormons), which have provided generous support for their institutions. The church support of the Roman Catholic colleges and universities is the poorest; only slightly more than one-half of the Catholic institutions receive actual monetary assistance from the Church or from religious organizations. The failure of American churches to provide for their educational institutions is deplorable. Income data for the 50 case-study institutions are shown in Table 22.

Table 22: Current and Capital Income of Representative Institutions

	MEDIAN	MEAN	RANGE	
Current income [a]	$1,072,312	$2,119,013	$117,910 –	$14,118,853
Percent received from student fees	64.0	62.0	11.0 –	91.0
Percent received from government	0.0	2.4	0.0 –	59.0
Percent received from endowment	4.0	7.6	0.0 –	34.0
Percent received from gifts, church	5.5	11.9	0.0 –	69.0
Percent received from gifts, other	10.0	13.0	0.0 –	68.0
Percent current-income increase, 1940–60	572.0	800.0	176.0 –	4,567.0
Capital funds received in last five years [b]	$1,622,301	$3,012,738	$ 7,600 –	$27,588,843
Percent received from church	7.0	22.0	0.0 –	98.0

[a] Total amount of current income received by 50 institutions—$105,950,665.
[b] Total amount of capital funds received by 49 institutions—$147,624,154.

One ominous aspect of the financing of church-sponsored institutions is the rapid increase in indebtedness since World War II. We have found many administrators concerned about this trend. The figures for indebtedness in the representative institutions surveyed are given in Table 23.

Table 23: Indebtedness of Representative Institutions

	MEDIAN	MEAN	RANGE
Amount of present indebtedness [a].........	$959,000	$1,701,498	$0 – $16,484,678
Percent debt owed Federal government...	61.5	68.6	0.0 – 100.0
Percent increase in debt, 1950–60 [b].....	287.0	1,452.5	−57.0 – 14,037.0

[a] Eight of these institutions had no debt. The remaining 42 institutions owed a total of $85,074,904.
[b] Number of institutions—21. Fourteen institutions with indebtedness in 1960 had none in 1950. Four institutions were established after 1950. Incomplete data received from 3.

Physical Facilities

This is an area in which church-related institutions have made remarkable strides since World War II. The rapid increase in indebtedness at many institutions is largely attributable to building programs. As one visits campuses today, he is impressed with the fine additions being made to physical plants almost everywhere. The means are being found at a number of institutions to create whole new campuses. Examples are Valparaiso University, St. Andrews Presbyterian College, Florida Presbyterian College, Furman University, and California Lutheran College. In general, it can be said that the physical plants of church colleges and universities are reasonably adequate, although they are not as elaborate as those of many public and independent institutions. Where physical plants are not adequate, the point of greatest weakness is often the library, a difficult facility for which to raise funds.

In the case studies we obtained data on expenditures for plants for the last five years and also projected figures for the next five years. This information is summarized in Table 24.

Table 24: Plant Expenditures of Representative Institutions

	MEDIAN	MEAN	RANGE
Plant expenditures for past five fiscal years [a]......................	$2,720,000	$4,493,940	$0 – $17,742,000
Plant expenditures for next five fiscal years [b]......................	$2,580,000	$4,143,000	$350,000 – $31,000,000

[a] Total capital expenditures for plant for 50 institutions—$224,697,000.
[b] Total anticipated capital expenditures for 45 institutions—$186,422,000.

We now turn from the antecedents of a strong educational program to the process of teaching and learning itself. What judgment can we make about the health of church-sponsored higher education in the light of the eight criteria employed?

INDICATORS OF QUALITY

Seriousness of Purpose

In the general sense of the faculty and students looking upon education as serious business, the church institutions are good and getting better. The heyday of football, fraternities, and fun (to use Hutchins' delightful phrase) is over in most colleges. In our interviews with students and faculty members we found a serious outlook. For the most part, students consider education important. The "Joe College" attitude is less prevalent than it used to be.

In this study we have also used the term "seriousness of purpose" in a deeper sense. Teaching and learning are not ends in themselves. A college ought to know what it stands for, and these values should be perceivable in the daily lives of the faculty and students. An important part of the assessment of an institution or group of institutions is the effort to apprehend the convictions or presuppositions having the greatest influence on what is thought and done. In general, this kind of seriousness of purpose in the deeper sense of dedication to well-defined values which transcend the daily task of teaching and learning is weaker than it should be in the colleges we have studied. There is a distinct lack of philosophical depth. Many of the church institutions are floundering in this respect as is higher education at large.

Clear Awareness of Distinctive Role

We find that church institutions are approximately equally divided between those that have clear roles and those that do not. Too many of the colleges are imitative, making for inconsistencies in program. Strangely enough, it is often the well-established colleges—those that have adequate funds and facilities—that are most intent on imitating other institutions. They tend to have a kind of status consciousness, to look to more highly respected colleges for the image of what they should become. The prestige image which they seek to follow is often a secular pattern, since most of the well-established private institutions in this country are secular in their outlook. Institutional imitation—failure to exploit the opportunity for individuality—is one of the basic problems in all of higher education and is not limited to the church-related segment. This problem, however, may be more serious for the church institutions because, in a secular academic world, uncritical imitation has the practical effect of drawing them away from their own distinctive purposes.

Care in Selection and Retention of Faculty

As we have observed procedures and talked to appointing officials, we have been depressed by the routineness of much faculty personnel administration. Typically, when a college is looking for a new faculty member, it goes to one or two nearby graduate schools and seeks candidates with the desired degree and satisfactory recommendations. The finer points of matching an applicant to a particular college and a particular teaching responsibility are often ignored. More often than not it seems to be a degree, not a person, that is being appointed. Great colleges cannot be developed in this way. The character of the teacher and his concern for the student are essential ingredients of quality.

Few church institutions provide sufficient opportunities for the professional improvement and refreshment of their faculties. Since many of the colleges are small, are located in isolated communities, and have small departments—conditions which limit scholarly stimulation of the faculty—special attention needs to be given to this point. How to keep a faculty alert and growing intellectually is a fine art that is being neglected. It requires money but, even more, it requires imagination and hard work. Low salaries and weak libraries, points that have already been mentioned, are serious handicaps in faculty development in many institutions.

In our case studies we obtained data on faculty size, distribution among ranks, training, and teaching load. This information is summarized in Table 25. From the table it is clear that the modal or typical teacher in a church-sponsored college is an assistant or associate professor with a master's degree and probably some additional study toward his doctorate. It is interesting to note the wide range in percentages of faculty members at the various ranks in this

Table 25: Faculty Data for Representative Institutions

	MEDIAN	MEAN	RANGE
Number of faculty members (full-time)	59	80	17 – 550
Faculty rank (percentage at each level)			
Instructor	20	20	0 – 36
Assistant Professor	29	31	13 – 71
Associate Professor	21	22	5 – 42
Professor	23	24	7 – 45
Faculty training (percentage at highest degree held)			
Doctor's degree	37	38	0 – 66
Master's degree	50	51	11 – 88
Bachelor's degree	9	11	0 – 30
Average teaching load (in hours)	13	12.7	6 – 16.5

group of institutions, although faculties tend to be approximately equally divided among the four principal ranks. (A few colleges, especially junior colleges, do not use faculty rank.) In interpreting the data on faculty training, it should be borne in mind that some of the institutions are junior colleges, and the training of their faculties is not, of course, comparable to that of four-year colleges.

One of the most encouraging things we have found during our visits is that even the weakest, humblest, struggling college seems always to have a nucleus of able, dedicated teachers who will stay with the institution through times of adversity as well as prosperity. These are persons who could, if they wished, move to better positions but who, for reasons that are not always clear, choose to stay where they are. Sometimes it is religious conviction that holds them, often it is loyalty to the kind of education and the kind of relationship with students that is possible in the small liberal arts college. The good small college can use these attractions not only to hold its staff in the face of increasing competition but also, occasionally, to entice men of renown from large, impersonal institutions. This is perhaps the greatest asset of the small college.

But small colleges, with their small departments, have built-in limitations, too. It is difficult for departments with one or two faculty members to provide the breadth of scholarly competence, the intellectual stimulation, and diversity of outlook which are essential ingredients of good education. The data on faculty size in the preceding table show clearly the extent of this problem. When it is considered that liberal arts colleges normally have between 20 and 25 departments and that the typical faculty has 59 members, it is clear that the departments in these institutions average 2 to 3 persons. In fields in which there are different schools of thought vying for academic ascendency and the allegiance of students, the different points of view can hardly be represented properly in one- or two-man departments. This is true, for example, in the social sciences where there are often differences in methodology or values between such groupings as "behaviorists" and "theoreticians," "liberals" and "conservatives." If an educational institution exercises its right to permit and even to encourage diversity in the scholarly conclusions of its faculty—and, as we have said before, this is indispensable to the whole process of sound teaching and learning—it faces special difficulties with small departments. The large university has the same problem in maintaining balance, but for other reasons.

While one- and two-man departments are limiting in some respects, they present opportunities, too. A few small colleges have capitalized on this condition by merging departments into large groupings and thus achieving better integration of curriculum. The administrators of large institutions know that excessive departmentalism is one of the prime causes of curricular fragmentation. A divisional form of organization which brings related disciplines and their teachers into closer working relations can promote interdisciplinary courses, thus helping to unify both curriculum and faculty. In this way the small institution can make a virtue of what at first appears to be a serious defect.

In the staffing of church colleges and universities, one of the difficult problems is that of appointing persons who have the requisite religious commitment. We commented extensively on this matter in the last two chapters, pointing out the importance of making explicit any religious qualifications that are expected of faculty members. We also dealt with the relationship of freedom to commitment. These are quite basic issues which should be carefully examined by every institution. The integrity of a college depends, in large measure, on having sound policies for safeguarding the several desiderata involved.

In general, we find that most church institutions lack firm and well-formulated policies in this respect. Institutions commonly seek some evidence of religious affiliation in prospective teachers, but too often nominal church membership is regarded as sufficient. What is lacking is the expectation that the faculty member will be an informed, thoughtful churchman and relate his subject to the Judeo-Christian tradition. Such persons are rare. This is one of the most basic problems of church institutions today.

The question of the proper relationship of freedom, responsibility, and institutional purpose has not been given the attention that it deserves by most institutions. Some colleges assume that "ventilation" is provided by simply ignoring the religious qualifications of faculty members, while others—and these are very few today—see no need for it at all. In this connection we must comment on the widespread impression, especially among educators who are not personally acquainted with church-affiliated colleges, that these institutions are narrowly sectarian, that they are engaged primarily in religious indoctrination, and that their faculties are selected only for their evangelistic zeal. This impression is very far from the truth. It would accurately describe not more than 10 percent of the church institutions in the United States. Many more institutions reflect a loose, vaguely defined religion and bend over backwards to avoid any suggestion of sectarianism. Very few colleges restrict faculty appointments to members of their own churches. People who think that rigid sectarianism is the principal defect of church-related higher education are 50 years behind the times.

Careful Selection of Students

The church institutions are becoming more selective in their admissions, as are institutions of other types. More and more colleges now find themselves in the position of having to turn away applicants. This is resulting in higher academic standards in undergraduate colleges. Faculties can now demand more of their students. In general, however, colleges are simply raising the level of test scores required for admission and are not giving sufficient attention in the selective process to other factors that are important in matching students with colleges.

There is no common yardstick by which students entering different colleges can be compared. However, College Entrance Examination Board scores, American College Testing Program scores, high school rank, and similar kinds of data for freshman classes do provide a rough basis for comparisons. Using these means, we tried to classify the academic abilities of students entering the 50 representative institutions. While the data are not strictly comparable, they do provide a reasonably good analysis of student academic quality in these institutions. The judgments are summarized in Table 26.

Table 26: Estimates of Student Academic Ability in Representative Institutions

ACADEMIC ABILITY	PERCENTAGE OF INSTITUTIONS WITH STUDENTS OF INDICATED LEVEL OF ABILITY
Below average.............................	29
Slightly below average....................	9
Average...................................	20
Slightly above average....................	18
Above average.............................	9
Superior..................................	15
Total..................................	100

It is worth noting that while approximately one-sixth of the institutions have become highly selective and two-fifths are above average, almost one-third are well below average. The latter fact tends to corroborate our firsthand observation that church-sponsored higher education includes a substantial number of "marginal" colleges which struggle to fill their freshman classes and continue operation. It is some of these institutions that are most vulnerable to competition from the junior colleges and expanding state colleges.

In some denominations there is a feeling that the church college is obliged to provide educational opportunity for almost all young churchmen, regardless of aptitude or interest. Thus the church institution often faces a problem similar to that of the state college or university when it is expected to provide education for almost all graduates of high schools in the state. As in the case of the state institutions, it would seem highly desirable for church colleges to require reasonable promise of entering students, explaining that colleges cannot properly accept the obligation of trying to educate all church members.

The careful matching of applicants and educational programs is not being attempted by more than a handful of church institutions. Our interviews with admissions officers left the clear impression that most institutions are seeking the same students regardless of educational purpose. In other words, the assumption is made that a good student is a good student, and that the distinctive educational purposes of the admitting college do not really matter. We believe this to be a prevalent weakness in most of American higher education. However, in the years ahead it will be particularly important for the church institutions, whose contribution must be defined not in size but in *kind* of education and *kind* of product, to select their students more carefully.

The financial problems facing private institutions have an important bearing on the question of which students are to be served. With the rising cost of higher education and the increasing of fees to help balance budgets, private institutions (including those connected with churches) find that the social and economic complexion of their students is shifting upward. How to preserve a reasonably representative clientele under these circumstances is a problem that is taxing the ingenuity of administrators and trustees. Some church colleges are literally pricing themselves out of their accustomed markets. Many students who would have attended private colleges in former days must now turn to public higher education for financial reasons. This is a point to which we shall return later.

The church-related institutions today serve predominantly the middle class. Many of the colleges are moving rapidly toward upper-middle-class student bodies. Only a few are serving primarily students from the lower social and economic groups. In our case studies we found that most of the institutions did not have systematically compiled data on the social and economic backgrounds of their students. Only a few have made careful analyses. The information that was provided us on this point was based largely on the general observations of student personnel officers. While not precise, this information is, however, helpful in describing the students who are being served by this group of institutions. About 60 percent of the colleges reported that their students were drawn primarily from professional and business families in urban and suburban communities—that is, predominantly middle- and upper-middle-class young people. Of the 50 institutions, perhaps three might be described as primarily upper-class institutions. In about 20 percent of the cases, personnel officers described the student bodies as drawn predominantly from semiskilled and farm families residing in small towns and rural areas. The student bodies in 10 percent of the institutions were described as broad, varied, and too heterogenous to be easily categorized, while in 10 percent of the cases the information available was too meager to permit useful description. Table 27 presents other data on the student bodies of these representative institutions.

Table 27: Composition of Student Bodies in Representative Institutions

	MEDIAN	MEAN	RANGE
Total full-time enrollment...........................	717	1,256	98 – 11,325
Percent summer school enrollment is of total full-time enrollment [a].................................	36	38	3 – 141
Percent enrollment increase, 1940–50 [b]............	51	79	−66 – 842
Percent enrollment increase, 1950–60 [c]............	43	77	−37 – 293
Percent enrollment increase, 1940–60 [d]............	99	187	−30 – 1,358
Number of states represented in student body..........	30	29	4 – 50
Number of foreign countries represented in student body..	7	12	0 – 58
Percent students from home state....................	59	51	7 – 95
Percent students from within 25 miles................	20	28	0 – 78
Number of other institutions within 25 miles............	4	5.7	0 – 28
Percent students belonging to sponsoring church [e].......	58	59	3 – 99

[a] Two institutions had summer session enrollments larger than their regular session enrollments. In 10 cases the summer enrollments were over one-half the size of their regular enrollments. Eleven colleges had no summer session.
[b] Two institutions showed a decrease in this period. Incomplete data received from 13 institutions.
[c] Six institutions showed a decrease in this period.
[d] Two institutions showed a decrease in this period. Incomplete data received from 14 institutions.
[e] In seven cases the denomination represented by the largest number of students was not the denomination sponsoring the institution.

These data emphasize certain points about the student bodies of the institutions. First, although most of the colleges are small, they have approximately doubled their size since 1940. They draw their students from wide geographical areas, including foreign countries. It is interesting to note that typically only about one-half of the students come from the state in which the institution is located and only about one-fifth from the immediate geographical area. A little over one-half of the students typically belong to the sponsoring church. However, in one institution only 3 percent of the students belonged to the denomination with which the institution was associated.

We asked the institutions to describe for us the religious values of their student bodies. This is a question which is difficult to answer with any precision, and we found that most of the institutions had not tried to study it systematically. The reports provide impressions gleaned from students and from college chaplains, a kind of description, of course, that is much more elusive than merely compiling statistics on denominational affiliation. Twenty percent of the institutions described their students as religiously conservative and traditional; 15 percent as conventional, average, reflecting society at large; 5 percent as strongly-committed religiously; and 2 percent as "liberal"; 20 percent reported insufficient information. Thirty-eight percent used a variety of descriptive terms—such phrases as "intellectually interested in religion," "better than average ethically," "committed Lutherans," "normal Catholics," "conscientious Catholics," "religious community," "much latent interest in religion," "antichurch but concerned about religion," "out of touch with the basic thrust of the church," "social concern," and "all Christian Scientists."

Curricular Design

In evaluating curricular design, we considered two things: (1) careful planning of curricula to assure proper treatment of the various kinds of human experience (in subject-matter terms, the humanities, the fine or creative arts, the social sciences, and the natural sciences); and (2) clear formulation by the faculty of the common body of knowledge, intellectual skills, and other learning which it considers essential to the liberally-educated person. Except for the fact that some church institutions, notably Roman Catholic and conservative Protestant colleges, have heavier than average requirements in religion and philosophy, the curricular pattern of church institutions is quite similar to that of other undergraduate colleges; specifically a balance among the broad fields of knowledge is usually provided through a plan of election within distribution requirements. The student is required to take so many hours of courses in the social sciences, so many hours in the sciences, and so forth; he samples the several broad fields of knowledge. A question may well be raised as to whether this gives him an understanding of the methods of inquiry, the presuppositions, and the essential facts of the broad fields. Does the typical course in economics, for example, serve as an adequate introduction to the whole field of the social sciences for the purposes of liberal education? For the most part, the faculties of church colleges have not seriously considered this question.

These institutions are weak, as are others, in the portion of the curriculum which is common to all students—the general or liberal core. This common body of knowledge, intellectual skills, and other learning is the heart of liberal education. In many colleges it has become so attenuated (often consisting of freshman composition, two years of physical education, and, in church colleges, a course in religion) that liberal arts education, as a common experience of educated people, has almost dwindled away. Graduate and professional schools find that few of their entering students, however carefully selected, bring with them a firm knowledge of the essentials of liberal learning in history, literature, and philosophy, and few students can demonstrate advanced proficiency in the fundamental disciplines of writing, reasoning, and careful reading.

It is difficult today to define the intellectual foundation which the Bachelor of Arts degree actually represents. An important point is that cost is not the chief obstacle to providing these essentials of a liberal education. What is required is a planned curriculum and conscientious teaching, but there is reason to believe that many of our most highly respected colleges are failing in this task. Church-sponsored colleges suffer, as do others, from faculty preoccupation with technical and specialized work. They are subject, too, to the criticism that much of undergraduate education is fragmented and purposeless, that there is little relationship between the announced objectives of institutions and what actually goes on in the classroom. There is perhaps less excuse for these defects in church colleges, which are presumed to have a clear philosophical basis, than in other institutions.

In this study we reviewed the development of the college curriculum over the last three centuries. The thing that impressed us most was the recurrence of the foregoing criticisms. When the pattern of the classical curriculum was broken in the nineteenth century, colleges failed to take the steps necessary to bring about a new curricular unity. Extending educational opportunity, requiring higher and higher levels of faculty training, building buildings, raising money, adding new and more specialized programs—all these things have their value, but none of them is a remedy for the deeper vacuity which comes from not having a coherent philosophy to tie the separate activities together and make them a rational whole. The most obvious symptoms of the problem are narrowly trained teachers, departmentalized introductory courses, premature specialization, emphasis on professional and vocational study, disjunction between stated purposes and actual curriculum, and technical as against liberalizing scholarship.

The point to emphasize here is that the criticisms are not new or isolated. A. Lawrence Lowell said much the same thing in 1887, as did Woodrow Wilson in 1894, John Dewey in 1902, Alexander Meiklejohn in 1920, Abraham Flexner in 1923, and Robert Maynard Hutchins and James Conant in the 1940's and 1950's. More often than not, critics have blamed the graduate school (the training ground of college teachers) for the difficulties we face in undergraduate education, but this is too simple an assignment of responsibility.

We made a careful analysis of the majors most frequently elected by students in the 50 representative institutions. The choice of majors by students shows the emphasis in an educational program. Although most of the case-study institutions are liberal arts colleges, the selection of major fields by students reflects a strong professional and occupational interest. The four departments in which students most often majored were, in order, (1) education, (2) English and business administration (tied), and (3) biology. The predominance of education as the favorite major field is an indication of the degree to which these colleges are functioning as teacher training institutions. The popularity of biology as a major is evidence of the prominence of preparation for medical schools in church institutions. The major in business administration is the choice of many men students, of non-bookish temperament, who see college as desirable preparation for entrance into the world of commerce.

Atmosphere of Intellectual Ferment

This quality, as we mentioned earlier, is manifested in the encouragement of independent study and thought, in the involvement of the faculty and students in the intellectual issues of the day, in freedom of discussion, in student interests, in the role played by the library, in the educational aspirations of graduates, and in other ways. Intellectual ferment is essential to liberal education. Overall, our evidence indicates that the church-affiliated institutions are doing a reasonably good job in this respect. Some exhibit remarkable intellectual vitality. Others have what would be expected with run-of-the-mill faculty teaching run-of-the-mill students in a run-of-the-mill program. Many of the church colleges do have the initial advantage here of relatively small size and close faculty-student relationships. As Astin, formerly of the National Merit Scholarship Corporation, showed, a number of the more productive undergraduate colleges (that is, scholarly productivity, as measured by graduate school records of alumni) are institutions of small enrollment.[4] The stimulation of direct confrontation between teacher and students can be an important factor in encouragement of intellectual activity.

Table 28 shows the sizes of classes in the case-study institutions.

Table 28: Class Size in Representative Institutions

	MEDIAN	MEAN	RANGE
Percentage of classes under 5	10.0	11.0	0.0 – 29.0
Percentage of classes under 10	29.0	29.0	6.0 – 48.0
Percentage of classes over 100	1.0	1.0	0.0 – 15.0

Almost 30 percent of the classes in these institutions have fewer than 10 students. Only 1 percent of the classes exceed 100 students. A great majority of the classes are in range of 10 to 25 students. While it is appropriate to raise the question as to whether these colleges can afford to teach as many very small classes as they do, from the point of view of personal relationship between teacher and student the conditions reflected in this table are almost ideal.

Most of the institutions we visited in the study have honors or independent study plans for their abler students. This is a curricular feature in which faculties are much interested. In some of the weaker colleges, however, the opportunity for teachers to work with individual students is limited by heavy teaching loads (for example, 15 hours or more). As we have already pointed out in Table 26, the median teaching load in the representative institutions is 13 hours. While this is by no means light, it is probably not excessive for a faculty member whose research activities are modest.

In many colleges, the religious dimension seems to make for greater faculty interest in the individual student—a responsible attitude toward him. We entered our inquiry with some skepticism on this point but have been persuaded by the testimony of teachers and

[4] Alexander W. Astin, "Differential College Effects on the Motivation of Talented Students to Obtain the Ph.D.", *Journal of Educational Psychology*, Vol. 54, No. 1 (1963), pp. 68-70.

students who have experienced both church and independent institutions.

Freedom of inquiry and discussion are an important condition for intellectual ferment. As a broad generalization, it may be said that a large measure of freedom exists in most areas on most of the campuses we visited. Moreover, the number of cases involving questions of freedom in church institutions, that have come to public and professional attention, is not disproportionate to the number of cases in all of higher education. We are of the opinion that church institutions have been so much criticized on this point in times past that most of their administrators are now quite fastidious about any infringement of freedom.

An important point in the appraisal of an institution or a group of institutions is the place occupied by the library. We have two observations to make on this question. In most of the colleges we visited, the libraries provide adequate resources for undergraduate students. Many of them, however, are weak from the point of view of nurturing the continuing scholarship of the faculty. The factual data on the libraries of the case-study institutions are shown in Table 29.

Table 29: Library Data for Representative Institutions

	MEDIAN	MEAN	RANGE
Annual expenditure for books [a]	$16,890	$30,398	$ 1,651 – $212,236
Percentage increase, 1940–60 [b]	556.0	952.0	84.0 – 6,795.0
Annual expenditure for salaries [c]	$27,145	$49,012	$ 4,183 – $308,527
Percentage increase, 1940–60 [d]	556.0	871.0	38.0 – 6,173.0
Number on professional staff	3	5.2	1 – 36
Number of student assistants	18	22	2 – 112
Number of volumes	62,898	105,498	11,255 – 488,300
Number of periodicals received	399	652	70 – 4,299

[a] Total amount spent for books by 50 institutions—$1,519,884.
[b] Number of institutions—30. Incomplete data received on 20.
[c] Total amount spent for library salaries by 50 institutions—$2,450,594.
[d] Number of institutions—20. Incomplete data received on 25.

We mentioned the educational aspirations of the graduates of an institution as a sign of intellectual vitality. If a college is serving an academically-able student body and has an alert faculty, a substantial fraction of the graduates will be stimulated to undertake more advanced study in graduate and professional schools. The record of an institution in this respect depends in part on the type of student admitted, as well as on the quality of the program, and direct comparisons between institutions without taking that fact into account would be improper. Yet the academic record of graduates is one index of institutional vitality.

The evidence on this point will be reviewed in detail in the next chapter. Here it will suffice to point out that some of the most productive institutions in the United States are church-sponsored colleges and that certain of the Protestant institutions, in particular, rank high in the scholarly achievements of their graduates. We wish that it were possible to cite evidence on other, broader outcomes. It would be helpful to know, for example, how the graduates of church institutions compare with other graduates in the breadth and depth of their intellectual interests, in their assumption of civic responsibility, and in their leadership in churches and charitable organizations. Unfortunately, data are not available on these questions. Few, if any, institutions have alumni records which are adequate for educational evaluation and planning. If there had been any way in which our study could have brought together existing information of this kind and interpreted it, we should have done so.

One point at which church institutions are weak, on the basis of information obtained from our visits, is the involvement of the faculty and students in ongoing civic responsibilities. While most colleges sponsor occasional lectures, and student interest in particular issues (such as civil rights and the war in Vietnam) runs high at times, preparation for assuming the normal responsibilities of citizenship is rather limited on most campuses. This is part of the broader need in American higher education to involve students more concretely in the affairs of their age. It should be said that on certain public issues of the day a minority of the students, at least, are thoughtful and vocal.

While we are considering intellectual climate, it is perhaps a logical point at which to comment on graduate education in church-related universities. We have been discussing primarily undergraduate colleges. There are twenty church-related universities offering extensive graduate and professional programs. These are chiefly associated with the Methodist and Roman Catholic churches. The following are the institutions offering the most extensive programs of university type: American University, Baylor University, Boston College, Boston

University, Brigham Young University, Catholic University, University of Denver, Duke University, Emory University, Fordham University, Georgetown University, Loyola University (Chicago), Marquette University, Northwestern University, University of Notre Dame, St. Louis University, Southern Methodist University, Syracuse University, Texas Christian University, and Yeshiva University. Five of these universities were included in our case studies.

Our own visits, however, afforded too little evidence on the quality of the graduate programs to justify judgments. The appraisal of graduate programs is a highly technical matter. Here we are forced to rely primarily on academic reputation as a clue to quality. A recent study by Allan M. Cartter, Vice President of the American Council on Education, sheds some light on the question. Cartter reported evaluations by 4,008 scholars of the graduate faculties and programs in 29 academic disciplines at 106 institutions. The univerities appraised are the major producers of doctorates. Graduate faculties were rated as "distinguished," "strong," "good," and "adequate plus". No church-related university was ranked as "distinguished" in any of the 29 fields surveyed. Five church-related universities were considered "strong" in one or more departments as follows: Northwestern in 16 departments, Duke in 7, Yeshiva in 4, Syracuse in 2, and Emory in 1. These five universities plus Boston, Catholic, Fordham, Georgetown, Notre Dame, and St. Louis were given "good" or "adequate plus" ratings in a total of 63 departments. The pattern of ratings for graduate programs (as distinct from graduate faculties) was similar.[5]

It may also be noted that there are only three church-related universities (Catholic, Duke, and Northwestern) holding membership in the Association of American Universities. Though not purporting to pass judgment on the quality of graduate schools, this organization of 40 institutions does include the American and Canadian universities generally regarded as having the most distinguished graduate schools. Information of this kind is not above criticism as a basis for evaluating graduate programs in individual universities, but it tends to corroborate our belief that church-related universities, with a few exceptions, are relatively weak at the doctoral level. They do not have the money to develop broad strength in graduate programs beyond the

---

[5] Allan M. Cartter, *An Assessment of Quality in Graduate Education* (Washington: American Council on Education, 1966).

master's degree. It should be mentioned that while all twenty of the universities listed confer the Ph.D. degree, ten also have medical schools granting the M.D. degree. In addition, another church-related institution, Wake Forest University, has a medical school. Thus a good fraction of the medical schools of the United States are conducted by church-related universities.

Institutional Self-Criticism

By the criterion, institutional self-criticism, we simply mean that a quality institution is constantly striving for improvement of its program. It uses the best techniques that have been developed for appraising educational results and is willing to experiment with promising new approaches to the art of teaching and the organization of courses. We have reported that most of the church institutions are working hard to improve themselves financially and physically. In the areas of academic and personnel affairs, however, many show a high degree of complacency. There is a good deal of curricular innovation in the sense of adding promising features to conventional curricula, but not much basic recasting of curricula. The church institutions should be doing much more in the area of educational evaluation. A later chapter will describe some of the more significant innovation and experimentation that is going on in church-affiliated institutions.

Ultimate Effect of a College on Its Students

When considering the ultimate effect of a college on its students we are looking at the process and outcomes of a liberal education in the most basic sense. It is widely assumed and often asserted that the consideration of fundamental questions and the development of a reasoned framework of belief are the most important activities of a liberal arts college and especially, one would think, of the church institutions. We have been disappointed to find relatively little of this kind of deeper inquiry and synthesis going on. Faculty people have not been prepared by graduate schools to do it themselves, and the departmental organization of the curriculum strongly inhibits a broad approach to human problems. The organization of the curriculum, proceeding from the general to the special, almost educates the student away from a willingness to look seriously at broad questions. Moreover, the tempo of college life today militates against reflective thinking.

Failure to accomplish this purpose is not a weakness of church colleges alone. It is common to American higher education across the board. However, one might expect that the church colleges, which purport to have a clear and time-tested view of life, would point the way for other institutions in this area. A few colleges are engaged in significant demonstrations, but, on the whole, church-related higher education is not doing much better in helping students face fundamental questions than are other institutions. Much of the confusion and uncertainty regarding this responsibility which one finds in public and independent colleges and universities, and indeed in the world at large, is also present in church-related institutions of higher learning.

Under this heading it would be logical to summarize our impressions on religion in church colleges and universities. However, this is such an involved question that it deserves a chapter of its own. At this point we shall say only that it is our considered opinion that religion is not as strong in the programs of church-related institutions as one would expect. In fact, there is good reason to believe that these institutions are, by and large, stronger academically (in the secular sense) than they are religiously. We shall have more extended comments to make on this aspect of their programs.

OVER-ALL ESTIMATE

The foregoing observations on the academic quality of the church-affiliated segment of higher education present a mixed picture. To summarize in general terms, the principal assets of church institutions are: freedom to experiment and to serve special purposes, close student-faculty relationships, a creditable record of preparation for graduate and professional study, concern for the progress of individual students, and espousal of humane values. Areas in which, generally speaking, these institutions are not sufficiently strong include: scholarly attainment of faculty, financial support, selection of students and faculty in relation to educational purpose, curricular design, implementation of religious aims, and self-evaluation.

It is our considered judgment that there is nothing inherent in church relationship that either assures or precludes quality in a college or university. A religious orientation should add a dimension to higher education that broadens and deepens the outlook of faculty and students alike, but we cannot say that this does in fact occur in most of the 817 institutions we have been studying.

Included among these 817 are *some* of the finest colleges in America, but also *many* of the poorest. Over 20 percent are not regionally accredited; accreditation, of course, is only a badge of acceptable quality, not of distinction. A reasonable estimate is that at least one-third of the whole group is marginal. Another one-third lies in the broad middle range of quality. The last one-third compares favorably with the best public and independent institutions. About 50 of this last group could properly be described as excellent colleges and universities—institutions ranking in the highest 10 percent of American higher education.

7

Studies
of
College
Graduates

Studies of college graduates are a useful source of data for the appraisal of individual institutions. The results of such studies should be interpreted cautiously, however. The research that has been done so far does not yield comprehensive information on the basis of which the success of institutions in achieving a broad range of educational objectives can be judged, but it does provide partial measures of certain types of effectiveness. In general, individual colleges and universities have been deficient in compiling and analyzing data on their graduates for purposes of evaluating their own programs. For comparisons among institutions, therefore, chief reliance must be placed on studies which, though touching on limited objectives, do include a large number of institutions. At the present time information is available which offers better clues to educational quality than those commonly accepted by academic people or by the general public. Additional research on the outcomes of collegiate education is urgently needed, if more precise judgments are to be made. The studies at hand, however, are sufficient to raise questions about some of the widely-held assumptions. It is therefore very much worthwhile to review the findings of several of the more systematic studies and to add to them certain analyses of our own. The original reports should be consulted for detailed descriptions of the research.

SOURCES OF SCHOLARS

In 1953 Robert H. Knapp and Joseph J. Greenbaum, of Wesleyan University, published a volume entitled *The Younger American*

Scholar: His Collegiate Origins, which embodied the results of a project financed by the Fund for the Advancement of Education. In brief, the investigators analyzed the undergraduate backgrounds of students who had received Ph.D. degrees or held significant fellowships at 25 prominent graduate schools during the six-year period beginning in 1946. They then ranked undergraduate colleges on the basis of the percentage of their graduates who had reached this level of achievement. Particular attention was given to the 50 institutions that ranked highest in the performance of their male graduates. A further analysis was made of graduates in science, social science, and the humanities. The results surprised many readers. The 50 highest institutions and the percentages of their male graduates who were "younger scholars," as defined by the study, are shown in Table 30.[1]

Table 30: Highest Ranking Institutions in
Production of Younger Scholars, 1946-51

INSTITUTION	PERCENTAGE OF MALE GRADUATES WHO ARE YOUNGER SCHOLARS
†Swarthmore College	61.2
Reed College	53.1
University of Chicago	48.4
Oberlin College	39.8
†Haverford College	39.5
California Institute of Technology	38.2
Carleton College	35.4
Princeton University	32.4
Antioch College	31.5
Harvard University	27.3
Yale University	27.2
Queens College (New York)	25.6
†Grinnell College	23.7
Wesleyan University	22.5
†Kenyon College	22.4
Johns Hopkins University	21.4
Massachusetts Institute of Technology	20.6
†University of the South	20.2
Knox College	19.6
†Cornell College	19.5

† Church-related institutions. See Appendix C.

[1] Robert H. Knapp and Joseph J. Greenbaum, *The Younger American Scholar: His Collegiate Origins* (Chicago: University of Chicago Press and Wesleyan University Press Incorporated, 1953), p. 16.

Table 30—Continued

INSTITUTION	PERCENTAGE OF MALE GRADUATES WHO ARE YOUNGER SCHOLARS
Cooper Union	18.0
†Beloit College	17.9
Columbia University	17.7
Pomona College	17.4
†College of Wooster	17.4
†Augustana College (Illinois)	17.3
†DePauw University	17.1
Amherst College	17.1
Williams College	17.1
Brooklyn College	16.5
Berea College	14.8
†Bethel College (Kansas)	14.7
†Trinity College (Connecticut)	13.3
Purdue University	12.8
†Bates College	12.8
University of Wisconsin	12.3
†Hope College	12.2
Alfred University	12.2
Hamilton College	12.0
Wabash College	12.0
College of William and Mary	11.9
Brown University	11.9
†Juniata College	11.7
University of Rochester	11.7
†Calvin College	11.6
†Monmouth College	11.5
†Kalamazoo College	11.0
University of Pennsylvania	10.7
Dartmouth College	10.6
†Coe College	10.2

For our purposes, it may be noted that 19 of the top 50 institutions have definite church affiliations and that most of these are located in the Middle West. Thirty-one are private colleges of arts and sciences. Five, including two municipal colleges, are basically public in their control and support. One (Alfred University) is partly public, partly private. Fourteen are institutions of university type; the remainder are primarily undergraduate colleges of simple organization. Although most of the 50 are colleges and universities that enjoy good national or regional reputations, a sizable fraction are colleges that are not well known to the general public, and some are institutions that might be regarded by most academic people as undistinguished or inconsequential. Several institutions that are highly regarded nationally do not appear in the top 50.

It should be emphasized that this study identifies only one kind of educational achievement, defined in rather narrow terms. It covers a brief period. Later we shall mention other factors that ought to be taken into account in interpreting such findings. However, this study was one of the first and is still one of the most significant impartial analyses of college graduates.

SOURCES OF PHYSICIANS

A second study, similar to the first in its method, is that of William A. Manuel and Marion E. Altenderfer, on *Baccalaureate Origins of 1950-1959 Medical Graduates*, published by the United States Public Health Service. Undergraduate colleges were ranked on the basis of the number and percentage of their graduates who received M.D. degrees during the period 1950-1959.

For our purposes the most useful part of the study is that concerned with the 100 undergraduate colleges having the highest percentage of male graduates receiving M.D. degrees during the period covered. This list and the percentage for each institution are shown in Table 31.[2]

Table 31: Undergraduate Colleges with the Highest Percentage of Male Graduates Receiving M.D. Degrees, 1950-59

COLLEGE	PERCENTAGE OF MALE GRADUATES RECEIVING M.D. DEGREES
†La Sierra College	25.3
†Pacific Union College	22.5
College of Charleston	20.9
†Hampden-Sydney College	18.0
†Emory University	17.5
†Carroll College (Montana)	16.7
†Creighton University	16.3
†Southwestern at Memphis	16.3
†Atlantic Union College	15.4
†Walla Walla College	14.9

[2] William A. Manuel and Marion E. Altenderfer, *Baccalaureate Origins of 1950-1959 Medical Graduates*. Public Health Monograph No. 66 (Washington: U.S. Government Printing Office, 1961), pp. 18-19.

Table 31—Continued

COLLEGE	PERCENTAGE OF MALE GRADUATES RECEIVING M.D. DEGREES
†Hendrix College	14.7
†Union College (Nebraska)	14.5
†Davidson College	14.4
†Hope College	14.2
†Haverford College	13.9
†Ursinus College	13.6
†Emmanuel Missionary College[a]	13.4
†Talladega College	13.0
Vanderbilt University	12.9
Reed College	12.0
Tulane University	12.0
Washington and Jefferson College	11.7
†Wake Forest College	11.7
†Franklin and Marshall College	11.0
Memphis State University	11.0
†Duke University	10.9
†Fisk University	10.8
Lincoln University (Pennsylvania)	10.7
†Westminster College (Missouri)	10.6
†Millsaps College	10.6
†Swarthmore College	10.2
†Washington Missionary College[b]	10.2
†Fairfield University	10.1
†Muhlenberg College	9.6
Johns Hopkins University	9.5
Howard University	9.3
†Loyola University (Louisiana)	9.1
Virginia Military Institute	9.1
Carleton College	9.0
Inter American University	9.0
†Roanoke College	8.7
Wesleyan University	8.7
University of Mississippi	8.7
†University of Richmond	8.4
University of Louisville	8.3
†Morehouse College	8.1
Oberlin College	8.1
†Randolph-Macon College	8.0
†Calvin College	8.0
†Bethany College (West Virginia)	7.9
†College of the Holy Cross	7.9
Amherst College	7.9
University of Virginia	7.9
Hamilton College	7.8
Tufts University	7.8

[a] Now Andrews University.
[b] Now Columbia Union College.

Table 31—Continued

COLLEGE	PERCENTAGE OF MALE GRADUATES RECEIVING M.D. DEGREES
Dartmouth College	7.8
University of South Dakota	7.8
Union College (New York)	7.7
Princeton University	7.7
†John Carroll University	7.5
†Allegheny College	7.5
†Dickinson College	7.5
†Bridgewater College	7.5
†University of the South	7.4
†College of St. Thomas	7.3
†Centre College	7.3
†Kenyon College	7.3
†Loyola University (Illinois)	7.3
†St. Vincent College	7.3
Harvard University	7.2
Rice Institute	7.1
†Baylor University	7.0
†Marquette University	7.0
†Centenary College	6.9
Wabash College	6.9
University of Vermont	6.8
†Loras College	6.7
†Mount St. Mary's College (Maryland)	6.6
Wheaton College (Illinois)	6.6
Indiana University	6.6
†Emory and Henry College	6.5
†Mississippi College	6.5
†DePauw University	6.5
Columbia University	6.5
†Willamette University	6.5
†College of Idaho	6.5
Lincoln Memorial University	6.5
†Manchester College	6.5
†Mercer University	6.4
†University of Scranton	6.4
University of Chicago	6.4
†Albion College	6.4
Williams College	6.4
Washington and Lee University	6.4
Stanford University	6.4
†College of Wooster	6.3
University of Alabama	6.3
†Spring Hill College	6.3
†Denison University	6.3
University of North Dakota	6.3

Manuel and Altenderfer concluded that "the ten colleges with the highest rates for male graduates with M.D. degrees tended to be rather small, church-controlled, coeducational colleges located in the South or West." Nine of the highest 10 are institutions with definite church relationships, while 17 of the top 20 and 62 of the top 100 are church affiliated. Thus it is clear that some of the church colleges and universities are preparing a disproportionate share of students for medical schools and subsequent medical practice. In absolute numbers, not percentage of graduates, the large public and independent universities tend to be the most productive, although 21 of the highest 100 in this respect are church institutions. It should be mentioned, of course, that, although the successful preparation of men for medical schools is to the credit of an institution academically, this is only one bit of evidence and ought not to be broadly interpreted as an indication of over-all educational effectiveness. It represents achievement of one kind.

SOURCES OF COLLEGE TEACHERS

The third study we should like to mention is that made by Allan O. Pfnister for the Association of American Colleges, entitled *A Report on the Baccalaureate Origins of College Faculties*. The results were published in 1961. The project was begun by Frank R. Kille and completed by Pfnister. It is an analysis of the undergraduate backgrounds of 17,749 faculty members during the academic year 1955-56. The persons studied were teaching one-half time or more at 255 representative American liberal arts colleges and teachers colleges or were members of the liberal arts or education faculties at 29 representative universities during the academic year 1955-56. Pfnister reported that the contribution made by colleges enrolling between 600 and 1,199 students to the ranks of college teachers was particularly noteworthy. Middle Western institutions also stood out as heavy producers of college teachers. Over one-half of the teachers in the sample came from 69 colleges—only 8.3 percent of the accredited degree-granting institutions. Private liberal arts colleges ranked high in the precentage of their graduates going into college teaching, 36 of the highest 50 being of that type. Twenty-three of the top 50 are church-related colleges, one-half of them located in the Middle West. Many of the same colleges that ranked high in the other two studies also gave a good account of themselves in this survey. As in the study of physicians, the largest producers, in total numbers, not percentages, were the large public and independent universities. The 50 institutions that produced the largest numbers of college teachers in relation to size (1955 enrollment) are listed in Table 32.[3]

Table 32: Highest Ranking Institutions in Production of College Teachers, as of 1955

INSTITUTION	COLLEGE TEACHERS PRODUCED PER 1,000 FULL-TIME UNDERGRADUATES
†Woodstock College	119.71
University of Chicago	108.04
George Peabody College for Teachers	93.33
Oberlin College	76.23
Reed College	71.55
Wesleyan University	69.85
†Greenville College	65.31
†Swarthmore College	61.24
Bowdoin College	58.44
†Southwestern University	56.07
†Haverford College	54.58
†Transylvania College	47.94
Carleton College	45.45
Amherst College	45.32
†Cornell College	44.88
Hamilton College	44.20
†Lawrence College	41.61
†College of Wooster	39.48
†College of the Pacific[a]	38.46
Princeton University	34.85
Knox College	33.59
Clark University	33.58
†Bates College	33.45
Williams College	33.42
University of Rochester	32.18
Columbia University	32.12
Goucher College	31.34
Johns Hopkins University	31.29
Harvard University	31.13
†Grinnell College	30.55

[3] Allan O. Pfnister, *A Report on the Baccalaureate Origins of College Faculties* (Washington: Association of American Colleges, 1961), pp. 30-31.

Table 32—Continued

INSTITUTION	COLLEGE TEACHERS PRODUCED PER 1,000 FULL-TIME UNDERGRADUATES
†St. Olaf College	29.23
†Davidson College	28.93
†Earlham College	28.24
†Birmingham-Southern College	27.80
†Ohio Wesleyan University	26.83
†Gonzaga University	26.62
Mount Holyoke College	26.47
†DePauw University	26.27
Colorado State College of Education	26.14
Pomona College	25.98
University of Iowa	25.44
Dartmouth College	25.44
Yale University	24.90
†Illinois Wesleyan University	24.80
Kansas State Teachers College, Emporia	24.74
Colorado College	24.19
Springfield College	24.19
†Catholic University	24.16
†Hope College	24.05
†Denison University	23.34

ª Now University of the Pacific.

This study yielded other findings which are of interest to us, although they do not throw light on the effectiveness of individual institutions. Pfnister found that in a sample group of 14,550 college teachers the percentage that had received their undergraduate degrees from four major types of institutions were as follows: public institutions, 47 percent; private institutions, 30.8 percent; Protestant institutions, 16.5 percent; and Roman Catholic institutions, 5.7 percent. The statistics on inbreeding are also informative. An analysis of 15,056 college teachers showed that 21.2 percent were teaching at the same institutions from which they had received their bachelor's degrees. It was found that over 40 percent of the faculty members at the 31 Roman Catholic senior colleges included in the study were teaching at the institutions from which they had received their baccalaureate degrees. The corresponding figures for other groups of institutions and the percentage of faculty members who had earned their baccalaureate degrees at the same institutions were as follows: 65 public institutions, 16.8 percent; 42 private, non-denominational senior colleges, 16.9 percent; and 45 Protestant institutions, 26 percent.

SOURCES OF MINISTERS

A fourth study that is illuminating for our purposes is the Lilly Endowment study of pre-seminary education, which investigated the preparation of students for theological schools. This research was sponsored by the American Association of Theological Schools and the National Association of Biblical Instructors, directed by Keith R. Bridston and Dwight W. Culver, and published in 1965 under the title *Pre-Seminary Education*. One portion of the study is an analysis of the sources of theological students—the identity of the institutions which send the largest numbers or percentage of their students to theological schools. The data on the undergraduate backgrounds of theological students were obtained directly from the seminaries. Roman Catholic seminaries were not included because they do not hold membership in the A.A.T.S. Thus this study sheds no light on the undergraduate backgrounds of Roman Catholic seminarians.

The research showed that 291 American colleges and universities had 20 or more graduates enrolled in member institutions of the A.A.T.S. in 1960-61. Thirty-two institutions had as many as 100 graduates in seminary that year. The names of these institutions and the numbers of their graduates in seminary are shown in Table 33.[4]

Table 33: Colleges and Universities with 100 or More Graduates Attending Theological Schools, Fall 1962

INSTITUTION	NUMBER OF GRADUATES IN SEMINARY, 1960–61
†Baylor University	496
†Concordia Senior College	442
†Oklahoma Baptist University	235
†Howard College	230
†Mississippi College	226
Asbury College	218
University of California	192
†Furman University	189
†Mercer University	186
Wheaton College (Illinois)	184
†Carson-Newman College	175
†Hardin-Simmons University	171
†St. Olaf College	166
†Capital University	160
†Wake Forest College	151

[4] Keith R. Bridston and Dwight W. Culver, *Pre-Seminary Education* (Minneapolis: Augsburg Publishing House, 1965), p. 204.

Table 33—Continued

INSTITUTION	NUMBER OF GRADUATES IN SEMINARY, 1960–61
†Wartburg College	140
†Gettysburg College	136
†Howard Payne College	128
University of Minnesota	126
†Texas Christian University	123
†University of Richmond	121
†Ouachita Baptist College	120
†Phillips University	110
†Louisiana College	108
†Davidson College	105
†Elmhurst College	105
†Concordia College (Moorhead, Minn.)	102
†Duke University	102
†Anderson College	101
†Calvin College	101
†Georgetown College	101
†Luther College	100

Several pertinent comments may be made about this list. It is clear that almost all of the largest producers of students for theological schools are church-affiliated institutions. Twenty-eight of the highest 32 have church connections, and two of the remaining colleges (Asbury and Wheaton) are closely identified with churches, though neither is related to a particular denomination. Two of the largest state universities complete the list of 32.

It is significant that 14 of these 32 institutions are Southern Baptist, while 6 of the top 10 are affiliated with that denomination. Seven of this group are colleges sponsored by Lutheran bodies. Nineteen of the 32 institutions are located in the South, 11 in the Middle West. Only two are located in other regions.

In another analysis of the undergraduate backgrounds of theological students Bridston and Culver related the number of graduates in seminary to the sizes of the institutions from which they graduated, arriving at a second ranking. The results, using the number of graduates enrolled in seminaries for 1960-61 and college enrollments for the Spring of 1961, are shown in Table 34.[5]

[5] *Ibid.*, pp. 196-203.

Table 34: Colleges and Universities with Highest Indices of Graduates Attending Theological Schools, 1960-61

INSTITUTION	INDEX
†Concordia Senior College	131.16 [a]
Asbury College	24.33
†Northwest Christian College	20.40
†Eastern Baptist College	18.71
†Oklahoma Baptist University	18.68
†East Texas Baptist College	17.59
Johnson Bible College	17.28
Gordon College	14.62
†University of Corpus Christi	14.46
†California Baptist College	14.43
†Wartburg College	14.08
†Carson-Newman College	13.93
†Mercer University	13.86
†Wayland Baptist College	13.45
†Mississippi College	13.14
†Furman University	12.56
†Capital University	12.49
†Elmhurst College	12.35
†Bethel College (Minnesota)	11.83
†Howard Payne College	11.76
†Howard College	11.71
†Grand Canyon College	11.65
†Union University (Tennessee)	11.47
†King College	11.46
†Hardin-Simmons University	11.14

[a] The extraordinarily high index for Concordia Senior College requires explana-tion. Not only is the preparation of men for theological study the primary function of this institution (which, in itself, would make for a high index), but Concordia is a two-year college, which means that the number of its graduates in seminary is greater than its enrollment. This explains the fact that its index is well over 100.

This table shows the 25 highest ranking institutions. It will be noted that there is a considerable amount of duplication between this list and the list of institutions producing the largest absolute numbers, but in the list based on percentages the public institutions drop out entirely. Thirteen of the colleges listed in Table 34 are Southern Baptist. Fifteen of the 25 institutions are located in the Southern states.

It should be observed that the institutions ranking high in pre-seminary education are, almost without exception, a different group from those that were found to be highly productive in the studies of younger scholars, medical graduates, and college teachers. There are a

few instances of overlapping, but not many. For example, Calvin
College, Baylor University, Wheaton College, and Mercer University
appear in both the medical and the seminary lists. Calvin College
ranks high in the three areas of younger scholars, physicians, and
seminarians.

The study of pre-seminary education uncovered other facts that
are of some interest in our own study. It was found that 58 percent
of seminary students in 1960-61 were graduates of church-affiliated
colleges and universities, 21 percent of public institutions, and 17
percent of independent institutions. In answer to a question about
their theological positions, seminary students responded as follows:
conservative, 36.5 percent; liberal, 20 percent; neo-orthodox, 12.3
percent; and fundamental, 2.9 percent. These figures probably indicate a marked shift toward a more conservative position since World
War II. The investigators also reported that there were strong and
frequent protest by theological students against the institutional
aspects of the contemporary church and often widespread theological
confusion and uncertainty among seminarians.[6]

SOURCES OF FELLOWSHIP HOLDERS

The records of systematically administered fellowship programs are
another source of data that can be suggestive as to the kind of education offered in institutions across the country. The number of students
selected from individual colleges and universities over a period of
years in competitive fellowship programs involving large numbers of
people provides one type of information useful in assessing institutions. With this in mind, we shall present rudimentary analyses of the
backgrounds of successful candidates for the Danforth Graduate Fellowships and the Woodrow Wilson Fellowships. As in the case of
other data on college graduates, the statistics on fellowships require
careful interpretation.

The Danforth Graduate Fellowships were initiated by the Danforth
Foundation in 1951 to attract to the teaching profession persons of
unusual intellectual promise, whose personal gifts indicate that they
possess a potential for effective teaching in the disciplines represented

---

[6] Keith R. Bridston and Dwight W. Culver, *Seminary Quarterly*, Vol. 4, No. 3
(Spring, 1963), p. 4.

in undergraduate colleges. The candidates are expected to possess a genuine interest in religion. Until 1955 fellowships were awarded to women as well as to men, and women have been eligible since 1965, but, for a period of ten years, all of the recipients were men. The program is open to seniors and graduates of accredited colleges in the United States, who have not yet begun their graduate study and seriously intend to go into college teaching. There are no limitations as to religious affiliation, race, citizenship, or marital status, but the candidates cannot be over 30 years of age. Approximately 100 new fellowships are awarded each year. Candidates are nominated by accredited undergraduate colleges, each institution having the right to nominate between two and five qualified men, depending on its size. Competition for the awards is keen, approximately one out of ten of the candidates having been selected for fellowships in recent years. Table 35 shows the institutions which produced five or more Danforth Fellows during the period 1952-62.[7]

Table 35: Colleges and Universities with Five or More
Graduates Elected Danforth Fellows, 1952-62

INSTITUTION	NUMBER OF GRADUATES ELECTED DANFORTH FELLOWS
Harvard University	15
†University of Notre Dame	15
†Duke University	14
Princeton University	14
†College of Wooster	13
Williams College	12
Yale University	12
†Davidson College	11
†Denison University	11
Pomona College	11
†St. Olaf College	11
Colgate University	10
University of Kansas	10
Brown University	9
Carleton College	9
†Haverford College	9
Oberlin College	9
†University of Redlands	9
†DePauw University	8
University of Colorado	7

[7] Data tabulated from *The Annual Report of The Danforth Foundation*, 1961-62 (St. Louis: The Foundation, 1962), pp. 25-66.

Table 35—Continued

INSTITUTION	NUMBER OF GRADUATES ELECTED DANFORTH FELLOWS
†Earlham College	7
†Kalamazoo College	7
Massachusetts Institute of Technology	7
Stanford University	7
†Brigham Young University	6
†Emory University	6
†Georgetown University	6
†Hamline University	6
†Luther College	6
University of Minnesota	6
†Ohio Wesleyan University	6
†University of the South	6
†Stetson University	6
†Swarthmore College	6
Wabash College	6
Wesleyan University	6
Amherst College	5
†Bates College	5
†Beloit College	5
Bowdoin College	5
Columbia University	5
Dartmouth College	5
†Drake University	5
†Grinnell College	5
Hamilton College	5
University of Michigan	5
Oklahoma State University	5
University of Oklahoma	5
University of Pennsylvania	5
Texas Agricultural and Mechanical University	5
†Texas Christian University	5
University of Utah	5
†Valparaiso University	5

Of the 53 colleges and universities from which as many as five of the Danforth Fellows came during the period under study, 26 are church affiliated. One church-related institution (Notre Dame) tied for first, while another (Duke) tied for second, and a third (the College of Wooster) ranked third. When the size of most of the church institutions is taken into account, the figures take on additional significance.

The Woodrow Wilson National Fellowship Foundation, established in 1945, is the largest private organization of its kind. During its early years it was closely identified with Princeton University. Since 1951, however, it has been national in scope, and the number of fellows appointed annually has increased to 1,000. In 1963-64 approximately 11,000 nominations were received from 904 different colleges and universities in the United States and Canada. Its purpose is to recruit able persons for the academic profession. Table 36 shows the 111 institutions, ten or more of whose graduates were selected as Woodrow Wilson Fellows for the academic years 1945-46 through 1960-61.[8]

Table 36: Colleges and Universities with Ten or More Graduates Appointed Woodrow Wilson Fellows, 1945-60

INSTITUTION	NUMBER OF FELLOWS
Princeton University	187
Harvard University	109
Yale University	97
Cornell University	85
Columbia University	76
University of Michigan	74
University of California at Berkeley	68
†University of Notre Dame	62
Oberlin College	58
University of Chicago	51
†Swarthmore College	47
Reed College	46
University of Texas	46
Stanford University	44
University of Minnesota	43
University of Wisconsin	43
University of Washington	42
University of Kansas	41
University of North Carolina	40
†Northwestern University	39
Rutgers University	38
Washington University	38
Pomona College	37
University of Pennsylvania	36
Amherst College	35

[8] Data tabulated from *Directory of Fellowship Awards for the Academic Years 1945/46-1960/61* (Princeton, New Jersey: Woodrow Wilson National Fellowship Foundation, 1960), pp. 476-83.

Table 36—Continued

INSTITUTION	NUMBER OF FELLOWS
University of California at Los Angeles	35
Barnard College	34
†Haverford College	33
University of Iowa	33
University of Illinois	32
University of Missouri	32
Brown University	31
Dartmouth College	30
Johns Hopkins University	30
Radcliffe College	30
Indiana University	29
Bryn Mawr College	28
Carleton College	28
Hunter College	28
†Kenyon College	28
Massachusetts Institute of Technology	28
Ohio State University	28
University of Colorado	28
Wellesley College	27
Brooklyn College	26
†Duke University	26
Wesleyan University	26
Williams College	26
Vanderbilt University	25
University of Rochester	23
City College of New York	22
Michigan State University	22
New York University	22
University of Oklahoma	22
University of Florida	21
Antioch College	20
†Davidson College	20
†Fordham University	20
Sophie Newcomb College	20
California Institute of Technology	19
College of William and Mary	19
†Occidental College	19
†St. Louis University	19
University of Hawaii	19
University of Virginia	19
†Emory University	18
Louisiana State University	17
Smith College	17
Brandeis University	16
Rice University	16

Table 36—Continued

INSTITUTION	NUMBER OF FELLOWS
University of Miami	16
University of Nebraska	16
University of Oregon	16
†University of the South	16
Knox College	15
†Grinnell College	15
University of Kentucky	15
Douglass College	15
Queens College (New York)	15
University of Pittsburgh	15
†Beloit College	15
University of Arkansas	14
†Georgetown University	14
Montana State University	14
Colgate University	14
Lawrence College	14
University of Alabama	13
Tulane University	13
Mount Holyoke College	13
Vassar College	13
Washington and Lee University	13
University of California at Riverside	12
†Trinity College (Connecticut)	12
Southwestern Louisiana Institute	12
Wayne State University	12
College for Women, University of North Carolina	12
University of Utah	12
†Agnes Scott College	11
University of Georgia	11
†Valparaiso University	11
Wabash College	11
Goucher College	11
†Kalamazoo College	11
†Denison University	11
†Augustana College (Illinois)	10
†Boston University	10
†DePauw University	10
†Lafayette College	10
†Millsaps College	10
†St. John's University (New York)	10
University of Southern California	10

These figures could be better interpreted if they were analyzed in terms of institutional enrollments, but it is difficult to do that because the data cover a long period whereas enrollments change from year to year. In considering their meaning, however, we can take into account the approximate sizes of institutions.

Forty-nine institutions had 25 or more Woodrow Wilson Fellows for the period studied. Thirty-four of these can be broadly termed universities. With three exceptions (Notre Dame, Northwestern, and Duke) they are large public and independent institutions. Fifteen of the 49 highest ranking institutions in number of Woodrow Wilson Fellows are essentially undergraduate colleges. Of these, three (Swarthmore College, Haverford College, and Kenyon College) are church affiliated. Thus of the top 49 institutions in total number of fellowships, only five are associated with religious bodies.

Thirty-two institutions produced from 15 to 24 Fellows. Of these 24 are state and independent institutions, while eight are connected with churches. These eight are Davidson College, Fordham University, Occidental College, St. Louis University, Emory University, the University of the South, Grinnell College, and Beloit College. The 32 institutions in this group tend to be somewhat smaller colleges and universities than those in the top 49.

Thirty institutions had 10 to 14 Woodrow Wilson Fellows during this period. Twelve of them are connected with churches.

The total number of colleges and universities in the United States that have had students selected as Woodrow Wilson Fellows is 538, which is somewhat more than one-third of all degree-granting institutions in the United States. Thus the 111 institutions included in the foregoing table are a rather highly selected group. Twenty-five, or about 23 percent of this group, are church-sponsored institutions; 18 of these are smaller undergraduate colleges.

INTERPRETATION AND CONCLUSIONS

Our examination of the findings of studies of graduates could be pressed much farther. More refined statistical treatment of the data at hand would yield additional understanding of the results achieved by individual institutions and groups of institutions. However, on the basis of what has been presented a few general observations can be offered.

The findings of the studies of college graduates that have been cited tend to place the independent and church-affiliated liberal arts colleges, *or at least some of them*, in a favorable light. Moreover, in terms of the criteria employed in these studies, certain of the smaller and less pretentious institutions appear to have an academic vitality which outstrips their reputations. This type of inquiry is valuable in focusing attention on impartial analysis of educational outcomes as distinguished from more superficial ways of viewing higher education. It probes beneath the surface of institutional notoriety and makes for a more critical scrutiny of outcomes.

The results of such studies must be interpreted cautiously. It is easy to jump to broad conclusions that are not justified. We need to keep in mind, for example, that the preparation of students for graduate and professional work is only one of the functions of collegiate education and, from the point of view of a sound conception of liberal education, not the most important.

Additionally, evidence of the success of graduates in one respect or another is not in itself a sufficient means of appraising educational effectiveness, even in the particular respect under consideration.

Finally, the scope as well as the quality of an institution affects its showing on such indices as those we have cited. Thus a liberal arts college has a distinct advantage over an institution with extensive programs in agriculture, business administration, and other fields in which the bachelor's degree is usually terminal.

An obvious illustration of the difficulty of interpretation can be drawn from the study of seminary students. The fact that certain church colleges send high percentages of their graduates on to theological schools does not *necessarily* show that the impact of those colleges is to encourage men to enter the ministry. Another explanation is that students who are planning to enter the ministry are more likely to choose a church college in the beginning. And so it is with other studies of graduates. It is difficult to separate cause and effect. Also, in the case of fellowships, a large number of graduates holding certain kinds of fellowships may be due in part to factors other than sheer academic achievement. Aggressive encouragement by a dean or other official to able students to seek fellowships can affect an institution's showing on fellowship appointments. These are illustrations of uncontrolled factors which may affect the findings of studies of graduates.

Recent explorations by Holland and Astin at the National Merit Scholarship Corporation cast doubt on some of the conclusions that have been drawn from studies of graduates. These investigators found that, if allowance is made for the aptitude, academic interests, and percentages of men and women entering various colleges, some of the institutions that have been credited with being particularly productive with respect to alumni doctorates are actually found to be "underproductive." [9] In other words, Holland and Astin have tried to refine the research method in order to isolate the influence institutions have on their students from the potential which students bring with them on entrance. This is an effort to separate the colleges which do a first-class job of education with the human material they receive from those that have able student bodies but do not stimulate their students to maximum achievement. What the college does for the students who come to it is the important thing.

Using more refined techniques for measuring actual institutional influence, Astin found that some institutions that had been regarded as highly productive of Ph.D.'s were, in fact, "underproductive." Dartmouth, Hamilton, Harvard, Princeton, Wesleyan, and Williams, for example, produced fewer than their expected numbers of Ph.D.'s. Brooklyn College, City College of New York, Queens College, Yeshiva University, Brigham Young University, the University of Utah, Utah State University, Antioch College, California Institute of Technology, Oberlin College, Reed College, Swarthmore College, and Wabash College were found, in his study, to be "overproductive"; more of the graduates of the latter institutions obtain doctorates than would have been predicted.

Astin concluded that ethnic and religious factors probably play an important role in academic motivation at some institutions, but that, in general, colleges may not differ greatly in the academic stimulation they provide. This line of research raises a host of new questions requiring further investigation. It does seem clear, however, that we are reaching deeper levels of understanding of institutions and their educational effects through more systematic analysis of student input and output.

[9] Alexander W. Astin, "A Re-Examination of College Productivity," *Journal of Educational Psychology*, Vol. 52, No. 3, pp. 173-78; Alexander W. Astin, " 'Productivity' of Undergraduate Institutions," *Science*, Vol. 136, No. 3511, pp. 129-35.

We wish that it were possible to cite evidence on other, broader outcomes of collegiate education. It would be helpful to know, for example, how the graduates of church-related institutions compare with other graduates in the breadth and depth of their intellectual interests, in their assumption of civic responsibility, and in their leadership in churches and charitable organizations. Unfortunately, data on these questions are not available. If there had been any way in which our study could have brought together existing information of this kind and interpreted it, we should have done so. Few institutions have alumni records that are adequate for educational evaluation.

From the evidence at hand, we are able to conclude, however, that some of the church-affiliated institutions, and especially certain Protestant colleges, have made a contribution to American educational and professional life out of all proportion to their size and resources. A significant number of church colleges have produced more than their share of the members of service professions. This has been an important contribution by church-affiliated higher education to the public welfare.

8

Religion in America:
Background of
Church-Sponsored
Higher Education

As this study proceeded, we found it more and more necessary to delve into the status of religion in the United States for explanations of influences we saw operating in church-affiliated colleges and universities. One cannot understand this segment of higher education without some acquaintance, at least in general terms, with the present situation and the problems of the churches. It is not our task to assess religion for its own sake but, rather, to provide a background for the religious evaluation of church colleges which is undertaken in the next chapter. What follows is a brief outline of those features of the American religious scene which we believe are most significant for the purposes of our analysis.

In recent years a steady stream of informative books diagnosing the condition of the churches today has come from the pens of sociologists, church historians, and theologians.[1] We shall draw but a few salient points from this rapidly growing body of literature.

A brief statement such as this, addressed primarily to the intellectual problems of the church in our day, cannot do full justice to the enormous contribution made to human welfare by thousands of dedicated clergymen and laymen throughout America. Churches and

[1] Among those who have made useful contributions to our understanding of the church in the last decade are the following: Peter L. Berger, Daniel Callahan, Harvey Cox, J. H. Fichter, S.J., Langdon Gilkey, C. Y. Glock, James Gustafson, Will Herberg, Gerhard Lenski, Franklin Littell, Martin Marty, Samuel H. Miller, Michael Novak, Victor Obenhaus, Michael Ramsey, Paul Tillich, A. R. Vidler, and Gibson Winter. Reference should also be made to the earlier work of H. Richard Niebuhr, Ernst Troeltsch, Joachim Wach, and Max Weber, who built much of the conceptual framework used by subsequent students of the subject.

churchmen are engaged in unheralded acts of kindness every day—
the visiting of the sick, the helping of the poor, the consoling of the
bereaved, and the guiding of the perplexed. This work goes on largely,
if not completely, apart from the struggle for clarification of theological issues. Any balanced picture of the church must accord an honored
place to these pastoral achievements. They receive limited attention
in this chapter, not because they are considered unimportant, but because they are less directly related to the central problems of academic
institutions.

This has been a period of intensive self-criticism within the
churches. The current has run strongly toward change in outlook and
structure. Analyzing what is wrong with the churches and proposing
sweeping reforms has been one of the principal activities of religious
writers. This preoccupation has been reflected in the pages of widely-
read magazines such as *Christianity Today, Christian Century,
Christianity and Crisis, America,* and *Commonweal.* Even popular
magazines have featured serious articles on the issues confronting
churchmen. *Time, The New Yorker, Newsweek, Reader's Digest,
Look, Fortune,* and *The Saturday Evening Post,* for example, have
given attention to the changing character of the ministry, recent developments in theological scholarship, the impact of Biblical criticism,
and the future of Protestantism. Whether these are indications of
grave sickness in the churches, as some informed observers believe, or
of new vitality, as others insist, is a question that cannot be answered
with assurance at this point. It may be a century before historians will
be able to label the middle of the twentieth century as a time of massive disintegration or of spectacular renewal for the Christian church
in America. It is clear, however, that a major change of some kind is in
the making.

Any discussion of the contemporary church is hampered by the
lack of agreed-upon language. One of the first things that impresses
a reviewer of the literature on this subject is the imprecision of definition of terms like Christianity, religion, church, denomination, sect,
God, secular, sacred, and theology. These terms often have different
meanings to persons from different traditions or schools of thought.
The non-professional reader may grow weary of what seems to him
to be the prolixity of much theological literature. Indeed, some theo-

logians have complained about this themselves.[2] Perhaps the difficulty
is inherent in a field which is as highly speculative as religion. We
apologize in advance to any of our readers, who, accustomed to the
prevalent style of American theological writing, find the following
treatment rather too neat and simple for their taste. Our aim here
is to sketch with bold strokes some of the more important characteristics of American religious life as identified by ecclesiastical scholars.

SCOPE AND VARIETY OF CHURCHES

The range and diversity of official belief, forms of worship, church
government, and religious attitudes in American churches is enormous. There is no established or dominant church. It could hardly
be said that there is an acknowledged norm for religion in this country,
although, as we shall see later, there are powerful influences that cut
across all the churches, tending to make them similar.

As of 1961, data were available on 258 religious bodies in the United
States.[3] The reports on church membership received from the official
statisticians of these bodies showed a total of 116,109,929 persons in
1961—63.4 percent of the estimated population of the United States.
The data from the various churches are not truly comparable, but
the total figure is satisfactory for our purposes. The 258 bodies included 28 distinct Baptist groups, 22 Eastern churches (such as the
Greek Archdiocese of North and South America and the Russian
Orthodox Greek Catholic Church of America), 22 Methodist
churches, and 11 churches with the word "Catholic" in their titles
(not including 7 Eastern churches so designated). The largest bodies
were the Roman Catholic Church (42,876,665), the Methodist
Church (10,046,293), the Southern Baptist Convention (9,978,488),
and the National Baptist Convention, U.S.A., Inc. (5,000,000).

Perhaps more striking to the observer than the formal differences
among churches in the United States are the incidental characteristics
which give the various groups their distinctive flavors. For example,
some of the Protestant denominations, such as the Methodists and the

---

[2] See, for example, Daniel Day Williams, *What Present-Day Theologians Are
Thinking* (New York and Evanston, Illinois: Harper & Row, 1959), p. 174.
[3] *Yearbook of American Churches: Information on All Faiths in the U.S.A.*, edited
by Benson Y. Landis. 31st Issue (New York: Office of Publication and Distribution,
National Council of the Churches of Christ in the U.S.A., 1963), pp. 247-55.

Baptists, have strongly discouraged the use of alcoholic beverages in their official teaching. The frontier traditions of a number of the Protestant denominations have given them pronounced attitudes toward such matters as the formality of worship. The rural and pietistic backgrounds of several of the larger Protestant denominations have greatly affected the tone and attitudes of those groups. The ethnic origins of some churches, such as several of the Lutheran bodies, have been significant factors in their development. Other communions, such as the Roman Catholic and the Episcopal, which have been primarily urban, have been influenced in different ways by their circumstances. The fact that the Roman Catholic Church in the United States is now becoming a middle-class church after a history of identification with working-class immigrants is changing the whole character of this large religious group. Economic and sociological factors have had a pronounced impact on the various segments of American religious life.

In this century the ecumenical movement has certainly made for greater cooperation and a spirit of good will among churches. With initial impetus coming chiefly from the conventional, middle-class Protestant denominations and being manifested in such organizations as local church federations, state councils of churches, and the National Council of Churches, this movement has now received strong encouragement from the new spirit stimulated in the Roman Catholic Church by the Second Vatican Council.

As has been suggested, the very existence of so many churches or denominations, each exercising its right of autonomy, deprives American religion of anything like a single authoritative voice and engenders in the popular mind the view that, although each church claims to be authoritative, none really is, and religion is pretty much a matter of personal opinion and preference. We shall dwell on this point at greater length in a moment, but suffice it to say here that diversity of beliefs and values with its accompanying interplay, compromise, and tolerance, tends to result in a kind of religious relativism. The processes by which this occurs are well known to students of the sociology of knowledge and have been described with particular clarity by Karl Mannheim.[4]

[4] See, for example, Mannheim's *Ideology and Utopia: An Introduction to the Sociology of Knowledge.* Translated from the German by Louis Wirth and Edward Shils (New York: Harcourt, Brace & World, Inc., 1936), pp. 5-20, 250-56.

ROLE IN A CHANGING SOCIETY

Most of the scholarly studies of the church as an institution have pointed out that the character of churches, denominations, and sects in the United States has changed in response to changing social conditions. The rural Protestant sects, for example, with their individualistic, informal, emotional religion of an earlier time, have been transformed as they have followed their people to the cities and suburbs in the twentieth century. They have tended to give up their separateness from a sinful culture and become middle-class denominations in the mainstream of the secular world. Their earlier insistence on a personal religious experience has been largely replaced by formal membership and formal worship. Likewise, the historic churches—Roman Catholic, Episcopal, and Lutheran—have assimilated some of the friendly, egalitarian, congregation-centered flavor of the sect-type religious bodies, as they have tried to adapt to their American environment. Thus both the church-type religious bodies and the sect-type groups have tended to become, under the pressure of contemporary culture, modern American denominational churches, a new kind of religious institution.[5] Perhaps the most typical of the American denominations are such Protestant bodies as the Methodist, Presbyterian, and Baptist churches.

A Highly Organized Church

Several characteristics of church life have been much discussed in the literature. First, the American church is highly organized. It has a multiplicity of committees, commissions, boards, guilds, clubs, circles, and meetings. Activities are available for every group—children, youth, young married people, employed women, the elderly, and so forth. Not only is the local church highly organized, but so also are the district or conference or diocese and the regional and national bodies. Much has been said about the "activism" of the church in the United States. The conventional term of praise for a churchman is to describe him as "active." It is not so much what a person is or believes as what he does that matters, and this is interpreted as participation in church organizations.[6]

[5] Langdon Gilkey, *How the Church Can Minister to the World Without Losing Itself* (New York and Evanston, Illinois: Harper & Row, 1964), pp. 4-20.
[6] John Huess, *The True Function of a Christian Church* (West Cornwall, Connecticut: Episcopal Center, n.d.), pp. 4-5.

The Ministry, A Problem Profession

Second, the ministry, especially in the freer Protestant churches, is a problem profession. Extensive research has been done on the lives and anxieties of clergymen. The basic difficulty seems to be that of defining the role of the minister (or priest or rabbi) under present conditions. As with the laity, the clergyman is expected to be active— to be doing useful things. The traditional responsibilities of the minister—officiating at services, instructing his people, and the like —are no longer sufficient. He must engage in practical activities that affect the lives of members of the congregation and of the community. He becomes a psychotherapist, an adviser on marital problems, a television performer, an organizer of recreational programs, and an administrator of financial campaigns and church organizations. His authority depends on his making a success of these activities. He no longer has authority simply as a spiritual leader. This is less true in the Roman Catholic, Episcopal, and Lutheran churches, in which the position of priest or pastor is fairly well defined, than in the typical Protestant denominations. To some degree, however, the problem of role-definition faces most clergymen and rabbis in the United States. The result is that an increasing percentage of clergymen are moving out of the local church or parish ministry into teaching or ancillary positions. Many leave the ministry entirely.[7]

Weakness of Educational Programs

Third, the educational programs conducted directly by the churches are, in general, weak. The two types of education most immediately related to the future strength of the churches are the religious instruction of the young in the local church and the theological training of candidates for the ministry.

During the last generation there have been many experiments in religious instruction, some of the most recent and ambitious of which have closely resembled the earlier progressive education movement in the public schools. The theory of religious education always seems to lag behind that of secular education. At any rate, few informed persons are satisfied with the results of the programs of re-

[7] An excellent summary of research on the ministry is available in James M. Gustafson, "The Clergy in the United States," *Daedalus*, Vol. 92, No. 4 (Fall, 1963). pp 732-34, 736.

ligious education conducted by local churches. In large churches, the senior clergy, disillusioned with religious education, almost uniformly delegate responsibility for this work to younger men just out of seminary or to women directors of education. The typical Sunday school consists of poorly-trained volunteer teachers, cajoled into accepting the teaching responsibility for a year or two, filling 35 minutes or so each Sunday morning with whatever information and discussion they can manage with minimal preparation.

College teachers of religion, who encounter the products of Sunday schools, report that the results of this process are almost negligible and often detrimental. Careful studies of the results of religious instruction tend to corroborate this impression. For example, on the basis of an evaluation of adult religious knowledge in a Middle Western community, Obenhaus reports an alarming lack of understanding of the Bible, even in denominations which describe themselves as Bible churches. Only about one-third of Protestant respondents could explain any difference between the Old and New Testaments. Less than one-half of the church members had any knowledge of the Old Testament prophets. Less than one-third understood the meaning of the Parable of the Good Samaritan. Obenhaus concluded that the Bible is almost an unknown book to most laymen.[8] The inability of the churches to develop effective programs of religious education for children and youth is one of the most disturbing symptoms of inner weakness. When a religious movement can no longer transmit its faith to the young, its future is problematic.

The position of theological education in the American churches is stronger than that of religious education in the local church, but it, too, is faced with difficulties. It is, to use President Pusey's phrase, "a depressed area" in higher education. The theological seminaries, even the most noted, are often unable to attract enough men of the quality they desire. A prominent theological educator, in private conversation, recently contrasted the recruitment success of the Peace Corps with the recruitment results of his own institution. Why cannot the stronger seminaries, he asked, attract even a small fraction of the able students who apply for service in the Peace Corps?

[8] Victor Obenhaus, *The Church and Faith in Mid-America* (Philadelphia: Westminster Press, 1963), pp. 72-79.

Conrad Bergendoff found in a recent study of theological education in the Lutheran Church in America that the typical seminarian had been a "C" student as an undergraduate—and this in a church with a long tradition of a learned ministry.[9] The Roman Catholic Church has had to draw its leadership almost entirely from the abler sons of culturally deprived parents.[10]

The mortality among able theological students appears to be high in some denominations. In education, social work, and elsewhere one encounters large numbers of capable men who began theological study but did not continue their ministerial careers. With the possible exception of three or four communions in which the ministry has a relatively well-established position and status, theological education and the ministry are not, by and large, attractive to promising young men today. Moreover, seminaries probably have more than their share of student psychological problems with which to contend. Spectacular exceptions can, of course, be cited in which first-rate students with extraordinary personal qualities enter theological seminaries and continue their careers in the ministry with firm resolve and complete dedication.[11] It should be mentioned, in passing, that some of the newer Protestant sects do not require graduate theological education of their ministers. Many pastors are trained in Bible colleges and institutes or enter the ministry without professional preparation. Of the learned professions, the ministry is probably the most heterogeneous in its educational requirements.

It is not entirely clear what the present-day theological curriculum ought to be. The tendency of the larger theological centers is to de-

---

[9] Conrad Bergendoff, *The Lutheran Church in America: A Report to the Board of Theological Education* (New York: Board of Theological Education, Lutheran Church in America, 1963), p. 18.

[10] Richard Hofstadter, *Anti-Intellectualism in American Life* (New York: Alfred A. Knopf, 1963), pp. 138-39.

[11] A valuable source on the quality of theological students is H. Richard Niebuhr, Daniel D. Williams, and James M. Gustafson, *The Advancement of Theological Education* (New York: Harper & Brothers, 1957). Though dismissing the recruitment and selection of students as the key problem in theological education, the authors reach the following conclusion from the point of view of the seminaries themselves: "Several denominations in the United States and apparently all the churches of Canada are plagued by the shortage of candidates for the ministry, or at least by the shortage of candidates who are willing and able to complete a theological course of study. More frequently the complaint is that too many men are entering the ministry without adequate preparation and that too many of those who are attending theological schools are either too poorly prepared or lacking in native gifts." (p. 204). However, the authors report that standards of admission were raised by seminaries during the period 1934-54.

velop broad programs which duplicate much that is offered elsewhere in the universities. For example, the divinity schools of universities often have faculty members and courses in such fields as psychology, sociology, education, philosophy, public speaking, and drama—subjects which might better be taught in regular university departments than offered in modified forms specifically for theological students. This tendency toward curricular diffuseness can be explained in part by the feeling on the part of theological faculties that if the interests peripheral to the central theological disciplines are left to other departments to be cultivated, they will be handled improperly, given the secularistic attitudes which pervade the contemporary university. Another issue in theological education concerns the framework of presuppositions within which the teaching is to be conducted. Should the faculty take certain Christian notions for granted and proceed from there? Or is there to be unlimited inquiry? Some of the larger non-denominational theological centers have operated on the latter principle, becoming, to a considerable extent, schools of religion and philosophy in a more general sense, not of the Christian faith exclusively.

The dissatisfaction with theological education in its present form may lead to basic changes in the next decade or two. Indeed, one responsible leader has proposed that the theological school, as a separate professional institution or division of a university, be eliminated. The student preparing for the ministry would complete an appropriate program of studies in the humanities in a graduate school. The courses in religion would not be oriented toward the church but would be taught as any other academic discipline in the university. Necessary devotional and ecclesiastical functions would be discharged through off-campus houses of study supported by churches. Such a plan would be consonant with some of the trends in the churches and in theology today.[12]

Separation from Mainstream of Everyday Life

The fourth aspect of the contemporary church which should be noted is its separation from the affairs of other major institutions in society. The actual bases on which important decisions of the day

[12] From an address entitled "A Model for Theological Education," delivered at the 125th anniversary celebration of the School of Theology, Boston University, March, 1964, by Walter D. Wagoner, of the Fund for Theological Education, Inc.

are made in government, business, and education are not usually the theistic values officially advocated by the churches. In government and education the legal principle of separation of church and state has accentuated the insulation of the church from these influential institutions. In a few instances, such as the movement for Federal legislation on civil rights, the church has taken effective action in matters of public policy, but these are exceptional.[13] Ordinarily the church is expected to play a supportive rather than a determinative role in large public decisions involving moral principles. As Robin Williams has stated it, perhaps somewhat too cynically: "The public generally assigns organized religion a special circumscribed place as the repository of values that are inherently of the highest good, but that should be safely insulated and restricted to ceremonial occasions ('Sunday religion') so that they cannot interfere too much with the ordinary business of the society." [14]

Efforts to Revive Influence

Before leaving this subject, we must mention four movements which have been significant as efforts to restore the religious influence of the church in the larger society. The first is the liturgical revival. Though the essential ideas of this movement are traceable at least as far back as Archbishop Cranmer, the Anglican reformer of the sixteenth century, the last two or three decades have seen an unprecedented blossoming of liturgical interest in this country. This has occurred not only in the Episcopal Church but on a wider scale in the Roman Catholic Church, the Lutheran churches, the Methodist Church, and others. The Liturgical Movement in the Roman Catholic Church, under such leaders as Father Virgil Michel, Father Godfrey Dieckmann, and their Benedictine associates at St. John's University, Collegeville, Minnesota, has been the most dramatic development in this field. It has resulted in the major liturgical changes approved at the Second Vatican Council. From our point of view in this discussion, perhaps the most important aspects of the liturgical revival are its emphasis on lay participation in public worship and

[13] Franklin Hamlin Littell, *From State Church to Pluralism: A Protestant Interpretation of Religion in American History* (Garden City, New York: Doubleday & Company, Inc., 1962), pp. 163-64.
[14] Robin M. Williams, Jr., *American Society: A Sociological Interpretation* (New York: Alfred A. Knopf, 1957), pp. 339-40.

on the consequences for daily living and social action which flow from liturgical celebration. Only time can tell whether this promising movement will affect in basic ways the practice of religion in the United States.

A second development is what might be called lay renewal in the life of the church. This has expressed itself not only in special programs such as the Yokefellows, Kirkridge, the Faith and Life Community, and the Detroit Industrial Mission, but in a greater awareness generally that the church can succeed only with responsible lay participation at all levels. Except in the local parish or congregation, the increasing professionalization and bureaucratization of almost all churches has proved to be a barrier to reform in this respect. The twin obstacles of lay apathy and clergy fear of lay domination seem likely to prevent any substantial lay involvement in policy-making at the higher levels in most churches in the foreseeable future. The Church of Jesus Christ of Latter-day Saints and the Society of Friends (neither of which really has a professional ministry) are notable exceptions. Perhaps the most striking evidence elsewhere of genuine lay interest is the agitation on the part of Roman Catholic intellectuals for a more influential role in their church. Several Roman Catholic journals and a number of books have reflected this attitude.[15]

The third effort of some consequence to relate the churches more closely to the larger society is the beginning of a systematic body of Christian social thought. In their more zealous days some of the American Protestant churches—notably, the Congregational and Methodist—played an active part in campaigns of social reform. The slavery issue is perhaps the best illustration of such interest. This enthusiasm for reform has lost much of its momentum in the twentieth century, but has, to some degree, been continued within the churches and in committees and commissions of the National Council of Churches. A more systematic analysis of social questions has, however, been begun by individual theologians of whom Reinhold Neibuhr has perhaps been the most influential in this country. By all odds the most impressive corporate effort to define Christian social principles is the growing body of papal encyclicals. The pronouncements of recent popes, beginning with Leo XIII at the turn of the

[15] See, for example, Michael Novak, A New Generation (New York: Herder and Herder, 1964).

century, are probably the closest thing we have to a comprehensive and carefully formulated social philosophy which has any claim on the consciences of a substantial segment of Christians.

A fourth effort is that of Christian intellectuals to relate religion to literature and the arts. Such persons as T. S. Eliot, W. H. Auden, E. Martin Browne, Nathan Scott, and Thomas Driver have been leaders in this undertaking. Though strongest in universities and seminaries, the movement has also found its way into the churches.

PROBLEM OF SECULARITY

We now come to the heart of the matter, the underlying cause of the frustration and ineffectiveness of the churches. Its principal manifestation is the inability of the churches to provide a convincing framework of belief other than the values of our secular culture. The church becomes an agency of social stability rather than of the judgment and mercy of God. Why?

Theologians have given us answers in various forms, but the general idea is much the same. Gustafson speaks of the minister's "normlessness . . . in the realm of belief"—the lack of "authoritative statements of belief which set the intellectual framework for his ministry." The dilemma is that the church represents "a historical tradition which in many respects is dissonant with contemporary knowledge and with the principles of practical life in the age of technology." The minister has to cope with the fact that "in the secularization of modern life God is very remote to most men. Indeed, it is difficult to be a clergyman in an age in which the death of God is one of the basic principles of life." [16]

The problem is not only one of what to do about a religiously illiterate laity. An intensified program of religious education could perhaps solve that problem. The difficulty is deeper. Theologians are not agreed as to the meaning or value of the word "God." Cobb points out that the problem of God for theologians used to be that of adducing evidence of His existence. Now the debate has shifted, and the urgent question is "whether the word 'God' has any meaning at all. Granted a certain sound is uttered from time to time, does any meaningful idea correspond to this sound?" [17] Cobb answers the

[16] James M. Gustafson, op. cit.
[17] From an unpublished manuscript by John B. Cobb, Jr., entitled "Affirming God in a Non-Theistic Age."

question in the affirmative, but some theologians do not. Paul Van Buren, a non-theistic theologian, has this to say:

Although traditional theology does have a historical, intentional, and ethical dimension, does it not include a good deal more? Where, as one reviewer asked of Professor Ramsey, is the transcendent God of Classical Christianity? Have we not reduced theology to ethics? Our answer takes the form of another question: In a secular age, what would that "more" be? It is our inability to find any empirical linguistic anchorage for that "more" that has led to our interpretation. If this is a reduction in the content of theology, it is the sort of reduction which has been made by modern culture in many fields.[18]

Other Christian atheists or "death-of-God" theologians frankly accept the non-theistic assumptions of the secular culture and urge the churches to give up the religious or transcendent dimension of their beliefs. In the words of the German theologian Dietrich Bonhoeffer, we need "Christianity without religion."

The profound discomfort of the church is precisely at this point. As Langdon Gilkey has said, the church, if it is to be itself and do its work, "must mediate to the world some Word, some Presence, some norm and standard, that are both transcendent in their origin—in some measure 'holy'—and also relevant to the world's life."[19] But the progressive secularization of life and thought in recent centuries has made this task impossible:

For multitudes of us (and they seem to be most characteristic of our age) no experience of God is either expected or felt, no word from God listened for or heard, and no command of God received or obeyed. To many the question of the existence or experience of these things is not even intelligible or meaningful.

Any discussion of the relation of the church to culture in our age must be set against the massive backdrop of this contemporary absence of God. The church now lives in a society for which God is elusive, if not quite unknown, and the categories of the holy and the transcendent are apparently meaningless, empty, and useless. And surely the deep religious problems of the church . . . are caused in large part by the fact that this secular spirit has penetrated into the mind and heart of the church as well as penetrating the world outside it.[20]

Is it any wonder that the church-sponsored colleges and universities, whose curricula are supposed to be undergirded and integrated by religion, have serious theological problems?

[18] Paul M. Van Buren, *The Secular Meaning of the Gospel* (New York: Macmillan Company, 1963), pp. 197-98.
[19] Langdon Gilkey, *op. cit.*, p. 2.
[20] *Ibid.*, pp. 21-22.

⑨

A Religious
Evaluation
of the
Institutions

In this study we have been greatly interested in the influence of different religious traditions on higher education. We believe that these differences have not been sufficiently recognized or explored in previous research. Much of the diversity of religious belief and practice in the United States is reflected in the church-sponsored colleges and universities. However, it would be a mistake to suppose that this influence is usually transmitted in the form of old-fashioned sectarianism. This is rarely the case. It is the distinctive attitudes and temperaments of the various communions and denominations which seem to have the most important effect on the character of church-related institutions. Most of the literature on the subject overlooks these subtle influences which are probably more significant educationally than the consequences of formal doctrine and church government.

It hardly need be said that the distinction between religion and other aspects of an institution's educational program is artificial. Religion, properly understood, is a pervasive element. For purposes of analysis, however, it is useful to look specifically at the religious dimension of the institutions with which we are concerned. We have assumed that each of the major religious traditions has something important to contribute to higher education—that each deserves to be taken seriously. Some churches can make special contributions to theological scholarship, some to liturgical refinement, others to a strong sense of freedom, still others to a deep social concern, and so forth. Our inquiry started with colleges—with firsthand observations of faculty and student attitudes. We sought to learn how religion affects what is done educationally, and why religion seems important in College A but not in College B. Differences from one denomination to another and from one college to another are often perplexing. We therefore found it necessary to delve into the condition of religion in America for explanations of influences we saw operating in church-affiliated colleges and universities. Thus the preceding chapter on religion was intended as background for the observations we shall present in this chapter.

What follows is based primarily on the studies made of the 50 case-study colleges and universities mentioned in Chapter 4. In this chapter we shall also report the results of the administration of a specially prepared test of religious knowledge, which was given at 31 institutions as part of our study, and the findings of a survey of formal religious requirements in a large sample of colleges.

During our visits to the 50 representative institutions we spent hundreds of hours interviewing individuals and groups of faculty members and students trying to discover how they viewed the place of religion in collegiate education. Faculty and student attitudes have much to do with the way in which religion is handled. As a matter of fact, faculty notions about religion are probably the most important single factor in determining what the religious impact of an institution on its students will be.

In our faculty and student interviews we discovered wide differences in attitudes toward the churches with which colleges are associated. In some colleges faculty members and students tend to be proud of their churches, while in others they are apologetic. These attitudes affect the emphasis placed on church relationships. If, for example, many members of a given faculty are somewhat contemptuous of the church which sponsors the college, they will "play down" the church relationship. The church connection seems to them to be something that does not bring credit to the institution and, perhaps unconsciously, they push it into the background. If, on the other hand, most members of the faculty are proud of the church with which they are associated, they tend to emphasize this in talking to students and in making educational decisions.

As a broad generalization, it may be said that attitudes of respect for the church are less pronounced in many of the free or liberal Protestant churches than they are in others. One finds more affirmative feelings among Lutherans, Episcopalians, and evangelicals or fundamentalists, to mention only a few instances. Most Roman Catholics view their church with respect, though criticism, both constructive and destructive, is more prevalent among Catholic intellectuals today than it used to be. The Second Vatican Council has encouraged a new spirit of freedom and criticism. This is reflected in Catholic colleges and universities. Attitudes in some of the denominations appear to be caused by rapid sociological change in those bodies. For example, several large Protestant denominations have altered their whole character in the last two or three generations and are hypersensitive to vestiges of rural pietism and frontier revivalism. The Roman Catholic Church is becoming an American middle-class church, and this is finding expression in Catholic institutions.

Some denominations seem not to be well equipped to sponsor colleges. Those churches that are loosely organized, have less well-defined theologies, lack a scholarly tradition, face a liberal-fundamentalist split in their ranks, or are unwilling to give substantially to church enterprises are distinctly handicapped in the sponsorship of colleges and universities. Denominations with strong theological emphases, with cohesion, with highly developed liturgies, and with a tradition of generous giving have built-in advantages in operating colleges. It is hard for the colleges connected with the freer, more liberal traditions to maintain their religious character. They tend to be assimilated into the secular culture and to become indistinguishable from avowedly secular institutions.

Many faculty members and students in church colleges and universities share the secular view that religion does not really belong in an educational institution. There is a widespread feeling, often unconscious, that religion is not genuinely concerned with truth, that by its very nature it is inharmonious with the purposes of an academic community. Many teachers in public or independent institutions think of church colleges as restricted environments. Although this impression is usually based on misinformation, it is sometimes a handicap in recruiting faculty members. The issue is often clouded by moralistic prohibitions (for example, rules against dancing or drinking in some church colleges), which restrict personal conduct more than they limit academic freedom. Even faculty people in church-related institutions sometimes assume that abridgment of freedom is characteristic of many institutions of this type, though they are quick to state that their own freedom is not abridged. They often believe that their institution is different in this respect from others.

What can be said about the effectiveness of religious programs in these colleges and universities? This is, of course, a question that touches on one of the central purposes of church-affiliated institutions. We shall consider the matter as evidenced in formal instruction, corporate worship, student religious groups, social concern, and intellectual presuppositions.

FORMAL INSTRUCTION IN RELIGION

A large majority of church institutions require the completion of courses in religion or theology for the bachelor's degree. A survey of the curricula of 196 representative colleges and universities showed that 87 percent require some formal instruction in this field for graduation. In Roman Catholic institutions the courses are usually entitled "theology," whereas in other colleges the term "religion" or "Bible" is commonly used. The requirements in the institutions surveyed are shown in Table 37.

It is perhaps surprising to learn that 26 of these 196 institutions have no course requirement in religion or theology. The explanation would appear to be two-sided. In a few colleges the election of courses in religion or theology is taken so much for granted that a requirement is unnecessary, while in other institutions, predominantly related to freer or more liberal denominations, instruction in religion is not regarded as essential in collegiate education. It is also interesting to note that course requirements are closely correlated with chapel requirements. Institutions with heavy requirements in one of these respects tend to have heavy requirements in the other, while colleges with light requirements in one typically also have light requirements in the other.

It is worthy of note that the requirements in Roman Catholic colleges are substantially greater than in other institutions. The average requirement in Catholic senior colleges is 13.1 semester hours, while the comparable figure for other colleges is 6.9. In junior colleges the average requirements are 10 semester hours (Catholic) and 5.7 (others).

Table 37: Course Requirements in Religion in 196 Church-Sponsored Institutions

SEMESTER HOURS REQUIRED	Roman Catholic		Others		Total Sample	
	Junior Colleges	Senior Colleges	Junior Colleges	Senior Colleges	Junior Colleges	Senior Colleges
2			1		1	
3			5	7	5	7
4		1	1	5	1	6
5				2		2
6	2	1	10	38	12	39
7		1				1
8	3	9	2	6	6	15
9				8		8
10		1		1		2
11			1	1	1	1
12	1	11	1	5	2	16
13		1				1
14		6		2		8
15		1				1
16	2	24		1	2	25
17		1				1
Required, but hours not specified	1	4	1	2	2	6
Strongly urged		1				1
No official statement	4	10	3	8	7	18
Total	13	72	25	86	38	158

In our visits to the 50 case-study institutions, we asked faculty members and students for evaluations of the instruction in religion on their campuses. The courses were reported to be academically strong at most of the Protestant colleges. The faculty members of departments of religion in these institutions are, on the whole, well trained. The day when teachers of religion in Protestant colleges were often retired ministers or clergymen who had wearied of the parish ministry has passed. Most of the teachers today are men who have completed graduate study in one of the large theological centers. Many hold Ph.D. degrees from the better universities. Students report that the courses are, for the most part, stimulating.

The appraisal of formal religious instruction in Roman Catholic institutions is more mixed. Students frequently complain that the courses are artificial and unrelated to contemporary interests. Many administrators believe that the teaching in undergraduate departments of theology would be better if the instructors were university trained instead of seminary trained. Most teachers of theology in Catholic colleges are graduates of conventional programs of preparation for the priesthood rather than for teaching. This, however, is slowly changing. Through the influence of the Society of Catholic College Teachers of Sacred Doctrine, the impact of changes in the Church at large, and the development of graduate programs at Marquette University and elsewhere expressly designed for the training of college teachers of religion, the courses in theology in Catholic colleges are undergoing major reorientation. There is also a trend toward an increase in the number of lay teachers of theology. In a few institutions more than one-half of the faculty members in theology are now laymen. This movement, no doubt, will continue and accelerate.

One of the more ambitious parts of our study was the preparation and administration of a test of religious knowledge. The purpose was to find out how much students know about religion, whether their knowledge increases during the four years of undergraduate study, and what differences exist among institutions in this respect. We learned from college teachers of religion that there was no generally recognized test of religious knowledge which would be useful for our purposes. With the expert assistance of C. Eugene Conover, Bernard A. Cooke, S.J., Paul L. Dressel, and other scholars, a 50-minute, short-answer test covering the principal areas of religious knowledge was prepared. The areas included were: Old Testament; New Testament; theology; church history, liturgics, and sacraments; Christian ethics or moral teaching; and non-Christian religions. The test was printed in two versions—one for use in Roman Catholic institutions and another for use in a reasonably wide range of Protestant institutions. While the two versions had a substantial core of common items, it was not found feasible to use a single test for all institutions. The sections on Old Testament, New Testament, and non-Christian religions were, however, almost identical in the two forms of the test.

The test was designed specifically for college undergraduates. It was intended to be a yardstick of religious knowledge, not of attitudes or commitment. The authors of the test were keenly aware of the limitations of a short-answer test which is to be completed in 50 minutes. They would have liked to include questions that probe more deeply the student's ability to interpret, to generalize, and to reason theologically. They recognized that the test was heavily weighted toward information.

A further limitation on the development of the test should be noted. Time did not permit preliminary testing followed by selection and revision of items. However, most of the items had been used by the authors of the test in course examinations and had proved to be discriminating. The validity of the test content must be regarded as adequate for the purpose, as judged by the authors. Since groups rather than individuals were to be compared, high reliability was not a matter of great concern, although the test in its present forms would not be adequate for use in assessing the performance of individuals.

This was the first attempt to develop a test which could be used in a variety of colleges and universities as a measure of the religious literacy of the general student—the student who is not specializing in religion or preparing for a church vocation. It would require several tests to do full justice to the spectrum of religious traditions in the United States. However, on the basis of a careful review of the test items by readers representing different traditions, it was estimated that the two versions of the test developed in this study, taken together, were suitable for perhaps 75 percent of American college students.

The test was administered in May, 1964, to 1,334 randomly selected seniors in 31 colleges and universities across the country. Twenty-five were church affiliated, three independent, and three public. The public institutions included a large state university, a medium-sized state university, and a large teacher-training institution. Nine of the church-sponsored institutions were Roman Catholic. In the fall of 1964, the same test was administered to 1,414 freshmen at 29 of the institutions which had participated the previous spring. The freshman sample was matched with the seniors on the basis of sex and of aptitude data obtained at the time of admission. Thus the two groups were reasonably comparable. The aim was to test the seniors immediately before graduation and the freshmen immediately after entrance and before they had had the benefit of extended college instruction. The results of the testing program were analyzed by Thomas Freeman, of the Office of Institutional Research, Michigan State University.

We shall comment here on some of the more obvious inferences to be drawn from the testing program without recourse to the usual tests of statistical significance. Tests of significance were made, however, and the significance of the reported differences was confirmed. Furthermore, we are more interested in the relationship of the differences found to other evidence than in the differences as such.

First, the range of student religious knowledge was found to be great, both among and within colleges. For example, among the 31 institutions in which the test was administered to seniors, the percentage of correct answers ranged from 33.28 as the average in one college to 73.18 in another. The broad range of scores within institutions is shown by the standard deviation which was calculated for each of the institutions. As an illustration, in one college in which the mean score for seniors was 40.00, the standard deviation was 15.35.

There were also wide variations in the difference in religious knowledge between the seniors tested and the matched sample of freshmen. In six of the institutions (including three church colleges), there was no significant difference in the scores of the two groups. By contrast, at three colleges the performance of the seniors was more than 40 percent above that of the freshmen. The mean scores for freshmen and seniors on the portion of the test which was common to both Roman Catholic and Protestant versions were 24.66 and 28.83, respectively, out of a possible score of 54. Thus the freshmen as a group got slightly less than one-half of the questions right, and the seniors slightly more than one-half.

The seniors at Roman Catholic and conservative Protestant colleges tended to do better than did seniors at liberal Protestant and public institutions. Moreover, the superiority of the seniors over the freshmen was much more marked in Roman Catholic and conservative Protestant colleges than in the other two groups. It appears that the increase in religious knowledge during the four undergraduate years is substantially greater in the first two groups of institutions. The data on freshman and senior performance by types of colleges are presented in Table 38.

Table 38: Freshman and Senior Performance on Test of Religious
Knowledge According to Groups of Institutions

GROUP OF INSTITUTIONS	FRESHMEN PERCENT CORRECT ANSWERS	SENIORS PERCENT CORRECT ANSWERS
Roman Catholic	47.85	57.65
Conservative Protestant	45.14	56.19
Liberal Protestant	38.93	45.13
Non-church-related	38.18	42.03

We realize that the classification of colleges as "conservative Protestant" and "liberal Protestant" is a somewhat arbitrary matter. These terms are not at all precise, though widely used. However, some division of Protestant institutions would appear helpful in interpreting the data. Included here as "liberal Protestant" are eight colleges related to the following religious bodies: Disciples of Christ, Methodist Church, Society of Friends, United Church of Christ, American Baptist Convention, and African Methodist Episcopal Church. Classified as "conservative Protestant" are nine institutions with the following relationships: Seventh-day Adventist, Lutheran, Southern Baptist, Episcopal, Presbyterian (U.S.), and evangelical or fundamental interdenominational. We recognize that two or three of the colleges do not fit neatly into either group.

It is a significant fact that the standing of seniors on the test and the number of courses completed in religion or theology were positively correlated. In other words, students who took more courses in religion or theology tended to do better on the test. As has already been mentioned in the discussion of course requirements, there are wide differences among institutions in the amount of religious instruction received by students. The data for four groups of colleges are shown in Table 39.

Each student taking the test was asked to supply certain information about himself. This made it possible to compare the performance

Table 39: Number of Courses in Religion Completed by Students
Taking Test According to Groups of Institutions

GROUP OF INSTITUTIONS	MEAN NUMBER OF COURSES COMPLETED
Roman Catholic	5.02
Conservative Protestant	4.37
Liberal Protestant	2.31
Non-church-related	.71

of various groups of students. For example, Table 40 shows comparative figures for freshmen who had attended public and private secondary schools. The private schools are, in most cases, Roman Catholic institutions.

Table 40: Performance of Freshmen with Public and Private School Backgrounds on Portion of Test Common to Roman Catholic and Protestant Versions

TYPE OF SCHOOL ATTENDED	NUMBER OF STUDENTS	MEAN SCORE
Private school..........................	497	27.32
Public school..........................	867	23.14

A comparison was also made of the performance of men and women students. The test results show that women did slightly better than men, both as freshmen and as seniors. Table 41 summarizes the data on this point.

Table 41: Performance of Men and Women on Portion of Test Common to Roman Catholic and Protestant Versions

GROUP OF STUDENTS	MEAN SCORES OF MEN	MEAN SCORES OF WOMEN
Freshmen.............................	23.79	25.41
Seniors.............................	28.38	29.21

An analysis of the performance of students according to their fields of academic interest provides illuminating insights. The data corroborate the generally held impression that religion as an academic discipline has a special affinity to the humanities. The standing of four groups of students according to major field is shown in Table 42.

Table 42: Performance on Common Portion of Test and Number of Courses in Religion Completed by Seniors According to Major Field

MAJOR FIELD	MEAN NUMBER OF COURSES COMPLETED	MEAN SCORE ON COMMON PORTION OF TEST
Humanities............................	3.78	31.48
Social sciences......................	3.73	29.54
Natural science......................	3.53	28.55
Professional.........................	3.25	26.54

The testing program yielded useful information on denominational differences in student religious knowledge. These differences are rather pronounced. Table 43 shows the performance of several groups of students classified according to broad religious categories.

Table 43: Performance of Seniors and Freshmen on Common Portion of Test According to Religious Preference

RELIGIOUS PREFERENCE	NUMBER OF SENIORS	MEAN SCORE OF SENIORS	NUMBER OF FRESHMEN	MEAN SCORE OF FRESHMEN
Roman Catholic................	446	30.56	490	26.57
Lutheran.....................	113	30.05	103	26.58
Other preferences.............	224	29.33	257	25.44
Baptist......................	163	29.31	166	24.08
Presbyterian..................	127	28.21	96	23.17
Episcopal....................	42	26.28	48	19.27
Methodist....................	139	25.02	153	21.13
No preference................	81	23.83	51	19.45

We have already commented on the limitations of a short-answer test designed to measure factual knowledge. It should be said, too, that religious knowledge, though basic in the treatment of religion by a college, is not the only factor in spiritual development. This test provides no appraisal of the daily conduct of students or of their attitudes on a variety of questions related to religion. Notwithstanding these limitations, the testing project did yield some evidence of the effectiveness of church-sponsored institutions in their programs of formal instruction in religion. The comparative data provide clues for the development of greater strength in this area.

CORPORATE WORSHIP

Our survey of religious practices in 196 representative colleges and universities showed a wide variety of requirements and expectations with respect to formal worship. It is characteristic of Roman Catholic institutions to consider attendance at Mass as a Church, not a college, obligation. The student is expected to attend Mass because he is a Roman Catholic, not because he is a student of College X. This is an important distinction; it places the Catholic institution in a very different position from that of the Protestant college.

Protestant institutions typically require chapel attendance twice a week. Of the 111 Protestant colleges whose policies were examined, about 14 percent require daily and 12 percent weekly chapel attendance. About 15 percent have placed weekday corporate worship on a wholly voluntary basis. Six percent give credit for chapel attendance. Only 12 percent require church attendance on Sunday. Colleges related to large Protestant denominations such as the Methodist and United Presbyterian churches tend to have minimal chapel requirements, while institutions connected with more cohesive religious bodies usually make heavier demands on their students.

A careful examination of the colleges that are without explicit requirements of worship showed the complexity of this matter. In some institutions participation in corporate worship is so much a part of the daily life of students and faculty that a formal policy is unnecessary. There would be no more point in requiring chapel attendance than in requiring the student to be present for meals in the dining hall. In other colleges, however, the lack of a chapel requirement is a symptom of secularity. Corporate worship is not regarded as an essential feature of the life of the academic community. The corporate spirit of the institution is expressed and nurtured in other ways. Cultural convocations, athletic contests, or other events take the place of worship as the focal point of communal life.

Formal worship is a weak area in most colleges in spite of the liturgical renewal which is going on in several of the larger churches. To many students and faculty members, the requirement of worship seems out of place in an academic setting. Students who readily accept requirements in such areas as English or physical education, frequently raise strong objections to required attendance at religious services. Students often complain that the chapel services are dull, childish, perfunctory, and passive. A number of the colleges we visited were in the throes of controversy over required chapel. Too often in Protestant colleges, the content of chapel services is a vague humanitarianism which does justice neither to the majesty of God nor the intellectual aspirations of a college. Many students are obviously looking for a more sophisticated level of worship than they are now offered in most college chapels. Others, lacking religious conviction, see no reason for engaging in worship at all. The revitalization of corporate worship is badly needed in many institutions.

It should be said that there are a few notable exceptions to this description. St. John's University, Collegeville, Minnesota, has been the acknowledged leader of the liturgical movement in the Roman Catholic church. Its University Church occupies a central position in the life of the institution. On our visit to St. John's we gained the impression that, although many students enter the University without a proper appreciation of the role that the Benedictine Fathers of St. John's Abbey have played in the whole church, the remarkable liturgical achievements of the University do affect the students' outlook by the time of graduation. The University Church, quite apart from what goes on inside, is a spectacular edifice which attracts thousands of visitors from throughout the country. Among the 50 colleges and universities of which we made case studies, St. John's must be mentioned as a brilliant example of what can be done with worship in an academic community.

Brigham Young University may be cited as exemplary in a different sense. Worship at this institution is characteristically American in the manner of the nineteenth century. Chapel is held in an athletic fieldhouse with the center of attention being the platform and speaker. It is as far from the liturgical movement as it could be, but the point is that corporate worship at Brigham Young does play a central role in the life of the University. It, probably more than anything else, unifies the institution. The President often presides, giving the occasion a dignity and importance which could not be achieved were this responsibility always delegated to someone else. Respected leaders of the Church of Jesus Christ of Latter-day Saints speak at chapel and are listened to with utmost seriousness.

A third example is Concordia Senior College, Fort Wayne, Indiana, where the spiritual life has been highly developed. Worship is thought of as the principal communal activity at Concordia. The following statement describes well not only the intention at Concordia but also the day-to-day practice:

Since the students of the College as well as its faculty, are professed Christians, the group life of the campus is that of community under the headship of Christ as Lord and Savior. This is symbolized by the central and predominant position of the chapel in the physical facilities and in the daily program. In this community the source of individual and corporate life in growth is found in the Holy Scriptures and the Sacraments. Corporate worship is provided each school-day morning and on Wednesday and Saturday evenings in the chapel and, for the dormitory families, in the dormitories themselves on the remaining weekday evenings. Facility for private meditation and prayer is provided by a small prayer chapel in each dormitory.[1]

This description of worship is followed immediately by a statement regarding interpersonal relations:

It is the objective of this community that each individual regard all others, whether students or staff members, as well as the community, as ends in themselves, and view only himself as a means to an end. The expression of this attitude is service to others; and the outcome is that all serve and are served, all teach and all learn. The common life of the campus, therefore, is regarded as a learning situation equal in importance to that of the classroom.[2]

Architecturally, the St. John's University Church and the Concordia Chapel are notable structures in the United States. Although very different, they both represent highly refined and majestic housing for group activities which the institutions regard as basic to everything else they do.

One of the most obvious characteristics of corporate worship in many colleges is its sameness. Remarkably little ingenuity has been shown in the development of new forms of worship for academic communities. The liturgical experimentation which is going on in many places seems not to have touched most college campuses. It would appear that so much emphasis has been given in the appointment of chaplains to personal qualities of congeniality and to interest in the intellectual problems of religion that liturgical skill has been largely overlooked.

Is it appropriate for a college to require student participation in formal worship? This is a question that is being debated on many Protestant campuses. On the one hand, it is pointed out that worship should be a voluntary act, that the praise of God becomes meaningless (or worse) if it is forced. On the other hand, the argument is advanced that many students will not have the valuable experience of observing and taking part in corporate worship unless this is required, just as students are required to take courses in music appreciation or English literature. There is no easy solution to the dilemma. If participation in worship is viewed as an important element in the student's educational experience, we believe a requirement can be defended. However, the ideal is probably a voluntary system in

---

[1] *Concordia Senior College Catalogue, 1964-1965,* p. 18.
[2] *Ibid.*

which corporate worship has somehow become the focal point of faculty and student life. This is not simple in our day and time, but it can be done; a few colleges have achieved it. One thing is clear. If corporate worship is to be more than a gesture, it must be indigenous, so to speak, in the institution. It cannot stand alone as window dressing. It must be in context, supported by a climate of conviction. Too often, however, it is vestigial—the last official pretense of institutional commitment.

STUDENT RELIGIOUS ORGANIZATIONS

Student religious organizations are weak and struggling on most campuses. In many places they are close to extinction. Pre-ministerial students and a few loyal women students often keep them going. On most of the campuses we visited, these organizations were not taken seriously. We found that the responsible officials—directors of religious activities, chaplains, and so forth—were more frequently than not perplexed as to what useful purpose organizations of this kind serve. It would appear that, in colleges where religion is vital and pervasive, the student religious organizations are superfluous and, in colleges where the administration and faculty assign a low priority to religion, student religious organizations can hardly be effective remedies.

On some campuses the National Federation of Catholic College Students is a notable exception to our general comments about student religious organizations. The Federation tries to relate social action to theological conviction in rather explicit terms and not infrequently attracts strong student leaders.

SOCIAL CONCERN

We found evidences of social concern on most of the campuses we visited, but it was often focused on two or three particular issues, especially civil rights and American policy in Vietnam. Students seem to have specialized social interests rather than a more general social sensitivity and awareness of responsibility. They respond more readily to a movement or an emotional appeal than to the less spectacular forms of social and public service. Students will rally to a cause that has been publicly dramatized—they may even rally in ways which are disturbing to administrative tranquility and the peace of the campus—but it is difficult to arouse them to the responsibility of normal citizenship. Student government, which might be a channel for such interests, languishes on many campuses. As with corporate worship, one could wish that there were a greater variety of manifestations of vitality in the area of social concern.

The disruption which occurred on some campuses during the last two years, though most highly publicized on state and independent university campuses, also occurred at some church-sponsored institutions. In several of the colleges of which case studies were made, student movements reached major proportions. In one college the administrative officers spent a considerable part of the academic year 1964-65 negotiating with students and trying to cope with the effects of adverse publicity.

One of the questions that we have pondered greatly in this study is the relationship of social concern to religious conviction. It is not clear to what extent there is a definite connection between student interest in social problems and religious belief. Christopher Dawson has observed that "men today are divided between those who have kept their spiritual roots and lost their contact with the existing order of society, and those who have preserved their social contacts and lost their spiritual roots." [3] This comment may be applicable to social concern on the campus.

Most officials responsible for the development of religion on campuses are grateful for expressions of social concern and tend to feel that the question of why students are concerned is unimportant and that social concern per se should be considered a sign of religious vitality. We believe that this is a matter that should be examined more carefully. As student discontent has more and more become a major administrative problem, thoughtful administrators have been searching for explanations of student behavior and are coming to see that motivation is important. Students motivated by love of God and love of neighbor are likely to behave very differently in a

---

[3] Quoted in Alec R. Vidler, *The Church in an Age of Revolution, 1789 to the Present Day.* Vol. 5, *The Pelican History of the Church* (Baltimore: Penguin Books, 1961), p. 273.

crisis situation from students motivated by the sheer frustration of our times or a desire for public attention.

We have already commented on the program of the National Federation of Catholic College Students. The effort of the Federation to help students view specific social problems in the context of a highly developed body of Christian social teaching is perhaps the best illustration of the kind of thing that we think needs to be done more widely.

INTELLECTUAL PRESUPPOSITIONS

The intellectual presuppositions which actually guide the activities of most church colleges are heavily weighted in the secular direction. In other words, religion as a world view or explanation of existence is not penetrating college education as its exponents would wish. The difficulty is that many academic people do not think of religion as concerned primarily with the truth about ultimate reality. Rather, it is regarded as a moral code, as a set of ideals, or as a quaint and antiquated body of ideas which educated people are supposed to have outgrown.

As was mentioned in the section on the selection of faculty, a basic, perhaps the most basic problem faced by church institutions which take religion seriously is that of finding informed, practicing Christians (or Jews) for teaching appointments. The number of such persons is too small to meet the requirements of church-college faculties. And yet, without these persons, it is impossible for an institution to make educational decisions in Christian terms. Well-meaning but largely uninformed churchmen on a faculty will tend to see religion and education as entirely separate activities.

To summarize our appraisal of the religious aspects of church-related institutions, it is our considered opinion that religion is not as strong in the programs of these institutions as one would expect. In fact, there is good reason to believe that the church colleges are, by and large, stronger academically (in the secular sense) than they are religiously. We realize that this conclusion is directly contrary to an assumption widely held by the general public and by academic people.

In all of our discussion of the religious aspects of church-sponsored higher education we have been troubled by semantic difficulties. We have tried to use language that would be understood by educational leaders and by laymen interested in education. However, it must be emphasized that modern theologians are redefining many terms, and words such as "God," "theology," and "religion" have different meanings to different people today. We have mentioned Bonhoeffer's insistence on "Christianity without religion." This kind of specialized use of language is confusing to many readers.

If one takes the position, as some contemporary theologians do, that Christianity and Judaism in an educational setting cannot be usefully examined in terms of such external manifestations as courses in religion or theology, corporate worship, religious organizations, and a body of values clearly derived from truths called religious—that indeed the effort to talk about religious matters in these terms is a distortion—then much of what we have been saying is beside the point. If the distinction between the sacred and the secular disappears —and there is a real possibility that this will happen in some religious traditions—the church institutions of higher education will face a radically different situation. In the last chapter we spoke of the prediction that theological education, as a separately organized enterprise, might disappear in the future. One can foresee the time when some church-sponsored colleges and universities may abolish courses in religion, formal worship, student religious organizations, and the like *on theological grounds*. The aim would be to eliminate the artificial separation of Christianity from the rest of life. There would then be no need for chaplains or even ministers or, ultimately perhaps, the church itself as a separate organization.

Some would say that this is the road to the elimination of Christianity as a significant force in the world. Others would hold that it is a desirable trend which might well be spearheaded by Christian colleges. Perhaps it is too soon for anyone to know exactly where such a movement might lead. This is but another illustration, at the deepest level, of the way in which what happens in churches and in theology impinges on church-affiliated colleges and universities. How Christianity or Judaism is defined influences how the religious dimension should be embodied in church-sponsored institutions and, indeed, whether such institutions are justified at all.

10

Faculty Evaluations of Church-Sponsored Colleges and Universities

As an additional means of assessing church institutions of higher learning, we asked 52 Danforth and Kent Fellows now teaching in colleges and universities affiliated with religious bodies to give us the benefit of their observations.[1] Specifically, they were asked to answer two questions: (1) What, in your judgment, are the most important assets and liabilities of the church institutions of higher education *with which you are personally acquainted?* (2) What are the principal satisfactions and frustrations, *as you have experienced them,* of being a faculty member in institutions of this type? It should be emphasized that we were not asking for generalized appraisals of church institutions but for evaluations based on personal experience in particular institutions.

This chapter is a summary and analysis of the responses of these 52 men and women who are teaching in 39 colleges and universities associated with 14 denominations. The institutions are located in 19 states distributed throughout the country. Although the respondents range in age from young persons just out of graduate school to teachers in their sixties, they are typically men and women in their

[1] The Danforth and Kent Fellows are a carefully selected group of men and women who are well known to the Danforth Foundation and in whose judgment we have confidence. They were appointed originally on the basis of superior academic qualifications. An interest in religion is one of the factors taken into account in the selection procedures of both fellowship programs. Thus the authors felt that the Danforth and Kent Fellows were well fitted, as a group, to make the judgments we requested.

thirties who have had several years of teaching experience. Most of them hold doctorates from leading graduate schools. They are teaching in all of the principal fields of the arts and sciences. Some report that they have held faculty positions in two or three church-affiliated institutions. Since the respondents were asked to be completely frank and were assured of anonymity, our summary will not attribute particular sentiments or statements to individuals.

The results of this inquiry are highly instructive. Almost without exception the statements submitted show careful thought and analysis. Their tone is judicious but straightforward. They have the ring of authenticity about them. They contain a minimum of clichés and platitudes. The statements reflect a high degree of individual judgment; they do not follow any pattern which might be considered ready-made or partisan. They include observations on a number of institutions that could not be visited and thus add significantly to our store of evaluative material.

Since the questions were intentionally broad, leaving the respondent free to comment on whatever topics seemed to him germane, the contents of the statements do not fall into neat categories. In general, though, they touch upon five principal topics, which, in order of frequency, are: (1) relationships with students; (2) the administration of institutions, including conditions of faculty service and faculty estimates of presidents and other officers; (3) institutional purposes, religious vitality, and unity; (4) freedom, as experienced by individual teachers and by institutions; and (5) church relationships, including faculty and administrative attitudes toward church officials. These areas of comment are not mutually exclusive, but they do give us a manageable framework within which to analyze the responses. In order to let the faculty members speak for themselves as much as possible, we shall rely heavily on quotations, using them wherever they express well the opinion of a number of respondents, or where they are especially illuminating.

RELATIONSHIPS WITH STUDENTS

About one-half of the respondents say that their greatest satisfaction as teachers is derived from their close relationships with individual students, and many feel that these relationships are enhanced by the religious purposes of their institutions. This view is well expressed by a young teacher of philosophy in a liberal arts college affiliated with the Disciples of Christ:

My principal satisfactions as a teacher in an institution of this type have come from the deeper personal relationship with the students than I found possible in a secular university. . . . I welcome the more frequent opportunities to know my own students out of class. Small classes contribute to this as well since it is almost impossible with really large classes. With less students of my own I also am able to know students not in my classes or department. More generally, as a faculty member, I have gotten a good deal of satisfaction out of contributing to the development of a series of humanities courses on an integrative approach, which will illustrate, among other things, the constant relevance of religion.

A senior faculty member in an Episcopal college puts it this way:

There is genuinely a personal touch. This may be due in part to the small size of the college (1,000 students), but I cannot help feeling, having taught in other small colleges, that it is due also to the college's Christian traditions. Where the student is concerned, I think it is safe to say there is no definite "_____ type".[2] This seems to me to be the purest evidence that the student is regarded as an individual and not poured into a kind of mold, academic or otherwise.

A number of respondents mention the advantages of working with students many of whom share their teachers' religious convictions. The following statement by a faculty member of a large Roman Catholic institution is representative of the views of a number of others:

This general basic agreement also makes it easier to deal with students, since one can predict many of their values and habits of mind—begin with some foundation in common which doesn't have to be thought out laboriously. This common ground is often, of course, more shifty than it initially appears; but that does not interfere much with the initial advantages for communcation with students.

However, a professor in a Lutheran college, a high percentage of whose students are members of the sponsoring church, sees some ill-effects of religious homogeneity. This condition, he says, "leads too often to resentment or ignoring of the non-Lutherans."

[2] Here and elsewhere a blank is used in order not to reveal the identity of the institution.

The Roman Catholic teacher who was just quoted makes the further point that many of his students seem "too respectful of authority, as a result of parochial-school education (which is obviously not a necessary concomitant of a Catholic university, but is nevertheless still a factual one)." A young instructor in a well-known Roman Catholic college for men makes a similar comment about his students:

The students here are quite talented, eager to learn, and very well behaved. This last point is a bit of a puzzle for sometimes I feel they might be too docile and have too much respect for authority, but I suspect this is more a result of their previous training than the fact that they are in a church school.

Several respondents speak unfavorably of the social-class characteristics of their students. This is a reflection of the upward movement in the social and economic backgrounds of students at many church-related institutions in the last 15 years. A teacher in a leading Methodist university reports that steady increases in tuition, without corresponding increases in scholarship assistance for needy students, have produced:

A more exclusively middle- and upper-class student body, with their peculiar strength and limitations. Most faculty members, I surmise, are of lower-middle-class backgrounds; I share their (class-biased?) opinion that our student body grows more well-prepared, well-heeled, pragmatic, conservative, and uninteresting.

Faculty members in a number of colleges, especially those connected with the Methodist and Presbyterian churches, speak critically of the regulations governing student conduct in their institutions. The words "moralistic" and "paternalistic" are used by several respondents in describing rules governing such practices as drinking, smoking, and dancing. However, a teacher in one Methodist college says:

The occasional extreme (I think) moralism which creeps into the school rules is due less to its ties with the church than with its location. This is seen in that the state university system has, in many instances, stricter college rules than —————.

ADMINISTRATION OF INSTITUTIONS

The area of administration is one in which the evaluations tend to be highly critical. At least one-half of the respondents are dissatisfied with the administrative leadership of their institutions. Whether they are more critical of administrators than are faculty members in other types of institutions is a difficult judgment to make. The following are illustrative of the adverse comments.

One of the stronger statements is that of a young scholar in a Roman Catholic college:

The frustrations generally have to do with the fact that religion is necessarily a body of teaching that speaks with authority, and this authority is often rightly and wrongly extended to its ministers, so that the administrators of Catholic colleges—particularly clerics who are used to literal obedience—may often justify ruthless suppression of academic freedom on spurious theological grounds. More often, in fact, the whole way of life of people with a public commitment to religion—that is, priests, nuns, etc.—leads them to be quite oblivious to the fact that they are riding rough-shod over the sensibilities of faculty members. Moreover, that Catholic colleges are highly unified by reason of the stronger authority possessed by the administrators and by reason of the common religious viewpoint, often induces a kind of pseudo-family relationship into faculty-administration contacts.

Several Roman Catholic educators referred to the difficulty of relationships between lay faculty members and clerical faculty and administrative officers. This is a matter that is coming to the fore in many institutions, in part as a result of the increasing number of lay teachers in colleges that were formerly staffed largely with religious. One respondent points out:

Particular problems exist at universities like _____, which are owned by religious communities: the clerical administration and clerical faculty feel that the university is a family affair, and they jealously guard the proprietorship, restricting the role of laity in policy-making decisions. Lay faculty are still too often second-class citizens in the Catholic college.

Sharp criticism of administrative officers is not, however, limited to Roman Catholic institutions. The following quotation from the statement of a young Ph.D. teaching in a Middle Western college is a remarkably incisive and sweeping critique that is representative of attitudes and observations found in less dramatic form in the evaluation of several other respondents:

A pervasive fact about the college at which I teach is its mediocrity; and the heart of this fact is the absence, especially among officialdom, of much of a passion, certainly anything like a single-minded one, for academic excellence.

Almost to the point of caricature, the dominant mentality of the institution, reflected in the type of people too numerous on the board of trustees and in the outlook of too many students, upon graduating as well as upon entering, is that of middle-class, predominantly business-minded culture. Moreover, the place is rotted with fraternities and sororities and has by tradition a certain style which appeals to bourgeois families to "send" their children for further upbringing.

And then there is the church. It is present in the dreary, pointless chapel-talks by visiting ministers, the trivial rules of conduct, such as that about drinking, the vague talk, usually by those who are least able to clear it up, about the school as somehow a Christian institution, and a hundred other inane but distracting things.

Such is the primary disability of the college. From it most other difficulties come:—(1) needless expansion of administrative staff; (2) the often paternalistic and inept approach of some of the deans toward students; (3) unnecessary rules about student morals, hours, and supposed well-being which generates disrespect among students; (4) special perquisites for administrative personnel and consequently a kind of second-class status for the faculty; (5) weak faculty and courses in some of the departments and the undemocratic disposition of power in the faculty, which revolves around the heads of departments who, by administrative preference, have their status permanently and some of whom are rather tradition-minded, intellectually weak, and also autocratic. It is despite these that there are certain strong departments and some highly competent faculty.

Several of the respondents dwell at some length on their misgivings about the part played by the faculty in the government of the institutions they serve. They feel that academic excellence would be more effectively promoted if faculties had a larger voice in educational decision-making. A teacher in a Presbyterian college has this to say about the position of the president:

Formally, all powers are in the hands of the college president. The actual operation of the college is fairly democratic, but this democracy exists only at the will of the president.

The problem of reconciling academic with public-relations considerations and the tendency of administrators (as seen by faculty critics) to favor the latter over the former is emphasized by several of the correspondents. A teacher in a Baptist college characterizes the administration as:

Hampered by lack of clear purpose, paternalism toward faculty and students, lack of clear lines of responsibility manifested in: (1) vague admissions policy, (2) unclear student discipline policy, (3) academically unjustifiable athletic policy, (4) apparent lack of definite plan of place for college in future and type of student desired, (5) tendency toward institutional hypocrisy—vague Christian ideals announced, but fraternity system, subsidized athletics, admission policies, scholarships and allocation of funds not in harmony with these ideals.

A professor in a Disciples of Christ college speaks of the discrepancy "between the official rhetoric of the pursuit of academic excellence and the day-to-day attitude to any proposed change as negative, destructive criticism of present policy and program."

A teacher at a college which has just passed through a period of administrative upheaval concludes his diagnosis with the following prescription:

What is needed, and I hope will grow as the recent crisis recedes, though I am dubious, are a less pretentious board, more restricted in its formal image of competence and thus more accurate in its substantive one; a more responsive faculty, more carefully chosen with the view to the college and not sheer scholarship, more permanent in its foreview, and more candidly risky about life and thought; and above all a stronger administration, more critical about the college's limitations, and willing to incur some displeasures and trouble in modifying them.

Some faculty members who consider themselves more liberal in their religious views than the trustees or presidents of their institutions report the discomforts of being in that position. This is apparently a difficulty that arises most often in colleges connected with denominations that are divided into liberal and conservative wings. An illustration is provided by a young assistant professor at a Baptist college, who lists the following as the frustrations involved in his work as a faculty member:

(1) An occasional gnawing sense that I am in the position of being a lackey of trustees who are so one-sidedly concerned about the religious emphasis, that I must exercise my intellectual freedom on a slightly surreptitious basis. The students themselves understand this, but I know the trustees who heard my lectures would be upset. A very bad incident occurred this year: a trustee heard that _____ had been invited to lecture, or speak in our chapel. This conservative trustee immediately managed to hold an "executive" session of some kind with other trustees, and had the invitation rescinded. This kind of arbitrary action, and the attempt at thought-control that inspired it, filled me with revulsion. (2) Strong personalities in the administration exercising ill-defined and rather arbitrary power, all the while stressing the "Christian" aspects of our educational aims.

A different type of negative appraisal is submitted by a senior professor in a Methodist college in a Western state:

The worst staff problems are the utterly disorganized head librarian and a president who hesitates to make decisions and carry them out. Perhaps the worst liability is the religious atmosphere or, rather, the lack of it. There is no moral leadership by the administration in terms of combating discrimination and cheating or stimulating real service among the faculty. All that remains is a perfunctory "chapel" once a week which has become a convocation for electing cheerleaders and hearing speeches.

It would be too sweeping to suggest that all of the comments on administration are unfavorable. A few are strongly affirmative. For example, a young mathematician in a well-known Presbyterian college asserts:

The administration has provided leadership which is obviously based upon what is morally right as well as on what is economically possible. But, more important, there has never been an instance (that I know of) of putting forth a second-rate plan and justifying it with the excuse that the school is church related. Fortunately, the administration regards "church relatedness" as a responsibility for providing the best that can be provided.

Likewise, a teacher in a Quaker college speaks of the "sensitive and imaginative administrative leadership" of his institution.

The liability which is most frequently cited in these evaluations of church colleges and universities is the lack of sufficient financial support. Again and again, references are made to low salaries, heavy teaching loads, lack of time for research and professional growth, and weak libraries. Most of the respondents lament the financial situations of their institutions; a few see some value in austerity. A department head in a Congregational college serving primarily a Negro constituency offers the following candid observations:

There is a gradual but continuous elimination of personnel without other than financial and self-glorification motivation, by transfer to institutions with higher salaries and more "prestige." Those who remain have to be either too incompetent to secure one of the numerous other openings or motivated by more than money and fame—and a few of the latter can make any college "great" in ways that really matter.

A teacher in a college operated by the Reformed Church states the case this way:

There is a particular breed of teacher who will make sacrifices to teach in such an institution. They are teachers who want to teach first and publish second if at all; teachers who see their role as comprehending, synthesizing, communicating the elements of their discipline rather than adding bits and pieces to it. There are also teachers who themselves hold to a fundamental religious philosophy of life. The basic problem facing religion in higher education in America today is keeping these people in the small church-related colleges. The opportunities for greater financial reward, wider community recognition, and a better situation for personal intellectual development available in universities are making these teachers, particularly the younger ones, more acutely aware of their "sacrifice." There are things that can be done to offset this and they must be done.

PURPOSE, VITALITY, AND UNITY

Of the five areas we are considering, institutional purpose, religious vitality, and unity is the one in which the most impressive affirmative statements are made by our respondents. What is said again and again is that the faculty member finds his relationships with other members of the teaching staff congenial because he and they share common religious convictions and educational values. Reading the statements, one gets the unmistakable impression that many of the 39 colleges and universities which are being assessed have a strong sense of community within the faculty. Some contrast this sense of community with the disunity and fragmented character of other institutions with which they have been associated. The sense of community in the institutions being described here seems to be the result of the fact that: (1) most of the institutions are relatively small, making for close personal relationships; (2) most are devoted primarily to liberal education and thus tend to attract to their faculties persons with reasonably similar views on education; and (3) in most of the institutions there seems to be a nucleus, at least, of faculty members sharing a common religious commitment. Moreover, as has already been mentioned, in many instances students also contribute to the faculty member's sense of community as junior partners, so to speak, in the sharing of common values and interests.

A teacher in a large Roman Catholic university discusses this in a rather personal way:

I find the social community to be much more satisfactory in the church-related college, with greater person-to-person love (I *do* find love—real love—at _____), and a sense, too, of community worship. I find myself, my family, and my students living a more fully integrated life—blending learning, play, and worship. And I find the community is a more morally-healthy one, with a less overwhelming atmosphere of—particularly—sexual immorality.

A teacher of the humanities in another Roman Catholic institution stresses similarity of values as the key to a sense of community:

The awareness of a common body of opinions and beliefs (the religious commitment) provides a principle of integration which is organic and obviates the need for constructing one artificially. I do not think this principle is to be found in the articulated theological system underlying such a school's program, but in the general temper, the attitude and comportment of sympathetic minds working towards a common—though perhaps never scientifically defined—goal.

A teacher in a Lutheran college emphasizes the unifying role of worship:

There is here a greater sense of community than elsewhere. It is not only a religiously oriented community but that is basic. The campus is not fragmented into sororities, fraternities, etc. A large proportion of the student body turns out each day for a voluntary chapel service in which, among other things, our unity as a community is celebrated.

The same observer, however, notes that this sense of community has its negative aspects. He points out that a common outlook can interfere with the exchange of ideas:

There is an absence of articulate representatives on campus of some points of view—there is a tendency for a kind of unconscious orthodoxy to develop. People with unconventional ideas are not stifled but they are discouraged. The faculty as a whole should be more encouraged to open up and more attention should be paid to unorthodox kinds of people. . . . There is not enough social and political ferment on campus. The religious fervor is for scholarship and creativity—some of it should be channeled into social and political areas. This may be due to the historical traditions of Lutheranism, but whatever the cause it is unfortunate.

An instructor in psychology at a Quaker college offers this opinion:

The greatest assets I see are the feelings of "community" fostered by _____. In many cases the helpfulness and concern of those in other disciplines is a great help to a new faculty member. From luncheons, meetings, and casual contacts outside of the usual faculty meetings one gets a feeling of common purpose and mutual respect. Much of what I have described may be appropriate for smaller institutions in general, but I suspect that the underlying religious approach to life has a great deal to do with fostering the feeling of community.

A number of the respondents speak favorably of the opportunities in their institutions to relate theological insights to secular disciplines.

A faculty member of a Methodist college, who is teaching temporarily in a theological school, contrasts a seminary and a college. In the theological school in which he is now teaching he misses the opportunity to converse with persons in the secular disciplines. He cites the advantages to be gained from a formal institutional commitment to a particular religious tradition. A young historian in a Lutheran college makes the same point:

I have been impressed with the dedication of most of this faculty both to academic discipline and to students as persons. A number of teachers are confronting students with religious and ethical challenges arising within the disciplines, and doing it as a result rather than an excuse for serious study. There is, among the faculty, a large nucleus of members vitally interested in religious and ethical problems; there is healthy interdepartmental discussion along these lines.

Commenting on the values implicit in two church-related institutions with which he has been associated, a teacher of international relations at a large Methodist institution has this to say:

The second asset [humane values] is not, of course, always realized. However, I have seen this spirit at work and I believe that it can help to create expertise without presumption, tutelage without pride, questioning without desire to harm, and knowledge modified by compassion. Pardon if this sounds high-flown. What I am trying to say is that the conception of the role of the institution of higher education, the conduct of its essential intellectual work, and the human products which are its sole reason for existing, all may be touched by a spirit of deep human searching which organized religion always tends to strive for and sometimes achieves. This leavening spirit may work wonders.

The chairman of the department of religion of a Baptist college, speaking of the unity which is possible in such an academic community, cites as important assets:

The opportunity to develop an undergraduate curriculum in the liberal arts in which inquiry into the Judeo-Christian tradition is integral and foundational to a number of undergraduate majors, especially in the humanities and the social sciences; and the possibility of developing a non-coercive consensus among faculty in varied subject matters as to major issues for continuing exploration in the effort to articulate a philosophy of Christian higher education relevant to the particular campus, the consensus here understood as inviting into conversation a number of non-Christian members of the faculty.

However, the unity which comes from a commitment to common values has not been achieved in all of the institutions from which we have reports. After referring to the importance of an open society, both on the campus and elsewhere, a professor in a college related to the Disciples of Christ presents the issue of freedom and commitment with remarkable clarity:

The second strength of the open society which the strong church-affiliated college may perpetuate is perhaps becoming less understood and appreciated among liberal Protestant colleges. It is easy enough in most cases these days for the college to be open and liberal, but more difficult to recognize that the open society is strong only so long as there are strong voices heard within its liberal framework. The open society and the college community are vital only when men stand for something and make themselves heard. If the first strength of the free society is to listen and to respect the other, the second is to speak and make one's convictions heard. Here, it seems to me, the liberal church-affiliated colleges have an important role to play: not simply to mirror the pluralism of the larger society, but to contribute a distinctive point of view from their religious heritages and convictions. Otherwise the claim to church relatedness becomes a dishonest affiliation and the result is to turn the college to a shade of gray which conforms to every other. If the church-controlled colleges err in claiming too great a distinction of religious perspective, the liberal church-affiliated institutions are now in danger of losing any religious consciousness at all. This is the problem we now face at _____ College, and we are not alone among similar colleges in facing the difficulty of articulating our stand.

The fact of being sponsored by a church does not assure consensus on basic values in a college. A disunited and unhappy faculty is described by a teacher in a medium-sized Methodist institution:

If one of the chief claims of a church-related college is the practice of higher education in an atmosphere of combined sympathy and criticism in questions and activities of religion, then this claim is ill served by a dominant circumstance at this college. While the sympathetic attitude seems confined to men who strike me as naively supportive of the _____ family of church, college, and national, middle-class, social fraternities, the critical attitude seems confined to men whose better instincts in the matter are vitiated by a kind of worldly cynicism. In the presence of unclear and therefore feared and despised supposed-threats and pressures from the Board, and thus the Church, these latter men whose minds are our best, and whose inner lives are not unsympathetic to the spiritual life, turn defensively cold and cynical both about religion as a part of education and about potential experimentation and imagination in academic and cocurricular life at the college.

STATUS OF FREEDOM

The matter of freedom is one on which church-sponsored institutions of higher education have been much criticized. The view has commonly been held in the academic world that freedom to teach and to learn is severely circumscribed in institutions conducted under religious auspices. The statements from the respondents to this inquiry are most informative. These indicate that most of the institutions have well-established traditions of freedom, and some of the respondents believe that their colleges have a broader freedom than that of public and independent institutions. Some negative comments on freedom in church institutions are cited elsewhere in this summary. All in all, the status of freedom in these institutions, as in others, is mixed; in some places freedom is strong, in others weak.

A teacher in a Lutheran college reports:

The University is free from religious indoctrination. Chapel attendance is voluntary, for example, though it is also daily. The sectarian influence is present among students active in Lutheran youth work and community service, but it is not dominant, as it tended to be upon occasion at my Alma Mater, _____ College.

A professor of economics at a Quaker college makes the following comments on freedom:

In summary, I would say that by all means the major characteristic which our religious affiliation has brought to us is one which we could hope to find in every institution of advanced learning, whether religiously affiliated or not: wholesome attitude toward freedom of thought and equality of people. The point is that although these qualities should not be unique to religiously oriented schools, and, indeed, are not unique to them, nevertheless they do stand out much more sharply at places like _____ and _____ because of our religious tradition and affiliation.

The author also comments on openness to points of view closely associated with Quaker positions:

The Quaker attitude toward war, although held by a very small minority of the faculty, is always treated with respect. When appropriate in relation to educational work this view would be included among others, whereas other colleges might generally omit it entirely. Similarly a genuine effort is made to bring religious values to the attention of students in many systematic ways although these are largely extracurricular.

A teacher in a large Methodist institution contributes these observations on freedom:

I have been blessed to see religious affiliation add to rather than detract from the two institutions I have been most closely associated with. But I am also aware of the stultifying effects of religious belief upon free academic inquiry. Religion is certainly not necessarily antithetical to free inquiry, but there is a decided tendency for it to be, and this tendency is a product of religion's epistemological underpinning which is very different from that of the freely inquiring scholar.

This faculty member perhaps summarizes the whole matter of freedom in church institutions when he says "a college or university will find affiliation with organized religion an advantage or liability depending entirely upon the quality of that religion."

Comparing conditions in a well-known women's college with those in the Methodist institution in which he is now teaching, a department head concludes, "academic freedom is just as sacred at both places."

An Episcopal college faculty member reports that his institution "has a degree of academic freedom which is often lacking elsewhere. By that I mean that religious subjects are not discriminated against." A faculty member at a Roman Catholic institution expands on this theme:

Although it may sound paradoxical, I, as a faculty member, feel *freer* in the church-related institutions (all Roman Catholic) with which I am familiar. It is a freedom to be myself—to explore and to communicate whatever religious dimensions, I, as a religiously oriented person, find or fail to find within my discipline. I did not feel this same freedom when I taught at non-church-related institutions, committed as the faculty and student bodies seemed to be to a secular materialistic humanism. I found myself squashing areas of investigation and perceptions of religious significance in literature which would have been either totally misunderstood or ridiculed in the secular environment. In the church-related college, religious meanings and interpretations are understood and encouraged without—and obviously this is essential—forcing them where they do not fit. So, to over-simplify it, *both* the religious and the secular are admitted to the church-related institution, while *only* the secular is admitted in the secular institution. The result I find to be a greater sense of exploration, a freer intellectual atmosphere, and a greater opportunity to find truth. And from the vantage point of within a church-related college, I feel freer to criticize the failings of my church.

A similar note is struck by a respondent who, at the time of our inquiry, was in the process of moving from a Presbyterian college to a large state university:

Let me close by noting an additional satisfaction of teaching in the Christian college which I well think may be inherent in that type of institution and hard to find in other types of colleges. It is easy to find other scholars who are interested in the questions of how their disciplines and professions relate to the Christian way of life and the Christian faith. One can talk directly and overtly about these questions rather than obliquely as I anticipate doing at a state university.

A senior staff member in a large Methodist institution, who had previously taught at two Presbyterian colleges, makes this observation:

The church institution usually has the characteristic of smallness, which may be either an asset or a liability. Both the student body and the faculty tend to be rather more "homogenized", culturally and religiously. This may encourage greater intimacy within the academic community, but it also diminishes the range and intensity of intellectual dialogue. In general, the pressures toward conformity of thought and behavior are stronger in the colleges closely bound to the church. I myself do not find such pressure ordinarily burdensome, but I can see that individual differences may not be permitted to express themselves with maximum freedom. However, I must testify that in no church-related institution have I experienced or observed any substantial repression of academic freedom.

A teacher of the humanities in a large Roman Catholic university comments as follows on freedom in his institution:

For reasons closely connected with the religious foundations of the university, the control of policy has been left almost exclusively in the hands of clergymen. In some cases, the resulting stability and relative invulnerability of the administration has been an advantage; but it naturally causes discontent among the faculty and students who are occasionally pinched by it, or who envision ways in which they might be pinched. . . . There have been problems (gradually diminishing, I must say) about the position of religious dogma and pseudo-dogma. Occasionally, the dogmatic allegiances of the institution have resulted in touches of anti-intellectualism, escapism, and intellectual complaisance.

A historian in a Quaker college makes one of the strongest statements on this subject when he points out the most important asset of his institution as:

The absolute academic freedom which prevails. Many board members are still Friends, and the non-Friends, I think, try to act as they think Friends should. I have never felt, nor have I known of, the slightest interference with the freedom of teaching what one believes to be true or useful here. . . . My principal satisfaction has been in my freedom in the classroom to teach as I wished, saying what I believed to be right, holding back nothing that was relevant. Another satisfaction has been in seeing students free to participate in religious activities as they wished. The College encourages this.

Several respondents see the freedom of the church-sponsored institution to define its own purposes as one of its strongest features. It does not have to serve everyone. A faculty member in a Methodist university elaborates this point:

A strength of this university, I think, is its ability to limit its scope of endeavor to whatever it thinks it can do well, and to leave other efforts (perhaps equally deserving, in themselves) to other private and especially to public colleges and universities. The state universities seem expected to do something with everything; the church-related or private university can do fewer things and do them with distinction. There are risks in selectivity, of course; but in the case that I know the advantages outweigh the harm.

A teacher in a Methodist college in the Middle West makes the following observation on his institution:

Certainly academic freedom is not impaired and no sectarian test of any kind is made of students or professors. The religious views of the faculty reflect the full scope of religious opinion in America—from indifference to militant atheism to devout methodism (the latter is a distinct minority).

A younger teacher in a Presbyterian college offers this comment on religious pressures in his institution:

The chief frustration that I have experienced is the loss of excellent faculty members because, in part, of their views on the separation of religion and education. There has been no effort to infringe on religious freedom, but they were uncomfortable in the community. (Most of the faculty members who have departed under these conditions were hired under a previous administration, and about half of them were of the Jewish faith.)

I do not believe that religion is a forced issue at my school. But, at least among the faculty, an atmosphere exists where those who are more than casually interested in their faith do not find themselves in an uncomfortable situation six days of the week. And several friends who are *only* casually interested have assured me that neither are they uncomfortable in our situation.

CHURCH RELATIONSHIPS

In considering church affiliations one is likely to find striking denominational differences. Such differences show up clearly in the 52 evaluations we are summarizing. Typical of the feelings of many faculty members in Protestant colleges is this statement from a teacher in a Methodist institution:

The primary and perhaps only advantage of my institution's association with the Methodist Church lies in the opportunity to draw upon church constituencies for student recruitment and limited financial support. However, all this seems to be offset by a number of strings that come from close contact with a church body. The Board of Regents is composed of a number of bishops and ministers. Official announcements and policy statements by the President of the University usually reflect a conscientious effort not to offend members of the Church. At commencement time there is always the spectacle of seeing a certain quota of honorary doctorates conferred upon district superintendents and ministers who "were nominated by their bishop."

From another Methodist institution comes this analysis of the situation:

Colleges of this type which I know (admittedly a limited understanding) all suffer from the same flaw—out-dated definitions of their "church relatedness." Extensive rethinking needs to be done by college administrators (especially), faculty, and even students, concerning what it means to be a church institution of higher education in the mid-twentieth century. For too long we have used definitions applied to these institutions in the nineteenth century, too often in the public eye today "church relatedness" involves primarily moralistic rules about drinking, compulsory chapel, and the like. These conceptions are inadequate and hinder the educational process. What is needed is for college officials to view their schools more fully and within a mature, sophisticated theological context. . . . In order to make "church relatedness" truly meaningful, the Christian faith *as an intellectual position* must be brought into creative dialogue and encounter with the educative process that goes on within a school. Thus college administrators must try to establish the relationship between Christian theology and the stated aims and goals of their schools, the curriculum being offered, the environment of student living units, etc., all part of the milieu of an institution.

I also believe that the churches bear a responsibility in this situation. They, too, should participate in this attempt to redefine what "church relatedness" should mean. At ———, for example, the chief outward evidences of the Methodists' relation to this school are large financial contributions each year, a concern over the fact that the Philosophy and Religion Department doesn't seem to be turning out enough pre-ministerial students, and large representation on the Board of Trustees. These are all mechanical, traditional expressions of the relationship. I am not necessarily advocating that these functions be abolished, but that they be placed within a larger intellectual context which justifies, from a theological point of view, the necessity of relationships established between the church and any given institution of higher education.

A department head in a Baptist college is deeply concerned about Protestantism as a basis for an educational program. He lists as the first liability of the institution he serves:

The atrophy of any sense of "Protestant heritage" as foundation for a relevant twentieth-century rethinking of the identity and educational stance of a Protestant church-related college of liberal arts; *example*: the need to recover and identify a free-church tradition as resource for exciting alternatives in educational program and institutional enrichment—as distinguishable from enlightenment rationalism and Deweyan instrumentalism, though not in direct conflict or opposition with either of these.

A Lutheran teaching in an Episcopal college views the task of the church in higher education in these terms:

The church's problem is not one of percentages—that is, one should not be concerned about maintaining a constant percent of all students in the country in church-related colleges. If the product of the church-related college is to be an active yeast which leavens the worldly loaf, what is important is the quality of the product and not its percent. . . . The church's job is not one of higher education per se—that is, one should not be concerned about higher education slowly disappearing as a direct activity of the church. If the church is to provide a catalyst for the reaction which unites man with God, and higher education is one kind of pot in which this reaction occurs, then the church might well welcome other sources taking over the responsibility and problems of providing these pots, so that the church can more efficiently concentrate its efforts on its catalytic activity.

The respondents argued both sides of the question of whether a church connection is good or bad for a college. A teacher in a Quaker institution cites as some of the hazards:

Frequent control by boards and churches which are conservative and rigid; who lack knowledge of, and are not sympathetic to principles of good education . . . distorted views of purposes of church-related colleges on part of church members; poor communication and suspicion between colleges and churches.

A Quaker teaching in an Episcopal college mentions the following benefits from the church connection of his institution:

Perhaps due in part to an accident of location, the college church really is to a considerable degree a church for the whole of any churchgoing faculty. This provides a religious focus for the college which I think is not elsewhere readily found except on campuses where religious conformity is deliberately imposed. The intelligence of the sermons is another satisfaction which surely in part results from the fact that it is a *college* church. Perhaps the opportunity to participate in religious discussion groups which involve more than a denominational fringe of the faculty and students is another benefit which can be attributed to the college's possession of an "established" church.

On the basis of his experience in several church institutions a professor in a large Methodist university writes:

I am not certain that the church element in most of our denominational colleges contributes anything of much importance to the educational process. The more rigorously dogmatic groups will continue to support their institutions, since they are willing to pay for support of strongholds against secular assimilation. But the more liberal institutions seem (in my observation) to depend less upon church support, and thus become undifferentiated from other private colleges . . . many of them have become increasingly similar to all other educational institutions, preserving only a facade of religious emphasis. This tendency has, in part, been forced upon them by the failure of the churches to provide significant financial support; in part, the process of secularization is probably the inevitable consequence of changing patterns in education and changing mores in our society.

A senior faculty member in a Baptist college makes this straightforward statement:

I am not personally conscious of any important assets and liabilities or satisfactions and frustrations by virtue of the fact that _____ is a church-related institution. This may be due to the type of ecclesiastical organization of the Baptist church with which _____ is related.

Similarly, a young social scientist in a United Church of Christ institution responds that he was not aware, until he received our inquiry, that his institution was connected with any church.

In all honesty, then, I must reply that as far as I can see _____'s relationship with the Congregational Church has almost no impact on everyday institutional life. There are no particular frustrations or assets involved in this relationship as far as most faculty members are concerned.

The two preceding responses are perhaps indicative of the predicament of some colleges in the free-church tradition, to which reference was made in earlier quotations. Several of the respondents imply that it is difficult for colleges in this tradition to maintain their religious character.

A faculty member in one of the larger Lutheran colleges thinks of the church relationship of his institution in the following way:

The faculty doesn't know how much influence the ecclesiastical brass of the church and the regents have on college policy—salaries, promotions, leaves, etc. Also, some administrative decisions seem based on consideration for public relations among the congregations rather than stated policy, especially in student discipline problems.

A humanities teacher at a Southern Baptist institution makes a rather critical comment as follows:

At times, official pronouncements seem directed toward maintaining good relationships with the church as an organization that contributes financially to the school, rather than to a true definition of the relationship between religion and education. There are perpetual rumors, undoubtedly exaggerated but not without empirical justification, of "placation" of the church. . . . In this respect, there is an undue insistence on the forms of religion, e.g. church membership, rather than on the spiritual actuality. Thus a truly dedicated teacher who does not belong to a church might not be hired for that very reason, whereas a person of lesser competence who did not care but conformed might be accepted.

The occasional effects of church relationship on the non-academic activities of faculty members are illustrated by the following remarks by a faculty member of a Methodist college:

Thus far I have observed only one attempt made to influence one's private life. This was a concern expressed by the dean of the faculty over members of the faculty drinking in local taverns. When the professors in question indicated that they considered this aspect of their life private and not within the scope of the college's concern, the issue was dropped and was not reopened. The professors continue to visit the taverns. This reflects the one major liability of the church connection; viz., a slight nervousness on the part of the administration. . . . Let me summarize in the words of a colleague who when asked about the influence of the Methodist Church at _____ replied that it is unobtrusive.

A senior professor in a southern Presbyterian college lists as one of the liabilities of church relationship "policymaking hampered by entrenched opinion in the church at large (for example, against admitting or hiring Negroes). . . . The allegedly Christian constituency may deter the college from taking significant Christian initiative in sensitive areas."

COMPOSITE EVALUATION

This concludes our analysis of the evaluations of a selected group of faculty members. We have tried to present a fair sample of their observations, as much as possible in their own words and with a minimum of interpretation. Quotations can convey nuances of thought that are lost in other forms of summarization.

The respondents have provided valuable insights into some of the fundamental issues confronting church-affiliated institutions today. The composite evaluation is mixed. The faculty members sampled derive greatest satisfaction from their relationships with students and staff colleagues. They see financial limitations and the academic deficiencies of administrators as widespread weaknesses of church-affiliated higher education. In Roman Catholic colleges and universities there is criticism of "heavy-handed" administration. In some Protestant institutions, perhaps especially Methodist and Baptist, faculty members are restive under moralistic policies relating to drinking, dancing, and other matters of social conduct. A number of respondents commented on the cleavage that exists between the lay and religious faculties in many Roman Catholic institutions, the lay faculties being treated as "second-class" members of the teaching staff.

Many of the respondents consider the sense of community which comes from shared religious convictions and shared allegiance to liberal education as an important asset. They believe that the church institutions with which they have been associated have greater unity than the secular institutions with which they are personally acquainted. However, some find themselves cramped by the expectation of conformity to the middle-class social values dominant in most church-related colleges and universities. Several of the respondents teaching in colleges identified with the free-church tradition mention the attenuated religious influence of their institutions.

Most of the faculty members who assisted in this inquiry believe that they have ample freedom to do their educational work, although several of the Roman Catholic institutions appear to be deficient in this respect. Some of the respondents emphasize the point that they are actually freer to investigate and discuss religious questions than are their colleagues in secular institutions. The degree of freedom in church-sponsored colleges and universities varies according to the character of the particular church involved. The faculty comments on church relationships reflect in some quarters a mild anti-clericalism and cynicism about administrative "window-dressing" to impress church constituencies. The sharpest criticism of this kind seems to come from faculty members in Methodist, Baptist, and Roman Catholic institutions.

In conclusion, we quote a history teacher in an Eastern college for men, who expresses well some of the more positive points mentioned by other respondents.

The great advantage of a college of this type is that it offers a serious explanation of theology, an essential element in man's life and heritage which other non-denominational schools are often forced to neglect. One can hope for a truly liberal education only in an environment which respects and promotes a sustained intellectual study of theological values. This religious dimension (usually coupled with history—the record of man's experience) offers a unifying factor to help understand the many diverse facets of knowledge. Unfortunately, this theological inquiry does constitute an additional scholastic burden for the student, a load many of his peers do not have to shoulder. However, this study does mean that I can often assume in my students a greater body of knowledge in this area than can my faculty colleagues in non-religious institutions. . . . The old problems concerned matters like regimentation and censorship and, while these may be real difficulties elsewhere, they have not troubled me. . . . I doubt that I would have been so optimistic had I written this report ten years ago. I have always believed in the value of the religious college, but it is only now that some of these schools are realizing the great potential they always possessed. We must make sure that the economic squeeze of our time does not force them from the field of education. I believe in the church college because it makes an essential contribution to a young man's intellectual growth which other institutions ignore.

11

Significant Innovation and Experimentation

Church-sponsored colleges and universities are often criticized for not being in the vanguard of educational improvement. While it is true that these institutions, as a group, provide too little leadership in the solution of educational problems and, like other colleges and universities, are often sluggish and unimaginative, it should also be said that some of them are engaged in highly significant innovation and experimentation. We could cite dozens of cases of promising departures in theory and practice undertaken by church-affiliated institutions. In a few instances the innovation is radical; in others variation from the established pattern takes the form of useful refinements which do not affect the basic fabric of an institution.

We have selected thirteen illustrations for special attention. This catalogue is not exhaustive; the examples we have chosen may not even be the most important. We believe, however, that they are constructive attacks on the problems facing church-sponsored higher education today. In a few instances the results of innovation can be evaluated with some precision and rigorously-scientific means are being used for that purpose, while in others appraisal must be based upon discerning observation and judgment as to success. The cases have been chosen as illustrative of different kinds of innovation—organizational and administrative, curricular, instructional, religious, financial, and evaluative. The brief descriptions are intended only to give a general notion of what is being done and why it is noteworthy. More detailed information can, of course, be obtained from the institutions themselves.

ORGANIZATIONAL INNOVATION

Intercommunity Cooperation at Marillac

Marillac College, located at Normandy, Missouri, a residential suburb of St. Louis, is conducted by the Community of Daughters of Charity of St. Vincent de Paul. It is a new institution and a new kind of institution. Its educational program, combining the intellectual, spiritual, social, and professional, exemplifies the goals of the Sister Formation movement of the Roman Catholic Church. All Marillac students are sisters.

In its conceptualization of itself Marillac College draws an explicit parallel with military education:

Soldiers are different. Sisters are different. To accomplish for each the prime purpose of a healthy and vigorous development, their education must be different. Good education requires a unifying element. For the soldier, the unifying element is patriotism, from which stems love of country, with a willingness to make even the supreme sacrifice of life to prove that love. For the Sister, the unifying element is Theology, from which stems love of God and the neighbor. She, too, must be ready, daily, for the supreme sacrifice. No curriculum teaches that, but every course, as taught in Marillac, can be made to contribute to it.[1]

Growing out of the idea of a distinctive education for sisters, not just the sisters of a single religious community but all sisters of the Roman Catholic Church, the most important feature of Marillac has been its plan of cooperation with a number of religious communities. The Sisters of Charity have invited other groups to join them in the conduct and benefits of Marillac College. The number of religious communities participating has increased steadily until now fifteen are represented in the faculty and thirty in the student body. This intercommunity approach to higher education obviates the necessity of each community's maintaining a small college for the education of its own personnel. Cooperative arrangements make for better education. The number of very small and weak colleges, many with fewer than 100 students, operated by religious communities is one of the most acute problems facing Roman Catholic higher education. The Marillac pattern is a major breakthrough in the solution of this problem.

[1] *Marillac College Catalogue, 1961-1964,* p. 32.

Interdenominational Sponsorship of Westminster

Westminster College, Salt Lake City, Utah, was established in 1875 as a Presbyterian institution. Through the years it has maintained its relationship with the United Presbyterian Church and is a member of the Presbyterian College Union. In 1953 it also became affiliated with the Methodist Church and is approved by the Methodist University Senate. Five years later it added a third affiliation—with the Congregational Christian Churches (now the United Church of Christ). The College is a member of the Council for Higher Education of the United Church of Christ, the official organization of United Church institutions. All three religious groups are represented on the Board of Trustees and provide annual and capital funds. In addition, the Bishop of the Episcopal Missionary District of Utah and a representative of the Associated Baptist Conventions of Utah-Idaho are members of the Board. Thus the College has formal relationships with three communions and enjoys the counsel of officials of two others.

While there are other instances of joint sponsorship of a college by more than one denomination, Westminster is the most notable example. In a state such as Utah, in which most churches lack sufficient strength to maintain institutions of their own, the Westminster pattern of relationships has obvious advantages. Multiple sponsorship is, however, a possibility that deserves serious consideration by colleges and churches elsewhere.

Structural Distinctiveness at Concordia

Concordia Senior College, Fort Wayne, Indiana, was established by the Lutheran Church-Missouri Synod in 1957. It offers a liberal arts curriculum in which acquaintance with the major fields of knowledge is combined with particular emphasis on language study. This is an innovating institution in a number of respects. Its campus and physical plant were designed and built as a unit in the most advanced architectural style. Chapel and worship occupy a place in the lives of faculty and students which is matched in few institutions. A student body of 500 is housed in 15 small dormitories with highly personal relationships among the students and between the students and the residential counselors. The educational objectives of the

College are defined with remarkable clarity and precision. Many of these features could profitably be described in much greater detail.

The most striking feature of this institution, however, is its over-all structure. It is a two-year college which includes only the junior and senior years, and its students are drawn principally from the ten junior colleges of the Missouri Synod. Almost all of its graduates proceed to Concordia Seminary in St. Louis. Thus Concordia Senior College is a carefully designed unit within a highly planned educational system. In few colleges is structure so clearly related to function.

Affiliated College Plan of the University of Waterloo

The University of Waterloo, Waterloo, Ontario, is a new and rapidly growing provincial university. It offers instruction at both the undergraduate and graduate levels in the arts and sciences and in selected professional fields. It receives provincial and federal funds. Of special interest to us is the arrangement which has been developed between the University and four church-sponsored liberal arts colleges —St. Jerome's College, Renison College, St. Paul's College, and Conrad Grebel College—which occupy sites granted to them by the University.

St. Jerome's College, conducted by the Roman Catholic Congregation of the Resurrection, is a federated college and has the closest relationship with the University. It has the power to confer degrees but exercises this authority only in the case of theology. The College has three buildings, a coeducational student body, and course offerings in eleven departments of the arts and sciences, including religious knowledge.

Renison College, an Anglican institution, has an affiliated relationship with the University. It has three buildings accommodating 80 students, is conducted by a staff of four, and offers a limited number of courses, chiefly in the humanities.

St. Paul's College, sponsored by the Hamilton Conference of the United Church of Canada, is an affiliated college offering elective courses in religious knowledge. All of its residential students are required to participate in a weekly seminar on the Christian faith and its implications for contemporary life and are expected to attend daily chapel. The College has two residence halls for 150 men and women and a wing containing offices, lecture rooms, chapel, library, and dining room.

Conrad Grebel College, the newest of the four institutions associated with the University, is supported by the Mennonites of Ontario. It plans to offer courses and seminars in Bible, church history, Christian theology, and ethics. Students registered in the College but not enrolled in a religious knowledge course are assigned to a weekly seminar on the Christian faith.

This plan of cooperation is mutually advantageous to the University of Waterloo and the colleges. Each college may integrate its academic offerings with those of the University, providing as many or as few courses as it wishes and as its financial resources permit. The colleges do not provide instruction in science or other expensive fields, depending instead on the University offerings in these fields. On the other hand, a University student wishing instruction in one of the federated or affiliated colleges may register for such courses in the college of his choice. The University library is used by students in all of the colleges, thus permitting each college to concentrate its funds on the development of a library collection suited to its own needs. There is free interchange of course credits between the colleges and the University. The student pays a single tuition fee which is allocated according to the courses for which he is registered.

In Canada the Federal Government makes grants for all colleges and universities on the basis of a per capita assessment distributed to the provinces and then to the individual institutions according to size. These moneys are used for current operating purposes. When colleges are federated or affiliated, as at the University of Waterloo, the Federal grants are either kept by the colleges or shared with the University according to arrangements worked out locally. However, grants made by the provinces are generally available only to non-church-related institutions. In the case of the University of Waterloo, for example, grants from the Province of Ontario must remain within the University and cannot be used by the federated and affiliated colleges. The colleges are, however, indirect beneficiaries in that they have access to the University's facilities and take advantage of the instruction it offers in the areas of science and applied science.

Under the University of Waterloo Act, the University itself is strictly non-denominational in management and control. No member of the staff of a federated or affiliated college is eligible for membership on the Board of Governors of the University. However, the University Senate, which is responsible for the educational policy of the University and determines the standards to which the colleges must adhere, has college representation. The dean of each federated or affiliated college is an ex-officio member of the Senate, and provision is made for faculty and alumni representation of the colleges in the Senate. The University confers all degrees except in theology.

The pattern developed at the University of Waterloo between a public university and church-sponsored colleges has advantages which might very well be explored by institutions in the United States. Not only does the arrangement afford substantial financial savings, particularly for the colleges, but also enriches the environment of the University and tends to sharpen the distinctive character of each cooperating college. It helps to bridge the gap between religiously oriented and secular education. It fits the realities of a religiously pluralistic society. The University of Waterloo plan is not unique in Canada, but there is no similar scheme of cooperation, at least none fully developed, in the United States.

CURRICULAR INNOVATION

Christianity and Culture Program at St. Andrews

St. Andrews is another of the new, innovating institutions. It was first known as Consolidated Presbyterian College, because it was the result of the merger of three existing institutions. At the time of its establishment, the Board of Trustees asked a panel of six leading educators to draw up a plan for the curriculum of the new institution. Working under a grant from the Fund for the Advancement of Education, the panel met daily for a month and with the help of twenty consultants produced a detailed report which has served as a blueprint for the development of St. Andrews' educational program. The heart of it is a 36 semester-hour sequence of interdepartmental courses extending through three and one-half years. Beginning with a study of the Hebraic and Greek sources of our culture and concluding with a study of contemporary culture, the program acquaints the student with the history of ideas in the perspective of Christianity. The sequence includes materials drawn chiefly from history, philosophy, religion, literature, psychology, sociology, anthropology, and art. The courses are organized in such a way as to show the interrelationships of the several disciplines. All candidates for the Bachelor of Arts degree are required to take this program.

Fourteen members of the faculty devote part of their time to teaching this sequence of courses, but they teach departmental courses as well. The team-teaching approach is used. Unusual breadth of interest and knowledge is required. The Christianity and Culture Program constitutes a strong backbone for liberal education at St. Andrews and is intended to assist the student in arriving at a Christian synthesis.

Core Course at Florida Presbyterian College

Another highly experimental institution is Florida Presbyterian College, St. Petersburg, Florida. Established in 1959, this is a coeducational liberal arts college related to the Presbyterian Church in the United States and the United Presbyterian Church in the U.S.A., acting cooperatively. Probably the most significant characteristic of Florida Presbyterian College is its aggressive search for the meaning of Christian community in an institution of higher education. As the College states in its catalogue:

We have a vision of *a Christian community* which is not monastic in separating dedicated persons from the world but which prepares dedicated people to go back into the world and witness through the exercise of their intellect. This witness, we pray, will prove to the world that a Christian education best fits people for life, liberty, and the pursuit of happiness for others.[2]

One of the means used by the College to promote this sense of community and to demonstrate the interrelatedness of knowledge is a series of "core courses" which extend through the four years of each student's undergraduate education. The core courses are taught cooperatively by instructors from art, biology, economics, history, literature, language, mathematics, music, philosophy, physics, political science, psychology, religion, and sociology. "In these, students pursue with the group and on their own a critical understanding of the major attempts of man to interpret his purpose and to organize his experience through the analytic and historical study of works and

[2] *Florida Presbyterian College, 1964-1965,* p. 5.

institutions." [3] As at St. Andrews, the sequence of courses forms the backbone of the liberal arts program and is the common experience of all students. The courses include participation in both large and small groups—both lecture and discussion. The four year-long courses have the following titles: "Western Civilization and Its Christian Heritage" (two courses), "Asian Studies," and "Christian Faith and Great Issues."

Though developed independently, the Christianity and Culture Program at St. Andrews and the core courses at Florida Presbyterian have many similarities. They are both efforts to bring back into liberal education a larger measure of integration and to relate this core to the Christian faith. Although there are similar programs at several other colleges, these are perhaps the most valuable illustrations of the carrying out of general education and Christian objectives. The fact that the two programs constitute a large portion of the undergraduate education of the students enrolled is, of course, an essential feature.

Program for Christian Culture at St. Mary's

St. Mary's College, Notre Dame, Indiana, is a residential liberal arts college conducted by the Sisters of the Holy Cross. It is one of the oldest Roman Catholic colleges for women.

In 1956 St. Mary's established the Program for Christian Culture, based on the insights of Christopher Dawson, the noted English historian. This program differs from those at St. Andrews and Florida Presbyterian in that it is a major for juniors and seniors. Like them, however, it is an interdepartmental program designed to integrate the undergraduate curriculum along religious-historical lines which are described as:

The development of Western civilization stressing the dynamic role played by Christianity in shaping social institutions and patterns of thought. The course integrates a number of significant aspects of Christian life: history, literature, art, philosophy, and theology . . . the student develops a deeper appreciation of the profound contribution Christianity has made to the growth of Western ideas and ideals. A program which enriches an understanding of the Christian past and develops religious sensitivity is appropriate to our pluralistic American society. [4]

[3] *Ibid.*, p. 9.
[4] *Bulletin of Saint Mary's College, 1962-1964*, p. 58.

The program includes a sequence of courses entitled "Christianity and Culture," a series of colloquies, several other courses, and an annual program of lectures by visiting scholars.

Curricular Design at Shimer

Shimer College, Mt. Carroll, Illinois, is a small, coeducational college affiliated with the Episcopal Church. While the educational program at Shimer is not wholly original—much of it was borrowed from the College of the University of Chicago in the early 1950's—it is a conspicuous example of rigorous curricular planning. The Shimer curriculum is based on a clear definition of liberal education. As the College itself says:

Shimer's distinctive kind of curriculum is achieved through a unique welding of general courses, comprehensive examinations, and specialized courses, into a complete academic experience, each element of which is essentially related to the whole.[5]

In brief, the student completes seventeen general courses in history, foreign language, philosophy, humanities, social sciences, mathematics, and natural sciences. He demonstrates his proficiency by performing satisfactorily on nine comprehensive examinations in analysis, logic, rhetoric, humanities, natural sciences, social sciences, foreign languages, history, and philosophy. His progress is determined by demonstrated achievement rather than by the mere completion of courses. In addition to satisfying the general requirements, the student takes a prescribed number of specialized courses which may lead to graduate or professional study.

The Shimer theory of education places primary emphasis on round-table classroom discussion as the principal means of instruction:

The discussion section offers a place and an atmosphere where minds may grow and mature by being given the opportunity to think through questions for themselves. The guidance and queries of the faculty member as well as the questions, insights, and criticisms of his colleagues, are the pedagogical devises which aid the student in acquiring the desired intellectual tools and attaining deeper understanding and richer appreciation of the materials in hand.[6]

[5] *Shimer College, 1964-1965*, p. 18.
[6] *Ibid.*, p. 66.

Demonstrations at Kalamazoo

In recent years Kalamazoo College, Kalamazoo, Michigan—an institution related to the American Baptist Convention—has been a center of innovation. It has incorporated into its program several distinctive features, which, though not entirely new, together constitute a major reorganization of program. These features have given Kalamazoo an experimental tone and have made it a beacon for many other institutions.

Perhaps the four most significant features of the educational program at Kalamazoo are the four-quarter academic calendar, of which Kalamazoo was one of the early exponents; the foreign-study program, which now includes almost all Kalamazoo students; the career-service quarter, also called the experiential quarter, which provides practical experiences in off-campus work and service assignments; and independent study and internships, which afford an opportunity for seniors to engage in special activities related to their occupational objectives. In seeking a more vital, more challenging educational experience for its students, Kalamazoo has been willing to move aggressively away from the conventional pattern of undergraduate education at several points. It has been a testing ground for ideas subsequently adopted by many colleges.

INSTRUCTIONAL INNOVATION

Improvement of Teaching at Earlham

Earlham College, Richmond, Indiana, an institution related to the Society of Friends, has recently launched a promising attack on the perennial problem of the evaluation and improvement of teaching. The project is designed to overcome the traditional objections to the discussion and assessment of the instructional activities of the individual teacher. This is, of course, a crucial problem in higher education today.

The basic idea is to arrange for "critic-advisors" to visit the classes of Earlham teachers, particularly beginning teachers, to analyze their course organization and methods of teaching, to appraise what is observed, to encourage those techniques which seem most effective, and to suggest remedies for weaknesses. Each visitor makes two trips to the Earlham campus. On his first trip he is solely concerned with helping the teacher who is being observed. Later in the year he makes a second visit, during which time he submits a report to the dean as well as to the teacher. Following the completion of the visit the instructor and the dean confer about the report that has been submitted.

A second part of the plan involves the exchange of "observer-consultants" with two other colleges. This feature is open to all ranks of teachers. Each college prepares a list of ten faculty members who are willing to be observed and who agree to serve as "observer-consultants" on another campus. This phase of the project does not involve reports to administrative officers.

This is a pioneering effort to overcome one of the most basic problems facing undergraduate institutions. It is a new project, the results of which should be of wide interest in the years ahead.

RELIGIOUS LEADERSHIP

Interdenominational Fellowship at Earlham

Another significant innovation at Earlham is the work of an organization known as the Yokefellow Associates, a nationwide interdenominational fellowship of Christian laymen. Although this program is legally separate from the College, it has been developed under Earlham faculty leadership and is housed on the Earlham campus. It is a demonstration of how a church-related college can assist in the renewal of the church. Members of the fellowship accept a personal discipline of religious devotion and action. Yokefellow institutes are attended by men and women of all professions and walks of life who wish to make a more effective Christian witness. The annual Yokefellow conference, which is held in the meeting house at Earlham, gives interested laymen an opportunity to hear some of the nation's most notable lay leaders and pastors. Although the Yokefellow approach reflects many of the values and methods of the Society of Friends, with which Earlham is associated, the movement has been interdenominational and points the way toward similar efforts at other institutions.

Student Religious Life at Brigham Young

Brigham Young University is an innovating institution in many areas, but one of the most highly developed aspects of the University is its program of student religious activities. It is striving to give students a religious experience which exemplifies the best in the Church of Jesus Christ of Latter-day Saints. The religious activities on the campus are part of the mainstream of church life, not a special student program which tends to set students apart. Mormon students are organized into three stakes, embracing 37 wards (congregations). Each ward is composed of 150 to 300 students, in which each student has a specific responsibility. Students are assigned to wards on the basis of their campus residence. The ward, over which a bishop presides, is a closely knit religious and social group with frequent meetings and sevices. Close personal relationships are nurtured in the wards. The bishops come to know their students well and counsel them on personal and religious problems. Tuesday evening and most of Sunday are devoted to ward activities.

Ward and stake participation not only gives the student a vital sense of religious and social belonging but also prepares him for church leadership upon graduation. Brigham Young graduates usually rise quickly to responsible lay posts wherever they go. A substantial portion of the top leadership of the Church has been drawn from the faculty and the alumni of the University, who are serving in such capacities as bishops of wards, presidents of stakes, mission presidents, general board members, and general authorities.

The assemblies held on Monday, Wednesday, and Friday in the Field House are major events in the life of the University community. The devotional assemblies on Wednesday bring members of the First Presidency and the Quorum of the Twelve Apostles to address the students. The attendance at these assemblies is 6,000–8,000 students and faculty members, an expression of religious solidarity which is probably unequalled at any other university in the world.

The role played by returned missionaries at Brigham Young should be of interest to other institutions. At the time of the authors' visit, the student body of the University included about 2,875 young men who had completed from two to two and one-half years of service as Latter-day Saint missionaries in the United States or abroad. These are carefully selected youths, who at the age of 19 or 20, were appointed by the President of the Church on the recommendation of their bishops to represent the Church in its missionary enterprise. As experienced and dedicated churchmen, they give a special tone to the campus life of the University. They have studied their faith and are articulate in explaining it to others. They play prominent roles in the ward and stake organizations at the University. Many are destined for higher leadership in the Church after graduation.

No institution of which we are aware has gone as far as Brigham Young in the organization of campus religious life.

INSTITUTIONAL EVALUATION

Self-Study at Mundelein

Mundelein College, Chicago, Illinois, was founded by the Sisters of Charity of the Blessed Virgin Mary in 1930 for the education of women. Challenged by the criticism of Roman Catholic education as not sufficiently intellectual, Mundelein initiated an elaborate institutional analysis in 1962 under the direction of its Vice-President. In this study detailed data were obtained from students, faculty, alumnae, husbands of alumnae, parents, and high school students on a wide variety of questions to throw light on what the educational program of Mundelein College was and what it should be. A committee of outside educators and a number of consultants were appointed to assist in the project. Seven faculty committees also participated in the study. Upon completion of the project, Mundelein College made major revisions in its educational program.

Hundreds of American colleges, encouraged by accrediting agencies and foundations, have undertaken institutional self-studies since World War II. There is no longer anything unusual about that. What was innovative and highly commendable about the Mundelein study was that it gave particular attention to information obtained from persons outside the institution—information that was helpful in the improvement of the educational program. The collection of data from alumnae and their husbands was notable. This is an extremely rare procedure among American colleges, although studies of the products of education are one of the best sources of clues for the strengthening of curriculum and instruction.

OTHER EXAMPLES

We have not found it easy to select these instances of significant innovation and experimentation from all of the cases that might be mentioned. Others could just as well have been described. The Ph.D. program for the preparation of college teachers of theology at Marquette University; the summer workshop in theology for faculty members at Goshen College; the University Church and leadership in the liturgical movement at St. John's University, Collegeville; the pioneering concepts of financial management at Parsons College (which was a United Presbyterian institution at the time of our visit, though it has now become independent); the Special Guidance Program at Culver-Stockton College for less able students; the Academy of Christian Thought and Service at Tarkio College for the development of stronger lay leadership in churches; the Arts and Service Program at Haverford College for fostering the non-academic development of its students; the Basic Studies Program at Austin College; the new Central States College Association, involving twelve church-related colleges in the Middle West in a systematic program of improvement; university-college cooperation at the University of Toronto and other Canadian institutions; the Associated Christian Colleges of Oregon, with its plan of cooperation action—these and many other examples could be cited with equal profit.

At their best the church-affiliated college and university are capable of making highly important contributions to the improvement of educational theory and practice. This is a capability that should be fully exploited.

12

Patterns
of
Institutional
Character

In our analysis of church-sponsored colleges and universities, we have discerned several distinct types of institutions—coherent patterns of purpose, clientele, staffing, program, financing, and other elements. These variations in institutional character are the result of many influences, among which founders' intentions, denominational affiliation, location, administrative leadership, and age are often prominent. Moreover, the character of an institution is determined as much by implicit as by explicit factors. The notions which the trustees, major administrative officers, and senior faculty members take for granted as they make important decisions are as crucial as the formal statements of institutional objectives which appear in articles of incorporation and catalogues.

In one sense every college or university is unique. As the authors have broadened their firsthand knowledge of institutions—and their personal acquaintance now includes several hundred colleges and universities—they have become more and more impressed with this fact. No two institutions are exactly alike. Thus it would be possible to describe as many patterns as there are institutions; for the purposes of our study this would not be a useful exercise. More helpful would be an effort to describe a few broad patterns or models which take account of the most significant variations.

Among the institutions of higher education associated with religious bodies in the United States, we observe four major types. Although not every institution fits neatly into one of these types, the four patterns do encompass the principal features which distinguish one church institution from another, including especially the various ways in which religion and church affiliation are treated.

The first type might be described as a *"defender of the faith college."* Its purpose is to provide an education in the arts and sciences for persons who will later take their places as leaders (lay or clerical) in a particular religious tradition. Its students and faculty are drawn entirely or almost entirely from the sponsoring group (though this is rarely a formal requirement). Before admitting students or appointing instructors, the college assures itself that they are committed to the specific religious beliefs for which the institution stands.

Such a college sees itself as distinct from the culture around it and in tension with the culture. It is training persons who will go out to defend and advance a clearly-defined religious position in a secular society. It seeks students and staff who will be staunchly loyal to this tradition. In some respects the concept is not unlike that of a military college.

Such an institution is explicitly and self-consciously theistic. It represents an orthodoxy which is not supported by the contemporary culture. While conflicting religious and philosophical points of view are presented in the classroom, they are evaluated in terms of the beliefs and principles officially espoused by the institution. In areas not touching directly on religion, the teaching may be much the same as in other colleges.

Worship and other religious practices are prominent and are a unifying factor in the academic community. All students and faculty are expected to participate in the common religious life. Student conduct tends to be closely supervised.

The curriculum follows the conventional pattern of liberal arts colleges except that the course requirements in religion or theology are substantial, often consisting of a sequence of courses extending over three or four years. Thus every student has the equivalent of a major or minor in religion in addition to the concentration in his chosen field. A good fraction of the graduates enter church vocations.

"Defender of the faith colleges" are usually controlled by single communions or denominations but sometimes by evangelical or fundamentalist groups that cut across denominational lines. Some Roman Catholic colleges are of this type, as are a few institutions associated with the newer conservative Protestant bodies. Their constituents often contribute financial support which is large in relation to their numbers and means. In return, they expect the institution to safeguard the faith and even the social practices of the constituency.

Colleges of this type have the advantage of clarity of purpose and a strong religious influence on students. The graduates are likely to be imbued with the values reflected in the educational program. On the other hand, student and faculty freedom is circumscribed; the student has limited opportunity to make up his own mind freely about the basic issues of life.

The number of institutions in the United States fitting this description is not large. Many of them are weak academically, but there are several which, judged by such conventional criteria of educational quality as faculty training, student aptitude, and success of graduates, are strong.

The second institutional pattern might be called that of the *"non-affirming college."* Though church related, an institution of this type gives relatively little formal attention to religion. Neither students nor faculty are attracted to the college because of its church connection. Students are admitted and faculty appointed without regard to religious interest or belief. The catalogue and other publications make brief mention of the church affiliation, but the statement of educational purposes is likely to omit any reference to religion or to speak in more general terms of moral and spiritual values.

The college has chapel services for those interested. However, most students and faculty members do not attend. Students may take courses in religion but are not always required to do so. The curriculum follows the conventional liberal arts pattern.

The church relationship of the institution is evidenced principally by the fact that a specified number of the trustees must be members of the associated denomination or elected by a denominational body, and a nominal fraction of the operating budget is provided by the church. The president and most of the faculty and students may be members of other denominations. For many years official descriptions of the institution have emphasized its non-sectarian character. Some of the faculty feel that the tenuous church connection should be severed entirely.

Campus life tends to reflect the values of contemporary culture.

Campus social regulations are permissive. Esprit de corps is developed through such means as athletics, periodic convocations (not primarily religious), and, most importantly, an allegiance to secular intellectual and social values.

Colleges fitting this general description have the advantage of being open-minded religiously. There is almost complete freedom of inquiry in the area of religion. No one is embarrassed by his religion or lack of it. It is possible for the college to serve a heterogeneous clientele. The chief disadvantage is that the college has no clear sense of identity. It is not quite sure where it fits into American higher education. It wonders about its role as a church-related institution. Some of the colleges related to the American Baptist Convention, the Disciples of Christ, the Methodist Church, the United Church of Christ, the United Presbyterian Church, and other denominations are of this general type.

A "non-affirming college" leaves the student's religion largely uncultivated. Academically, the institution may be weak or strong, though many faculty people assume that the adoption of such a pattern leads to educational strength.

The third type might be called a *"free Christian college"* (or *"free Jewish college,"* as the case may be). It is free because it does not control thought; Christian because it has a definite commitment. Most of its faculty share its religious purposes and consider them to be important in the life of the college. Students are attracted by the dual emphasis on academic excellence and religious vitality. The college surrounds its students with opportunities for full development —intellectual, religious, moral, artistic, social.

While chapel attendance may not be required, the chapel is a focal point of student and faculty interest. Worship is viewed as essential. The department of religion is composed of well-trained teachers who play an active role in faculty affairs. The courses in religion are rigorous and stimulating and are an integral part of the academic program. The college does not tell its students what they must believe, but it does expect them to grapple with the basic religious and philosophical questions and arrive at a considered position of their own. Much attention is given to the relationship between religion and the intellectual problems of our day. Religion and liberal learning are regarded as mutually supportive.

In making appointments to the faculty, the college prefers scholar-teachers who see the relationship of religion to their own disciplines, but may welcome a few constructive critics of religion to challenge colleagues and students. Once appointed, faculty members have the widest freedom consistent with law and good taste.

The institution has a cordial association with its church. A number of the faculty hold positions of leadership in the church and often serve it on important study commissions. Appreciative of the contribution of the college to the education of Christian laymen, the church makes a substantial annual appropriation to the institution. The college values its association with the church and would wish to continue the relationship even if there were no church support.

The curriculum is built around a common body of knowledge and skills which all students are required to master. The common portion extends through the four years and culminates in a senior course which helps the student integrate his undergraduate education.

The "free Christian (or Jewish) college" combines the chief assets of the other two models while it tries to avoid their liabilities. It stands unapologetically for religion and liberal education, but it relies on example, persuasive presentation of ideas, and a climate of conviction, rather than on conformity, to accomplish its ends. Many colleges purport to be this kind of institution, but only a minority actually exemplify it.

These three patterns or types, as the sketches make clear, are primarily descriptions of undergraduate colleges. The church-related university, as distinct from the college, is sufficiently different to necessitate a fourth pattern.

The archetype of the *"church-related university"* is an urban institution with a heterogenous student body. It serves primarily a community or a region rather than a particular religious group. It draws its financial support from a wide range of sources, including many donors who have little if any interest in its function as a church-related institution. Though it is associated with a Christian church, some of its most generous donors may be persons of the Jewish faith or of no faith who see it as an important cultural asset.

The "church-related university" is much larger than the college. It enrolls between 5,000 and 20,000 students. The scope of its educational offerings is broad. It provides programs in many of the professional and occupational fields, such as business administration, engineering, law, social work, journalism, music, and perhaps medicine, nursing, pharmacy, dentistry, and others, as well as programs in the arts and sciences. It may include a school of theology. It offers graduate study leading to master's and doctor's degrees in a number of fields and often has a large evening program for part-time students.

Many of its students live at home and commute to the university. Thus it takes on much of the diverse character of the city itself. The student body is not a homogeneous residential group as in many liberal arts colleges. The students are regarded as adults, and the discipline with respect to social conduct is minimal. The university does not assume responsibility for the behavior of its students except at points that directly affect the welfare of the institution.

Religiously, the church-related university is pluralistic. It is unlikely to have religious requirements which apply to all students. Many opportunities for participation in religious activities are provided, but these are optional except in Roman Catholic universities where the requirements may apply to all students of that faith.

The relationship of the university to its church is tenuous. In the case of a Roman Catholic institution the connection is usually with a religious order or religious community rather than with the Church directly. In other cases there may be church representation on the board, historic identification with a church, some connection through a divinity school, or membership in a group of church-related institutions. Financial support from the church, if indeed there is any, is negligible in relation to the size of the budget. And yet the university, whatever its general tone or specific relationship, does consider itself in some sense church related.

The two important groups of church-related universities are Methodist and Roman Catholic. Including several universities associated with other religious bodies, the total number of such institutions is about twenty.

Here are four constructs—combinations of purpose, clientele, faculty, educational program, financial support, treatment of religion, and church affiliation—which describe in broad terms the principal types of church-related institutions. These are not sketches of particular colleges and universities. As explained earlier, they do not exhaust the possibilities, and many institutions combine features of two or more of the patterns as described.[1] Institutions are often in transition from one pattern to another. Sometimes they are in fact one type but hold up another as their ideal. Not infrequently institutions find themselves enmeshed in two patterns, unable to extricate themselves from inconsistencies of purpose and program. They may be trying to respond to conflicting sets of pressures which are driving them in two directions at once.

The subject of models was discussed at length and with profit by college officials in the regional conferences sponsored by the Commission. While the titles we have used to designate the four principal types were generally accepted as descriptive, several conference participants suggested alternative names. Proponents of the first model mentioned, for example, "witness to the faith college" as having a more positive tone than "defender of the faith college." Likewise, "non-affirming college" had an unnecessarily negative ring to a few persons who were otherwise attracted to that pattern. The matter of titles is, however, secondary for our purposes.

In our final section on recommendations, we shall have further comments to make on models or patterns of institutional character. This whole subject is basic to the future welfare of the church-sponsored colleges and universities. Many administrators, trustees, and faculty committees are engaged in an intensive examination of the character of the institutions for which they are responsible. The position taken on this central question determines the decisions that are made on hundreds of lesser matters.

[1] For example, the presidents and other representatives of 17 evangelical colleges met in Washington on August 13-14, 1965, at the invitation of Carl F. H. Henry, Editor, *Christianity Today*, and formulated a fifth model which they felt more accurately described their type of institution than any of the four models sketched in this chapter. They formulated a model entitled "The Affirming College," which appeared in *Christianity Today*, September 10, 1965, pp. 25-26.

13

Conclusions
and
Recommendations

The position of church-sponsored higher education in this country today is mixed. It includes elements of strength and weakness, of achievement and failure, of hope and discouragement.

The 817 colleges and universities are affiliated with 64 different religious bodies. Approximately 42 percent are Roman Catholic, while about 57 percent are connected with Protestant and other Christian groups and about 1 percent with Judaism. The institutions are located in 48 of the 50 states, but most of them are in the eastern half of the country. They constitute more than one-third of the 2,238 colleges and universities in America; they enroll between one-fifth and one-sixth of the students. They range in size from fewer than 100 students to large universities with student bodies of over 10,000. Their average enrollment is approximately 1,000. They are growing but not as rapidly as American higher education as a whole. They draw their students primarily from the middle social and economic class. Although, in the aggregate, they offer a wide range of graduate and professional programs, the typical church-affiliated institution is an undergraduate college emphasizing the functions of pre-professional and teacher education.

We have seen that the church institutions, considered as a whole, have substantial assets: freedom to experiment and to serve special purposes; responsiveness to able leadership, when provided; close student-faculty relationships; a good record (in some colleges) of preparation for graduate and professional study; concern for the progress of individual students; and espousal of humane values. Previous chapters have also shown that these institutions, as a group, are insuffi-

198

ciently strong in scholarly attainment of faculties, financial support, selection of students and faculty in relation to educational purposes, curricular design, implementation of religious aims, and self-evaluation. This segment of higher education includes some of the best colleges in the United States, and many of the poorest. About 50 could properly be described as institutions of high quality. Their excellence is chiefly at the undergraduate level. Hanging like a cloud over the whole group of 817 institutions, and affecting them at many points, is the uncertain status of the church and religion in the contemporary, secular world.

Viewed in historical perspective, the church-sponsored institutions belong to the great tradition of collegiate education in the arts and sciences illuminated by the Christian faith. It is a conception of education which, in its essentials, has stood the test of some fifteen centuries. It combines learning in the fundamental fields of knowledge with the insights of the Christian faith, the aim being to cultivate the humane person. Its subject matter changes, but its purposes are fairly constant. At its best it is a broad and general education in that it stresses the arts of thought and communication and the principles which should govern personal and public affairs. It is the most useful kind of education, in the best sense of the word "useful," for its worth is not restricted to a particular occupation, a particular time or place, a particular stratum of society. It should be a liberating, a freeing education. It should provide good preparation for responsible living in a rapidly changing world such as ours. Soundly conceived, it gives the student an understanding of the values that are most worth conserving in our heritage and of how they may be the guiding principles of the future. If there is a single word that describes the highest aspiration of colleges of this type for their graduates, that word is probably "wisdom."

During the three centuries since this tradition was brought to America from the English colleges of the seventeenth century the strength of this kind of education has been sapped by several large movements in modern culture and education. The Enlightenment philosophies of the eighteenth century, the influence of the German university idea with its emphasis on technical and specialized scholarship, the rapid growth of public higher education, a diminution in the influence of the church and religion—all these factors and others have affected the position of church-related institutions. Stated simply, in this period of history the private college, the religiously oriented college, the college offering a broad liberal education in the British tradition is rowing upstream on all three counts.

On the basis of what we know about the present status of church-related higher education and the forces acting upon it, should we be pessimistic about the future of these institutions? To be sure, public higher education will overshadow the private colleges and universities in size, facilities, total financial support, and, in some areas, quality. The church institutions will continue to educate a minority of the college students, as will private higher education as a whole. The percentage of the student population enrolled in church institutions, as well as in private institutions generally, will probably decline slowly for some years to come. The low fees of public institutions make it difficult for private colleges and universities to compete for students of modest means. The establishment of new public junior colleges and the transformation of state teachers colleges into state colleges and state universities accentuates the problem. All these factors complicate the operation of church institutions and call for wise policies and astute administration, but we are convinced that they are not insuperable. The church institutions can and should play an important leavening role in American education and American life.

How are they to do this? It is not possible to give a detailed answer for every one of the 817 colleges and universities. Each has its own tradition and circumstances. From the many suggestions which might be drawn from the findings of this study, we have selected 15 points on which to offer specific recommendations. We believe the matters considered in these recommendations are crucial to the future strength and contribution of the church-sponsored segment of American higher education.

ADMINISTRATION AND ORGANIZATION

A More Experimental Approach

In order to make the most of their assets and overcome their weaknesses, the church-affiliated college and university, in our judgment, need to take a more experimental approach to their work. Private institutions have more freedom to experiment than public institutions, but they are not taking full advantage of this opportunity. The church institutions must become problem-oriented, rather than merely imitative of educational patterns laid down by others. It is not only that they imitate but that they imitate in ways that ill serve their purposes. Let them strive for distinctive programs which will point the way to better educational theory and practice. To become experimental and distinctive in the best sense requires wise administrators and committed faculties more than it requires money and prestige. Some of the most valuable experiments in education have been conducted under conditions of poverty. With experimentation and distinctiveness will come more productive service and an indispensable niche in American higher education.

Experimentation in the treatment of religion, especially worship, is urgently needed. This, as we have seen, is an area of particular weakness in many church-affiliated institutions. Each college must proceed in its own way. A Quaker college in Oregon might attack the problem quite differently from a Roman Catholic college in New York or a Southern Baptist college in Alabama. The important thing is that the church institutions start work immediately on efforts to revitalize the devotional life of their students and somehow give their students a sense of the reality of religious experience. Our belief is that this is more likely to be accomplished through imaginative and perhaps radically different forms of expression than through theological debate. The spectacular revival of the arts on the American college campus may provide clues for the launching of a religious renewal.

To act upon this recommendation will require stronger academic leadership than most of the institutions have at the present time. We urge that trustees, in searching for presidential material, and presidents, in looking for prospective deans, seek out energetic men who are young in mind and who have been involved in significant experimentation. We are strongly of the opinion that, at this juncture of history, it is most important to recruit to major administrative posts men of ideas and conviction—men who are resolute as to purpose but creative as to means.

The experimental theme is reflected in all of the recommendations that follow. We realize that it does no good merely to exhort educators to be experimental. This is like urging people to be original or imaginative. It was to give this concept some concreteness that we included an extensive review of specific instances of significant innovation in Chapter 11.

Restructuring of Administration

The complexity of administrative responsibilities today, the heavy toll of presidential failure and physical breakdown, and the administrative understaffing of many colleges call for a new, more flexible concept of college administration.

We urge trustees and administrators to give serious thought to the advantages of a group-leadership pattern in which the day-to-day work of the president would be more realistically defined. Perhaps a chancellor-president combination like that of the chairman-president relationship in business and industry holds promise for higher education. The chancellor might be a policy-initiating officer and the president the operating head of the institution. The chancellor, who would be a salaried officer, might or might not also be chairman of the board.

Another possibility with which institutions might experiment is that of team leadership by a committee of major officers, of which the president would in effect be the chairman. Such an executive committee might consist of the chief policy officer, the chief executive officer, and the chief academic administrator as a tightly knit group who would guide and operate the institution in close consultation.

In our judgment the time-honored principles of college administration are much too rigid and doctrinaire to cope successfully with modern conditions of administration. We realize that some presidents may resist proposals for a more realistic sharing of authority and responsibility on the grounds that this would tend to weaken their position. This objection, it seems to us, is less telling than the deficiencies of the present form of organization. A more flexible approach is needed. If what we are proposing is to be accomplished, more attention will have to be given to the appointment of groups of administrators with complementary personalities and capabilities and less to the selection of a single man around whom the whole organization will be developed.

We have been gratified to learn that several colleges have begun to act upon this proposal since it was discussed in tentative form at the regional conferences sponsored by the Commission in March and April, 1965.

Roman Catholic higher education has special administrative and organizational problems of its own—for example, the composition and authority of boards of trustees and the relationship of lay and religious faculty members. These are matters requiring careful study in each institution.

Institutional Planning and Development

At the very least every college or university should have a development officer with responsibility for continuous cultivation of donors. The day when old-fashioned spasmodic campaigns could be relied upon to produce needed income has long since passed. Fund-raising must be a well-organized process in which the financial requirements of an institution are brought to the attention of alumni, business and industry, foundations, governmental agencies, individual donors, and other sources of funds on a continuing basis.

As a necessary tool not only for effective fund-raising but also for general administration, the institution must have a long-range plan, outlining in some detail the proposed development of the student body, program, faculty, and facilities for a number of years ahead. The plan should include estimated expenditures and income, so that steps can be taken to obtain the resources needed. Through the efforts of the Fund for the Advancement of Education, the Ford Foundation, and other organizations, the techniques of planning have been refined in recent years. It is recommended that medium-sized and larger institutions have offices of institutional research which can provide expert assistance to administrators, trustees, and faculty committees in studies leading to policy formation.

In Roman Catholic institutions there is special need for the improvement of institutional planning and development. The Catholic colleges have lagged particularly in their adoption of modern tools of management.

More Efficient Operation

The recent experience of a number of institutions has demonstrated that the financial status of colleges and universities can be markedly improved through more efficient operation. Among the steps that accomplish this end are: a reduction in the number of courses offered, more required courses, fewer very small classes (with less than ten students), and better utilization of plant. The first three measures not only reduce unit costs but also strengthen undergraduate curricula and teaching. We strongly recommend that more institutions look into these opportunities for achieving better use of resources.

Clarification of Relationship of Freedom, Responsibility, and Purpose

From the faculty point of view, the central problem of Christian higher education is: How can a college do justice to its avowed purpose as a Christian institution, a purpose which carries with it commitment to a set of beliefs, and at the same time maintain the freedom of inquiry which most academic people think is necessary for good education? This is a dilemma that every college, whether religiously oriented or not, ultimately faces. In the case of the church institution the problem is more obvious. Perhaps what we are saying is that for many academic people religious commitment seems more hampering to freedom of inquiry than other types of commitment because of the teacher's unconscious reservations about theological truth. In any event, the problem is one that is so sharply confronted that it cannot be ignored.

We are convinced that the cause of church-sponsored higher education would be greatly helped if every institution formulated a clear statement of its policies with respect to this matter. The problem has been treated in greater detail in an earlier chapter. Here it is sufficient to say that many church institutions have proved the feasibility of reconciling freedom, responsibility, and institutional purpose, as these are involved in the religious character of a college. This is done by (1) seeing to it that a substantial nucleus of the persons appointed to the faculty are intelligent, practicing Christians (or Jews) and are sympathetic with the religious purposes of the institution; (2) insisting on freedom of inquiry for faculty and students; (3) creating a climate in which the underlying philosophy of the institution is reasonably and persuasively presented in a variety of ways, but without pressing for acceptance; and (4) encouraging faculty and students to explore the relationships between religion and other facets of modern life.

The chief obstacle to accomplishing this reconciliation is the tendency of many people to treat commitment or freedom as absolute, thus making them mutually exclusive in an educational setting. Wise administrators and mature teachers know how to avoid this pitfall.

Experimentation with New Types of Faculty Training

The persistent and informed criticism of the advanced work in graduate schools as being narrow and poorly organized cannot be ignored. As the supply of persons with this training becomes less and less adequate to meet the demand for college teachers, we are confronted with an opportunity to develop a better kind of preparation. The present doctoral program is not as important for undergraduate teaching as many institutions have supposed. A strong case can be made for a broader type of preparation, such as that represented by a properly planned master's degree and certain types of non-academic experience.

We recommend to the administrators of church-affiliated institutions, both colleges and universities, that they not wait until the increasingly inadequate supply of conventionally trained candidates forces hasty improvisation of new patterns of preparation for teaching. Now is the time to take the steps necessary to work out new patterns of graduate training suited to the broader purposes of liberal education. Action by groups of undergraduate colleges in cooperation with nearby graduate schools offers one promising avenue for accomplishing this end. Such efforts are already in progress at the University of Chicago and elsewhere but need to be extended. The provisions for supervised teaching apprenticeships for graduate students at Michigan, Yale, Washington (St. Louis), Harvard, Virginia, Emory, Duke, and other universities are also hopeful signs but, again, are too limited. Another interesting variation in preparation for college teaching is the internship program of the Woodrow Wilson National Fellowship Foundation, conducted in cooperation with a group of predominantly Negro colleges in the South. These are forward-looking experiments.

There are several steps that individual institutions can take to improve faculty quality. Those few church-related universities with extensive graduate programs have an opportunity to work out broader patterns of preparation for undergraduate teaching to meet the demand for more and better teachers. Liberal arts colleges can provide in-service training for their own faculties and financial assistance to promising younger teachers who are eager to complete their graduate study. Administrators should recognize that they may be able to build stronger faculties by recruiting at the junior ranks alert young M.A.'s than by appointing less able Ph.D.'s.

Elimination of Haphazard Establishment of New Colleges

Some way must be found to control the whimsical and unplanned founding of new institutions within denominations. We say this even though several of the newer colleges are highly significant ventures. Can anyone justify the operation of four Presbyterian colleges in Iowa, five United Presbyterian institutions in Missouri, nine Methodist colleges in North Carolina (including two brand-new ones), and three Roman Catholic colleges for women in the city of Milwaukee? Much of the damage was done in the nineteenth century, but such unplanned establishment of colleges is still going on in some churches. The problem is perhaps most acute in Roman Catholic higher education where the various religious orders and communities are free to begin new colleges without any central restraint, and bishops often encourage the founding of institutions for which they have no financial responsibility. The result is a dissipation of available resources and the maintenance of many weak institutions.

Often the establishment of new colleges seems to be the result of a lack of precedent for cooperation among like-minded groups. This probably explains the proliferation of colleges by religious orders and communities. However, the new Marillac College in St. Louis, conducted by an intercommunity faculty and serving 25 different religious communities, provides a promising pattern for replication elsewhere. The diocesan and order cooperation at Bellarmine College and the plan for united efforts at the University of Dallas are likewise constructive experiments. Among Protestant institutions, Westminster College at Salt Lake City, now related to three denominations, suggests a feasible plan of ecumenical sponsorship that deserves to be studied carefully by other institutions.

In our judgment the Association of American Colleges, a respected organization representing colleges of all denominations, working in close collaboration with the National Catholic Educational Association and the Council of Protestant Colleges and Universities, is in the best position to encourage restraint in the founding of new institutions. If the churches and church educational agencies would lend their support, and if the effort were widely publicized, we believe that a valuable service could be performed for church-related higher education.

Financial Responsibility of Churches

The differences among churches in their support of colleges are enormous. Some churches provide almost no funds; others contribute more than 50 percent of operating budgets and capital funds. One church underwrites its principal institution at the rate of $1,000 per student per year. As we have already reported, 26 percent of the church-sponsored colleges and universities receive no annual appropriations from their churches; the average amount given to those that are assisted is only 12.8 percent of their operating budgets.

Clearly, the differences among the churches in their support of higher education are not due to differences in economic status. In fact, the opposite is closer to the truth. The churches whose members have modest means often show the greatest financial responsibility in higher education.

We think the time has come for most churches to reconsider their obligations to church-sponsored colleges and universities and to increase their appropriations substantially. How long can self-respecting churches permit other donors to bear the primary responsibility for the support of these institutions?

A new factor has entered the financing of church-related higher education—large Federal funds. It remains to be seen what effect this will have on the character of institutions. We may reasonably suppose, however, that governmental support will increase the pressure toward secularity. Militant secularist groups can be expected to raise questions about every manifestation of religious commitment in institutions receiving Federal funds. Church-sponsored institutions will be tempted to "play down" religion in order to avoid trouble. College officials will not wish to risk withdrawal of Federal funds. Thus the enormously involved problem of the place of religion in higher education will be still further complicated by financial and political considerations.

Cooperation among Institutions for Mutual Benefit

The experience of such groups as the Associated Colleges of the Midwest, the Great Lakes College Association, and the Associated Mid-Florida Colleges, has demonstrated the practical value of co-operation among similar institutions—cooperation designed to accomplish particular purposes, not cooperation merely for the sake of cooperation. Such relationships are much more widespread among private colleges than is generally recognized, but further development can bring new strength to many institutions. Although in some instances cooperative programs have yielded significant economies through large-scale buying, the major benefit to be derived from such arrangements is probably enrichment of programs.

We commend to the thoughtful consideration of church-affiliated institutions another type of relationship which, though well developed in other countries, has been largely overlooked in the United States. This is the idea of creating a cluster of small colleges around a university. A dramatic illustration of this idea is the new University of Waterloo in Ontario, where a constellation of Anglican, Roman Catholic, United Church, and Mennonite colleges is being built around the larger university. The University of Toronto is another impressive example. For the many colleges that are disadvantageously located, relocation next to a strong and friendly institution with complementary purposes may be the solution to many problems. This plan should be tested more widely.

CURRICULUM AND TEACHING

Commitment to Teaching as the Primary Function

In this day when the teaching of undergraduates has clearly taken second place to research and perhaps third place to research and service in universities, liberal arts colleges, including the church colleges, can make an educational contribution of the first order by giving priority to teaching. They are in an excellent position to exploit this opportunity. A Christian estimate of the importance of the individual student should give this goal a special urgency for church colleges.

An excessive individualism has perhaps been a weakness in some denominations in times past, but carried over into the sphere of higher education it can be a valuable asset. In an age of bigness and impersonality, the church-sponsored college has at its disposal a view of the worth and dignity of the individual which can give to undergraduate teaching an ingredient badly needed. It helps to safeguard the college from becoming a factory-like institution in which the individual student is only a statistic or an I.B.M. card.

The small college is in a favorable position to offer effective educational and personal counseling. We hear more and more these days about the inability of the large public high school and the large university to give the individual student proper guidance in the shaping of his educational program and the charting of his future. The work of the faculty adviser often becomes hopelessly routine, and for all practical purposes the student is on his own without adult guidance. This is a serious defect of large-scale education. More and more parents, students, and educators are realizing the importance of proper counseling, in which the counselor comes to know the student with whom he is working. The church college, by virtue of its philosophy and its typical size, is well equipped to preserve the personal element in higher education. This is not, however, achieved automatically. Effort is required to take advantage of the opportunity.

The church-related institutions are, on the whole, doing a good job in this respect. The absence in most undergraduate colleges of influences which seriously divert the faculty member from his teaching responsibilities protects him from the acute schizophrenia of many university teachers whose loyalties are divided between teaching duties and the greater career opportunities of research and publication. By the same token, undergraduate college faculties should not rest until the quality of their teaching is unmistakably superior to that found in multi-purpose institutions.

In emphasizing the importance of faculty-student relationships, we do not mean to overlook the place of professional counseling. Every college should have a well-trained staff for student personnel services. Nor do we intend to suggest that the college teacher is to be only a big brother to his students. He is to be a good teacher, a good scholar, and a good adviser.

Emphasis on the Humanities and Responsible Citizenship

Thoughtful students of American higher education have been saying for a long time that the humanistic dimensions of life are being neglected in undergraduate curricula. This is an area in which the church institutions have compelling reasons for seeking strength. The humanities, properly taught, provide a supportive and nurturing environment for religious thought and action. Courses in literature, history, and philosophy should lead the student to an intelligent appreciation of the place of religion in his education. Thus it would seem to us that, at a time when the humanities are fighting a losing battle in higher education, having been eclipsed by other disciplines and ways of viewing reality, the 817 church colleges and universities could not only serve their own purposes but also help to preserve balance in the whole educational system by stressing that field. We urge them to become citadels of the humanities—effective champions of the humanistic view of life.

It would be entirely in keeping with the long tradition of both liberal education and the Christian religion if church-sponsored colleges and universities also stressed the importance of public affairs throughout their programs. This is an area in which they are now weak. The aim would be to prepare students better for the responsibilities of intelligent citizenship. The country would be well served if more college graduates assumed active roles of public service. This need not and should not be a partisan undertaking. Properly done, it would contribute markedly to the revitalization of teaching in the social sciences and the humanities. The opportunity for constructive experimentation is nowhere more apparent. The possibilities for sound and exciting programs are almost limitless. They only await imaginative development.

To say that the humanities and public affairs should be emphasized is not at all to suggest, of course, that the sciences should be neglected.

The Common Experience of Educated Men

Several of the most serious weaknesses identified in this report concern the organization of the liberal arts curriculum and the thoroughness of teaching. We believe that the first step in the curricular strengthening of most liberal arts colleges (including church colleges) is the clear formulation by their faculties of the common body of knowledge, intellectual skills, and other learning which should be required of all students seeking a liberal arts degree. Great ideas and the methods of productive inquiry should be prominent in such a formulation. This common core is the heart of liberal education. In many colleges it has been neglected.

More attention should be given to those liberal arts which used to be called the trivium—grammar, logic, and rhetoric—or translated into present-day terms—writing, reading, speaking, and critical thinking. Most college graduates have not mastered these arts to the point of advanced proficiency. More thorough instruction is required. We are not talking here about a faddish plan—something new and fancy—simply an insistence that students have a good command of the intellectual skills which have always been recognized as essential to the liberally educated person.

At a time when many colleges aspire to educate only the superior student, the nation badly needs first-rate programs of liberal education tailored to the average student. There is nothing inherent in the idea of good education which requires that it be limited to the student of high aptitude. A liberal arts program designed for the average student may properly be described as "excellent" if well conceived and executed. We ought to have many more colleges dedicated to this kind of excellence. The future of representative government and humane living depends as much on finding effective means of transmitting the essentials of liberal education to a large segment of our young people as it depends on perfecting the education of the few who will enter the learned professions. Without in any way depreciating the latter function, we urge the church colleges to keep in sight the broader responsibility of higher education.

A Reasoned Framework of Belief

We recommend that church-sponsored institutions make definite provision in their curricula for helping students develop a philosophy of life, a faith, a coherent and reasoned understanding of fundamental matters. It is now assumed by most colleges that this goal is attained indirectly and fortuitously, that it is not an objective toward the achievement of which the student can be assisted in an orderly way. This assumption is fallacious. The student is no more likely to arrive at a sound world view effortlessly and by chance than he is to master calculus as a by-product of studying psychology or music.

Presumably in a Christian institution a special effort will be made to assist the student in arriving at a Christian synthesis. In this connection we commend to the attention of faculties and administrators the first three curricular innovations described in Chapter 11.

Systematic Studies of Students and Alumni

The analysis of data on students and alumni can provide valuable clues to the improvement of an institution's educational program. We urge colleges and universities to develop more complete files of information on such matters as the social and economic backgrounds of their students, the psychological characteristics of students, the occupations of alumni, and the civic and church involvement of alumni. Properly used for the purpose of institutional research, such data can help to answer many questions about the impact of an institution on its students.

Intellectual Leadership for the Churches

It is time for the colleges to turn their attention to the churches that have nurtured them and not merely regard the churches as sources of students and money. The grave problems faced by the churches have already been outlined. To reverse or redirect or adapt to a change in world view as profound as that through which we are passing cannot be simple. It may take a century for the church to chart its course of action.

We cannot expect church administrators and pastors to give the answers. They are too much involved in the day-to-day activities of the church. They are called upon to work out *ad hoc* solutions to immediate problems. They are supposed to inspire others; they must not admit to discouragement or perplexity. This role precludes the dispassionate examination of large historical and philosophical trends in perspective—the work necessary to frame proposals commensurate with the church's problems. Nor does it seem likely that the needed guidance can come from seminary faculties and professional theologians. The manpower available in theological schools is too meager and its outlook necessarily limited.

In our judgment the faculties of church-related colleges are in the most favorable position to provide intellectual leadership in the study of the issues facing the church and the hammering out of proposals for action. The church college lives in both the "church world" and the "outside world." Its faculty, in the aggregate, has the breadth of knowledge required to see the church in perspective. College faculties include historians, philosophers, artists, theologians, psychologists, sociologists, literary critics, political scientists, economists—scholars whose business it is to be sensitive to ideas and to understand the meaning of the world around us. They are in touch with secular thought, but at their best they care about the church and its future.

We urge the faculties of church-affiliated institutions to view themselves as scholarly task forces for assessing the status of the Christian Church in the changed and changing world. Let the faculties do in a more comprehensive and thorough way the kind of diagnosis we have attempted in this report. It is not now being done on a systematic basis. Let them make their scholarly contribution to the sound development of Christian social thought—a requisite in this age of turbulence. Some colleges are already providing certain types of leadership to the churches, but much more is required.

INSTITUTIONAL MODELS

Patterns of Institutional Character

We have suggested that one of the difficulties of church colleges is that of seizing upon secular images—conceptions of collegiate education borrowed from other institutions whose purposes are different. This is a matter of the first importance. Church institutions sorely need models of their own to serve as broad conceptual frameworks. These should provide internally consistent patterns of purpose and program, not as blueprints to be followed slavishly by institutions—we have already inveighed against imitation—but as illustrations of the proper relationship of ends and means.

Whole conferences have been held on such themes as "What Is A Christian College?" and "The Nature of Christian Higher Education," as though there were one correct answer. Early in our study we concluded that there is no single model or definition of a Christian college that is appropriate for all such institutions. The American religious and educational scenes are much too complex. In an earlier chapter we sketched the four models or patterns that are required to describe the principal types of church-affiliated institutions—the "defender of the faith college," the "non-affirming college," the "free Christian (or Jewish) college," and the "church-related university."

Our final recommendation is that each institution devise for itself a coherent pattern which relates purposes, clientele, staff, program, and church relationship in some such manner as these models. Many colleges have adopted ends and means that are not consistent. Each of the models we have tried to sketch has its assets and liabilities. But we believe that many more church institutions should aspire to the third model or something like it. Enough colleges and universities have achieved this combination of commitment and freedom to show beyond doubt that it can be done. We believe that this is the key to the future of church-related higher education in the United States—the way in which the great tradition of liberal education infused with the Christian faith can, at this point in history, better serve God and man.

Questionnaire
on Relationships
with
Religious Bodies

The following is a copy of the questionnaire that was used in the study of the Danforth Commission on Church Colleges and Universities to obtain up-to-date information on the church relationships of American institutions of higher education. This questionnaire was sent to the presidents of all private institutions (1,189) in the United States. In the case of Roman Catholic colleges and universities a separate and subsequent inquiry was also made regarding financial questions peculiar to that group of institutions.

Please check below the items that describe the nature of your affiliation, if any, with a church body. Leave unchecked items that are not applicable to your institution. The term "church" is used here for convenience. It is intended to embrace all religious groups, including branches of Judaism. If you wish to expand your response to any of these statements, or if you wish to make additional comments on your relationship to a church body, please use the reverse side of this sheet.

........1. The provisions governing the composition of your board of trustees require that:
.... of a total board membership of .... be members of your church.
.... of a total board membership of .... be nominated and/or elected by an official body of your church.
........2. Your institution is owned by the church, a division of the church, or a religious order or congregation.
........3. Your institution receives financial support from official church sources.
Approximately .... per cent of your annual budget for educational and general purposes is provided by the church.
.... Substantial amounts are provided by your church for capital purposes from time to time.
........4. Your institution is affiliated with an organization (council, association, etc.) which includes colleges related to your church and which bears the name of the church.

.......5. Your institution subscribes to a set of standards or a statement of policy adopted by your church for its colleges.

.......6. The statement of your educational purposes makes it clear that yours is a religiously oriented institution.

.......7. In the selection of faculty and administrative personnel preference is given to members of the church.

.......8. None of the foregoing statements applies to your institution. At the present time it should not be classified as church related.

Church body with which institution is affiliated..

B

List
of Fifty
Case-Study
Institutions

The case-study institutions, which, through their cooperation, contributed so greatly to the study, were:

Agnes Scott College, Decatur, Georgia

Andrews University, Berrien Springs, Michigan

Arkansas College, Batesville, Arkansas

Austin College, Sherman, Texas

Bard College, Annandale-on-Hudson, New York

Bellarmine College, Louisville, Kentucky

Bridgewater College, Bridgewater, Virginia

Brigham Young University, Provo, Utah

Cabrini College, Radnor, Pennsylvania

California Lutheran College, Thousand Oaks, California

Catholic University of America, Washington, D. C.

College of the Holy Cross, Worcester, Massachusetts

College of St. Joseph on the Rio Grande, Albuquerque, New Mexico

Concordia Teachers College, Seward, Nebraska

Covenant College, St. Louis, Missouri (now Lookout Mountain, Tennessee)

Culver-Stockton College, Canton, Missouri

Doane College, Crete, Nebraska

East Texas Baptist College, Marshall, Texas

Fisk University, Nashville, Tennessee

Florida Memorial College, St. Augustine, Florida

Furman University, Greenville, South Carolina

Hamline University, St. Paul, Minnesota

Hannibal-LaGrange College, Hannibal, Missouri

Haverford College, Haverford, Pennsylvania

Heidelberg College, Tiffin, Ohio

Hesston College, Hesston, Kansas

Iowa Wesleyan College, Mount Pleasant, Iowa

Kalamazoo College, Kalamazoo, Michigan

Loretto Junior College, Nerinx, Kentucky

Manhattanville College of the Sacred Heart, Purchase, New York

Marquette University, Milwaukee, Wisconsin

Morris Brown College, Atlanta, Georgia

Occidental College, Los Angeles, California

Oklahoma Christian College, Oklahoma City, Oklahoma

Parsons College, Fairfield, Iowa

Principia College, Elsah, Illinois

Roanoke College, Salem, Virginia

Rocky Mountain College, Billings, Montana

Rosary College, River Forest, Illinois

217

St. Andrews Presbyterian College, Laurinburg, North Carolina
St. Francis College, Biddeford, Maine
St. John's University, Collegeville, Minnesota
Texas Christian University, Fort Worth, Texas
University of Dallas, Dallas, Texas

Wesley College, Dover, Delaware
Westminster College, Salt Lake City, Utah
Wheaton College, Wheaton, Illinois
Willamette College, Salem, Oregon
Wittenberg University, Springfield, Ohio
Yeshiva University, New York, New York

C

Procedure
for
Institutional
Self-Study

One of the more fruitful movements in higher education since World War II has been that of institutional self-study. With encouragement from foundations, accrediting agencies, the American Association of University Professors, and others, more and more institutions have come to see the value of subjecting their own programs to periodic scrutiny, of developing their plans on the basis of systematic and critical analysis. For many institutions such studies have provided the leverage for significant improvement. An important value in this approach to the solution of educational problems is that, properly organized, it yields not only better answers to questions but also, as a result of the process itself, motivation to act upon the findings.

Many colleges have been handicapped in undertaking self-study by not knowing how to compile relevant data. The following questionnaire, which was used in the case studies described earlier in this report, may be suggestive to institutions that are planning analyses of their programs. These forms were originally prepared for a survey of private colleges in Indiana, conducted by Norman Burns and Manning M. Pattillo, Jr., for Lilly Endowment. Portions of them were subsequently adopted by the North Central Association of Colleges and Secondary Schools and by others engaged in institutional evaluation. When the Danforth study was being planned, the questionnaire was revised for use especially with church-affiliated institutions.

As was emphasized in Chapter 4, institutional data are not self-interpretive. They must be interpreted in the light of criteria, such as those outlined in that chapter. The forms merely provide a convenient means for gathering factual material on some of the questions that many colleges face. They can be adapted to the special requirements of particular studies.

(The forms have been compressed here in order to save space.)

SURVEY FORMS

ENROLLMENT DATA   REGISTRAR

1. How many students are currently enrolled in your institution?

	Freshmen	Sophomores	Juniors	Seniors	Graduate Students	Total
Full-time students						
Part-time students						

2. Does your institution conduct a summer session? If so, how many students were enrolled last summer?

3. What was your enrollment of full-time students in each of the following years:
   1940-41 ....;   1950-51 ....;   1960-61 ....?

4. From which states and foreign countries have you drawn students in the present academic year? How many students from each state and country?

5. How many students in the present academic year came from an area within 25 miles of the institution?

6. What other colleges are located within 25 miles?

7. Which churches or denominations are most heavily represented in your student body?

8. What curricula and majors are offered, leading to a certificate, diploma, or degree, and how many students are enrolled in each?

Certificate, Diploma or Degree	Curriculum or Major Leading to Certificate, Diploma, or Degree	Current Enrollment in Curriculum or Major
(Example: Bachelor of Arts	History	15)

9. What is the distribution of classes by size during the current term?

Size of Classes	Number of Classes of this Size
Under 5 students	
5–10 students	
11–25 students	
26–50 students	
51–100 students	
Over 100 students	

STUDENT DATA   DIRECTOR OF ADMISSIONS

10. If you have exact information about the academic quality of your entering students in comparison with the quality of students in other colleges
and universities, please summarize the data here. (College Entrance
Examination Board scores, American College Testing Program scores,
etc.)

DEAN OF STUDENTS

11. What is the social and economic background of your students, considered as a group? (Urban, suburban, small-town, rural; ethnic factors; professional, business, farm families; homogeneous or heterogeneous, etc.)

Have you made any systematic studies of the backgrounds of your students? (Please attach copies of any reports available.)

12. From your knowledge of the students or from formal studies made of
them, what can be said about the religious and other values of your
entering students? (Please attach copies of any reports available.)

STUDENT ACHIEVEMENT DATA   DEAN OR ACADEMIC
                                             VICE-PRESIDENT

13. What information do you have on the academic achievement of your
students in comparison with the achievement of students in other colleges and universities? (Graduate Record Examination, graduate and
professional school records, competitive fellowships, etc.)

LIBRARY DATA   LIBRARIAN

14. What has been the trend in library expenditures at your institution?

Purpose	1940–41	1950–51	1960–61	Last Completed Fiscal Year
Library materials, including books, periodicals, binding				
Salaries of library personnel, including student assistants				
Library supplies and equipment, excluding operation and care of building				

15. How large is your library staff?

Professionals........................
Clerical helpers........................
Student assistants........................

16. What is the total number of books in the library? ....
How many periodicals are regularly received? ....

FINANCIAL DATA   BUSINESS OFFICER

17. What were the major sources of current income of your institution for the last completed fiscal year? Please indicate amounts received from the following:

Student fees $........................
Government $........................
Endowment income $........................
Gifts and grants (church) $........................
Gifts and grants (other) $........................
    Total current income $........................

18. What was the total amount of current income in 1940–41? $........................
1950–51? $........................
1960–61? $........................

19. What is the total amount of capital funds received in the last five completed fiscal years? .... How much of this was provided by the church? ....

20. What was the amount of indebtedness at the end of each of the following fiscal years?

Fiscal Year	Total Amount Owed to Outside Parties	Reason for Which Debt Incurred	Amount Owed to Federal Government
1950–51 1960–61 Last completed fiscal year			

21. If the institution has made significant additions to its physical plant in the last ten years, what were these additions? What was the cost of each? What were the sources of the funds?

22. If the institution has plans for the construction of any new buildings in

the next five years, what buildings are planned? What are the estimated costs? What are the anticipated sources of funds?

23. What are the present ranges of salaries for full-time faculty members by rank?

RANK	SALARIES		
	Mean	Highest	Lowest
Instructor			
Assistant Professor			
Associate Professor			
Professor			

These salaries are for .... months of service.
The mean salary for the entire faculty is $............................ .

INSTITUTIONAL PURPOSES AND POLICIES   TRUSTEES

24. What do you see as the special role or distinctive place of your institution in higher education?

25. What are the most pressing problems the board faces at the present time?

26. How do you, as an individual trustee, define your responsibility to the institution?

27. In what respects do you feel your institution is especially strong, and in what respects does it need further development?

28. What is your view of the proper relationship between an institution of higher education and a church with which it is associated?

GENERAL ADMINISTRATION   PRESIDENT

29. What are the most pressing problems you face at the present time?

30. What do you see as the special role or distinctive place of your institution in higher education?

31. What plans do you have for the long-range development of the institution? (Scope and character of educational program, size and type of student body, faculty, plant, financial support, etc.)

32. What is the precise relationship of your institution to the church (or religious order or congregation)?

Board composition
Church ownership

Financial support
Subscription to church standards
or use of church name
Educational aim
Selection of personnel
Other

33. What are the major contributions of the institution to the church and to religion generally? What are you trying to accomplish religiously? (Training of committed laymen, instruction in religion as one of the fields of knowledge, provision of religious activities for students interested, preparation for church vocations, research and other services for the church, etc.)

34. What strength or values does the institution derive from its association with the church (or religious order or congregation)?

35. What problems, if any, are there in connection with your religious affiliation?

36. What is the religious complexion of the faculty? (Planned, unplanned, heterogeneous, all or mostly members of one religious body, proportion of clergy, nuns, and laymen, etc.)

37. What would you regard as an ideal relationship between a college or university and a religious body and an ideal religious program for this institution?

38. In what respects would you like particularly to see your institution stronger, and in what respects do you feel that it is already quite strong?

39. How are members of the board of trustees elected?

40. What is the present composition of the Board?

Name of Board Member	Address (City and State)	Occupation	Term of Office

41. What are the policies governing invitations to outside speakers?

42. What other colleges and universities are under the same religious sponsorship as yours? Synod, diocese, religious order, or congregation, etc.) Do you have an assigned geographical area for fund-raising?

ACADEMIC ADMINISTRATION

DEAN OR ACADEMIC VICE-PRESIDENT

43. What are the requirements which all students (regardless of field of specialization) must meet in order to graduate from your institution?

44. What curricular features or devices do you feel distinguish your institution from others? Have you developed any special programs or emphases? Have there been any recent innovations or significant changes in curriculum that should be noted? Has your institution been particularly successful in its use of any special methods, such as comprehensive examinations, tutorials, independent study plan, honors program, study abroad, integrative courses, or senior seminars or papers?

45. In what specific ways is the religious character of the institution reflected in its academic program?

46. What level of academic preparation is possessed by full-time members of the faculty?

RANK	TOTAL NUMBER	NUMBER WHOSE HIGHEST DEGREE IS				
		Doctor's	Master's	Professional Bachelor's	First Bachelor's	Other
Professor						
Associate Professor						
Assistant Professor						
Instructor						
Other						

(If not shown in catalogue, what are the institutions from which degrees received?)

47. What is the normal teaching load of full-time faculty members in semester (quarter) hours? ....

48. Have any members of the faculty completed significant scholarly projects or received academic honors in the last three years? (E.g., authorship of books, membership on important committees outside the institution, distinguished lectureships.)

49. What do you consider the most notable strengths of your faculty? Weaknesses?

50. In what respects is the religious character of your institution an asset or a liability in attracting and retaining able faculty persons?

51. What are the principal means employed by your institution to stimulate the professional growth and scholarly refreshment of the faculty? (Sab-

batical leaves, financial assistance for graduate study, research assistance, travel grants, etc.) How much money is budgeted for such purposes this year?

52. What limitations does your institution place on freedom of teaching? Are there, for example, limitations on the political, economic, religious, or moral doctrines that may be taught or the manner in which controversial questions may be handled?

53. What has been the average turnover per year in your faculty in the last three years?

54. What is the procedure by which new faculty members are selected and appointed? What type of person are you seeking for your faculty?

55. What are the policies governing tenure for members of the faculty?

56. What are the provisions of your faculty retirement plan?

57. What is the approximate age distribution of the faculty?

> 20's................................%
> 30's................................%
> 40's................................%
> 50's................................%
> 60's................................%

58. Has your institution made any systematic studies of the occupations of its graduates and of their success in vocational, professional, religious, civic, and other respects after the completion of their formal education? (Obtain copies, if possible.) Please summarize findings.

FACULTY   FACULTY MEMBERS

59. What are the advantages and disadvantages of teaching in an institution which is associated with a church (or religious order or congregation)?

60. From your observation of individual students, what impact do you think this institution has on its students (undergraduates)? In what ways do they seem to change?

STUDENTS   DIRECTOR OF ADMISSIONS

61. Are the admission requirements, as stated in your current catalogue, an accurate description of the bases on which you are actually admitting students? If not, what stated requirements are not being currently enforced and what unstated criteria are being employed for admission purposes?

62. Does the institution place any limitation on the size of its student body or on the number of students that will be admitted to the Freshman class or to any division or curriculum?

63. In your opinion, what features or characteristics of your institution are the chief attractions for students?

64. What features or characteristics of the institution handicap you in the recruitment of the type of students you want?

65. What institutions "compete" most directly with yours for students?

66. What percentage of the applicants who met your formal requirements for admission last fall were admitted?

67. If the church with which your institution is associated maintains secondary schools, what percentage of your entering students are graduates of such schools? ....

68. Under the terms of its church relationship, does your institution have an assigned territory for student recruitment?

REGISTRAR

69. If you have made any studies of student attrition, what have been found to be the principal reasons for withdrawal of students from your institution? (Obtain copies of reports, if possible.)

LIBRARY   LIBRARIAN

70. In what fields are the greatest demands made on the library by faculty and students? What special studies, if any, have been made of library use?

71. Are there features of the curriculum that seem to encourage greater use of the library? (Honors programs, independent study, etc.)

72. In what areas, as you see it, is the library strongest in its holdings? Weakest?

73. Are there any types of reading materials which the library, as a matter of institutional policy, does not purchase or does not make freely available to students? (E.g., books considered objectionable on philosophical, political, economic, religious, or moral grounds.)

STUDENT LIFE   DEAN OF STUDENTS

74. Which are the strongest extra-curricular activities on the campus?

75. Have any studies been made of the effect of the college experience on the values, outlook, etc. of your students during their undergraduate years? (Obtain copies, if possible.) In general, what do these show?

76. To what extent, in your judgment, is religion a vital force on the campus? How does this show up in the daily lives of the students?

77. Do you have a formal religious program for students (apart from courses in religion)? In your judgment, how successful is this? Which aspects of the program seem most effective? What is the student attitude toward the program? The faculty attitude?

78. What are the major personal problems of your students, as they show up in counseling sessions, disciplinary cases, informal discussions, etc.?

79. From your observation, what are the things in which your students are most deeply interested? (Social activities, marriage, discussion of controversial issues, career preparation, the arts, athletics, public affairs, etc.)

80. How well acquainted is your staff with individual students, apart from problem cases? In your opinion, how well do faculty members know individual students as persons? (Evidence?)

81. What role do your students play in the determination of institutional policy or the government of student affairs? (Obtain published statements, if possible.)

82. What percentage of your students live in buildings operated by the institution?................. In fraternity and sorority houses?................. In off-campus rooming and boarding houses?................. At home?.................

83. Which of the following classes of students are given preference in the awarding of scholarships, the remission of fees, or the granting of other types of financial aid?

Children of staff members ....

Children of ministers ....

Athletes ....

High-ranking students, regardless of need ....

Needy students, regardless of academic record ....

Others ....

84. What opportunities are provided for your students in the way of visiting lecturers, musical events, dramatic performances, and similar activities? (Obtain copies of announcements, if possible.)

85. What provisions do you make for safeguarding the health of your students?

STUDENT OPINION   STUDENTS

86. What attracted you to this particular college?

87. In what respects do you feel that this institution does a good job? How might it be improved?

88. What is your appraisal of its religious program?

89. How well do you know your instructors?

90. What do you plan to do after graduation?

91. How has this institution influenced your attitude, interests, outlook? As you look back on your development while a student here, what specific changes in yourself can you see?

RELIGION   CHAPLAIN, CHAIRMAN OF DEPARTMENT OF RELIGION

92. Would you kindly outline the religious program of this institution? (Courses, chapel, graduation requirements, clubs, sodalities, study groups, retreats, lectures, service organizations, counseling, publications, choir, conferences, religious emphasis week, evangelistic efforts, etc.) What evidence have you on the effectiveness of the program?

93. What is the total number of staff persons involved in the religious program? .... What qualifications do you look for in making staff appointments?

94. How much money has been budgeted for the support of the religious program this year (other than salaries)? ....

95. What seem to be the attitudes of the administration, the faculty, the students, toward the program?

96. How well prepared religiously are your entering students?

FINANCIAL DEVELOPMENT   DEVELOPMENT OFFICER

97. What problems do you encounter in presenting this institution to its constituency?

98. What are the supporting groups, and what is their "image" of the institution?

PHYSICAL PLANT   STAFF APPRAISAL

99. Adequacy of present plant (classrooms, laboratories, dormitories, offices, general units) and site (suitability, possibility of future expansion).

100. Maintenance of plant and campus.

American Colleges
and Universities
Associated with
Religious Bodies

The types of relationship that exist between each institution and the religious body with which it is associated are indicated as follows:

1. Board of control includes members of church and/or members nominated and/or elected by church body.
2. Ownership of the institution by the religious body.
3. Financial support by the religious body.
4. Acceptance by the institution of denominational standards or use of the denominational name.
5. Institutional statement of purpose linked to a particular denomination or reflecting religious orientation.
6. Church membership a factor in selection of faculty and administrative personnel.

The following institutions reported the listed types of association as of 1963:

Institution	Types of Association
Abilene Christian College, Abilene, Texas	1, 5, 6
Academy of the New Church, Bryn Athyn, Pennsylvania	1, 5, 6
Adrian College, Adrian, Michigan	1, 3, 5, 6
Agnes Scott College, Decatur, Georgia	1, 4, 5
Alaska Methodist University, Anchorage, Alaska	1, 2, 3, 4, 5
Albertus Magnus College, New Haven, Connecticut	1, 2, 3, 4, 5, 6
Albion College, Albion, Michigan	4, 5, 6
Albright College, Reading, Pennsylvania	1, 3, 4, 5, 6
Alderson-Broaddus College, Philippi, West Virginia	1, 3, 4, 5, 6
Allegheny College, Meadville, Pennsylvania	1, 3, 4, 5
Allen University, Columbia, South Carolina	1, 2, 3, 4, 5, 6
Alma College, Alma, Michigan	1, 3, 4, 5
Alma White College, Zarephath, New Jersey	2, 3, 4, 5, 6
Alvernia College, Reading, Pennsylvania	2, 5, 6
Alverno College, Milwaukee, Wisconsin	1, 2, 5, 6

230

Institution	Types of Association
American University, Washington, D.C.	1, 2, 3, 4, 5
Anderson College, Anderson, South Carolina	1, 2, 3, 4, 5, 6
Anderson College and Theological Seminary, Anderson, Indiana	1, 2, 3, 4, 5, 6
Andrew College, Cuthbert, Georgia	2, 3, 4, 5
Andrews University, Berrien Springs, Michigan	1, 2, 3, 4, 5, 6
Anna Maria College for Women, Paxton, Massachusetts	1, 2, 3, 4, 5, 6
Annhurst College, South Woodstock, Connecticut	2, 4, 5
Aquinas College, Grand Rapids, Michigan	2, 3, 4, 5, 6
Arkansas College, Batesville, Arkansas	1, 2, 3, 4, 5, 6
Ashland College, Ashland, Ohio	1, 3, 5, 6
Assumption College, Worcester, Massachusetts	1, 2, 4, 5
Assumption College, Richardton, North Dakota	1, 2, 5, 6
Assumption College for Sisters, Mendham, New Jersey	1, 2, 3, 4, 5, 6
Athenaeum of Ohio, Cincinnati, Ohio	2, 3, 4, 5, 6
Athens College, Athens, Alabama	1, 2, 3, 4, 5, 6
Atlantic Christian College, Wilson, North Carolina	1, 3, 4, 5
Atlantic Union College, South Lancaster, Massachusetts	1, 2, 3, 4, 5, 6
Augsburg College, Minneapolis, Minnesota	1, 2, 3, 5, 6
Augustana College, Rock Island, Illinois	1, 2, 3, 4, 5, 6
Augustana College, Sioux Falls, South Dakota	1, 2, 3, 4, 5, 6
Aurora College, Aurora, Illinois	1, 5, 6
Austin College, Sherman, Texas	1, 2, 3, 4, 5, 6
Averett College, Danville, Virginia	3, 4
Avila College, Kansas City, Missouri	1, 2, 5
Bacone College, Bacone, Oklahoma	1, 3, 4, 5, 6
Baker University, Baldwin City, Kansas	1, 3, 4, 5, 6
Baldwin-Wallace College, Berea, Ohio	1, 3, 4, 5, 6
Barat College of the Sacred Heart, Lake Forest, Illinois	2, 5, 6
Barber-Scotia College, Concord, North Carolina	1, 2, 3, 4, 5
Bard College, Annandale-on-Hudson, New York	3, 4
Barry College, Miami, Florida	1, 2, 4, 5, 6
Bates College, Lewiston, Maine	4
Baylor University, Waco, Texas	1, 2, 3, 4, 5, 6
Beaver College, Glenside, Pennsylvania	1, 3, 4, 5, 6
Belhaven College, Jackson, Mississippi	1, 2, 3, 4, 5, 6
Bellarmine College, Louisville, Kentucky	1, 2, 3, 4, 5, 6
Bellarmine College, Plattsburgh, New York	1, 2, 3, 4, 5, 6
Belmont Abbey College, Belmont, North Carolina	1, 2, 5
Belmont College, Nashville, Tennessee	1, 2, 3, 4, 5, 6
Beloit College, Beloit, Wisconsin	4, 5
Benedict College, Columbia, South Carolina	1, 3, 4, 5
Benedictine Heights College, Tulsa, Oklahoma	1, 2, 3, 4, 5, 6
Bennett College, Greensboro, North Carolina	1, 3, 4, 5, 6
Bethany College, Lindsborg, Kansas	1, 2, 3, 4, 5, 6
Bethany College, Bethany, West Virginia	4, 5, 6
Bethany Lutheran College and Theological Seminary, Mankato, Minnesota	1, 2, 3, 4, 5, 6
Bethany-Nazarene College, Bethany, Oklahoma	1, 2, 3, 4, 5, 6

Institution	Types of Association
Bethel College, North Newton, Kansas	1, 5, 6
Bethel College, Hopkinsville, Kentucky	1, 2, 3, 4, 5, 6
Bethel College, McKenzie, Tennessee	1, 2, 3, 4, 5
Bethel College, Inc., Mishawaka, Indiana	1, 2, 3, 4, 5, 6
Bethel College and Seminary, St. Paul, Minnesota	1, 2, 3, 4, 5, 6
Bethune-Cookman College, Daytona Beach, Florida	1, 2, 3, 4, 5, 6
Birmingham-Southern College, Birmingham, Alabama	1, 2, 3, 5
Bishop College, Dallas, Texas	1, 3, 4, 5, 6
Blackburn College, Carlinville, Illinois	1, 3, 4, 5
Blessed Sacrament College, Cornwells Heights, Pennsylvania	1, 2, 3, 4, 5, 6
Bloomfield College, Bloomfield, New Jersey	1, 2, 3, 4, 5, 6
Blue Mountain College, Blue Mountain, Mississippi	1, 2, 3, 4, 5, 6
Bluefield College, Bluefield, Virginia	1, 2, 3, 4, 5, 6
Bluffton College, Bluffton, Ohio	1, 3, 4, 5, 6
Borromeo Seminary of Ohio, Wickliffe, Ohio	1, 2, 3, 4, 5, 6
Boston College, Chestnut Hill, Massachusetts	1, 2, 4, 5, 6
Boston University, Boston, Massachusetts	3, 4, 5
Brentwood College, Brentwood, Long Island, New York	1, 2, 3, 4, 5, 6
Brescia College, Owensboro, Kentucky	2, 5, 6
Brevard College, Brevard, North Carolina	2, 3, 5, 6
Briar Cliff College, Sioux City, Iowa	1, 2, 4, 5, 6
Bridgewater College, Bridgewater, Virginia	1, 2, 3, 4, 5, 6
Brigham Young University, Provo, Utah	1, 2, 3, 4, 5, 6
Buena Vista College, Storm Lake, Iowa	1, 3, 4, 5, 6
Buffalo Diocesan Preparatory Seminary, Buffalo, New York	1, 2, 4, 5, 6
Butler University, Indianapolis, Indiana	4, 5
Cabrini College, Radnor, Pennsylvania,	1, 2, 4, 5, 6
Caldwell College for Women, Caldwell, New Jersey	1, 2, 4, 5, 6
California Baptist College, Riverside, California	1, 3, 4, 5, 6
California Concordia College, Oakland, California	1, 2, 3, 4, 5, 6
California Lutheran College, Thousand Oaks, California	2, 4, 5, 6
California Western University, San Diego, California	1, 3, 4, 5
Calvin College, Grand Rapids, Michigan	1, 2, 3, 4, 5, 6
Campbell College, Buies Creek, North Carolina	1, 2, 3, 4, 5, 6
Campbellsville College, Campbellsville, Kentucky	1, 3, 4, 5, 6
Canisius College, Buffalo, New York	1, 2, 4, 5, 6
Capital University, Columbus, Ohio	1, 2, 3, 4, 5, 6
Capuchin Seminary of St. Mary, Crown Point, Indiana	1, 2, 3, 4, 5, 6
Cardinal Cushing College, Brookline, Massachusetts	1, 2, 4, 5
Cardinal Glennon College, St. Louis, Missouri	1, 2, 3, 4, 5, 6
Cardinal Stritch College, Milwaukee, Wisconsin	1, 2, 3, 5, 6
Carroll College, Helena, Montana	2, 4, 5, 6
Carroll College, Waukesha, Wisconsin	1, 3, 4, 5
Carson-Newman College, Jefferson City, Tennessee	1, 2, 3, 5, 6
Carthage College, Carthage, Illinois (now Kenosha, Wisconsin)	1, 2, 3
Catawba College, Salisbury, North Carolina	1, 3, 4, 5
Cathedral College of the Immaculate Conception, Brooklyn, New York	1, 2, 3, 4, 5, 6
Catherine McAuley College, Rochester, New York	1, 2, 5, 6

Institution	Types of Association
Catherine Spalding College, Louisville, Kentucky	2, 5
Catholic Teachers College, Providence, Rhode Island	1, 2, 3, 4, 5
Catholic University of America, Washington, D.C.	1, 2, 3, 4, 5
Cedar Crest College, Allentown, Pennsylvania	1, 3, 4, 5
Centenary College, Shreveport, Louisiana	1, 2, 3, 4, 5, 6
Centenary College for Women, Hackettstown, New Jersey	1, 3, 4, 5, 6
Central College, Pella, Iowa	1, 2, 3, 5
Central College, McPherson, Kansas	1, 4, 5
Central Methodist College, Fayette, Missouri	1, 3, 4, 5
Central Wesleyan College, Central, South Carolina	1, 2, 4, 5, 6
Centre College of Kentucky, Danville, Kentucky	1, 3, 4, 5
Chaminade College of Honolulu, Honolulu, Hawaii	1, 2, 4, 5, 6
Chapman College, Orange, California	1, 3, 4, 5
Chestnut Hill College, Philadelphia, Pennsylvania	1, 4, 5, 6
Chowan College, Murfreesboro, North Carolina	1, 2, 3, 4, 5, 6
Christ the Savior Seminary, Johnstown, Pennsylvania	1, 2, 3, 5, 6
Christian Brothers College, Memphis, Tennessee	1, 2, 5, 6
Christian College, Columbia, Missouri	3, 4
Church College of Hawaii, Laie, Oahu, Hawaii	1, 2, 3, 4, 5, 6
Claflin College, Orangeburg, South Orange	1, 2, 3, 4, 5
Clark College, Atlanta, Georgia	1, 3, 4, 5, 6
Clarke College, Dubuque, Iowa	1, 2, 4, 5, 6
Clarke Memorial College, Newton, Mississippi	1, 2, 3, 4, 5, 6
Coe College, Cedar Rapids, Iowa	3, 4, 5
College Misericordia, Dallas, Pennsylvania	1, 2, 4, 5, 6
College of Emporia, Emporia, Kansas	1, 2, 3, 4, 5, 6
College of Great Falls, Great Falls, Montana	1, 2, 4, 5, 6
College of Idaho, Caldwell, Idaho	1, 3, 4, 5, 6
College of Mount St. Joseph-On-The-Ohio, Mount St. Joseph, Ohio	2, 5
College of Mount St. Vincent, New York, New York	1, 5
College of New Rochelle, New Rochelle, New York	1, 2, 4, 5, 6
College of Notre Dame, Belmont, California	1, 2, 5
College of Notre Dame of Maryland, Baltimore, Maryland	2, 5, 6
College of Our Lady of Mercy, Burlingame, California	1, 2, 5, 6
College of Our Lady of the Elms, Chicopee, Massachusetts	1, 2
College of St. Benedict, St. Joseph, Minnesota	1, 3, 4, 5, 6
College of St. Catherine, St. Paul, Minnesota	1, 2, 4, 5
College of St. Elizabeth, Convent Station, New Jersey	1, 2, 3, 4, 5, 6
College of St. Francis, Joliet, Illinois	2, 4, 5, 6
College of St. Gertrude, Cottonwood, Idaho	1, 2, 3, 4, 5, 6
College of St. Joseph on the Rio Grande, Albuquerque, New Mexico	1, 2, 4, 5, 6
College of Saint Mary, Omaha, Nebraska	1, 2, 4, 5, 6
College of St. Mary of the Springs, Columbus, Ohio	1, 2, 4, 5, 6
College of Saint Rose, Albany, New York	1, 2, 4, 5, 6
College of St. Scholastica, Duluth, Minnesota	2, 5, 6
College of St. Teresa, Winona, Minnesota	1, 2, 4, 5, 6

Institution	Types of Association
College of St. Thomas, St. Paul, Minnesota	2, 3, 5
College of Steubenville, Steubenville, Ohio	1
College of the Holy Cross, Worcester, Massachusetts	1, 2, 4, 5, 6
College of the Holy Names, Oakland, California	1, 2, 5
College of the Holy Names, Albany, New York	2, 5, 6
College of the Ozarks, Clarksville, Arkansas	1, 2, 3, 4, 5, 6
College of Wooster, Wooster, Ohio	1, 3, 4, 5, 6
Colorado Woman's College, Denver, Colorado	1, 3, 4, 5
Columbia College, Columbia, South Carolina	1, 2, 3, 4, 5, 6
Columbia Union College, Takoma Park, Maryland	1, 2, 3, 4, 5, 6
Concordia College, Moorhead, Minnesota	1, 2, 3, 4, 5, 6
Concordia College, St. Paul, Minnesota	1, 2, 3, 4, 5, 6
Concordia College, Portland, Oregon	1, 2, 3, 4, 5, 6
Concordia College, Milwaukee, Wisconsin	1, 2, 3, 4, 5, 6
Concordia Junior College, Bronxville, New York	1, 2, 3, 4, 5, 6
Concordia Senior College, Fort Wayne, Indiana	1, 2, 3, 4, 5, 6
Concordia Teachers College, River Forest, Illinois	1, 2, 3, 4, 5, 6
Concordia Teachers College, Seward, Nebraska	1, 2, 3, 4, 5, 6
Cornell College, Mount Vernon, Iowa	1, 3, 4
Covenant College, St. Louis, Missouri (now Lookout Mountain, Tennessee)	1, 3, 4, 5, 6
Creighton University, Omaha, Nebraska	1, 4, 5, 6
Crosier Seminary, Onamia, Minnesota	1, 2, 4, 5, 6
Culver-Stockton College, Canton, Missouri	1, 3, 4, 5, 6
Cumberland College, Williamsburg, Kentucky	1, 2, 3, 4, 5, 6
Dakota Wesleyan University, Mitchell, South Dakota	2, 3, 4, 5, 6
Dana College, Blair, Nebraska	1, 3, 4, 5, 6
Daniel Payne College, Birmingham, Alabama	1, 2, 3, 4, 5
David Lipscomb College, Nashville, Tennessee	1, 5, 6
Davidson College, Davidson, North Carolina	1, 3, 4, 5, 6
Davis and Elkins College, Elkins, West Virginia	1, 3, 4, 5, 6
Decatur Baptist College, Decatur, Texas	1, 2, 3, 4, 5, 6
Defiance College, Defiance, Ohio	1, 3, 4, 5, 6
De Lima Junior College, Oxford, Michigan	1, 2, 4, 5, 6
De Lourdes College, Des Plaines, Illinois	1, 2, 3, 4, 5, 6
Denison University, Granville, Ohio	1, 3, 4, 5
DePaul University, Chicago, Illinois	1, 2, 5, 6
DePauw University, Greencastle, Indiana	1, 3, 4, 5
Dickinson College, Carlisle, Pennsylvania	3, 4, 5
Dillard University, New Orleans, Louisiana	3, 4, 5
Divine Word Seminary, Conesus, New York	1, 2, 4, 5, 6
Doane College, Crete, Nebraska	1, 3, 4, 5
Dominican College, Racine, Wisconsin	1, 2, 4, 5
Dominican College of Blauvelt, Blauvelt, New York	1, 2, 5
Dominican College of San Rafael, San Rafael, California	1, 2, 4, 5
Don Bosco College, Newton, New Jersey	1, 2, 3, 4, 5, 6
Donnelly College, Kansas City, Kansas	1, 3, 5, 6
Dordt College, Sioux Center, Iowa	1, 2, 3, 4, 5, 6
Drake University, Des Moines, Iowa	3, 4

Institution	Types of Association
Drew University, Madison, New Jersey	1, 3, 4, 5
Drury College, Springfield, Missouri	3, 4, 5, 6
Duchesne College of the Sacred Heart, Omaha, Nebraska	1, 2, 4, 5, 6
Duke University, Durham, North Carolina	1, 3, 4
Dunbarton College of Holy Cross, Washington, D.C.	1, 2, 5
Duns Scotus College, Southfield, Michigan	2, 3, 4, 5, 6
Duquesne University, Pittsburgh, Pennsylvania	1, 2, 4, 5
D'Youville College, Buffalo, New York	1, 2, 4, 5
Earlham College, Richmond, Indiana	1, 3, 4, 5
East Texas Baptist College, Marshall, Texas	1, 2, 3, 4, 5, 6
Eastern Baptist College, St. Davids, Pennsylvania	1, 3, 4, 5, 6
Eastern Mennonite College, Harrisonburg, Virginia	1, 2, 3, 4, 5, 6
Eastern Nazarene College, Wollaston, Massachusetts	1 3, 5, 6
Edgewood College of the Sacred Heart, Madison, Wisconsin	2, 4, 5, 6
Edward Waters College, Jacksonville, Florida	1, 2, 3, 4
Elizabeth Seton College, Yonkers, New York	1, 2, 4, 5, 6
Elizabethtown College, Elizabethtown, Pennsylvania	1, 2, 3, 4, 5
Elmhurst College, Elmhurst, Illinois	1, 3, 4, 5, 6
Elon College, Elon College, North Carolina	1, 2, 3, 4, 5
Emmanuel College, Franklin Springs, Georgia	1, 2, 3, 4, 5, 6
Emmanuel College, Boston, Massachusetts	2, 4, 5, 6
Emory and Henry College, Emory, Virginia	1, 3, 4, 5, 6
Emory University, Atlanta, Georgia	1, 2, 4, 5
Epiphany Apostolic College, Newburgh, New York	1, 2, 3, 4, 5, 6
Erskine College, Due West, South Carolina	1, 2, 3, 4, 5, 6
Eureka College, Eureka, Illinois	3, 4, 5, 6
Evangel College, Springfield, Missouri	1, 2, 3, 4, 5, 6
Evansville College, Evansville, Indiana	1, 3, 5
Eymard Preparatory Seminary, Hyde Park, New York	1, 2, 3, 4, 5, 6
Fairfield University, Fairfield, Connecticut	1, 2, 5, 6
Felician College, Chicago, Illinois	1, 2, 3, 4, 5, 6
Ferrum Junior College, Ferrum, Virginia	1, 2, 3, 4, 5, 6
Findlay College, Findlay, Ohio	1, 3, 5
Fisk University, Nashville, Tennessee	1, 3, 4
Florida Christian College, Temple Terrace, Florida	1, 5, 6
Florida Memorial College, St. Augustine, Florida	1, 3, 4, 5, 6
Florida Southern College, Lakeland, Florida	1, 2, 3, 4, 5, 6
Fontbonne College, St. Louis, Missouri	1, 2, 5, 6
Fordham University, New York, New York	1, 2, 4, 5
Fort Wayne Bible College, Fort Wayne, Indiana	1, 2, 3, 4, 5
Franklin College of Indiana, Franklin, Indiana	1, 3, 4, 5
Franklin and Marshall College, Lancaster, Pennsylvania	1, 3, 4, 5
Freed-Hardeman College, Henderson, Tennessee	1, 5, 6
Freeman Junior College, Freeman, South Dakota	1, 4, 5, 6
Friends University, Wichita, Kansas	1, 2, 3, 4, 5, 6
Furman University, Greenville, South Carolina	1, 2, 3, 4, 5, 6
Gannon College, Erie, Pennsylvania	2, 3, 4, 5
Gardner-Webb Junior College, Boiling Springs, North Carolina	1, 2, 3, 4, 5, 6

Institution	Types of Association
Geneva College, Beaver Falls, Pennsylvania	1, 2, 3, 4, 5, 6
George Fox College, Newberg, Oregon	1, 2, 3, 4, 5, 6
Georgetown College, Georgetown, Kentucky	1, 2, 3, 4, 5, 6
Georgetown University, Washington, D.C.	2, 4, 5
Georgetown Visitation Junior College, Washington, D.C.	1, 2, 5, 6
Georgian Court College, Lakewood, New Jersey	1, 2, 5
Gettysburg College, Gettysburg, Pennsylvania	1, 3, 4, 5, 6
Gonzaga University, Spokane, Washington	1, 2, 5, 6
Good Counsel College, White Plains, New York	1, 2, 5, 6
Goshen College, Goshen, Indiana	1, 2, 3, 4, 5, 6
Grace Theological Seminary and Grace College, Winona Lake, Indiana	1, 3, 4, 5, 6
Graceland College, Lamoni, Iowa	1, 2, 3, 5, 6
Grand Canyon College, Phoenix, Arizona	1, 2, 3, 4, 5, 6
Grand View College, Des Moines, Iowa	1, 4, 5
Green Mountain College, Poultney, Vermont	1, 3, 5, 6
Greensboro College, Greensboro, North Carolina	1, 2, 3, 4, 5, 6
Greenville College, Greenville, Illinois	1, 3, 4, 5, 6
Grinnell College, Grinnell, Iowa	3, 4
Grove City College, Grove City, Pennsylvania	3, 4, 5, 6
Guilford College, Guilford College, North Carolina	1, 3, 5, 6
Gustavus Adolphus College, St. Peter, Minnesota	1, 2, 3, 5, 6
Gwynedd-Mercy College, Gwynedd Valley, Pennsylvania	1, 2, 5, 6
Hamline University, St. Paul, Minnesota	1, 3, 4, 5
Hampden-Sydney College, Hampden-Sydney, Virginia	1, 3, 5
Hannibal-LaGrange College, Hannibal, Missouri	1, 2, 3, 4, 5, 6
Hanover College, Hanover, Indiana	1, 3, 4, 5, 6
Hardin-Simmons University, Abilene, Texas	1, 2, 3, 4, 5, 6
Harding College, Searcy, Arkansas	1, 5, 6
Hartwick College, Oneonta, New York	1, 3, 4, 5
Hastings College, Hastings, Nebraska	1, 3, 4, 5, 6
Haverford College, Haverford, Pennsylvania	1, 5
Hebrew Union College, Cincinnati, Ohio	3, 5
Heidelberg College, Tiffin, Ohio	1, 3, 4, 5
Hendrix College, Conway, Arkansas	1, 2, 3, 4, 5, 6
Hesston College, Hesston, Kansas	1, 2, 3, 4, 5, 6
High Point College, High Point, North Carolina	1, 2, 3, 4, 5, 6
Hillsdale College, Hillsdale, Michigan	3, 4, 5, 6
Hiram College, Hiram, Ohio	3, 4, 5
Hiwassee College, Madisonville, Tennessee	1, 2, 3, 4, 5, 6
Hobart and William Smith Colleges, Geneva, New York	1, 5, 6 (Hobart only)
Holy Family College, Philadelphia, Pennsylvania	1, 2, 4, 5
Holy Family College, Manitowoc, Wisconsin	2, 6
Holy Family Seminary, West Hartford, Connecticut	1, 2, 3, 4, 5, 6
Holy Names College, Spokane, Washington	1, 2, 4, 5, 6
Hood College, Frederick, Maryland	1, 3, 4, 5
Hope College, Holland, Michigan	1, 2, 3, 5
Houghton College, Houghton, New York	1, 2, 3, 4, 5, 6

Institution	Types of Association
Howard College, Birmingham, Alabama	1, 2, 3, 4, 5, 6
Howard Payne College, Brownwood, Texas	1, 2, 3, 4, 5, 6
Huntingdon College, Montgomery, Alabama	1, 2, 3, 4, 5, 6
Huntington College, Huntington, Indiana	1, 2, 3, 4, 5, 6
Huron College, Huron, South Dakota	1, 2, 3, 4, 5, 6
Huston-Tillotson College, Austin, Texas	1, 2, 3, 4, 5, 6
Illinois College, Jacksonville, Illinois	3, 4, 5, 6
Illinois Wesleyan University, Bloomington, Illinois	1, 3, 4, 5, 6
Immaculata College, Bartlett, Illinois	1, 2, 4, 5, 6
Immaculata College, Hamburg, New York	1, 2, 5
Immaculata College, Immaculata, Pennsylvania	1, 2, 4, 5, 6
Immaculata Junior College, Washington, D.C.	2, 5, 6
Immaculate Conception College, Inc., Oconomowoc, Wisconsin	2, 3, 4, 5, 6
Immaculate Conception Junior College, Lodi, New Jersey	2, 4, 5, 6
Immaculate Conception Seminary, Conception, Missouri	2, 5, 6
Immaculate Heart College, Los Angeles, California	1, 2, 4, 5, 6
Incarnate Word College, San Antonio, Texas	1, 2, 3, 4, 5, 6
Indiana Central College, Indianapolis, Indiana	1, 3, 4, 5, 6
Iona College, New Rochelle, New York	2, 5, 6
Iowa Wesleyan College, Mount Pleasant, Iowa	1, 2, 3, 4, 5, 6
J. P. Campbell College, Jackson, Mississippi	1, 2, 3, 4, 5
Jamestown College, Jamestown, North Dakota	3, 4, 5, 6
Jarvis Christian College, Hawkins, Texas	1, 3, 4, 5
John Carroll University, Cleveland, Ohio	1, 2, 4, 5, 6
Johnson C. Smith University, Charlotte, North Carolina	3, 4, 5
Judson College, Marion, Alabama	1, 2, 3, 5, 6
Juniata College, Huntingdon, Pennsylvania	1, 3, 5
Kalamazoo College, Kalamazoo, Michigan	1, 3, 4, 5, 6
Kansas Wesleyan University, Salina, Kansas	1, 2, 3, 4, 5, 6
Kendall College, Evanston, Illinois	1, 3, 4, 5, 6
Kentucky Wesleyan College, Owensboro, Kentucky	1, 2, 3, 4, 5, 6
Kenyon College, Gambier, Ohio	4, 5
Keuka College, Keuka Park, New York	4, 5
Kilroe Seminary of the Sacred Heart, Honesdale, Pennsylvania	2, 4, 6
King College, Bristol, Tennessee	1, 2, 3, 4, 5, 6
King's College, Wilkes-Barre, Pennsylvania	1, 2, 5, 6
Knoxville College, Knoxville, Tennessee	1, 2, 3, 4, 5, 6
Ladycliff College, Highland Falls, New York	1, 2, 4, 5, 6
Lafayette College, Easton, Pennsylvania	3, 4
LaGrange College, LaGrange, Georgia	1, 2, 3, 4, 5, 6
Lake Forest College, Lake Forest, Illinois	3, 4, 5
Lakeland College, Sheboygan, Wisconsin	1, 3, 4, 5
Lambuth College, Jackson, Tennessee	1, 2, 3, 4, 5, 6
Lane College, Jackson, Tennessee	1, 2, 3, 5
La Salette Seminary, Altamont, New York	1, 2, 3, 4, 5, 6
LaSalle College, Philadelphia, Pennsylvania	1, 2, 4, 5, 6
La Sierra College, Arlington, California	1, 2, 3, 4, 5, 6
Latter-day Saints Business College, Salt Lake City, Utah	2, 3, 4, 6

Institution	Types of Association
La Verne College, La Verne, California	1, 3, 4, 5, 6
Lawrence University, Appleton, Wisconsin	3, 4
Lebanon Valley College, Annville, Pennsylvania	1, 3, 4, 5, 6
Lee College, Cleveland, Tennessee	1, 2, 3, 4, 5, 6
Lees Junior College, Jackson, Kentucky	1, 2, 3, 4, 5, 6
Lees-McRae College, Banner Elk, North Carolina	1, 3, 5, 6
Le Moyne College, Syracuse, New York	1, 4, 5
Le Moyne College, Memphis, Tennessee	1, 2, 3, 4, 5
Lenoir-Rhyne College, Hickory, North Carolina	1, 2, 3, 5, 6
Lewis College, Lockport, Illinois	1, 4, 5, 6
Lewis and Clark College, Portland, Oregon	1, 2, 3, 4, 5, 6
Lindenwood College for Women, St. Charles, Missouri	3, 4, 5, 6
Lindsey Wilson College, Columbia, Kentucky	1, 2, 4, 5, 6
Linfield College, McMinnville, Oregon	1, 3, 4, 5, 6
Livingstone College, Salisbury, North Carolina	2, 3, 5
Loma Linda University, Loma Linda, California	1, 2, 3, 4, 5, 6
Lon Morris College, Jacksonville, Texas	2, 3, 4, 5, 6
Loras College, Dubuque, Iowa	1, 2, 3, 4, 5, 6
Loretto Heights College, Loretto, Colorado	2, 5
Loretto Junior College, Nerinx, Kentucky	1, 2, 4, 5, 6
Los Angeles Pacific College, Los Angeles, California	1, 3, 4, 5, 6
Louisburg College, Louisburg, North Carolina	1, 2, 3, 4, 5, 6
Louisiana College, Pineville, Louisiana	1, 2, 3, 4, 5, 6
Loyola College, Baltimore, Maryland	2, 4, 5, 6
Loyola University, Chicago, Illinois	1, 2, 4, 5
Loyola University, New Orleans, Louisiana	1, 2, 4, 5, 6
Loyola University of Los Angeles, Los Angeles, California	1, 2, 4, 5, 6
Luther College, Decorah, Iowa	1, 3, 4, 5, 6
Lutheran Concordia College, Austin, Texas	1, 2, 3, 4, 5, 6
Lycoming College, Williamsport, Pennsylvania	1, 2, 3, 4, 5
Lynchburg College, Lynchburg, Virginia	1, 3, 4, 5, 6
Macalester College, St. Paul, Minnesota	3, 4, 5
MacMurray College, Jacksonville, Illinois	3, 4, 5
Madison College, Madison, Tennessee	1, 2, 3, 4, 5, 6
Madonna College, Livonia, Michigan	1, 2, 4, 6
Mallinckrodt College, Wilmette, Illinois	2, 5, 6
Malone College, Canton, Ohio	1, 2, 3, 5, 6
Manchester College, North Manchester, Indiana	1, 2, 3, 4, 5
Manhattan College, New York, New York	1, 2, 4, 5, 6
Manhattanville College of the Sacred Heart, Purchase, New York	1, 2, 4, 5
Manor Junior College, Jenkintown, Pennsylvania	2, 5
Maria College of Albany, Albany, New York	1, 2, 4, 5, 6
Marian College, Indianapolis, Indiana	1, 2, 3, 4, 5, 6
Marian College of Fond du Lac, Fond du Lac, Wisconsin	1, 2, 4, 5, 6
Marillac College, Normandy, Missouri	1, 2, 5, 6
Marion College, Marion, Indiana	1, 2, 3, 4, 5, 6
Marion College, Marion, Virginia	1, 2, 3, 4, 5, 6

Institution	Types of Association
Marist College, Poughkeepsie, New York	3, 5
Marist College and Seminary, Framingham Centre, Massachusetts	1, 2, 4, 5, 6
Marquette University, Milwaukee, Wisconsin	2, 4, 5, 6
Mars Hill College, Mars Hill, North Carolina	1, 2, 3, 4, 5, 6
Martin College, Pulaski, Tennessee	1, 2, 3, 4, 5
Mary Baldwin College, Staunton, Virginia	1, 3, 4, 5
Mary College, Bismarck, North Dakota	1, 2, 4, 5, 6
Mary Hardin-Baylor College, Belton, Texas	1, 3, 4, 5, 6
Mary Holmes Junior College, West Point, Mississippi	2, 3, 4, 5, 6
Mary Immaculate Seminary, Northampton, Pennsylvania	1, 2, 3, 4, 5, 6
Mary Manse College, Toledo, Ohio	2, 4, 5, 6
Marycrest College, Davenport, Iowa	2, 5, 6
Maryglade College, Memphis, Michigan	1, 2, 3, 4, 5, 6
Marygrove College, Detroit, Michigan	1, 2, 4, 5, 6
Maryknoll Seminary, Glen Ellyn, Illinois	1, 2, 3, 4, 5, 6
Maryknoll Teachers College, Maryknoll, New York	1, 2, 5, 6
Marylhurst College, Marylhurst, Oregon	2, 5, 6
Marymount College, Palos Verdes Estates, California	2, 4, 5
Marymount College, Salina, Kansas	2, 4, 5, 6
Marymount College, Tarrytown, New York	2, 5, 6
Marymount College, Arlington, Virginia	2, 4, 5
Marymount Manhattan College, New York, New York	1, 2, 5
Maryville College, Maryville, Tennessee	1, 3, 4, 5, 6
Maryville College of the Sacred Heart, St. Louis, Missouri	2, 4, 5, 6
Marywood College, Scranton, Pennsylvania	1, 2, 5, 6
Mater Christi Seminary, Albany, New York	1, 2, 3, 4, 5, 6
Mater Dei College, Ogdensburg, New York	2, 4, 5
Maunaolu College, Paia, Maui, Hawaii	1, 2, 3, 4, 5, 6
McKendree College, Lebanon, Illinois	1, 2, 3, 4, 5, 6
McMurry College, Abilene, Texas	1, 2, 3, 4, 5, 6
McPherson College, McPherson, Kansas	1, 3, 4, 5, 6
Meharry Medical College, Nashville, Tennessee	1, 3
Mercer University, Macon, Georgia	1, 2, 3, 4, 5
Mercy College, Detroit, Michigan	2, 5, 6
Mercy College, Dobbs Ferry, New York	1, 2, 3, 4, 5
Mercyhurst College, Erie, Pennsylvania	2, 4, 5
Meredith College, Raleigh, North Carolina	1, 2, 3, 4, 5, 6
Merrimack College, North Andover, Massachusetts	1, 2, 4, 5, 6
Messiah College, Grantham, Pennsylvania	1, 2, 3, 4, 5, 6
Methodist College, Fayetteville, North Carolina	1, 2, 3, 5, 6
Midland College, Fremont, Nebraska	1, 2, 3, 4, 5
Midway Junior College, Midway, Kentucky	1, 3, 4, 5, 6
Miles College, Birmingham, Alabama	1, 2, 3, 4, 5
Milligan College, Milligan College, Tennessee	5, 6
Millikin University, Decatur, Illinois	1, 3, 4, 5, 6
Millsaps College, Jackson, Mississippi	1, 2, 3, 5, 6
Miltonvale Wesleyan College, Miltonvale, Kansas	1, 2, 3, 4, 5, 6

| | Types of Association |
Institution	
Mississippi College, Clinton, Mississippi.	1, 2, 3, 5, 6
Mississippi Industrial College, Holly Springs, Mississippi	1, 2, 3, 4, 5
Missouri Valley College, Marshall, Missouri	1, 2, 3, 4, 5, 6
Molloy Catholic College for Women, Rockville Centre, New York	1, 2, 4, 5, 6
Monmouth College, Monmouth, Illinois	1, 3, 4, 5, 6
Montreat-Anderson College, Inc., Montreat, North Carolina	1, 2, 3, 4, 5, 6
Moravian College, Bethlehem, Pennsylvania	1, 3, 4, 5, 6
Morehouse College, Atlanta, Georgia	5, 6
Morningside College, Sioux City, Iowa	1, 2, 3, 4, 5, 6
Morris Brown College, Atlanta, Georgia	1, 2, 3, 4, 5, 6
Morris College, Sumter, South Carolina	1, 2, 3, 4, 5
Morristown College, Morristown, Tennessee	3, 4, 5
Mount Aloysius Junior College, Cresson, Pennsylvania	1, 2, 5
Mount Alvernia College, Chestnut Hill, Massachusetts	1, 2, 3, 4, 5, 6
Mount Angel College, Mount Angel, Oregon	2, 5
Mount Angel Seminary, St. Benedict, Oregon	2, 5
Mount Marty College, Yankton, South Dakota	1, 2, 4, 5, 6
Mount Mary College, Milwaukee, Wisconsin	1, 2, 4, 5
Mount Mercy College, Cedar Rapids, Iowa	1, 4, 5, 6
Mount Mercy College, Pittsburgh, Pennsylvania	2, 5
Mount Olive Junior College, Mount Olive, North Carolina	1, 2, 3, 4, 5, 6
Mount Saint Agnes College, Baltimore, Maryland	1, 2, 5
Mount St. Alphonsus Seminary, Esopus, New York	1, 2, 3, 4, 5, 6
Mount St. Clare College, Clinton, Iowa	1, 2, 3, 4, 5
Mount St. Joseph Teachers College, Buffalo, New York	2, 4, 5
Mount St. Mary College, Hooksett, New Hampshire	1, 2, 4, 5, 6
Mount Saint Mary College, Newburgh, New York	2, 4, 5
Mount St. Mary's College, Los Angeles, California	1, 2, 4, 5, 6
Mount St. Mary's College, Emmitsburg, Maryland	2, 4, 5, 6
Mount St. Scholastica College, Atchison, Kansas	1, 2, 3, 4, 5, 6
Mount Union College, Alliance, Ohio	1, 3, 4, 5, 6
Muhlenberg College, Allentown, Pennsylvania	1, 3, 4, 5, 6
Mundelein College, Chicago, Illinois	1, 2
Muskingum College, New Concord, Ohio	3, 4, 5
Natchez Junior College, Natchez, Mississippi	1, 2, 3, 4, 5, 6
National College, Kansas City, Missouri (now closed)	1, 2, 3, 4, 5
Nazareth College, Nazareth, Michigan	2, 4, 5, 6
Nazareth College, Rochester, New York	2, 5
Nazareth College and Academy, Nazareth, Kentucky	1, 3, 4, 5, 6
Nebraska Wesleyan University, Lincoln, Nebraska	1, 2, 3, 4, 5
Ner Israel Rabbinical College, Baltimore, Maryland	1, 5, 6
Newberry College, Newberry, South Carolina	1, 2, 3, 4, 5, 6
Newton College of the Sacred Heart, Newton, Massachusetts	2, 5
Niagara University, Niagara University, New York	1, 2, 5, 6
Norman College, Norman Park, Georgia	1, 2, 3, 4, 5, 6
North Carolina Wesleyan College, Inc., Rocky Mount, North Carolina	1, 2, 3, 4, 5, 6

Institution	Types of Association
North Central College, Naperville, Illinois	1, 2, 3, 4, 5, 6
North Greenville Junior College, Tigerville, South Carolina	1, 2, 3, 4, 5, 6
North Park College and Theological Seminary, Chicago, Illinois	1, 2, 3, 5, 6
Northland College, Ashland, Wisconsin	4, 5
Northwest Christian College, Eugene, Oregon	1, 2, 3, 4, 5, 6
Northwest Nazarene College, Nampa, Idaho	1, 2, 3, 4, 5, 6
Northwestern College, Orange City, Iowa	1, 2, 3, 4, 5, 6
Northwestern University, Evanston, Illinois	1
Notre Dame College, St. Louis, Missouri	1, 2, 3, 4, 5, 6
Notre Dame College, Manchester, New Hampshire	2, 4, 5
Notre Dame College, Cleveland, Ohio	1, 2, 5, 6
Notre Dame College of Staten Island, Staten Island, New York	1, 2, 4, 5, 6
Notre Dame Seminary, New Orleans, Louisiana	1, 2, 3, 5
Novitiate of St. Isaac Jogues, Wernersville, Pennsylvania	1, 2, 3, 4, 5, 6
Oakland City College, Oakland City, Indiana	1, 2, 3, 4, 5, 6
Oakwood College, Huntsville, Alabama	2, 3, 4, 5, 6
Oblate College, Washington, D.C.	2, 3, 4, 5, 6
Oblate College and Seminary, Bar Harbor, Maine	1, 2, 3, 4, 5, 6
Occidental College, Los Angeles, California	3, 4, 5
Ohio Northern University, Ada, Ohio	1, 2, 3, 4, 5, 6
Ohio Wesleyan University, Delaware, Ohio	1, 3, 4, 5
Oklahoma Baptist University, Shawnee, Oklahoma	1, 2, 3, 4, 5
Oklahoma Christian College, Oklahoma City, Oklahoma	1, 5, 6
Oklahoma City University, Oklahoma City, Oklahoma	1, 2, 3, 4, 5, 6
Okolona College, Okolona, Mississippi	3, 4, 5
Olivet College, Olivet, Michigan	3, 4, 5
Olivet Nazarene College, Kankakee, Illinois	1, 2, 3, 4, 5, 6
Ottawa University, Ottawa, Kansas	1, 4, 5, 6
Otterbein College, Westerville, Ohio	1, 3, 5, 6
Ottumwa Heights College, Ottumwa, Iowa	1, 2, 4, 5, 6
Ouachita Baptist College, Arkadelphia, Arkansas	1, 2, 3, 4, 5, 6
Our Lady of Cincinnati College, Cincinnati, Ohio	2, 4, 5
Our Lady of Holy Cross College, New Orleans, Louisana	2, 4, 5
Our Lady of the Lake College, San Antonio, Texas	1, 2, 3, 4, 5, 6
Owen College, Memphis, Tennessee	1, 2, 3, 5
Pacific Christian College, Long Beach, California	1, 4, 5, 6
Pacific College, Fresno, California	1, 2, 3, 4, 5, 6
Pacific Lutheran University, Tacoma, Washington	1, 2, 3, 4, 5, 6
Pacific Oaks College, Pasadena, California	3, 4, 5
Pacific Union College, Angwin, California	1, 2, 3, 4, 5, 6
Pacific University, Forest Grove, Oregon	3, 4, 5
Paine College, Augusta, Georgia	1, 2, 3, 4, 5, 6
Park College, Parkville, Missouri	1, 3, 4, 5
Parsons College,[1] Fairfield, Iowa	1, 4, 5, 6
Pasadena College, Pasadena, California	1, 2, 3, 4, 5, 6

[1] Parsons College is no longer related to a church. Its connection with the United Presbyterian Church was severed in 1964.

Institution	Types of Association
Paul Quinn College, Waco, Texas	2, 3, 4, 5, 6
Peace College, Raleigh, North Carolina	1, 2, 3, 4, 5, 6
Pepperdine College, Los Angeles, California	1, 5, 6
Pfeiffer College, Misenheimer, North Carolina	1, 2, 3, 5, 6
Philander Smith College, Little Rock, Arkansas	3, 4, 5
Phillips University, Enid, Oklahoma	3, 4, 5
Piedmont College, Demorest, Georgia	1, 3, 4, 5, 6
Pikeville College, Pikeville, Kentucky	1, 2, 3, 4, 5, 6
Pontifical College Josephinum, Worthington, Ohio	1, 2, 3, 4, 5, 6
Presbyterian College, Clinton, South Carolina	1, 2, 3, 5
Presentation Junior College, Aberdeen, South Dakota	1, 2, 5, 6
Principia College, Elsah, Illinois	1, 5, 6
Providence College, Providence, Rhode Island	1, 2, 3, 4, 5, 6
Queen of Apostles College and Seminary, Dedham, Massachusetts	1, 2, 4, 5, 6
Queen of the Apostles College, Harriman, New York	2, 5, 6
Queen of Apostles Seminary, Madison, Wisconsin	2, 4, 5, 6
Queens College, Charlotte, North Carolina	1, 2, 3, 4, 5, 6
Quincy College, Quincy, Illinois	1, 2, 3, 5
Randolph-Macon College, Ashland, Virginia	1, 3, 4, 5, 6
Randolph-Macon Woman's College, Lynchburg, Virginia	3, 4, 5
Regis College, Denver, Colorado	1, 2, 5
Regis College, Weston, Massachusetts	2, 3, 5, 6
Reinhardt College, Waleska, Georgia	1, 3, 4, 5, 6
Ricker College, Houlton, Maine	3, 4, 5
Ricks College, Rexburg, Idaho	1, 2, 3, 4, 5, 6
Ripon College, Ripon, Wisconsin	3, 4
Rivier College, Nashua, New Hampshire	1, 2, 4, 5, 6
Roanoke College, Salem, Virginia	3, 4, 5
Roberts Wesleyan College, North Chili, New York	1, 3, 4, 5, 6
Rockhurst College, Kansas City, Missouri	1, 2, 5, 6
Rocky Mountain College, Billings, Montana	1, 3, 4, 5, 6
Rosary College, River Forest, Illinois	5, 6
Rosary Hill College, Buffalo, New York	1, 2, 4, 5
Rosemont College, Rosemont, Pennsylvania	1, 2, 4, 5, 6
Rust College, Holly Springs, Mississippi	2, 3, 4, 5
Sacred Heart College, Cullman, Alabama	1, 2, 6
Sacred Heart College, Wichita, Kansas	2, 5
Sacred Heart Dominican College, Houston, Texas	1, 2, 4, 5, 6
Sacred Heart Junior College and Academy, Belmont, North Carolina	5
Sacred Heart Novitiate, Monroe, Michigan	2, 4, 5, 6
Sacred Heart Seminary, Detroit, Michigan	2, 3, 5, 6
St. Ambrose College, Davenport, Iowa	1, 4, 5, 6
St. Andrews Presbyterian College, Laurinburg, North Carolina	1, 2, 3, 5, 6
St. Anselm's College, Manchester, New Hampshire	2, 4, 5
St. Augustine's College, Raleigh, North Carolina	1, 3, 4, 5
St. Basil's College, Stamford, Connecticut	1, 2, 3, 4, 5, 6
St. Bede College, Peru, Illinois	2, 5

Institution	Types of Association
St. Benedict College, Ferdinand, Indiana	1, 2, 4, 5, 6
St. Benedict's College, Atchison, Kansas	2, 4, 5, 6
St. Bernard College, St. Bernard, Alabama	1, 2, 4, 5
St. Bernardine of Siena College, Loudonville, New York	1, 2, 3, 4, 5, 6
St. Bernard's Seminary and College, Rochester, New York	1, 2, 3, 4, 5, 6
St. Bonaventure University, St. Bonaventure, New York	1, 2, 3, 4, 5, 6
St. Catharine Junior College, St. Catharine, Kentucky	2, 5
St. Charles Borromeo Seminary, Philadelphia, Pennsylvania	1, 2, 4, 5, 6
Saint Clare College, Williamsville, New York	1, 2, 4, 5, 6
St. Columbian's College and Seminary, Milton, Massachusetts	2, 4, 5, 6
St. Edward's University, Austin, Texas	1, 2, 4, 5
St. Fidelis College and Seminary, Herman, Pennsylvania	1, 2, 3, 4, 5, 6
St. Francis College, Fort Wayne, Indiana	2, 5, 6
St. Francis College, Biddeford, Maine	2, 3, 4, 5, 6
St. Francis College, Brooklyn, New York	1, 2, 3, 4, 5
St. Francis College, Loretto, Pennsylvania	1, 2, 4, 5
St. Francis College, Burlington, Wisconsin	1, 2, 3, 4, 5, 6
St. Francis Seminary, Milwaukee, Wisconsin	1, 2, 3, 5, 6
St. Gregory's College, Shawnee, Oklahoma	1, 2, 5
St. Hyacinth College and Seminary, Granby, Massachusetts	1, 2, 3, 4, 5, 6
St. John College of Cleveland, Cleveland, Ohio	1, 2, 3, 4, 5, 6
St. John Fisher College, Inc., Rochester, New York	2, 3, 4, 5
St. John Vianney Seminary, East Aurora, New York	1, 2, 4, 5, 6
St. John's Seminary, Camarillo, California	1, 2, 3, 4, 5, 6
St. John's College, Winfield, Kansas	1, 2, 3, 4, 5, 6
St. John's Seminary, Brighton, Massachusetts	1, 2, 3, 4, 5, 6
St. John's University, Collegeville, Minnesota	1, 2, 4, 5, 6
St. John's University, Jamaica, New York	1, 2, 4, 5, 6
St. Joseph College, West Hartford, Connecticut	1, 2, 4, 5, 6
St. Joseph College, Emmitsburg, Maryland	1, 2, 4, 5, 6
St. Joseph College of Orange, Orange, California	2, 4, 5, 6
Saint Joseph Seminary, Saint Benedict, Louisiana	1, 2, 3, 4, 5, 6
St. Joseph's College, Rensselaer, Indiana	1, 2, 4, 5, 6
St. Joseph's College, North Windham, Maine	1, 2, 5, 6
St. Joseph's College, Princeton, New Jersey	1, 2, 3, 5, 6
St. Joseph's College, Philadelphia, Pennsylvania	1, 2, 4, 5, 6
St. Joseph's College for Women, Brooklyn, New York	1, 5, 6
St. Joseph's Seminary, Westmont, Illinois	1, 2, 4, 5, 6
St. Joseph's Seminary and College, Yonkers, New York	1, 2, 3, 4, 5, 6
St. Joseph's Seminary of Washington, D.C., Washington, D.C.	1, 2, 3, 4, 5, 6
St. Joseph's Seraphic Seminary, Callicoon, New York	1, 2, 3, 4, 5, 6
St. Lawrence Seminary, Mount Calvary, Wisconsin	1, 2, 4, 5, 6
St. Leo College, St. Leo, Florida	2, 4, 5, 6
St. Louis University, St. Louis, Missouri	1, 2, 4, 5
St. Martin's College, Olympia, Washington	2, 4, 5, 6
Saint Mary College, Xavier, Kansas	1, 2, 4, 5, 6
St. Mary of the Lake Seminary, Mundelein, Illinois	1, 2, 4, 5, 6
St. Mary of the Plains College, Dodge City, Kansas	1, 2, 4, 5, 6

Institution	Types of Association
St. Mary-of-the-Woods College, Saint Mary-of-the-Woods, Indiana	1, 2, 4, 5, 6
St. Mary's College, Notre Dame, Indiana	2, 4, 5
St. Mary's College, Orchard Lake, Michigan	1, 2, 4, 5, 6
St. Mary's College, Winona, Minnesota	1, 2, 3, 4, 5, 6
St. Mary's College of California, St. Mary's College, California	1, 2, 4, 5, 6
St. Mary's Dominican College, New Orleans, Louisiana	1, 2, 3, 5
St. Mary's Junior College, O'Fallon, Missouri	2, 5
St. Mary's Junior College, Raleigh, North Carolina	1, 3, 5
St. Mary's Seminary, Techny, Illinois	1, 2, 3, 4, 5, 6
St. Mary's Seminary, Perryville, Missouri	2, 5, 6
St. Mary's Seminary and University, Baltimore, Maryland	1, 2, 3, 4, 5, 6
St. Mary's University of San Antonio, San Antonio, Texas	1, 2, 4, 5
St. Meinrad Seminary, St. Meinrad, Indiana	1, 2, 3, 4, 5, 6
St. Michael's College, Santa Fe, New Mexico	1, 2, 3, 4, 5, 6
St. Michael's College, Winooski, Vermont	1, 2, 4, 5, 6
St. Norbert College, West De Pere, Wisconsin	1, 2, 4, 5, 6
St. Olaf College, Northfield, Minnesota	1, 2, 3, 4, 5, 6
St. Patrick's Seminary, Menlo Park, California	1, 2, 3, 4, 5, 6
St. Paul's College, Washington, D.C.	1, 2, 4, 5, 6
St. Paul's College, Concordia, Missouri	1, 2, 3, 4, 5, 6
Saint Paul's College, Lawrenceville, Virginia	3, 4, 5, 6
St. Peter's College, Baltimore, Maryland	1, 2, 4, 5, 6
St. Peter's College, Jersey City, New Jersey	1, 2, 4, 5, 6
St. Pius X Seminary, Garrison, New York	2, 3, 4, 5, 6
St. Procopius College, Lisle, Illinois	1, 2, 3, 5
St. Thomas Aquinas College, Sparkill, New York	2, 5, 6
St. Thomas Seminary, Denver, Colorado	1, 5, 6
St. Thomas Seminary, Bloomfield, Connecticut	1, 2, 4, 5, 6
St. Vincent College, Latrobe, Pennsylvania	1, 2, 5, 6
St. Xavier College, Chicago, Illinois	1, 2, 5, 6
Saints Junior College, Lexington, Mississippi	1, 2, 3, 4, 5
Salem College, Winston-Salem, North Carolina	1, 2, 3, 5
Salem College, Salem, West Virginia	5
Salve Regina College, Newport, Rhode Island	2, 5
Sancta Maria Junior College, Buffalo, New York	2, 4, 5, 6
San Diego College for Women, San Diego, California	1, 2, 4, 5, 6
San Francisco College for Women, San Francisco, California	2, 5, 6
San Luis Rey College, San Luis Rey, California	1, 2, 3, 4, 5, 6
Scarritt College for Christian Workers, Nashville, Tennessee	1, 2, 3, 4, 5, 6
School of the Ozarks, Point Lookout, Missouri	3, 5
Schreiner Institute, Kerrville, Texas	1, 2, 3, 5
Seat of Wisdom College, Litchfield, Connecticut	2, 4, 5, 6
Seattle Pacific College, Seattle, Washington	1, 3, 4, 5, 6
Seattle University, Seattle, Washington	1, 2, 3, 4, 5, 6
Seminary of Our Lady of Providence, Warwick, Rhode Island	1, 2, 3, 5, 6
Servite College, Omaha, Nebraska	2, 4
Seton Hall University, South Orange, New Jersey	2, 4

Institution	Types of Association
Seton Hill College, Greensburg, Pennsylvania	2, 4, 5, 6
Shaw University, Raleigh, North Carolina	2, 3, 5, 6
Sheldon Jackson Junior College, Sitka, Alaska	1, 2, 3, 4, 5, 6
Shenandoah College, Winchester, Virginia	1, 2, 3, 4, 5
Shimer College, Mount Carroll, Illinois	4, 5
Shorter College, North Little Rock, Arkansas	1, 2, 3, 4, 5, 6
Shorter College, Rome, Georgia	1, 3, 5, 6
Siena College, Memphis, Tennessee	1, 2, 4, 5, 6
Siena Heights College, Adrian, Michigan	1, 2, 5, 6
Simpson College, Indianola, Iowa	1, 3, 4, 5
Sioux Falls College, Sioux Falls, South Dakota	1, 3, 4, 5, 6
Snead Junior College, Boaz, Alabama	1, 2, 3, 4, 5, 6
Southeastern Junior College, Laurel, Mississippi	1, 2, 3, 5, 6
Southern Baptist College, Walnut Ridge, Arkansas	1, 2, 3, 4, 5, 6
Southern California College, Costa Mesa, California	1, 2, 3, 4, 5, 6
Southern Methodist University, Dallas, Texas	1, 2, 3, 4, 5
Southern Missionary College, Collegedale, Tennessee	1, 2, 3, 4, 5, 6
Southwest Baptist College, Bolivar, Missouri	1, 2, 3, 4, 5, 6
Southwestern College, Winfield, Kansas	1, 2, 3, 4, 5
Southwestern Union College, Keene, Texas	1, 2, 3, 4, 5, 6
Southwestern at Memphis, Memphis, Tennessee	1, 2, 3, 5, 6
Southwestern University, Georgetown, Texas	1, 2, 3, 4, 5, 6
Spartanburg Junior College, Spartanburg, South Carolina	2, 3, 4, 5, 6
Spelman College, Atlanta, Georgia	1, 3, 5
Spring Arbor College, Spring Arbor, Michigan	1, 3, 4, 5, 6
Spring Hill College, Spring Hill, Alabama	1, 2, 4, 5, 6
Springfield Junior College, Springfield, Illinois	1, 2, 5
Sterling College, Sterling, Kansas	1, 2, 3, 4, 5, 6
Stetson University, De Land, Florida	1, 3, 4, 5, 6
Stillman College, Tuscaloosa, Alabama	1, 2, 3, 4, 5, 6
Stonehill College, North Easton, Massachusetts	2
Sue Bennett College, London, Kentucky	2, 3, 4, 5, 6
Sulpician Seminary of the Northwest, Kenmore, Washington	2
Suomi College, Hancock, Michigan	1, 2, 3, 5, 6
Susquehanna University, Selinsgrove, Pennsylvania	1, 3, 4, 5, 6
Swarthmore College, Swarthmore, Pennsylvania	5
Syracuse University, Syracuse, New York	1, 3, 4
Tabor College, Hillsboro, Kansas	1, 2, 3, 5, 6
Talladega College, Talladega, Alabama	3, 4, 5
Tarkio College, Tarkio, Missouri	1, 3, 4, 5
Taylor University, Upland, Indiana	1, 3, 4, 5, 6
Tennessee Temple College, Chattanooga, Tennessee	3, 5, 6
Tennessee Wesleyan College, Athens, Tennessee	1, 2, 3, 4, 5
Texas Christian University, Fort Worth, Texas	1, 3, 4, 5
Texas College, Tyler, Texas	1, 2, 3, 4, 5
Texas Lutheran College, Seguin, Texas	1, 2, 3, 4, 5, 6
Texas Wesleyan College, Fort Worth, Texas	1, 2, 3, 4, 5, 6
Thiel College, Greenville, Pennsylvania	1, 3, 4, 5, 6

Institution	Types of Association
Tift College, Forsyth, Georgia	1, 2, 3, 4, 5, 6
Tombrock Junior College, Paterson, New Jersey	1, 2, 3, 4, 5, 6
Tougaloo Southern Christian College, Tougaloo, Mississippi	1, 2, 3, 4, 5
Transylvania College, Lexington, Kentucky	1, 3, 4
Trevecca Nazarene College, Nashville, Tennessee	1, 3, 4, 5
Trinity College, Hartford, Connecticut	3, 4, 5
Trinity College, Washington, D.C.	2, 4, 5, 6
Trinity College, Burlington, Vermont	2, 5
Trinity Theological Seminary and Trinity College, Chicago, Illinois	1, 2, 4, 5, 6
Trinity University, San Antonio, Texas	1, 2, 3, 4, 5
Tusculum College, Greenville, Tennessee	1, 3, 4, 5, 6
Union College, Barbourville, Kentucky	1, 3, 4, 5, 6
Union College, Lincoln, Nebraska	1, 2, 3, 4, 5, 6
Union University, Jackson, Tennessee	1, 2, 3, 4, 5, 6
University of Chattanooga, Chattanooga, Tennessee	3, 4, 5
University of Corpus Christi, Corpus Christi, Texas	1, 2, 3, 4, 5, 6
University of Dallas, Dallas, Texas	2, 3, 5
University of Dayton, Dayton, Ohio	1, 2, 4, 5
University of Denver, Denver, Colorado	1, 4, 5
University of Detroit, Detroit, Michigan	2, 4, 5, 6
University of Dubuque, Dubuque, Iowa	1, 2, 3, 4, 5, 6
University of Notre Dame, Notre Dame, Indiana	1, 2, 3, 4, 5
University of Portland, Portland, Oregon	1, 2, 4, 5
University of Puget Sound, Tacoma, Washington	1, 3, 4, 5
University of Redlands, Redlands, California	1, 3, 4, 5, 6
University of Richmond, Richmond, Virginia	1, 3, 4, 5, 6
University of St. Thomas, Houston, Texas	1, 2, 5, 6
University of San Diego College for Men, San Diego, California	1, 2, 3, 4, 5, 6
University of San Francisco, San Francisco, California	1, 2, 3, 4, 5, 6
University of Santa Clara, Santa Clara, California	1, 4, 5
University of Scranton, Scranton, Pennsylvania	1, 2, 4, 5
University of the Pacific, Stockton, California	1, 3, 4, 5, 6
University of the South, Sewanee, Tennessee	1, 2, 3, 4, 5, 6
University of Tulsa, Tulsa, Oklahoma	3, 4, 5
Upland College, Upland, California	1, 3, 5
Upsala College, East Orange, New Jersey	1, 2, 3, 4, 5, 6
Ursinus College, Collegeville, Pennsylvania	3, 4, 5
Ursuline College, Louisville, Kentucky	1, 2, 5, 6
Ursuline College, Cleveland, Ohio	2, 5, 6
Valparaiso University, Valparaiso, Indiana	1, 2, 3, 5, 6
Vermont College, Montpelier, Vermont	1, 3, 4, 5
Villa Julie College, Stevenson, Maryland	1, 2, 4, 5, 6
Villa Madonna College, Covington, Kentucky	2, 4, 5, 6
Villa Maria College, Erie, Pennsylvania	1, 2, 3, 4, 5, 6
Villa Maria College of Buffalo, Buffalo, New York	1, 2, 5, 6
Villanova University, Villanova, Pennsylvania	1, 2, 4, 5, 6
Villa Walsh College, Morristown, New Jersey	6

Institution	Types of Association
Virginia Intermont College, Bristol, Virginia	1, 2, 3, 5, 6
Virginia Seminary and College, Lynchburg, Virginia	2, 3, 5
Virginia Union University, Richmond, Virginia	1, 3, 4, 5, 6
Viterbo College, La Crosse, Wisconsin	2, 5, 6
Voorhees School and Junior College, Denmark, South Carolina	1, 2, 3, 4, 5
Wagner College, Staten Island, New York	1, 2, 3, 4, 5, 6
Wake Forest College, Winston-Salem, North Carolina	1, 2, 3, 4, 5
Waldorf College, Forest City, Iowa	1, 2, 3, 4, 5, 6
Walla Walla College, College Place, Washington	1, 2, 3, 4, 5, 6
Walsh College, Canton, Ohio	1, 2, 4, 5, 6
Warner Pacific College, Portland, Oregon	1, 2, 3, 5
Warren Wilson College, Swannanoa, North Carolina	1, 2, 3, 4, 5, 6
Wartburg College, Waverly, Iowa	1, 2, 3, 4, 5
Wayland Baptist College, Plainview, Texas	1, 2, 3, 4, 5, 6
Waynesburg College, Waynesburg, Pennsylvania	1 3, 4, 5, 6
Webster College, Webster Groves, Missouri	1, 2, 3, 4, 5
Wesley College, Dover, Delaware	1, 3, 5, 6
Wesleyan College, Macon, Georgia	1, 3, 4, 5, 6
Wessington Springs College, Wessington Springs, South Dakota	1, 3, 4, 5, 6
West Virginia Wesleyan College, Buckhannon, West Virginia	1, 2, 3, 5, 6
Western Maryland College, Westminster, Maryland	1, 3, 4, 5
Westmar College, Le Mars, Iowa	2, 4, 5, 6
Westminster College, Fulton, Missouri	1, 2, 3, 4, 5
Westminster College, New Wilmington, Pennsylvania	1, 3, 4, 5, 6
Westminster College, Salt Lake City, Utah	3, 4, 5, 6
Wheeling College, Wheeling, West Virginia	1, 2, 4, 5, 6
Whittier College, Whittier, California	1, 5
Whitworth College, Spokane, Washington	1, 3, 4, 5, 6
Wilberforce University, Wilberforce, Ohio	1, 2, 3, 4, 5
Wiley College, Marshall, Texas	1, 2, 3, 4, 5, 6
Willamette University, Salem, Oregon	1, 3, 4, 5, 6
William Carey College, Hattiesburg, Mississippi	1, 2, 3, 4, 5, 6
William Jewell College, Liberty, Missouri	1, 2, 3, 4, 5, 6
William Penn College, Oskaloosa, Iowa	1, 3, 5, 6
William Woods College, Fulton, Missouri	1, 3
Wilmington College, Wilmington, Ohio	1, 4, 5
Wilson College, Chambersburg, Pennsylvania	1, 3, 4, 5
Wingate College, Wingate, North Carolina	1, 2, 3, 4, 5, 6
Wittenberg University, Springfield, Ohio	1, 2, 3, 4, 5
Wofford College, Spartanburg, South Carolina	1, 3, 4, 5, 6
Wood Junior College, Mathiston, Mississippi	1, 2, 3, 4, 5, 6
Xavier University, New Orleans, Louisiana	1, 2, 5, 6
Xavier University, Cincinnati, Ohio	1, 2, 5
Xaverian College, Silver Springs, Maryland	1, 2, 3, 5, 6
Yankton College, Yankton, South Dakota	4
Yeshiva University, New York, New York	1, 3, 5, 6
York College, York, Nebraska	1, 5, 6
Young Harris College, Young Harris, Georgia	1, 2, 3, 4, 5, 6

SUPPLEMENTARY LIST OF RELIGIOUSLY-ORIENTED INSTITUTIONS
NOT RELATED TO PARTICULAR RELIGIOUS BODIES [2]

Name	*Location*
Asbury College	Wilmore, Kentucky
Barrington College	Barrington, Rhode Island
Bob Jones University	Greenville, South Carolina
Bryan College	Dayton, Tennessee
Cascade College	Portland, Oregon
College of Jewish Studies	Chicago, Illinois
Dropsie College	Philadelphia, Pennsylvania
Gordon College	Beverly Farms, Massachusetts
Hebrew Teachers College	Brookline, Massachusetts
John Brown University	Siloam Springs, Arkansas
Lander College	Greenwood, South Carolina
LeTourneau College	Longview, Texas
Shelton College	Ringwood, New Jersey
Trinity Christian College	Palos Heights, Illinois
Wellesley College	Wellesley, Mass.
Western College for Women	Oxford, Ohio
Westmont College	Santa Barbara, California
Wheaton College	Wheaton, Illinois

[2] These institutions were not included in the 817 church-sponsored colleges and universities, nor were they considered to come within the purview of the Danforth study. They are listed here because their presidents reported affirmatively on Item 5 concerning religious orientation of institutional statement of purpose. No doubt, other colleges of similar character could be identified.

National Church
Agencies for
Higher Education

In the course of the study a large body of information was compiled on the agencies responsible for maintaining relationships with colleges and universities in the various churches. This material, most of which was assembled in 1963, is brought together here for reference purposes.[1]

The nomenclature of national church agencies differs from one religious body to another. The terms "board," "division," "department," "association," and "commission" are commonly used. Likewise, there are marked differences in the roles played by the various agencies. The Board for Higher Education of the Lutheran Church-Missouri Synod, for example, exercises a high degree of control over the fourteen institutions under its authority. It holds legal title to their physical properties and approves their policies, curricular changes, faculty appointments, plans for physical development, and budgets. The Board is clearly the most influential factor in achieving the goal of the Church in higher education, namely, the provision of a supply of workers for the teaching and preaching ministry. In contrast, the Board of Higher Education of the Christian Churches (Disciples of Christ) exercises no control over the eighteen colleges and universities of that communion. Its function is to promote cooperation among the institutions and maintain communication between them and the churches. The Board itself operates no colleges, and its by-laws state:

Nothing in the Articles of Incorporation or in these by-laws shall in any way be construed as interfering with or violating the complete autonomy of any cooperating institution in the free and unhindered management of its own affairs by its own board of trustees.[2]

As a matter of fact, so tenuous is the relationship between the church and the college that it is difficult in some instances to determine precisely why

---

[1] The reader is also referred to the valuable study by James C. Messersmith, *Church-Related Boards Responsible for Higher Education*, OE-53021, Bulletin 1964, No. 13 (Washington: Office of Education, U.S. Department of Health, Education, and Welfare, 1964).

[2] "By-Laws," Board of Higher Education, Disciples of Christ, Article XI, Section 1.

the college is identified as being related to the Christian Churches (Disciples of Christ).

LEGAL AND EXTRA-LEGAL FUNCTIONS

Preparing Descriptive Information

The publication and distribution of promotional literature is one of the most common activities of the church agencies. Often this material includes information on the location, physical facilities, purpose and scope of educational program, costs, financial aid available, and attractive features of individual institutions for distribution to students and parents through local churches and high schools. Many church agencies also publish more general statements on the aims and problems of Christian higher education for the information and stimulation of their constituents.

Listing Officially Recognized Institutions

Another common activity is the publication of the list of institutions affiliated with the church, together with an explanation of the criteria for inclusion. Often the agency also determines the requirements for official recognition.

Gathering Statistical Information

Many of the church agencies gather statistical information from their affiliated colleges. Usually included are data on finance, students, and faculty. Sometimes the data are used as a basis for the allocation of church funds to individual institutions, but more often they are compiled for purely informational purposes in the church.

Raising and Distributing Funds

When a church provides national support for its institutions of higher learning, the board, division, or department of higher education serves as the agency through which the funds are distributed. Four possible kinds of support involved are (1) unrestricted funds; (2) capital funds, contributed by the church for endowment purposes or for additions to physical plant; (3) student-aid funds in the form of either scholarships or student loans, to be used by institutions under policies established by the church or as the individual institutions see fit, or as grants made directly to students; and (4) special grants, either for particular projects in individual institutions or for a given area of concern in all affiliated institutions, such as the improvement of libraries. Agencies also conduct campaigns to raise funds for the capital or current needs of church-related colleges, providing fund-raising counsel and handling publicity.

Determining Institutional Policy

A less frequent function is that of setting institutional policy. Typically the church-related college in America is free of close control of internal policy by its church. However, in a few instances, church agencies have considerable authority in the management of institutions, including such matters as the approval of changes in curriculum and the appointment of faculty members. The case of the Lutheran Church-Missouri Synod has already been mentioned as an illustration of such broad control. More often, however, control is exercised in a more limited way, frequently through the acceptance by colleges of standards adopted by the church as criteria for affiliated status. In some churches, for example, standards for related institutions include a requirement that a given number of hours in religion must be completed by the student as a requirement for a degree.

Providing Stimulation and Counsel

Many of the church agencies state that one of their responsibilities is to stimulate the improvement of their affiliated institutions. This may be accomplished through conferences for faculty members and administrative officers, evaluative surveys of institutions, and other means of stimulation. The Division of Higher Education of the Methodist Board of Education, for example, encourages its institutions to undertake surveys and even requires one when a new president assumes office. The agency may offer financial support for programs or facilities designed to improve the quality of instruction. It may make available to institutions the services of consultants, either for the program as a whole or for a special area, such as business management.

Serving as Liaison

When matters of general policy regarding the church's role in higher education are to be considered by the church, it is the higher education agency that normally acts as intermediary between the church and the institutions. It must interpret the role of the colleges to the church and must carry out the wishes of the church as they relate to the colleges.

Planning in Higher Education

One of the most important, though less frequent, functions performed by church agencies is the planning of the church's efforts in the field of higher education. This includes the determination of how, when, and where new institutions are to be established; decisions as to whether weak institutions should be closed or merged with others; the initiation of important modifications in existing institutions; and similar matters.

There is no complete list of national church agencies for higher education. The *Information Service* of the National Council of the Churches of Christ lists 37 agencies in the denominations affiliated with the Council, to which may be added a lesser number of agencies representing Roman Catholic, Jewish, and Protestant groups not members of the Council. In the following pages are described the agencies of churches which sponsor ten or more colleges and universities. Most of the information has been provided by responsible officials of the churches or agencies involved.

BAPTISTS

The term "Baptist" refers to one of the largest groups of Christians in the United States, composed of 27 different denominations and sects. Among these groups the American Baptist Convention and the Southern Baptist Convention are the most active in higher education.

American Baptist Convention

The official agency responsible for overseeing the Convention's interests in higher education is the Department of Schools and Colleges of the Board of Education and Publication, located at Valley Forge, Pennsylvania. The staff is composed of a director, an assistant director, and a consultant.

In addition to secondary schools and seminaries, the Department lists 29 institutions of higher education as related to the Convention, of which four are junior colleges and 25 senior colleges or universities. However, of these, only 22 have taken official action adopting a statement entitled "What is a Baptist College?" prepared by representatives of the colleges and the Board of Education and Publication. This document defines a Baptist college as one whose faculty, administration, and trustees are committed to the following goals:

1. To maintain a thoroughly accredited curriculum based on recognized high academic standards of scholarship and teaching.
2. To develop a philosophy of Christian higher education; curriculum and teaching based on an avowedly Christian perspective.
3. To create a Christian community in the whole life of the college.
4. To provide a comprehensive program of religious life and training on campus, as well as in the local church and community.

5. To produce a vital relationship with the denomination and, through the denomination, with the ecumenical movement.
6. To anticipate active support from the American Baptist Convention through the Board of Education and the area constituency.[3]

The American Baptist Convention exercises no direct control over the colleges and universities related to it. Instead, it exerts its influence in informal ways affecting policy through advice and counsel, stimulating growth and development in certain areas through special grants, and otherwise helping institutions improve their programs. The Convention believes that each of its institutions should determine its own character and should define its purposes clearly. Moreover, it encourages the church-related colleges to seek able students and focus their programs on the cultivation of leadership for church and commonwealth. To this end, the colleges are expected to offer curricula preparing for humane leadership in key areas, such as journalism, government, and the church. The Department of Schools and Colleges favors the small college as the type of institution best fitted to develop "community."

In 1962 the Convention's budget provided $201,700 for its schools and colleges, plus an additional $146,742 in direct grants to institutions. A revolving loan fund, which is expected to reach $500,000, is maintained for emergencies in the colleges. Also, the Board holds endowment funds for certain institutions. It nominates persons for membership on the boards of trustees of some of the institutions. The Convention provides public relations services and expert counsel to assist colleges in their fund-raising efforts. It underwrites Christian emphasis programs in individual institutions up to $250 for visiting leaders and supports other special projects, such as Islamic studies and student exchange programs.[4]

Southern Baptist Convention

The Southern Baptist Convention itself owns seven theological seminaries but no colleges and universities. Ownership of collegiate institutions rests in the 28 cooperating state conventions. The state conventions own, operate, and support 33 senior colleges and 19 junior colleges.

Although the Southern Baptist Convention has adopted no official general statement defining its role in higher education, from the time of its organization in the middle of the nineteenth century there has been a

[3] *What Is a Baptist College Related to the American Baptist Convention?* (New York: Division of Christian Higher Education, Board of Education and Publication, American Baptist Convention, 1957).
[4] This statement is based on material provided by Elmer G. Million, Director, Department of Schools and Colleges, Board of Education and Publication, American Baptist Convention.

continuing interest in the promotion of higher education. The Convention has recognized the importance of providing Christian higher education under Baptist sponsorship to supply the church with an informed laity and a trained ministry. The high degree of autonomy in the state conventions composing the Southern Baptist Convention does not easily lend itself to the formulation of a statement of policy which would be binding on the Convention as a whole. Leaders are hopeful, however, that a general statement on the Convention's interests in higher education may eventually be adopted.

The agency responsible for the Convention's activities in higher education is the Education Commission, with offices in Nashville, Tennessee. The Commission is composed of 18 members, and its affairs are administered by an Executive Secretary-Treasurer and an Associate Secretary. It is responsible directly to the Convention. It has a four-fold program as follows: (1) promotion and information; (2) school and college studies and surveys; (3) teacher recruitment and placement; and (4) assistance in student recruitment. Ownership and financial support by a state convention are the basis for inclusion on the list of institutions related to the Southern Baptist Convention.

The Commission has no authority over the colleges. It receives no funds from the Convention for the support of the current operations of its related colleges, although the Convention does appropriate about $20,000 annually to the Commission for graduate fellowships for faculty members. The Commission sponsors a Baptist College Sunday in February when attention is directed to the institutions, but no offering is taken for college purposes. Church support for the colleges comes directly from the state conventions. In 1963 the Texas Convention, for example, began a three-year campaign with a goal of $28,000,000 for its colleges. A number of other state conventions were raising as much as $12,000,000 each. Some of the Southern Baptist colleges, however, receive very limited church support.[5]

CHRISTIAN CHURCHES (DISCIPLES OF CHRIST)

The higher educational interests of the Christian Churches are represented in the program of the Board of Higher Education, in which 16 senior colleges and universities and three junior colleges hold membership. In education, as in other areas of their work, the Christian Churches have always emphasized maximal freedom and minimal ecclesiastical control.

[5] The authors are indebted to Rabun L. Brantley, Executive Secretary, Education Commission, Southern Baptist Convention, for the material on which the foregoing statement is based.

Most of the Disciples institutions have self-perpetuating boards which govern their affairs and own their assets. They report to the International Convention of the communion through the Board of Higher Education, which has headquarters at Indianapolis, Indiana. Its officers are the President, Assistant Executive Secretary, Assistant Executive Secretary-Treasurer, and a secretarial assistant. It is organized into five departments: Department of Administration and Research, Department of Christian Institutions, Joint Commission of Campus Christian Life, Department of Christian Vocations, and Department of Publications and Public Relations.

If a college holds membership in the Board of Higher Education, it is then entitled to seek financial support from the churches in an assigned geographical area. Membership, however, does not imply central control in any sense of the word; indeed, control by the Board is specifically prohibited by its charter. The board is an instrumentality which provides avenues through which cooperation among the institutions and between them and the churches may be facilitated. The Articles of Incorporation of the Board state:

The object of this corporation shall be to promote comity, cooperation, and unity among other institutions; to inform Disciples of Christ as to the importance of these institutions in promoting Christian education; to encourage adherence to high educational standards; to publish such literature as may be deemed advisable; to aid colleges and other educational institutions fostered by the Disciples of Christ by securing for them gifts of endowment and betterments of various kinds; for current expenses necessary to the successful administration of these institutions; and to provide ways and means of mutual helpfulness to those engaged in the task of Christian education among the Disciples of Christ.[6]

In addition to the colleges and universities, the Disciple schools of religion, Bible chairs, and foundations on non-Disciple campuses are affiliated with the Board of Higher Education.[7]

EPISCOPAL CHURCH

The Episcopal Church does not have an official agency within its structure which is responsible for the total program of higher education, although there are ten colleges with some relationship to the Church. The responsibility for four of these colleges, which were established for the education of Negroes, is vested in the American Church Institute. The other six colleges are recognized as Episcopal either on historical grounds

[6] "Articles of Incorporation," Board of Higher Education, Disciples of Christ. Article 11.
[7] The information and publications on which this section is based were provided by Harlie L. Smith, President, Board of Higher Education, Disciples of Christ.

or by virtue of an informal relationship agreed on by the college and the Church and sometimes evidenced by clerical representation on the board of trustees. Recently, the Association of Episcopal Colleges was founded for the purpose of raising funds for the eight degree-granting colleges of the Church. The Association is not an official church agency, nor does it pretend to discharge the functions commonly performed by the boards of higher education in other communions.

The American Church Institute is a corporation of the Episcopal Church responsible to the Executive Council and the General Convention. It is also an integral part of the Division of Domestic Missions of the Home Department of the Executive Council. As mentioned earlier, the Institute is responsible for the four predominantly Negro colleges affiliated with the Church. A statement prepared by officials of the Institute describes its functions as follows:

In some ways, the Institute functions like a holding company in the public utility field; it attempts to do for the educational organizations certain tasks that it is better equipped to handle than any individual school. It directs fund-raising campaigns and attempts to secure grants for the individual schools from educational and other charitable foundations. It handles the investments for a number of the schools and makes a strong effort to aid the school authorities in meeting emergencies which inevitably arise where the schools have limited financial resources.[8]

The Institute does not own any of the colleges under its supervision, nor does it control them directly. It does, however, attempt to exert a strong influence by encouraging their boards and administrations to provide better educational programs, and it furnishes advice and counsel to this end. The Director and Associate Director of the Institute are members of three of the four boards of trustees, and the Director is a "visitor" at the fourth. During 1963 the Institute provided $465,000 for the support of the colleges, some of it for capital purposes. In addition, it contributed $40,000 toward the support of faculty retirement plans.[9]

LUTHERANS

Three of the Lutheran Churches are quite active in American higher education. In addition, an inter-Lutheran agency—the National Lutheran Educational Conference—plays a significant role.

---

[8] From a typewritten statement prepared by officials of the Institute.
[9] The authors are grateful to Charles M. Guilbert, Secretary, Executive Council, Protestant Episcopal Church, for preparing materials on which the foregoing statement is based.

American Lutheran Church

The American Lutheran Church has no official statement of policy defining its interests in higher education. However, the Constitution of the Church clearly reflects an interest. Among others, there are provisions for ownership of colleges by the Church and for requiring that "the teaching and life in these institutions shall be in conformity with the doctrines of the American Lutheran Church." [10]

The agency of the Church responsible for its program of higher education is the Board of College Education, with offices in Minneapolis, Minnesota. It is composed of 12 members elected by the Convention and is responsible for formulating the general policies governing American Lutheran colleges. The professional staff includes an Executive Director and an Assistant Director.

The Board controls ten degree-granting colleges and one junior college, plus one college operated jointly with the Lutheran Church in America. Each of these institutions has its own board of regents (elected by corporate bodies consisting of representatives of congregations from sections of the Church or the entire Church), which has full legal and ecclesiastical authority to operate the college within the general policies of the Board of College Education. The Executive Director of the Board is a member of each of the separate governing boards, thus providing a most effective relationship between the colleges and the Board. The President of the Church and the Chairman of the Board of College Education participate in the election of the presidents of all American Lutheran colleges.

Through the Board of College Education and under policies established by it, the colleges receive substantial amounts of money for current and capital purposes. In 1963 funds for current operation amounted to $115 per student for the 15,000 students enrolled in the colleges affiliated with the Church. The Board audits the accounts of each institution annually. It sponsors annual workshops for presidents, deans, business managers, development officers, and others. In conversation with the authors, the Executive Director remarked that he and his assistant knew all of the administrators and trustees and 75 percent of the faculty in the twelve institutions.

The Board is guided by two general principles: (1) a college should have its own legal identity with its own integrity and its own sense of responsibility; and (2) the Church should have a measure of control over the colleges because they are a part of the program of the Church—they are the Church in higher education. The Board attempts to keep these

[10] Constitution of the American Lutheran Church, Article XIII, Section 5A (2). *Handbook of the American Lutheran Church*, Edition 1960, Revised.

two principles in balance, which probably accounts for the vigor that appears to characterize the American Lutheran Church program in higher education.[11]

Lutheran Church in America

The agency of the Lutheran Church in America responsible for higher educational activities is the Board of College Education and Church Vocation, which has offices in New York City. The professional staff consists of the Executive Secretary of the Board and the Secretary of College Education. Nineteen senior colleges and three junior colleges in the United States are listed as related to this church. As mentioned earlier, one of the senior colleges is a cooperative venture with the American Lutheran Church. The definition of a college related to the denomination is largely historical, although efforts are now being made to define the relationship more precisely. The nature of the relationship varies from ownership by the Church, in some cases, to an institutional by-law requiring the presidency to be filled by a Lutheran in others. For the most part, the question of church relationship has been left to the synods.

Although the Board has less control over the colleges than do the synods, it does exercise influence through the allocation of funds, the establishment of standards, and consultation. In 1963 the Board distributed $300,982 to the colleges in amounts ranging from $3,200 to $74,000.[12]

Lutheran Church-Missouri Synod

At its 1962 convention the Synod adopted a statement outlining its convictions with respect to higher education. This statement sets forth 30 basic assumptions which are intended as the framework for long-range planning and general policy formation. The following passage from that document explains the Synod's view of higher education as an integral part of the church program:

The work of the synodical colleges and seminaries is church work in a vital and even essential sense as they, on behalf of all congregations and pastors, fulfil the divine obligation to enlist, teach, and guide consecrated and competent persons into the service of the Lord and His church.

Although pastors and teachers in parish service constitute the great majority of the graduates of the synodical professional training program, estimates are also necessary to plan for persons in specialized ministries such as synodi-

[11] The foregoing statement is based on material supplied by Sidney A. Rand, formerly Executive Director, Board of College Education, American Lutheran Church.

[12] The foregoing sketch is based on information obtained from E. Theodore Bachman, Executive Secretary, Board of College Education and Church Vocation, Lutheran Church in America.

cal professors, community high school instructors, directors of the workers in religious education, military and institutional chaplains, synodical and District executives, and lay and church workers.

An adequate forecast will include an estimate of the numbers of students who should be graduated from the Synod's theological seminaries and colleges, so that the estimated needs for pastors, teachers, and deaconesses can be met.[13]

The Board for Higher Education is the official agency of higher education in the Church. It has a professional staff of two, with offices in St. Louis. The Board has commissions in the following areas: curriculum, advisory council, student personnel services, business management, and recruitment policies.

The Board controls nine junior colleges, four senior colleges, and two seminaries in the United States, and one junior college in Canada. These institutions are called "synodical colleges." Another institution, Valparaiso University, Valparaiso, Indiana, although not controlled by the Board, may be considered as related to the Lutheran Church-Missouri Synod. It does not receive direct synodical support, but a "Valparaiso Sunday" is sponsored annually by the Synod to promote the cause of the University.

The Board exercises a large degree of control over its institutions. It plans the establishment of new synodical colleges. It controls the general character of the educational program offered, the staffing of the colleges, their budgets, and plant additions or alterations. The responsibility of the Board is to operate a system of higher education designed to provide an adequate supply of competent teachers, pastors, and other professional workers for the Church.

Through the Board the Church provides substantial funds for the operation of the colleges and underwrites the cost of new physical facilities. About 50 percent of the funds for current operation come from the Synod. In 1963 these funds totaled $7,200,000. For the same year the Church provided $3,450,000 for construction on new campuses.

There are few, if any, agencies in other churches which control the colleges related to their churches as completely as does the Board for Higher Education of the Lutheran Church-Missouri Synod. The policies of the Church with respect to higher education are definite, and the Church is ready to provide the financial support necessary to carry out the program. The Board has been given responsibility for planning and broad authority to act.[14]

[13] "Reports and Memorials, Cleveland, Ohio, June 20–30, 1962. II. Review and Preview, A. Basic Assumptions." (The 1962 Convention of the Lutheran Church-Missouri Synod. Mimeographed.)
[14] This statement was prepared from material provided by Arthur M. Ahlschwede, Executive Secretary, Board for Higher Education, Lutheran Church-Missouri Synod.

National Lutheran Educational Conference

Although it is not an agency concerned with the higher educational program of a single church, the National Lutheran Educational Conference should be mentioned as an organization which influences church-related higher education. A statement by the Council describes it as "the oldest inter-Lutheran agency in America. Its membership includes 17 seminaries, 30 colleges, five junior colleges, two other schools, four boards of college and theological education, and a number of interested individuals." [15]

The Council has no authority over its member colleges. Instead, its purpose is to stimulate and assist Lutheran colleges to improve their programs. The Council administers, for example, a fellowship program open to faculty members and seniors in member colleges who wish to work for doctorates and who agree to teach in Lutheran colleges or seminaries when they have completed their graduate study.

METHODIST CHURCH

The Division of Higher Education of the Board of Education, with offices in Nashville, Tennessee, is the agency of the Methodist Church responsible for higher education. The Division is divided into three departments: Educational Institutions, College and University Religious Life, and Ministerial Education. The Division has nine staff members who have direct contact with colleges and universities. Eight universities, 76 colleges, and 21 junior colleges are related to the Methodist Church.

According to the *Discipline of the Methodist Church* the Division of Higher Education represents the Church in all activities connected with secondary, higher, and ministerial education. The relationship between the Division and the institutions is advisory and correlative.

The *Discipline* sets forth the following objectives of the Division:

I. To develop an educational plan and purpose which definitely relates the institutions to the church.

II. To foster within these institutions highest educational standards and soundest business practices.

III. To aid the institutions to create and maintain an atmosphere conducive to the development of a Christian philosophy of life.[16]

---

[15] "More Power at Lutheran Colleges and Seminaries." (Washington: National Lutheran Educational Conference, n.d.)

[16] Quoted in Division of Higher Education, Board of Education, The Methodist Church, "Functions of the Division of Higher Education, Methodist Board of Education," (Nashville, Tennessee, n.d.), p. 2. (Typewritten)

The services performed by the Division include the following:

1. Initiation and prosecution of nationwide effort to gain understanding and support from church sources for Methodist schools, colleges, and Wesley Foundations. In this function the Division seeks to create a national attitude of appreciation for Christian higher education and a conscience regarding moral and financial support. Within such a framework local efforts prosper more readily.
2. Counsel and service to over 700 units of the Methodist Student Movement and Wesley Foundations; advisory and survey work with foundations and supporting annual conferences; liaison with the United Student Christian Council and the World Student Christian Federation.
3. An expanding program in ministerial and theological education, including provisions for in-service training (over 18,500 involved in 1960-61), and a growing emphasis on recruitment.
4. Counsel to boards of trustees and college presidents on fundamental educational matters—academic, administrative, financial. Additional outside consultants are supplied when requested. Consultation services upon request in every area of college life—business management, plant and building problems, endowment management, personnel, curriculum, religious program, public relations and fund-raising, library and others. Regional and state-wide trustee conferences are held regularly as well as consultation services to individual trustee boards.
5. Counsel to annual conferences regarding related educational institutions, to conference boards of education, to commissions on Christian higher education.
6. Counsel to presidents, deans, directors of religious life regarding campus religious cultivation.
7. Field work in regional and district conferences on educational problems. An annual Institute of Higher Education at Nashville, dealing with all types of administrative concerns.
8. Institutional surveys and studies, including institution-wide and limited-area, as well as state and conference studies.
9. Assistance with faculty conferences of all types.
10. Exchange of information regarding new and important ideas and practices, especially through a number of publications.
11. Administration in cooperation with schools and colleges, of the largest (approximately five and one-half millions of dollars) single student loan fund in the United States. In 1960–61 over $967,940 was loaned.
12. Cultivation and administration of the National Methodist Scholarship program—nearly $300,000 in scholarships granted in 1960–61.
13. A program to identify increasing numbers of promising teaching candidates for Methodist schools, colleges, and Wesley Foundations.
14. Liaison with leading educational agencies of the United States, such as the American Council on Education, the National Education Association, the American Alumni Council, the American College Public Relations Association. (One of the Division staff was a recent member of the executive committee of the American Council on Education.)
15. Close cooperation with other church educational agencies including the

National Council of Churches. Represents the schools, colleges, universities, and Wesley Foundations to various World Service and other Methodist Agencies, such as the Central Office of Promotion; the Television, Radio and Film Commission; the Methodist Publishing House; and the Methodist Press.[17]

The Methodist University Senate, existing separately from the Division of Higher Education but working closely with it, is composed of 21 "practical" educators. It serves an accrediting and standardizing function for Methodist higher education. The purposes of the Senate are as follows:

1. To accredit and classify institutions related to the Methodist Church, or adjudged to be so related.
2. To protect the church against educational malpractice by these institutions, or against ill-timed and ill-conceived educational expansion.
3. To serve as counselor of the Board of Education on "matters of educational policy."
4. To serve as a "consultant and counselor on all educational matters to all educational institutions related to the church."

In order to carry out these responsibilities, the Senate holds broad investigative powers. It may on its own initiative or upon the request of any general board of the church investigate "the personnel, scholastic requirements, resources, and procedure of any designated educational institution (claiming or adjudged to be) related to the Methodist Church." The Senate has rarely used these powers.

The Senate is today more closely linked with the Division of Higher Education than was originally the case. Earlier Senate members were appointed by the bishops, but now only ten of the twenty-one members are appointed by the Council of Bishops, the remaining eleven being elected by the Board of Education. No member of the Board of Education may be a member of the Senate, but the General Secretary of the Division of Higher Education is the Executive Secretary of the Senate.[18]

PRESBYTERIANS

Two Presbyterian bodies—the Presbyterian Church in the U.S. and the United Presbyterian Church—are especially well represented in higher education. Seventy-four collegiate institutions are related to these two churches.

Presbyterian Church in the United States

Throughout its history the Presbyterian Church in the U.S. has fostered higher education, supporting colleges in earlier days to supply an

[17] *Ibid.*
[18] This section describing the Methodist Church and its program of higher education is based largely on material provided by Myron F. Wicke, General Secretary, Division of Higher Education, Board of Education, The Methodist Church, Nashville, Tennessee.

educated ministry and in more recent times to provide higher educational opportunities for the youth of the Church under Christian influences. A statement of the Church's concern in higher education has been issued by its Board of Christian Education.[19] This statement recognizes the peculiar role of the college—that it must be a genuine intellectual community, free to seek and disseminate the truth. It seeks to promote a covenant relationship between the Church and the college, rather than a contractual one, implying "mutual confidence, respect, the giving and the accepting in good faith of responsibilities, and the endeavor of both sides to live up to commitments." The Church recognizes that the college has the right to expect understanding and financial support, concern for its welfare, program, and progress. The Church, in turn, expects from its colleges fidelity to the covenant relationship, unashamed witnessing of the Christian faith, educational programs of first-rate quality, the development of a mature Christian faith in its youth who will assume leadership in the Church, and scholarly assistance in keeping the life of the Church relevant and effective in a world of confusion.

The agency responsible for higher educational activities in the Presbyterian Church in the U.S. is the Division of Higher Education of the Board of Christian Education, with offices in Richmond, Virginia. The Division is comprised of the Departments of Christian Vocation, Schools and Colleges, Enlistment, and Campus Christian Life. The executive officer is the Secretary of the Division, who is also the President of the Presbyterian Educational Association of the South.

The Division publishes a set of standards or requirements which must be met by institutions wishing to be listed as "Presbyterian" colleges. These are:

1. Two-thirds of the trustees of the institution are to be elected, nominated, or ratified by one or more presbyteries or synods of said church.
2. The president or chief officer is to be a member of the Presbyterian Church in the United States.
3. All regular members of the faculty are to be active members of some evangelical church, a majority being Presbyterians.
4. The college shall provide thorough courses in the Bible and shall require at least one of these for graduation.
5. The college shall submit annually to the Executive Committee of Christian Education and Ministerial Relief full financial information on forms supplied by the committee, with a full audit if the committee so desires.

[19] "Higher Education and the Church," a statement prepared by General Assembly's Advisory Council on Higher Education (Richmond, Virginia: Board of Christian Education, Presbyterian Church in the U.S., n.d.).

6. The college shall be fully accredited by the regional accrediting agency.[20]

To be recognized as an "affiliated Presbyterian college" an institution must subscribe to a similar set of standards which, however, differ with respect to the composition of the board of control and to the church membership of faculty persons. The "affiliated" status is less demanding than "Presbyterian" status. Fifteen senior colleges and five junior colleges are recognized as Presbyterian institutions. Three others, one of which is a junior college, are affiliated with the Church.

The Division of Higher Education plays only a minor role in the financial support of these institutions. Church contributions come to the colleges directly from the synods. The Board of Christian Education, however, has available a challenge fund of about $100,000 which is used for such purposes as scholarship and fellowship aid, lecture series, and special needs. This is shared by the colleges with the seminaries and the Campus Christian Life program. The Division lends its assistance in the organization and promotion of campaigns for financial support undertaken by the colleges or the synods.[21]

United Presbyterian Church

The agency responsible for higher education in the United Presbyterian Church is the General Division of Higher Education of the Board of Christian Education, located in Philadelphia. The staff includes the Secretary of the Division, an Associate Secretary, and one assistant. In addition, there are four field representatives of the Division, whose responsibilities include working with the colleges, and two other staff members responsible for specialized programs directly involving the colleges. Forty-five colleges are related to the Church through the Board of Christian Education, all of which are four-year institutions. Legally, these institutions are related, in varying degrees, to the several synods of the Church rather than to the Church as a national body.

The Board of National Missions of the Church also has a responsibility in the field of higher education. Six colleges, three of them junior colleges, are affiliated with this board.

Church funds in the amount of $1,250,000 were distributed through the Division in 1962-63 to the colleges for general operational support. Another $1,300,000 was raised by the synods and other judicatories for

---

[20] *Minutes of the Forty-Eighth Annual Meeting of the Presbyterian Educational Association of the South* (Richmond, Virginia: Division of Higher Education, Board of Christian Education, Presbyterian Church in the U.S., 1962).

[21] For the material on which this section is based we are indebted to Hunter B. Blakely, formerly Secretary, and Robert Bluford, Jr., Acting Secretary, Division of Higher Education, Board of Christian Education, Presbyterian Church in the U.S.

the current support of these institutions. In addition, capital funds are raised from time to time in the synods and presbyteries through special campaigns.

A statement setting forth the Church's position with respect to higher education, prepared by a special committee, was adopted by the General Assembly in 1961.[22] On the basis of this statement a reappraisal of each of the colleges related to the Church has been undertaken in an effort to clarify the relationship between the Church and the colleges and to determine the importance and cost of the Church involvement in the support and sponsorship of its colleges.

For some time the Division used a set of standards, approved by the Board of Christian Education and the Presbyterian College Union (the association of presidents of the related colleges), as a criterion for determining whether an institution was entitled to be identified as Presbyterian Church related and to receive financial support. These standards have undergone considerable revision and have been adopted in their new form by the Board of Christian Education as "Administrative Guidelines for Colleges Related to the United Presbyterian Church, U.S.A." The essential portions of this statement are as follows:

I. General Policy
  A. Colleges related to the United Presbyterian Church in the U.S.A. shall have the declared purpose to fulfill the conditions and expectations set forth for the church-related colleges in the official statement, *The Church and Higher Education,* adopted by the 173rd General Assembly (1961).
  B. The purpose of this church-college relationship, in keeping with the Reformed tradition, is to affirm that the Lordship of Christ over the life and work of man includes his intellectual pursuits and to assist these colleges to be free, responsible, and creative institutions of higher learning. This purpose can be fully realized only through academic excellence in the college and through the academic freedom which will provide each student and teacher opportunity for independent initiative in his search for truth and in his encounter with the world.
  Integral elements in this freedom must be the opportunity to participate in an active exchange between the realm of faith and the academic disciplines and the opportunity to experience religious conviction in community.
  C. It is recognized that the educational concern of the Church, through the colleges related to it, is expressed in varying circumstances. Uniformity in the manner of the Christian witness of the colleges may be no more possible or desirable than uniformity in academic policies and practices. Each church-related college, however, will seek to be a

[22] *The Church and Higher Education.* An official statement approved by the 173rd General Assembly of the United Presbyterian Church in the United States of America. (Philadelphia: United Presbyterian Church in the U.S.A., 1961).

learning community which in word and act will provide for intellectual advancement and religious growth, and will undertake to carry out the ethical implications of the faith it represents.

II. Administrative Policies and Procedures
   A. The purpose of the institution as a college related to the United Presbyterian Church in the U.S.A. shall be clearly stated in the college catalogue and other appropriate publications of the institution.
   B. The church-related college will seek to have well-qualified faculty members, administrative officers, and trustees who are dedicated to its declared institutional purpose and will faithfully serve the primary objective of academic excellence in a community which encourages true piety with integrity of thought and character.
   C. Accreditation by a regional accrediting agency shall be required, but it is to be regarded as a minimum indication of the quality to be sought by a college related to the United Presbyterian Church in the U.S.A.
   D. The college shall provide courses in religious studies, including study of the Bible, and shall require of each student a mature classroom encounter with the Judaic-Christian heritage.[23]

The United Presbyterian colleges and universities are one of the larger groups of church-related institutions.[24]

ROMAN CATHOLIC CHURCH

The popular assumption that Roman Catholic higher education is centrally controlled is not at all accurate. On the contrary, Catholic institutions are established and administered by many subdivisions of the Church—orders, congregations, dioceses—each of which operates with a high degree of independence in educational matters.

It is difficult to determine the exact number of Roman Catholic agencies for higher education. *The Official Catholic Directory, 1963,* listed 93 orders and congregations of priests, 19 of brothers, and 295 of religious women, or a total of 407 religious communities in the United States.[25] Many of these carry on work at one or more levels of education. Some of them operate institutions at all levels, while others restrict their teaching ministry to one or two, such as the operation of high schools or colleges. The National Catholic Educational Association lists 14 agencies in the

[23] *Administrative Guidelines for Colleges Related to the United Presbyterian Church in the U.S.A.* (Philadelphia: General Division of Higher Education, Board of Christian Education, United Presbyterian Church in the U.S.A., 1963).

[24] This sketch of the United Presbyterian Church and its program of higher education is based in part on information and publications provided by Harold H. Viehman, Secretary, General Division of Higher Education, Board of Christian Education, United Presbyterian Church in the U.S.A.

[25] *The Official Catholic Directory, 1963* (New York: P. M. Kenedy and Sons, 1963), pp. 878–929.

field of Catholic higher education, but the list is incomplete. The exact number is not known.

In contrast to the Protestant denominational agencies that exercise a variety of functions with respect to their affiliated institutions, the Roman Catholic agencies are organized chiefly to facilitate communication among the membership—to provide an opportunity to exchange ideas, coordinate educational effort, conserve and promote the values of Catholic higher education, and present the Catholic philosophy of life in general. Only occasionally do they exercise legislative power. For the most part, they act in a consultative and advisory capacity.

Because many of the Catholic orders and congregations maintain extensive systems of elementary and secondary education as well as colleges, their educational associations are concerned with the entire range of education from the elementary schools through the college and university level. However, a committee or commission within the agency is often set up to deal specifically with the interests of the higher institutions. Meetings of the several agencies are customarily held in conjunction with the conventions of the National Catholic Educational Association. Two organizations—the Dominican Education Association and the Jesuit Educational Association—are described here as important examples of Catholic agencies in higher education.

Dominican Education Association

The Dominican Education Association was established to interpret and promote the educational principles and practices of the Dominican Order among its members—Dominican priests and sisters engaged in education in the United States.

The Dominican Order, officially entitled the Order of Preachers, has been associated with education since the thirteenth century. The first Dominicans came to this hemisphere in 1510. Most American Dominican priests are assigned to the teaching of philosophy and theology in their own seminaries and houses of study, in other seminaries, and in colleges and universities throughout the United States. Also, there are approximately 17,000 Sisters of the Third Order of St. Dominic in the United States, most of whom are engaged in teaching. They conduct 26 colleges and many secondary and elementary schools in addition to institutes and schools devoted to special education.

The Dominican Education Association is the agency through which the Dominican Order channels its interests in education. The annual meeting is held in conjunction with the convention of the National Catholic Educational Association and consists of two sections. One of these is of a general character at which a scholarly paper is read and discussed. The other is comprised of three separate meetings for elementary, secondary, and higher education. Higher education is served through the College Section of the Association. Among the topics which have been discussed by the College Section are freedom and responsibility in the college, the place of Biblical studies, and psychology in liberal education. All members of the staff of the Association are part-time. An executive secretary coordinates its activities. The Association publishes a quarterly, the *Dominican Education Bulletin*.[26]

Jesuit Educational Association

This organization is comprised of the 137 educational institutions operated by the Society of Jesus, one of the largest of the teaching orders. The Jesuits conduct 28 colleges and universities in the United States.

The Jesuit Educational Association is primarily a service and advisory agency, as its Constitution makes clear:

1. In general, the objectives of the Association are to promote and make more efficient all educational activities of American Jesuits.
2. Specifically, the objectives are the following:
   a. Cooperation of member institutions in furthering the aims of Catholic education.
   b. Promotion of scholarship and research in Jesuit institutions, and publication of the results of such scholarship and research.
   c. Conservation of the permanent essential features of the Jesuit educational tradition, and the necessary adaptation of its accidental features to national and local needs of the time.
   d. Increased academic efficiency of all Jesuit institutions.
   e. Effective presentation of the Catholic philosophy of life.
   f. Corporate cooperation with other educational associations, Catholic and secular.
   g. Collaboration with Jesuit educators and Jesuit educational institutions in other countries on the common problems of Jesuit education.
   h. Experimental study of educational problems in America.
   i. Provision for wider knowledge in the United States of the Jesuit educational system, its theory and its practice.[27]

The Association is divided into regional and provincial groups and has departments of higher and secondary education. In addition, five permanent commissions have been organized: secondary schools, liberal arts colleges, professional schools, seminaries, and graduate schools.

---

[26] The authors are indebted to Sister Mary Peter, O.P., President, Dominican Education Association, for providing the material on which the foregoing statement is based.

[27] *Constitution of the Jesuit Educational Association* (New York: The Association, 1948), p. 1.

The Constitution provides for a Board of Governors, consisting of the Provincial Superior of each of the Jesuit provinces of the United States; an Executive Director; and an Executive Committee. The Association publishes the *Jesuit Educational Quarterly*.[28] Its offices are located in New York City.

A complete list of all the organizations representing the interests of orders, congregations, and communities in Roman Catholic higher education is not available. From what is known, however, it may be said that the two just described, the Dominican Education Association and the Jesuit Educational Association, are typical of the majority of the Catholic higher education agencies. Some of them are formally organized, as in the two illustrative cases, but others are quite informal. A number of the orders and communities direct their efforts in education primarily toward the elementary or secondary level and so maintain only one or two colleges. The Norbertine Educational Association, for example, includes one college and eleven secondary schools, whose representatives meet informally in connection with the National Catholic Educational Association. Some of the groups do not have a separate organization for promoting their interests in higher education, using instead the existing structure of the orders for this purpose. Illustrative of this approach is the informal educational association of the Religious of the Sacred Heart of Mary whose activities are coordinated through the Provincial Council.

A partial list of Catholic agencies is given here to suggest the scope of the organizational effort of the Church in higher education:

American Benedictine Academy
Augustinian Educational Association
Basilian Educational Conference
Christian Brothers Education Association
Christian Brothers of Ireland Education Association
Congregation of the Sisters of the Holy Cross, Board of Higher Education
Diocesan College Group (no official title; informally organized group of colleges supported by dioceses)
Educational Conference of Religious Sisters of Mercy
Educational Conference of the Priests of the Congregation of the Holy Cross
Franciscan Educational Conference
Marianist Education Conference
Norbertine Educational Association
Notre Dame de Namur Educational Association
Oblates of St. Francis de Sales Education Association

[28] The foregoing statement is based on information provided by Edward B. Rooney, S.J., President, Jesuit Educational Association.

Religious of the Sacred Heart of Mary (has an informal educational association)

Sisters of St. Joseph of Carondelet (has an unincorporated educational conference)

Vincentian Educational Meeting

Xaverian Brothers Educational Conference.[29]

GENERAL CONFERENCE OF SEVENTH-DAY ADVENTISTS

The General Conference includes in its national organization a Department of Education with responsibility for the total educational program of the Church: pre-school education, elementary and secondary schools, and colleges. The Department has an Advisory Committee, Quadrennial Councils, and a Board of Regents. The Board serves as the executive committee of the Association of Seventh-day Adventist Institutions of Higher Education and Secondary Schools. It also provides leadership for the Commission on Seventh-day Adventist Graduate Education in the United States.

Although the Seventh-day Adventist Church believes in decentralized administration, and each of its universities and colleges has its own board of trustees and enjoys institutional autonomy, annual, biennial, and quadrennial advisory and legislative bodies counsel and coordinate the overall educational program of the Church.

An Associate Secretary of the Department of Education is in charge of relationships with the ten senior colleges and one junior college affiliated with the denomination. Although the colleges are legally autonomous, the Department does exercise some control over the institutions through its support of their budgets. Each institution receives $50,000 a year from the General Conference. In addition, it receives from $150,000 to $400,000 from its own sponsoring conferences. Usually five or six state conferences of the Church operate a college, hence the word "union" is included in the title of some of the institutions (for example, Atlantic Union College). As a means of assuring quality construction, the Department must approve all plans for new buildings. Further, it has established a policy that institutions cannot proceed with building plans unless 75 percent of the money is in hand. Federal funds may not be used, and no borrowing program may exceed three years.

A new Adventist institution, Andrews University, offering programs at

[29] The writers are indebted to George F. Donovan, Professor of Higher Education, Catholic University of America, and William J. Dunne, S.J., former Associate Secretary, College and University Department, National Catholic Educational Association, for providing information on which this list is based.

the undergraduate and graduate levels, is being built in Michigan. The Church has contributed about $7,000,000 toward its support in the last three years.[30]

UNITED CHURCH OF CHRIST

The interests of the United Church of Christ in higher education are centered in the Division of Higher Education of the Board for Homeland Ministries and in the American Missionary Association. The latter association is the agency through which the former Congregational Christian Church administered its program of Negro higher education. Thirty-one colleges are affiliated with this denomination. The administrators of the colleges, together with the administrators of the seminaries and academies, constitute the Council for Higher Education. To maintain close liaison with the Board for Homeland Ministries, the Council includes as voting members some of the members of the Board.

The Council for Higher Education, in outlining its criteria for membership, defines the ideals of United Church colleges. An institution may become a member of the Council if it satisfies the following:

1. Evidences the highest regard for academic excellence as a college of the liberal arts and sciences and achieves at least the minimum standard for accreditation in its regional association.
2. Has a policy of complete openness to all students and faculty qualified for its academic program, and desires a variety of racial and economic groups for its academic community.
3. Recognizes religion as an integral part of the liberal arts and sciences; affirms its belief in religious and academic freedom; and provides a competent and commanding exposition of the Christian faith in terms relevant to the academic community and provocative to rival faiths and assumptions.
4. Openly acknowledges membership in this Council as one evidence of its relationship to the United Church of Christ.

On its part, the Council assures its member colleges that:

1. It is a voluntary association of colleges which wish to associate themselves with the tradition of excellence in the liberal arts and sciences represented by the uniting groups.
2. It signifies a common concern among its members for the importance of religion as a part of the intellectual and spiritual heritage but without the ecclesiastical controls sometimes associated with church colleges.
3. The church and college are independent entities, each with a special mis-

---

[30] Much of the preceding material was drawn from a statement prepared by T.S. Geraty, Associate Secretary, Department of Education, General Conference of Seventh-day Adventists.

sion to perform in society, and that each can better perform its mission if it is in communication with the other.[31]

OTHER PROTESTANT DENOMINATIONAL AGENCIES

In addition to the foregoing agencies, there are others which sponsor fewer than ten institutions in each case. They perform functions similar to those described for the larger agencies. Often a single board of the church includes supervision of higher education among its responsibilities for Christian education. Typically, the staff is quite small; indeed, in some cases the president of one of the institutions affiliated with the denomination serves as chairman or executive officer of the group. In the course of the study we have corresponded with the following:

African Methodist Episcopal Church—Division of Educational Institutions, General Board of Education

Associate Reformed Presbyterian Synod—Department of Christian Education

Church of the Brethren—Christian Education Commission, General Brotherhood Board

Church of God—Commission on Christian Higher Education, Executive Council

Church of Jesus Christ of Latter-day Saints—Department of Education, Church Board of Education, Unified Church School System

Church of the Nazarene—Department of Education

Evangelical United Brethren Church—Board of Christian Education

Free Methodist Church of North America—Department of Educational Institutions, Commission on Christian Education of the Board of Education

The General Conference Mennonite Church—Board of Education and Publication

Moravian Church in America—The Board of Christian Education, Provincial Elders' Conference

Reorganized Church of Jesus Christ of Latter Day Saints—Committee on Higher Education

Seventh Day Baptist General Conference

Church of the United Brethren in Christ—Department of Christian Education

Wesleyan Methodist Church of America—Board of Administration

[31] Adopted by the Council for Higher Education, United Church of Christ, October 2, 1963. The foregoing description is based on information provided by Wesley A. Hotchkiss, General Secretary, Division of Higher Education and the American Missionary Association, United Church Board for Homeland Ministries, United Church of Christ.

A few of the smaller denominations, ordinarily sponsoring only one college, do not have formal arrangements for the supervision of higher education. Some of the functions performed by the larger church agencies, such as gathering comparative statistical information, are not required when only one college is involved. Other functions, such as preparing descriptive information about the college, are performed by the administrative staff of the college itself. Among these smaller church groups are the following:

Brethren Church
Christian Reformed Church
Cumberland Presbyterian Church
Evangelical Lutheran Synod
Reformed Church in America
Society of Friends
Synod of the Reformed Presbyterian Church of North America

OTHER AGENCIES

Each of the foregoing organizations is an agency of a specific religious group, either a whole church or denomination or a Roman Catholic order or congregation. Each has been described in order to show how the church in a great variety of ways has organized itself to promote its interests in higher education. In addition to these agencies, there are four other organizations that should be mentioned because of their close association with church-related higher education.

Association of American Colleges

Although it is not a church agency, the Association of American Colleges should be included in this appendix because of its important involvement in the goals of church-sponsored higher education. It probably exerts a greater influence than any other organization on the whole range of church institutions—Protestant, Roman Catholic, and others. The Association is primarily concerned with liberal arts education, as are most church institutions:

The purpose of the Association shall be the promotion of higher education in all its forms in the colleges of liberal arts and sciences which shall become members of this Association, and the prosecution of such plans as may make more efficient the institutions included in its membership.[32]

[32] "Constitution of the Association of American Colleges, Inc." *Liberal Education*, Vol. L, No. 1 (March 1964), p. 161.

The membership of the Association (835 institutions in 1963) includes colleges of liberal arts and sciences in public institutions as well as those which are privately controlled and denominationally affiliated.

The Association is governed by a Board of Directors comprised of the officers, the retiring Chairman, and four Directors elected at the annual meeting. The chief executive officer is the President, who has offices in Washington, D.C. An annual meeting is held in January.

The Association carries on its work through standing commissions, one of which is the Commission on Religion in Higher Education. The interest of the Association in church-sponsored colleges is reflected in numerous ways—in purpose, in program, and in personnel.[33]

Commission on Higher Education

The Commission on Higher Education of the National Council of the Churches of Christ describes its purpose as follows:

The Commission is the agency through which the denominations may express their common concerns, develop a united strategy, carry out cooperative programs, and initiate experiments, consultation, and surveys in the area of faith and learning as it concerns the churches. It also provides a forum in which the participating denominations may study and discuss vital issues and problems in higher education.[34]

The Commission operates through a number of committees and program units, most of which are concerned with phases of campus Christian work, plus one entitled "Associated Section of Denominational Board Secretaries on Higher Education," which provides an opportunity for Board secretaries to share experience and information. The governing body of the Commission is the Administrative Committee, composed of representatives of church boards of higher education and of program units. Leadership is given by a General Director, assisted by an Associate General Director. The Commission, which has offices at the National Council headquarters in New York, publishes *The Christian Scholar*, a quarterly devoted to the discussion of problems of faith and learning.[35]

Council of Protestant Colleges and Universities

Established in 1959 and affiliated with the National Council of the

---

[33] The foregoing account is based in part on information provided by F. L. Wormald, Vice President, Association of American Colleges.

[34] *The Commission on Higher Education, A Descriptive Statement.* (New York: National Council of the Churches of Christ in the United States of America, n.d.), p. 2.

[35] The authors are indebted to Hubert C. Noble, General Director, Commission on Higher Education, National Council of the Churches of Christ, for providing materials on which this section is based.

Churches of Christ, the Council of Protestant Colleges and Universities provides a means by which institutions which have sprung from a Protestant educational philosophy may achieve an identity in American higher education. Through it, also, member institutions may seek to assess the distinctive roles they play in achieving the broader goals of higher education in general.

The Council's program includes (1) representation of the membership at the national level in higher education; (2) sponsorship of a Quadrennial Convocation, the themes of which center on major problems of the member institutions; (3) an Annual Meeting held in conjunction with meetings of the Association of American Colleges; (4) cooperation with the Commission on Higher Education of the National Council of the Churches of Christ in the promotion of National Christian College Day; (5) support of the Cooperative College Faculty Registry; and (6) the pursuit of studies in the field of Christian higher education.

The Council publishes annual *Proceedings*. It has offices in Washington, D.C. Administrative leadership is provided by the President of the Council. The membership was comprised of 286 institutions in 1963.[36]

National Catholic Educational Association

Among the many Roman Catholic agencies in the field of higher education, the one all-inclusive organization is the National Catholic Educational Association. Founded in 1904, the objectives of the Association are:

To promote the welfare of Catholic education.
To provide Catholic education with national and regional representation.
To enable Catholic educators to work together for professional growth.
To foster cooperation between Catholic education and other professional agencies in the field of education.
To facilitate the interchange of ideas.
To conduct educational research.
To enable Catholic education to interpret itself to the public.[37]

The Association embraces the entire range of education from the elementary through the graduate school levels. In 1963, 258 colleges and universities were included in its membership. These institutions enrolled about 40 percent of all Catholic students in higher education.

The Association is organized into seven departments: Major Seminary, Minor Seminary, College and University, School Superintendents, Ele-

[36] This section is based on materials provided by James M. Godard, President, Council of Protestant Colleges and Universities.
[37] *National Catholic Educational Association.* (A descriptive leaflet issued by the Association.)

mentary School, Secondary School, and Special Education. As circumstances require, commissions and *ad hoc* committees are established to consider important problems and to conduct special studies.

The Association maintains offices in Washington, D.C. The chief administrative officer is the Executive Secretary, who is assisted by full-time Associate Secretaries representing each of the departments of the Association. It holds an annual national convention and regional meetings for the discussion of educational problems; provides a clearing house for ideas; and publishes bulletins, newsletters, directories, and other materials of interest to educators.

One of the problems of considerable concern to many in the Association is the proliferation of Catholic institutions of higher education. The Association has no power to prevent the establishment of new institutions, but it feels it renders a service by providing an opportunity to discuss the problems involved in the creation of new colleges, such as the need for adequate financial support and the availability of competent faculty. Related to this problem is the desirability of regional and national planning in Catholic education. The Association attempts to encourage full discussion of such matters and facilitates a measure of cooperation among Catholic institutions of higher education.[38]

CONCLUDING COMMENT

As we have reviewed the work of the several national church agencies in higher education, we have come to the conclusion that, by and large, they have not been an important factor in shaping church-sponsored higher education in this country. In a small minority of cases, they have been given definite control over their affiliated institutions and exercise a strong influence on them. But for the most part, they appear to play a relatively minor role. Specifically, the following observations may be made.

There is great diversity in the organizational status of the various agencies. Some are integral parts of the administrative structure of their parent churches, while others are affiliated with churches in more tenuous ways.

Most of the agencies lack the authority, budget, and staff to enable them to be influential agencies in their churches' programs of higher education. Again, there are exceptions. A few are well equipped to carry on their work and to assume leadership in planning and supporting an effective program, but they are not representative of the whole group of agencies.

[38] This section is based largely on information supplied by Frederick G. Hochwalt, Executive Secretary, National Catholic Educational Association.

In some churches the role of the church colleges and their proper relationships to the churches are so ill-defined that the agencies are almost powerless to exercise constructive influence. The confusion within these churches as to the function of the colleges makes it well-nigh impossible for educational agencies to define their own tasks.

In view of the wide variation in polity among American religious bodies, it is impossible to suggest a single organizational pattern that would be appropriate for all church agencies of higher education. Each communion must develop a pattern of relationship to its colleges that is appropriate to its own tradition.

In most denominational groupings of colleges and universities the presidents of the institutions are in a stronger position to take the initiative in charting the course of church-related higher education than are church agencies.

Bibliography

The scholarly literature on American church-related higher education, as such, is quite limited. There are, however, numerous publications in a variety of fields that illuminate particular aspects of the problems of church colleges and universities. In the bibliography that follows, we have tried to bring together much of the systematic literature of this type, together with the few items dealing specifically with higher education under church auspices. The references are drawn from the fields of education, history, philosophy, theology, psychology, sociology, political science, and economics. This is a selective bibliography; the authors have included the items they have found most helpful in the Danforth study. This by no means exhausts the serious literature on the subject.

For purposes of convenience, the materials have been classified under five broad headings: History of Higher Education, Liberal Education, Church and Higher Education, Religion and Values in Higher Education, and Administration and Financing of Higher Education.

HISTORY OF HIGHER EDUCATION

Brubacher, John S., and Rudy, Willis. *Higher Education in Transition: An American History: 1636–1956.* New York: Harper & Brothers, 1958.

Butts, R. Freeman. *The College Charts Its Course.* New York: McGraw-Hill Book Company, 1939.

Butts, R. Freeman, and Cremin, Lawrence A. *History of Education in American Culture.* New York: Henry Holt and Company, 1953.

Clapp, Margaret, editor. *The Modern University.* Ithaca: Cornell University Press, 1950.

Cowley, William H. "European Influences on American Higher Education," *Educational Record,* XX, April, 1939, pp. 165–190.

Dawson, Christopher. *The Crisis of Western Education.* New York: Sheed and Ward, 1961.

Gauss, George E., S.J. *Saint Ignatius' Idea of a Jesuit University: A Study in the History of Catholic Education* . . . Milwaukee: Marquette University Press, 1954.

Godbold, Albea. *The Church College of the Old South.* Durham: Duke University Press, 1944.

Gross, John O. *Methodist Beginnings in Higher Education.* Nashville: Division of Educational Institutions, Board of Education, The Methodist Church, 1959.

Harbison, E. Harris. *The Christian Scholar in the Age of the Reformation.* New York: Charles Scribner's Sons, 1956.

Harper, William Rainey. *The Trend in Higher Education.* Chicago: University of Chicago Press, 1905.

Haskins, C. H. *The Rise of Universities.* Ithaca: Cornell University Press, 1957.
Hofstadter, Richard, and Hardy, C. DeWitt. *The Development and Scope of Higher Education in the United States.* New York: Columbia University Press, 1952.
Hofstadter, Richard, and Metzger, Walter P. *The Development of Academic Freedom in the United States.* New York: Columbia University Press, 1955.

Morison, Samuel Eliot, and Commager, Henry Steele. *The Growth of the American Republic.* New York: Oxford University Press, 1950.

Power, Edward J. *A History of Catholic Higher Education in the United States.* Milwaukee: Bruce Publishing Company, 1958.

Rashdall, Hastings. *The Universities of Europe in the Middle Ages,* edited by F. M. Powicke and A. B. Emden. 3 vols. New York: Oxford University Press, 1936.
Rudolph, Frederick. *The American College and University: A History.* New York: Alfred A. Knopf, 1962.

Schmidt, George P. *The Liberal Arts College: A Chapter in American Cultural History.* New Brunswick: Rutgers University Press, 1957.
Snavely, Guy E. *The Church and the Four-Year College: An Appraisal of Their Relation.* New York: Harper & Brothers, 1955.
Storr, Richard J. *The Beginnings of Graduate Education in America.* Chicago: University of Chicago Press, 1953.

Tewksbury, Donald G. *The Founding of American Colleges and Universities before the Civil War.* New York: Teachers College Press, 1932.
Thomas, Russell. *The Search for a Common Learning: General Education 1800–1960.* New York: McGraw-Hill Book Company, 1962.

Ulich, Robert. *History of Educational Thought.* New York: American Book Company, 1950.

LIBERAL EDUCATION

Astin, Alexander W. "A Re-Examination of College Productivity," *Journal of Educational Psychology,* Vol. 52, No. 3, pp. 173–178.
———. "Productivity of Undergraduate Institutions," *Science,* Vol. 136, No. 3511, pp.129-135.

Barker, Sir Ernest. *Traditions of Civility.* London: Cambridge University Press, 1948.
Berelson, Bernard. *Graduate Education in the United States.* New York: McGraw-Hill Book Company, Inc., 1960.
Bloom, Benjamin S., editor. *Taxonomy of Educational Objectives: The Classification of Educational Goals. Handbook 1: Cognitive Domain.* New York: Longmans, Green and Co., 1956.
Butterfield, Victor L. *The Faith of a Liberal College.* Middletown, Conn.: Wesleyan University, 1955.

Carmichael, Oliver C. *Graduate Education: A Critique and a Program*. New York: Harper & Brothers, 1961.

Cooper, Russell M., editor. *The Two Ends of the Log: Learning and Teaching in Today's College*. Minneapolis: University of Minnesota Press, 1958.

Culler, A. Dwight. *The Imperial Intellect: A Study of Newman's Educational Ideal*. New Haven: Yale University Press, 1955.

Dressel, Paul L., and Associates. *Evaluation in Higher Education*. Boston: Houghton Mifflin Company, 1961.

Farrell, Allan P. *The Jesuit Code of Liberal Education*. Milwaukee: Bruce Publishing Company, 1938.

Fletcher, C. Scott, editor. *Education for Public Responsibility*. New York: W. W. Norton & Company, Inc., 1961.

Flexner, Abraham. *Universities: American, English, German*. New York: Oxford University Press, 1930.

Foerster, Norman. *The Future of the Liberal College*. New York: D. Appleton-Century Company, Inc., 1938.

French, Sidney J., editor. *Accent on Teaching: Experiments in General Education*. New York: Harper & Brothers, 1954.

General Education in School and College: A Committee Report by Members of the Faculties of Andover, Exeter, Lawrenceville, Harvard, Princeton, and Yale. Cambridge: Harvard University Press, 1953.

General Education in a Free Society. Report of the Harvard Committee. Cambridge: Harvard University Press, 1945.

Greene, Theodore M., et al. *Liberal Education Re-Examined*. New York: Harper & Brothers, 1943.

Griswold, A. Whitney. *Liberal Education and the Democratic Ideal and Other Essays*. New Haven: Yale University Press, 1959.

Highet, Gilbert. *The Art of Teaching*. New York: Alfred A. Knopf, 1950.

Hutchins, Robert M. *The Conflict in Education in a Democratic Society*. New York: Harper & Brothers, 1953.

Hutchins, Robert M. *The Great Conversation: The Substance of a Liberal Education*. Vol. I, *Great Books of the Western World*. Chicago: Encyclopedia Britannica, 1952.

————. *The Higher Learning in America*. New Haven: Yale University Press, 1936.

Jones, Arthur J. *The Education of Youth for Leadership*. New York: McGraw-Hill Book Company, Inc., 1938.

Keniston, Hayward. *Graduate Study and Research in the Arts & Sciences at the University of Pennsylvania*. Philadelphia: University of Pennsylvania Press, 1958.

Klapper, Paul. "The Professional Preparation of the College Teacher," *Journal of General Education*, XXIV (1949), pp. 228–244.

Knapp, Robert H. *The Origins of American Humanistic Scholars*. Englewood Cliffs, New Jersey: Prentice-Hall, Inc., 1964.

Knapp, Robert H., and Goodrich, H. B. *Origins of American Scientists.* Chicago: University of Chicago Press, 1952.

Knapp, Robert H. and Greenbaum, Joseph J. *The Younger American Scholar: His Collegiate Origins.* Chicago: University of Chicago Press, 1953.

Kunkel, B. W. and Prentice, D. B. "The Colleges in 'Who's Who in America'", *School & Society,* LXXIV, October 20, 1951, p. 241.

Liberal Education: Summary of a Discussion by the Trustees of the Carnegie Foundation for the Advancement of Teaching. New York: The Foundation. 1956.

Livingstone, Richard. *Education for a World Adrift.* London: Cambridge University Press, 1944.

————. *Some Thoughts on University Education.* London: Cambridge University Press, 1948.

Manuel, William A. and Altenderfer, Marion E. *Baccalaureate Origins of 1950–1959 Medical Graduates.* Public Health Monograph No. 66. Washington: U.S. Government Printing Office, 1961.

Mayhew, Lewis B. *The Smaller Liberal Arts College.* Washington: Center for Applied Research in Education, Inc., 1962.

McGrath, Earl J. *Are Liberal Arts Colleges Becoming Professional Schools?* New York: Teachers College Press, 1958.

————. *The Graduate School and the Decline of Liberal Education.* New York: Teachers College Press, 1959.

Maritain, Jacques. *Education at the Crossroads.* New Haven: Yale University Press, 1943.

Murphy, Gardner. *Freeing Intelligence Through Teaching: A Dialectic of the Rational and the Personal.* John Dewey Society Lectureship, No. 4. New York: Harper & Brothers, 1961.

Murphy, Lois B., and Raushenbush, Esther. *Achievement in the College Years: A Record of Intellectual and Personal Growth.* New York: Harper & Brothers, 1960.

Ness, Frederic W. and James, Benjamin D. *Graduate Study in the Liberal Arts College.* Washington: Association of American Colleges, 1962.

Newman, John Henry Cardinal. *The Idea of a University.* Garden City, New York: Doubleday & Company, Inc., 1959.

Norwood, Cyril. *The English Tradition of Education.* New York: E. P. Dutton and Company, 1930.

Ortega y Gasset, José. *Mission of the University.* Translated by H. L. Nostrand. Princeton: Princeton University Press, 1944.

Pfnister, Allan O. *A Report on the Baccalaureate Origins of College Faculties.* Washington: Association of American Colleges, 1961.

Prose, Sister M. Redempta. *The Liberal Arts Ideal in Catholic Colleges for Women in the United States.* Washington: Catholic University of America, 1943.

Pusey, Nathan M. *The Age of the Scholar: Observations on Education in a Troubled Decade.* Cambridge: Belknap Press of Harvard University Press, 1963.

Rattigan, Bernard Thomas. A Critical Study of the General Education Movement. Washington: Catholic University of America Press, 1952.

Reeves, Floyd W., et al. The Liberal Arts College. Chicago: University of Chicago Press, 1932.

Rudy, Willis. The Evolving Liberal Arts Curriculum: A Historical Review of Basic Theories. New York: Teachers College Press, 1960.

The St. John's Program: A Report. Annapolis, Maryland: St. John's College Press, 1955.

Severinghaus, Aura E., Carman, Harry J., and Cadbury, William E. Preparation for Medical Education: A Restudy. The Report of the Committee on the Resurvey of Preprofessional Education in the Liberal Arts College, Association of American Medical Colleges. New York: McGraw-Hill Book Company, Inc., 1961.

Smith, Huston. The Purposes of Higher Education. New York: Harper & Brothers, 1955.

Snow, C. P. The Two Cultures and the Scientific Revolution. New York: Cambridge University Press, 1961.

Special Studies Project, Report V, Rockefeller Brothers Fund, Inc. The Pursuit of Excellence. Garden City, New York: Doubleday and Company, Inc., 1958.

Spencer, Herbert. "What Knowledge Is of Most Worth, Selections," Great Issues in Education: Readings for Discussion, II, pp. 75-112. Chicago: Great Books Foundation, 1956.

Stanley, Arthur P. The Life and Correspondence of T. Arnold. New York: Charles Scribner's Sons, 1889.

Strachey, Lytton. "Dr. Arnold," in Eminent Victorians. Garden City, New York: Garden City Publishing Co., Inc., n.d.

Torrance, E. Paul. Guiding Creative Talent. Englewood Cliffs, New Jersey: Prentice-Hall, Inc., 1962.

Trueblood, Elton. The Idea of a College. New York: Harper & Brothers, 1959.

Tyler, Ralph W. Basic Principles of Curriculum and Instruction. Chicago: University of Chicago Press, 1950.

Ulich, Robert. Three Thousand Years of Educational Wisdom. Cambridge: Harvard University Press, 1961.

Van Doren, Mark. Liberal Education. New York: Henry Holt and Company, 1943.

Warner, Rex. English Public Schools. London: Collins, 1945.

Whewell, William. On the Principles of English University Education. Second Edition. London: J. W. Parker, 1838.

Whitehead, Alfred North. Adventures of Ideas. New York: Macmillan Company, 1933.

———. The Aims of Education and Other Essays. New York: Mentor Books, 1949.

Wriston, Henry M. The Nature of a Liberal College. Appleton, Wisconsin: Lawrence College Press, 1937.

CHURCH AND HIGHER EDUCATION

Bender, Richard N. "The Scholar and the Life of the Church," *Religious Education*, LVI, No. 5 (September-October, 1961), pp. 323–329.

Bridston, Keith R. and Culver, Dwight W. *Pre-Seminary Education*. Report of the Lilly Endowment Study. Minneapolis: Augsburg Publishing House, 1965.

Brown, Robert McAfee. "The Reformed Tradition and Higher Education," *The Christian Scholar*, XLI, No. 1 (March, 1958), pp. 21–40.

Butterfield, Herbert. *Christianity and History*. New York: Charles Scribner's Sons, 1950.

Butts, R. Freeman. *The American Tradition in Religion and Education*. Boston: Beacon Press, 1950.

Cauthen, Kenneth. *The Impact of American Religious Liberalism*. New York and Evanston, Illinois: Harper & Row, Publishers, 1962.

Cogley, John, editor. *Religion in America*. New York: Meridian Books, 1958.

Cox, Harvey. *The Secular City: Secularization and Urbanization in Theological Perspective*. New York: Macmillan Company, 1965.

Cuninggim, Merrimon. *The Protestant Stake in Higher Education*. Washington: Council of Protestant Colleges and Universities, 1961.

Davies, Horton. *The Challenge of the Sects*. Philadelphia: Westminster Press, 1961.

Doescher, Waldemar. *The Church College in Today's Culture*. Minneapolis: Augsburg Publishing House, 1963.

Duley, John S. "The Work of the Church in the University", *The Christian Scholar*, XLII, No. 3 (September, 1959), pp. 201–214.

Eby, Frederick, editor. *Early Protestant Educators; the Educational Writings of Martin Luther, John Calvin, and Other Leaders of Protestant Thought*. New York: McGraw-Hill Book Company, 1931.

Ellis, John Tracy. *American Catholics and the Intellectual Life*. Chicago: Heritage Foundation, 1956.

The Faith, the Church and the University: A Report of a Conversation Among University Christians. Prepared for publication by Stephen F. Bayne, Jr., Cincinnati, Ohio: Forward Movement Publications, 1959.

Ferré, Nels F. S. "Contemporary Theology and Christian Higher Education," *The Christian Scholar*, XLI, No. 2 (June, 1958), pp. 142–157.

Fremantle, Anne, editor. *The Social Teachings of the Church*. New York: New American Library, 1963.

Gilkey, Langdon. *How the Church Can Minister to the World Without Losing Itself*. New York and Evanston, Illinois: Harper & Row, Publishers, 1964.

Gross, John O. "The Church and the College—A Partnership," *The Christian Scholar*, XXXVI, No. 1 (March, 1953), pp. 47–52.

Gustafson, James M. "The Clergy in the United States," *Daedalus*, Vol. 92, No. 4 (Fall, 1963), pp. 724–744.

Hazo, Samuel, editor. *The Christian Intellectual: Studies in the Relation of Catholicism to the Human Sciences.* Pittsburgh: Duquesne University Press, 1963.

"Higher Education and the Church," a statement prepared by General Assembly's Advisory Council on Higher Education. Richmond: Board of Christian Education, Presbyterian Church in the U.S., n.d.

Huess, John. *The True Function of a Christian Church.* West Cornwall, Connecticut: Episcopal Center, n.d.

Littell, Franklin Hamlin. *From State Church to Pluralism: A Protestant Interpretation of Religion in American History.* Garden City, New York: Doubleday & Company, Inc., 1962.

Mary Florence, S.L., editor. *Religious Life in the Church Today: Prospect and Retrospect.* Notre Dame, Indiana: University of Notre Dame Press, 1962.

McCluskey, Neil G., S.J., editor. *Catholic Education in America: A Documentary History.* Classics in Education, No. 21. New York: Bureau of Publications, Teachers College, Columbia University, 1964.

McKenna, David L. "Evangelical Colleges: The Race for Relevance," *Christianity Today*, Vol. VIII, No. 11 (February 28, 1964), pp. 13–17.

Means, Richard L. "Intellectuals Within the Church," *Religious Education*, LV, No. 5 (September-October, 1960), pp. 341–344.

Meyers, Bertrande, D.C. *Sisters for the 21st Century.* New York: Sheed and Ward, 1965.

Miller, Samuel H. *The Dilemma of Modern Belief.* New York and Evanston, Illinois: Harper & Row, Publishers, 1963.

Mollegen, Albert T. *Christianity and Modern Man: The Crisis of Secularism.* Indianapolis and New York: Bobbs-Merrill Company, Inc., 1962.

Nichols, James H. *History of Christianity (1650–1950): Secularization of the West.* New York: Ronald Press, 1956.

————. *Primer for Protestants.* New York: Association Press, 1947.

Niebuhr, H. Richard. *Christ and Culture.* New York: Harper & Brothers, Publishers, 1951.

Niebuhr, H. Richard, Williams, Daniel Day, and Gustafson, James M. *The Advancement of Theological Education.* New York: Harper & Brothers, Publishers, 1957.

Novak, Michael. *A New Generation: American and Catholic.* New York: Herder and Herder, 1964.

Obenhaus, Victor. *The Church and Faith in Mid-America.* Philadelphia: Westminster Press, 1963.

Pfnister, Allan O. "The Church in Higher Education—Imperative or Not?" *Lutheran Quarterly*, XIV, May, 1962, pp. 99–120.

Ramm, Bernard. *The Christian College in the Twentieth Century.* Grand Rapids, Michigan: William B. Erdmans Publishing Company, 1963.

Reddick, DeWitt C. *Church and Campus.* Richmond: John Knox Press, 1956.

Robinson, John A. T. *Honest to God.* London: SCM Press Ltd., 1963.

Scaff, Marilee K., editor. *Perspectives on a College Church*. New York: Association Press, 1961.
Shepherd, Massey H. *Liturgy and Education*. New York: Seabury Press, 1965.
Sister Ritamary, C.H.M., editor. *The Mind of the Church in the Formation of Sisters*. New York: Fordham University Press, 1956.
Swidler, Leonard. "Catholic Colleges: A Modest Proposal," *Commonweal*, Vol. LXXXI, No. 18 (January 29, 1965), pp. 559-562.

Temple, William. *Christianity and the Social Order*. Harmondsworth, Middlesex, England: Penguin Books, 1956.
The Church and Higher Education. An official statement approved by the 173rd General Assembly of the United Presbyterian Church in the United States of America.
The Official Catholic Directory, 1963. New York: P. M. Kenedy and Sons, 1963.
Tillich, Paul. *The Protestant Era*. Chicago: University of Chicago Press, 1948.

Van Buren, Paul M. *The Secular Meaning of the Gospel*. New York: Macmillan Company, 1963.

Wakin, Edward. *The Catholic Campus*. New York: Macmillan Company, 1963.
Wedel, Theodore O. *The Christianity of Main Street*. New York: Macmillan Company, 1950.
Weigel, Gustave. "American Catholic Intellectualism—A Theologian's Reflections," *Review of Politics*, XIX, July, 1957, pp. 275–306.
Wicke, Myron F. *The Church-Related College*. Washington: Center for Applied Research in Education, Inc., 1964.
Williams, Daniel Day. *What Present-Day Theologians Are Thinking*. Revised edition. New York and Evanston, Illinois: Harper & Row, Publishers, 1959.
Williams, George H. *The Theological Idea of the University*. New York: Commission on Higher Education, National Council of the Churches of Christ, 1954.

RELIGION AND VALUES IN HIGHER EDUCATION

Allport, Gordon W. *The Individual and His Religion: A Psychological Interpretation*. New York: Macmillan Company, 1960.
Austin, C. Grey. *A Century of Religion at the University of Michigan: A Case Study in Religion and the State University*. Ann Arbor, Michigan: University of Michigan, 1957.

Baillie, John. *The Mind of the Modern University*. University Pamphlets No. 1. London: SCM Press Ltd., 1946.
Barton, Allen H. *Studying the Effects of College Education: A Methodological Examination of Changing Values in College*. New Haven: Edward W. Hazen Foundation, 1959.
Beach, Waldo. *Conscience on Campus*. New York: Association Press, 1958.
Becker, Howard, and Geer, Blanche. "The Fate of Idealism in Medical School," *American Sociological Review*, XXIII, February, 1958, pp. 50–56.

Bender, Richard N. " 'Illumined' Liberal Education," *The Christian Scholar*, XLI, No. 2 (June, 1958), pp. 101–108.

Bergendoff, Conrad. *The Idea of a Christian College*. Rock Island, Illinois: Augustana College, 1962.

Blanshard, Brand, editor. *Education in the Age of Science*. New York: Basic Books, Inc., 1958.

Brinton, Crane. *The Shaping of the Modern Mind: The Concluding Half of Ideas and Men*. New York: Prentice-Hall, Inc., 1950.

Bronowski, Jacob. *Science and Human Values*. New York: Harper & Brothers, 1959.

Brown, Charles. "Biblical Faith and the University's Purpose," *The University Bookman*, II, No. 4 (Summer, 1962), pp. 81–86.

Brown, Kenneth I. *Not Minds Alone: Some Frontiers of Christian Education*. New York: Harper & Brothers, 1954.

Brown, Merle E. "Objectivity and Commitment," *The Christian Scholar*, XLII, No. 1 (March, 1959), pp. 7–15.

Brownell, Baker. *The College and the Community*. New York: Harper & Brothers, 1952.

Buckley, William F., Jr. *God and Man at Yale: The Superstitions of "Academic Freedom"*. Chicago: Henry Regnery Company, 1951.

Butler, J. Donald. "The Church, the College, and Human Values," *The Christian Scholar*, XLII, No. 3 (September, 1959), pp. 215–220.

Buttrick, George A. *Biblical Thought and the Secular University*. Baton Rouge, Louisiana: Louisiana State University Press, 1960.

Buttrick, George A., et al. "Toward A Philosophy of the Church-Related University," *The Christian Scholar*, XLV, No. 2 (Summer, 1962), pp. 90–97.

Carpenter, Marjorie. "How Can Teachers Realistically Seek to Affect Student Attitudes and Values Through Courses in the Various Disciplines?" in *Current Issues in Higher Education*, 1958. Proceedings of the Thirteenth Annual National Conference in Higher Education, Association for Higher Education, pp. 108–115.

Carpenter, Marjorie, editor. *The Larger Learning: Teaching Values to College Students*. Dubuque, Iowa: William C. Brown Company, Publishers, 1960.

Casserley, J. V. Langmead. "The Theology of Education," *The Christian Scholar*, XXXVII, No. 2 (June, 1954), pp. 142–150.

Clark, G. Kitson. *The Kingdom of Free Men*. London: Cambridge University Press, 1957.

Convocation of Christian Colleges 1962, Advance Preprints. Washington: Council of Protestant Colleges and Universities, 1962.

Clough, Shepard B. *Basic Values of Western Civilization*. New York: Columbia University Press, 1960.

Cogley, John, et al. *Natural Law and Modern Society*. Cleveland, Ohio, and New York: World Publishing Company, 1962.

Coleman, A. J. *The Task of the Christian in the University*. New York: Association Press, 1947.

College Reading and Religion. New Haven: Yale University Press, 1946.

"A Complete Report of the First Quadrennial Convocation of Christian Colleges," *The Christian Scholar*, XXXVII, Supplement issue, Autumn, 1954.

Cuninggim, Merrimon. *The College Seeks Religion.* New Haven: Yale University Press, 1947.

Deferrari, Roy J., editor. *Essays on Catholic Education in the United States.* Washington: Catholic University of America Press, 1942.

Dewey, John. *A Common Faith.* New Haven: Yale University Press, 1960.

Diederich, Paul. "Methods of Studying Ethical Development," *Religious Education*, I, No. 3 (May–June, 1955), pp. 162–166.

Ditmanson, Harold H., et al. *Christian Faith and the Liberal Arts.* Minneapolis: Augsburg Publishing House, 1960.

Donohue, John W., S.J. *Jesuit Education: An Essay on the Foundations of Its Idea.* New York: Fordham University Press, 1963.

Eddy, Edward. *The College Influence on Student Character.* Washington: American Council on Education, 1959.

Ensley, F. Gerald: *The Marks of Christian Education.* Nashville: Methodist Publishing House, 1958.

English, Raymond: *Of Human Freedom.* Fifth Series, Faculty Papers. New York: National Council, Protestant Episcopal Church, 1959.

Espy, R. H. Edwin. *The Religion of College Teachers.* New York: Association Press, 1951.

Evans, M. Stanton. *Revolt on the Campus.* Chicago: Henry Regnery Company, 1961.

Fairchild, Hoxie N. *Religious Perspectives in College Teaching.* New York: Ronald Press Co., 1952.

Fitzpatrick, Edward A. *The Catholic College and the World Today.* Milwaukee: Bruce Publishing Company, 1954.

Freedman, Mervin B. *Impact of College.* New Dimensions in Higher Education, No. 4. Washington: Office of Education, U.S. Department of Health, Education, and Welfare, 1960.

Frye, Roland Mushat. "The Church College and the Revival of Humane Learning," *The Christian Scholar*, XL, No. 2 (June, 1957), pp. 93–100.

Fuller, Edmund, editor. *The Christian Idea of Education.* New Haven: Yale University Press, 1957.

Funkenstein, Daniel, King, Stanley H., and Drolette, Margaret. *Mastery of Stress.* Cambridge, Massachusetts: Harvard University Press, 1957.

Gaebelein, Frank E. *Christian Education in a Democracy.* New York: Oxford University Press, 1951.

Gauss, Christian, editor. *The Teaching of Religion in American Higher Education.* New York: Ronald Press Company, 1951.

Geier, Woodrow A., editor. *A Perspective on Methodist Higher Education.* Nashville: Division of Educational Institutions, Board of Education, The Methodist Church, 1960.

Geren, Paul. "Christianity, Communism, and College Students," *Liberal Education*, XLV, No. 3 (October, 1959), pp. 361–368.

Getzels, J. W., and Jackson, P. W. *Creativity and Intelligence.* New York: John Wiley & Sons, 1962.

Gleason, John P. "The Study of Christian Culture: A New Approach to General Education," *The Educational Record,* XL, No. 2 (April, 1959), pp. 155–158.

Goldsen, Rose K., et al. *What College Students Think.* Princeton, New Jersey: D. Van Nostrand Co., Inc., 1960.

Greeley, Andrew M. "Catholic Scholars of Tomorrow: Report on a Survey," *The Critic,* XX, No. 5 (April–May, 1962), pp. 24–26.

————. *Religion and Career: A Study of College Graduates.* New York: Sheed and Ward, 1963.

Griffith, Gwilym O. *Makers of Modern Thought.* London and Redhill, England: Lutterworth Press, 1948.

Hale, Oron J. "Faculty and Students: A Mid-Century Family Portrait," *The Christian Scholar,* XLI, No. 1 (March, 1958), pp. 5–14.

Hallowell, John H. "Christian Apologetics and the College Campus," *The Christian Scholar,* XXXVIII, No. 4 (December, 1955), pp. 259–269.

————. *Main Currents in Modern Political Thought.* New York: Henry Holt and Company, 1950.

————. "The Christian in the University," *Motive,* Vol. XXIII, No. 6 (March, 1963), pp. 36-43.

————. *The Moral Foundation of Democracy.* Chicago: University of Chicago Press, 1954.

Havemann, Ernest, and West, Patricia Salter. *They Went to College: The College Graduate in America Today.* New York: Harcourt, Brace and Co., 1952.

Henle, Robert J., S.J. "The Christian Tradition in Education," *Marquette University Magazine,* IV, No. 1 (Fall, 1962), pp. 16–19.

Hocking, William Ernest. *What Man Can Make of Man.* New York: Harper & Brothers, 1942.

————. *The Strength of Men and Nations.* New York: Harper & Brothers, 1960.

Hodges, H. A. *Christianity and the Modern World View.* New York: Macmillan Company, 1950.

————. *Objectivity and Impartiality.* University Pamphlets No. 2. London: SCM Press Ltd., 1946.

Hofstadter, Richard. *Anti-Intellectualism in American Life.* New York: Alfred A. Knopf, 1963.

Hong, Howard. *Integration in the Christian Liberal Arts College.* Northfield, Minnesota: St. Olaf College Press, 1956.

Hutchison, John. *Faith, Reason, and Existence: An Introduction to Contemporary Philosophy of Religion.* New York: Oxford University Press, 1956.

Jaspers, Karl. *Man in the Modern Age.* New York: Doubleday & Company, 1957.

Jacob, Philip. *Changing Values in College: An Exploratory Study of the Impact of College Teaching.* New York: Harper & Brothers Publishers, 1957.

Jeffreys, M. V. C. *Personal Values in the Modern World*. Baltimore: Penguin Books, 1962.

Katz, Wilber G. *Natural Law & Human Nature*, with comments by John Wild and Henry L. Shepherd. A Faculty Paper. New York: National Council, Episcopal Church, n.d.
Knight, Douglas M. "The College as a Community," *The Christian Scholar*, XL, No. 2 (June, 1957), pp. 85–92.

Lazarsfeld, Paul F., and Thielens, Wagner, Jr. *The Academic Mind*. Glencoe, Illinois: Free Press, 1958.
LeFevre, Perry. *The Christian Teacher*. New York: Abingdon Press, 1958.
Lewis, C. S. *The Abolition of Man*. New York: Macmillan Company, 1947.
Lilge, Frederic, *The Abuse of Learning*. New York: Macmillan Company, 1948.
Lippmann, Walter. *Essays in the Public Philosophy*. A Mentor Book. New York: New American Library, 1956.
Linton, Ralph, editor. *The Science of Man in the World Crisis*. New York: Columbia University Press, 1945.
Loew, Cornelius. *Modern Rivals to Christian Faith*. Philadelphia: Westminster Press, 1956.
Lowry, Howard. *The Mind's Adventure: Religion and Higher Education*. Philadelphia: Westminster Press, 1950.

Malik, Charles. "The Christian Educator and the Task of Evangelism," *The Christian Scholar*, XLI, No. 1 (March, 1958), pp. 56–57.
Mannheim, Karl. *Ideology and Utopia: An Introduction to the Sociology of Knowledge*. Translated from the German by Louis Wirth and Edward Shils. New York: Harcourt, Brace & World, 1936.
McGannon, J. Barry, S.J., Cooke, Bernard J., S.J., and Klubertauz, George P., S.J. *Christian Wisdom and Christian Formation: Theology, Philosophy, and the Catholic College Student*. New York: Sheed and Ward, 1964.
McGucken, William J., S.J. "Philosophy of Catholic Education," in *Philosophies of Education*, Forty-First Yearbook of the National Society for the Study of Education. Part I, pp. 281–282. Chicago: University of Chicago Press, 1942.
McLean, Milton D. and Kimber, Harry H. *Teaching of Religion in State Universities: Descriptions of Programs in Twenty-Five Institutions*. Ann Arbor, Michigan: Office of Religious Affairs, University of Michigan, 1960.
Martin, James Alfred, Jr. *Fact, Fiction and Faith*. New York: Oxford University Press, 1960.
Maslow, Abraham H. *New Knowledge in Human Values*. New York: Harper & Brothers, 1959.
Merriam, Thornton W., et al. *Religious Counseling of College Students*. American Council on Education Studies, Series VI—Student Personnel Work—No. 4. Washington: American Council on Education, 1943.
Merton, R. K., Reader, G. G., and Kendall, Patricia L., editors. *The Student Physician: Introductory Studies in the Sociology of Medical Education*. Cambridge, Massachusetts: Harvard University Press, 1957.

Mickey, Robert G. "Questions About the Christian College," *The Christian Scholar*, XLI, No. 1 (March, 1958), pp. 15–20.

Miller, Alexander. *Faith and Learning: Christian Faith and Higher Education in Twentieth Century America*. New York: Association Press, 1960.

Moberly, Walter. *The Crisis in the University*. London: SCM Press Ltd., 1949.

Mueller, William R. "Invitation to Theological Learning," *The Christian Scholar*, XLIII, No. 2 (Summer, 1960), pp. 128–134.

———. *The Prophetic Voice in Modern Fiction*. New York: Association Press, 1959.

Nash, Arnold S. *The University and the Modern World*. New York: Macmillan Company, 1943.

Newcomb, Theodore M. *Personality and Social Change: Attitude Formation in a Student Community*. New York: Dryden Press, 1943.

Niebuhr, Reinhold. *The Nature and Destiny of Man*. New York: Charles Scribner's Sons, 1943.

Ong, Walter J., S.J. "Religion, Scholarship, and the Resituation of Man," *Daedalus*, XCI, No. 2, (Spring, 1962), pp. 418–436.

Pace, C. R. "Methods of Describing College Cultures," *Teachers College Record*, LXIII, No. 4 (January, 1962), pp. 267–277.

Pace, C. R., and Stern, G. G. *A Criterion Study of College Environment*. Syracuse, New York: Psychological Research Center, Syracuse University, 1958.

Peck, R. F., and Havighurst, R. J. *The Psychology of Character Development*. New York: John Wiley & Sons, Inc., 1960.

Phenix, Philip H. *Education and the Common Good*. New York: Harper & Brothers, 1961.

Poteat, William H., et al. "Symposium: Can and Should a College Be Christian?" *The Christian Scholar*, XXXVII, No. 1 (March, 1954), pp. 12–33.

Power, Edward J. "Are Catholic Colleges Academically Respectable?" *Homiletic and Pastoral Review*, LVI (June, 1956), pp. 734–742.

Pusey, Nathan M. "Education and Religious Faith," *Trustee*, XIV, No. 4 (September, 1960).

Redden, John D. and Ryan, Francis A. *A Catholic Philosophy of Education*. Milwaukee: Bruce Publishing Company, 1956.

Riesman, David. *Constraint and Variety in American Education*. Garden City, New York: Doubleday and Company, Inc., 1958.

———. *The Lonely Crowd: A Study of the Changing American Character*. New Haven: Yale University Press, 1950.

Riesman, David, Jacob, Philip, and Sanford, Nevitt. *Spotlight on the College Student*. Washington: American Council on Education, 1959.

Ross, Murray G. *Religious Beliefs of Youth*. New York: Association Press, 1950.

Ryan, John. *The Idea of a Catholic College*. New York: Sheed and Ward, 1945.

St. Olaf College Self Study Committee. *Integration in the Christian Liberal Arts College.* Northfield, Minnesota: St. Olaf College Press, 1956.

Sanford, Nevitt. *The American College: A Psychological and Social Interpretation of the Higher Learning.* New York: John Wiley & Sons, Inc., 1962.

Sebaly, A. L. *Teacher Education and Religion.* Oneonta, New York: American Association of Colleges for Teacher Education, 1959.

Shuster, George N. *Education and Moral Wisdom.* New York: Harper & Brothers, 1960.

Smith, John E. *Value Convictions and Higher Education.* New Haven: Edward W. Hazen Foundation, 1959.

Smith, Seymour A. *Religious Cooperation in State Universities: An Historical Sketch.* Ann Arbor, Michigan: University of Michigan, 1957.

Stace, W. T. *Religion and the Modern Mind.* Philadelphia: J. B. Lippincott Company, 1960.

Stern, George G., Stein, Morris I., and Bloom, Benjamin S. *Methods in Personality Assessment.* Glencoe, Illinois: Free Press, 1956.

Stewart, Randall. "Doctrines of Man in American Literature," *Religious Education,* LVI, No. 2 (March–April, 1961), pp. 83–89.

"Symposium: The Humanities and Religious Education," *Religious Education,* LII, No. 6 (November–December, 1958), pp. 483–514.

Taylor, Jerome. "Religion in College," *The Commonweal,* LXXXI, No. 18 (January 29, 1960), pp. 483-486.

Tead, Ordway. *Character-Building and Higher Education.* New York: Macmillan Company, 1953.

"The Affirming College," *Christianity Today,* Vol. 9, No. 24 (September 10, 1965), pp. 25–26.

Tucker, Louis Leonard. *Puritan Protagonist: President Thomas Clap of Yale College.* Chapel Hill: University of North Carolina Press, 1962.

"The Vocation of the Christian College: Addresses and Reports of the Second Quadrennial Convocation of Christian Colleges," *The Christian Scholar,* XLI, Special issue, Autumn, 1958.

Von Grueninger, John Paul. *Toward A Christian Philosophy of Higher Education.* Philadelphia: Westminster Press, 1957.

Walsh, Chad. *Campus Gods on Trial.* Revised and enlarged edition. New York: Macmillan Company, 1962.

Walter, Erich A., editor. *Religion and the State University.* Ann Arbor, Michigan: University of Michigan Press, 1958.

Whitehead, Alfred North. *Science and the Modern World.* New York: Macmillan Company, 1925.

Wild, John. "The New Vocation to Leisure," *Modern Age,* VI, No. 3 (Summer, 1962), pp. 305–312.

Wilder, Amos N., editor. *Liberal Learning and Religion.* New York: Harper & Brothers, 1951.

Williams, George H. *Wilderness and Paradise in Christian Thought.* New York and Evanston, Illinois: Harper & Row, 1962.

Williams, Robin, Jr. *American Society: A Sociological Interpretation.* New York: Alfred A. Knopf, 1957.

Wise, W. Max. *They Come for the Best of Reasons—College Students Today*. Washington: American Council on Education, 1958.
Witmer, S. A. *The Bible College Story: Education with Dimension*. Manhasset, New York: Channel Press, Inc., 1962.

ADMINISTRATION AND FINANCING OF HIGHER EDUCATION

Barnard, Chester I. *The Functions of the Executive*. Cambridge, Massachusetts: Harvard University Press, 1958.
Bokelman, W. Robert. *Higher Education Planning and Management Data, 1960–61*. Washington: U.S. Government Printing Office, 1961.
Bolman, Frederick deW. *How College Presidents Are Chosen*. Washington: American Council on Education, 1965.
Brumbaugh, A. J. *Problems in College Administration*. Nashville: Division of Educational Institutions, Board of Education, The Methodist Church, 1956.
Burns, Gerald P., editor. *Administrators in Higher Education: Their Functions and Coordination*. New York: Harper & Brothers, Publishers, 1962.

Caplow, Theodore, and Reece, J. McGee. *The Academic Market Place*. New York: Basic Books, Inc., 1958.
Cartter, Allan M., editor. *American Universities and Colleges*. 9th edition. Washington: American Council on Education, 1964.
Cole, Luella. *The Background for College Teaching*. New York: Farrar & Rinehart, Inc., 1940.
Corson, John J. *Governance of Colleges and Universities*. New York: McGraw-Hill Book Co., 1960.

Davis, Paul H. "Changes Are Coming in the Colleges," *Journal of Higher Education*, XXXIII, No. 3 (March, 1962), pp. 141–147.
Deferrari, Roy J. *College Organization and Administration*. Washington: Catholic University of America Press, 1947.
Dimock, Marshall E. *Administrative Vitality: The Conflict with Bureaucracy*. New York: Harper & Brothers, 1959.
Dodds, Harold W. *The Academic President—Educator or Caretaker?* New York: McGraw-Hill Book Co., 1962.
Donovan, George F. *Selected Problems in Administration of American Higher Education*. Washington: Catholic University of America Press, 1964.
Donovan, J. D. *The Academic Man in the Catholic College*. New York: Sheed and Ward, 1964.

Educational Policies Commission. *Higher Education in a Decade of Decision*. Washington: National Education Association, 1957.

Gordon, Thomas. *Group-Centered Leadership*. Boston: Houghton Mifflin Company, 1955.

Harris, Seymour E. *Higher Education: Resources and Finance*. New York: McGraw-Hill Book Company, Inc., 1962.

————. *Higher Education in the United States.* Cambridge, Massachusetts: Harvard University Press, 1960.

Henderson, Algo D. *Policies and Practices in Higher Education.* New York: Harper & Brothers, 1960.

Higher Education for American Democracy, A Report of the President's Commission on Higher Education. Washington: Government Printing Office, 1947.

Hill, Alfred T. *The Small College Meets the Challenge: The Story of CASC.* New York: McGraw-Hill Book Company, Inc., 1959.

Hughes, Raymond M. A. *Manual for Trustees of Colleges and Universities.* Ames: Iowa State College Press, 1951.

Hungate, Thad Lewis. *Financing the Future of Higher Education.* New York: Columbia University Press, 1957.

Jones, Thomas E., Stanford, Edward V., O.S.A., and White, Goodrich C. *Letters to College Presidents.* Englewood Cliffs, New Jersey: Prentice-Hall, Inc., 1964.

Keezer, Dexter M. *Financing Higher Education, 1960-70.* New York: McGraw-Hill Book Company, Inc., 1959.

Kerr, Clark. *The Uses of the University.* Cambridge, Massachusetts: Harvard University Press, 1964.

Knight, Douglas M. *The Federal Government and Higher Education.* Englewood Cliffs, New Jersey: Prentice-Hall, Inc., 1960.

Mayhew, Lewis B. "Destiny of the Liberal Arts College," *Liberal Education,* XLVIII, No. 3 (October, 1962), pp. 408–414.

McGrath, Earl J. "The Future of the Protestant College," *Liberal Education,* XLVII, No. 1 (March, 1961), pp. 45–57.

————. *The Predominantly Negro Colleges and Universities in Transition.* New York: Teachers College Press, 1965.

Messersmith, James C. *Church-Related Boards Responsible for Higher Education.* O. E. 53021, Bulletin No. 1964, No. 13. Washington: Office of Education, U.S. Department of Health, Education, and Welfare, 1964.

Miles, Matthew B. *Learning to Work in Groups: A Program Guide for Educational Leaders.* New York: Teachers College Press, 1959.

Millett, John D. *Financing Higher Education in the United States.* New York: Columbia University Press, 1952.

Mushkin, Selma J. *Economics of Higher Education.* Washington: Office of Education, U.S. Department of Health, Education, and Welfare, 1962.

Rivlin, Alice M. *The Role of the Federal Government in Financing Higher Education.* Washington: Brookings Institution, 1961.

Ruml, Beardsley, and Morrison, Donald H. *Memo to a College Trustee: A Report on Financial and Structural Problems of the Liberal College.* New York: McGraw-Hill Book Company, Inc., 1959.

Russell, John Dale. *The Finance of Higher Education.* Chicago: University of Chicago Press, 1954.

Selden, William K. *Accreditation: A Struggle Over Standards in Higher Education.* New York: Harper & Brothers, 1960.

Stanford, Edward V., O.S.A. *A Guide to Catholic College Administration.* Westminster, Maryland: Newman Press, 1965.

Stoke, Harold W. *The American College President.* New York: Harper & Brothers, 1959.

Tasch, Alcuin W. *Religious Constitutions and Institutional Control.* Ph.D. dissertation, Department of Education, University of Chicago, 1953.

The Appraisal of Teaching. Ann Arbor, Michigan: University of Michigan, 1959.

Tickton, Sydney G. *Needed: A Ten Year College Budget.* New York: Fund for the Advancement of Education, 1961.

Upton, Miller. *"Quality in Higher Education," North Central Association Quarterly,* XXXVII, No. 4 (Spring, 1963), pp. 307–314.

White, Goodrich C. *The Education of the Administrator.* Nashville: Division of Educational Institutions, Board of Education, The Methodist Church, 1957.

Wicke, Myron F. *Handbook for Trustees of Church-Related Colleges.* New York and Nashville: Commission on Christian Higher Education, National Council of the Churches of Christ in the U.S.A., and Division of Educational Institutions, Board of Education, The Methodist Church, 1957.

Wilsey, H. Lawrence. *Long Range Planning for Colleges and Universities.* Washington: American College Public Relations Association, 1961.

Index

academic quality, summary of 100-101
accreditation
  distribution of institutions by
    agencies 23, 26
  history of 54-56
  lack of, in church-sponsored
    institutions 101
  methodology 56
acknowledgements vii-xiii
administrative officers 27-28, 158-163,
  202-203
  see also organization of institutions
admissions 63-65, 88-90, 211
African Methodist Episcopal Church
  145, 272
  see also Methodist institutions
Agnes Scott College 217, 230
  studies of graduates 119
Alabama, University of
  studies of graduates 107, 119
Albion College 230
  studies of graduates 107
Alfred University
  studies of graduates 104
Allegheny College 230
  studies of graduates 107
Altenderfer, Marion E. 105-108
alumni 102-123, 189, 212
America 125
American Association of Theological
  Schools 111
American Association of University
  Professors 81, 219
American Baptist Convention, 21,
  145, 194, 252-253
  Department of Schools and Colleges
    252-253
  see also Baptist institutions
American Lutheran Church 21, 47,
  257-258
  Board of College Education 257-258
  see also Lutheran institutions
American University 97, 231
Amherst College
  studies of graduates 104, 106, 109,
    116, 117
Anderson College 231
  studies of graduates 112

Andrews University 217, 231
  studies of graduates 106
Anglicans see Episcopalians
Antioch College
  studies of graduates 103, 118, 122
Aquinas College 47, 231
Arkansas, University of
  studies of graduates 119
Arnold, Thomas 7
Asbury College
  studies of graduates 111, 112, 113, 122
Assemblies of God 16, 24
  see also "newer groups," institutions of
Associate Reformed Presbyterian
  Church 24, 272
  see also Presbyterian institutions
Associated Christian Colleges of
  Oregon 190
Associated Colleges of the Midwest 208
Associated Mid-Florida Colleges 208
Association of American Colleges 108,
  206, 273-274
Association of American Universities 98
Astin, Alexander W. 95, 122
Atlantic Union College 231
  studies of graduates 105
Augustana College (Illinois) 231
  studies of graduates 104, 119
Austin College 190, 217, 231
Aydelotte, Frank 64

Baptists 126, 128
  association with colonial colleges 3
  establishment of institutions by 15
  religious knowledge of students 147
Baptist institutions 3, 15, 16, 21
  description of 24-26
  faculty evaluations of 160, 161,
    165, 172, 173, 174, 175, 176
  forms of relationships 32-34, 35-37,
    39, 41, 44, 46, 48, 51
  innovation at 186
  national agencies for 252-254
Barnard College
  studies of graduates 117
Bates College 231
  studies of graduates 104, 109, 116
Baylor University 231
  graduate education at 97

ownership of 42
studies of graduates 107, 111, 114
Bean, Walton E. 4
Bellarmine College 217, 231
cooperation at 206
Beloit College 64
studies of graduates 104, 116, 119, 120
Benedictine Fathers of St. John's
Abbey 149
see also St. John's University
(Minnesota)
Berea College
studies of graduates 104
Bergendoff, Conrad 131
Bethany College (West Virginia) 231
studies of graduates 106
Bethel College (Kansas) 51, 232
studies of graduates 106
Bethel College (Minnesota) 232
studies of graduates 113
Bible colleges and institutes 16, 32n
Birmingham-Southern College 232
studies of graduates 110
board of trustees 31, 34-42, 52, 58,
77-79, 193
see also organization of institutions
Bonhoefer, Dietrich 136, 154
Boston College 232
graduate education at 97
Boston University 132n, 232
graduate education at 97-98
studies of graduates 119
Bowdoin College
studies of graduates 109, 116
Brandeis University
studies of graduates 118
Brethren Church 273
Bridgewater College 217, 232
studies of graduates 107
Bridston, Keith R. 111-114
Brigham Young University 217, 232
chapel at 149
graduate education at 98
religious program at 187-189
studies of graduates 116, 122
British collegiate tradition 2, 6, 10,
12, 13, 16, 67, 199-200
see also liberal education
Brooklyn College
studies of graduates 104, 118, 122
Brown University
charter of 3
curriculum of 8
studies of graduates 104, 115, 118

Bryn Mawr College
studies of graduates 118

California Baptist College 232
studies of graduates 113
California Institute of Technology
studies of graduates 103, 118, 122
California Lutheran College 217, 232
campus of 83
California, University of, Berkeley
research on creativity at 64, 111
studies of graduates 117
California, University of, Los Angeles
studies of graduates 118
California, University of, Riverside
studies of graduates 119
Calvin College 47, 232
studies of graduates 104, 112, 114
Cambridge University 2, 13
Capital University 232
studies of graduates 111, 113
Carleton College
studies of graduates 103, 106,
109, 115, 118
Carmichael, Oliver C. vi, 10, 61n
Carnegie Foundation for the Advancement of Teaching 54
Carroll College (Montana) 232
studies of graduates 105
Carson-Newman College 232
studies of graduates 111, 113
Cartter, Allan M. 40n, 42n, 98
case studies 76-77, 138
list of institutions 217-218
Catholic University in Dublin see
Newman, John Henry
Catholic University of America 47,
217, 233
control of 31, 38
graduate study at 98
studies of graduates 110
Central States College Association 190
Centenary College 233
studies of graduates 107
Centre College 233
studies of graduates 107
Charleston, College of
studies of graduates 105
Chase, Philander 79
Chicago, University of
faculty training at 205
founding of 9
studies of graduates 103, 107, 109, 117
survey of 55

Christian Century 125
Christian Churches *see* Disciples of Christ
Christian Reformed Church 273
Christian social thought 134-135, 213
Christianity and Crisis 125
Christianity Today 125, 197
Church financial support of institutions
 15, 31, 34, 35, 43-47, 52, 207, 222
Church of Christ, Scientist 18, 50
 see also Principia College
Church of God 16, 24, 272
 see also "newer groups," institutions of
Church of God in Christ 24
 see also "newer groups," institutions of
Church of Jesus Christ of Latter-day
 Saints 18, 82, 134, 272
 see also Brigham Young University
Church of the Brethren 272
Church of the Nazarene 16, 272
Church of the United Brethren in
 Christ 272
"church-related university" model
 195-196, 214
church relationships 230-247
 board of trustees 34-42
 definition of 30-32
 denominational standards or name
  47-48
 educational aims 48-50
 faculty evaluation of 170-174
 financial support 43-47, 82
 frequency of forms of 32-34
 history of 2-4
 models 191-193, 194, 195,
  196, 213-214
 ownership 42-43
 personnel 50-51
 questionnaire on 215-216
 summary on 52-53
 terminology 18-19
 see also Westminster College (Utah)
churches in the United States
 126-128, 132-136, 138-139, 212-213
 see also names of individual religious
 bodies
Churches of Christ 16, 18, 24, 50-51
 see also "newer groups," institutions of
Churches of God in North America 24
 see also "newer groups," institutions of
Clark University
 founding of 9
 studies of graduates 109
class size 95, 204, 220
Cobb, John B., Jr. 135-136

Coe College 233
 studies of graduates 104
coeducational colleges 21-22, 25-26, 108
Colgate University
 studies of graduates 115, 119
College of Jewish Studies 19-20, 248
College of the Holy Cross 217, 234
 studies of graduates 106
College of the Pacific *see* University of
 the Pacific
Colonial colleges 2-4
Colorado College
 studies of graduates 110
Colorado State College of Education
 studies of graduates 110
Colorado, University of
 studies of graduates 115, 118
Columbia Union College 234
 studies of graduates 106
Columbia University
 development into university 9
 founding of 3
 studies of graduates 104, 107,
  109, 116, 117
Colwell, Ernest C. vi
Commager, Henry Steele 5-6
Commission on Higher Education *see*
 National Council of Churches
Commonweal 125
Community of Daughters of Charity of
 St. Vincent de Paul *see* Marillac
 College
community, sense of 163-166, 175, 183
Conant, James 94
Concordia College (Moorhead, Minn.)
 234
 studies of graduates 112
Concordia Senior College 234
 chapel of 149-150
 financial support of 45
 structural distinctiveness of 179-180
 studies of graduates 111, 113
Congregation of the Holy Cross 42, 269
 see also Notre Dame, University of;
 St. Mary's College (Indiana)
Congregationalists
 association with colonial colleges 3
 see also United Church of Christ
Conover, C. Eugene 142
Conrad Grebel College 181
 see also Waterloo, University of
Cooke, Bernard A., S.J. 142
cooperation among institutions and
 religious groups 178-179, 180-182,
 190, 208

see also ecumenical movement;
    organization of institutions
Cooper Union
    studies of graduates 104
co-ordinate colleges 21-22, 25
Cornell College 234
    studies of graduates 103, 109
Cornell University
    founding of 8-9
    studies of graduates 117
Corpus Christi, University of 246
    studies of graduates 113
Council of Protestant Colleges and
    Universities 207, 274-275
creativity, student 64-65
Creighton University 234
    studies of graduates 105
criteria for appraising colleges 57-69
Culver, Dwight W. 111-114
Culver-Stockton College 190, 217, 234
Cumberland Presbyterian Church 24, 273
    see also Presbyterian institutions
Cuninggim, Merrimon vi, vii

Dallas, University of 217, 246
    cooperation at 206
Danforth Commission on Church
    Colleges and Universities vi
Danforth Foundation v, vi, x, xi, xii,
    114, 155
Danforth Graduate Fellowships 114-116,
    155-156
Dartmouth College
    case 5
    founding of 3
    studies of graduates 104, 107,
        110, 116, 118, 122
Davidson College 234
    studies of graduates 106, 110,
        112, 115, 118, 120
Dawson, Christopher 1n, 152, 184
"defender of the faith college" model
    192-193, 214
degrees conferred 23-24, 25, 26
    comparison with other sectors 27
    see also doctor's degree
Denison University 234
    studies of graduates 107, 110, 115, 119
Denver, University of 234
    graduate education at 98
DePauw University 234
    studies of graduates 104, 107,
        110, 115, 119
development program 203, 223, 229
Dewey, John 94

Dickinson College 234
    studies of graduates 107
Disciples of Christ (Christian Churches)
    21, 55, 145, 194, 254-255
    Board of Higher Education 249-250,
        254-255
Disciples institutions 194
    faculty evaluation of 157, 161, 166
Diestler, Theodore A. vi
diversity in church-sponsored higher
    education 18-26, 53, 191-197,
        213-214
    broad categories 24-26
    program 23-24, 25, 59-60
    size 21
    student body 21-22, 25-26
doctor's degree
    as measure of faculty competence
        60-61, 85-86, 206
    history of 9-11
    in theology at Marquette 190
    undergraduate background of holders
        of 102-105, 108, 122
    see also graduate education; graduate
        schools in church-sponsored
        universities
Dominican Education Association 267-268
    see also Rosary College
Douglass College
    studies of graduates 119
Drake University 234
    studies of graduates 116
Dressel, Paul 12, 71n, 142
Duke University 235
    graduate study at 98
    studies of graduates 106, 112,
        115, 116, 118, 120
    teaching apprenticeships at 205

Earlham College 235
    improvement of teaching at 186-187
    interdenominational fellowship at 187
    studies of graduates 110, 116
East Texas Baptist College 217, 235
    studies of graduates 113
Eastern Baptist College 235
    studies of graduates 113
Eastern Mennonite College 47, 235
ecumenical movement 127
efficiency of operation 203-204
Elmhurst College 235
    studies of graduates 112, 113
Emmanuel Missionary College *see*
    Andrews University

Emory and Henry College 235
  studies of graduates 107
Emory University 235
  graduate education at 98
  studies of graduates 105, 116, 118, 120
  teaching apprenticeships at 205
enrollments 16
  comparison with other sectors 26-27
  in case-study institutions 91
  in church-related universities 195
  in church-sponsored institutions
    21, 198
Episcopal Church 21, 42, 47-48, 127,
    128, 129, 133, 139, 145, 179,
    255-256
  American Church Institute 255-256
  Association of Episcopal Colleges
    47, 256
  see also Episcopal institutions; Shimer
    College; Trinity College (Connecti-
    cut); University of the South
Episcopal institutions 21, 47-48, 145
  faculty evaluation of 157, 168, 172
  innovation at 180, 185, 208
Episcopalians
  association with colonial colleges 3
  establishment of institutions by 15
  see also William and Mary
  religious knowledge of students 147
establishment of institutions 1-5, 8-9,
    15-16, 22, 206-207
evaluation of institutions 54-57
  antecedents of quality 58, 77-84
  curricular design 65, 92-94, 210-211
  distinctive role 59-60, 84-85, 201
  effect of program on students 69,
    99-100
  faculty selection and retention 54-55,
    60-63, 85-88
  intellectual ferment 65-68, 94-99
  purpose, seriousness of 58-59, 84
  self-criticism 68-69, 99, 189
  student selection 63-65, 88-92
Evangelical Lutheran Synod 273
  see also Lutheran institutions
Evangelical Presbyterian Church 24
  see also Presbyterian institutions
Evangelical United Brethren Church 272
Evansville College 235
  trustees of 40
expenditures for plant 83
experimentation see innovation and
  experimentation

faculty-student relationships 27, 66-67,
    73, 74-75, 95-96, 100, 156-158, 209
faculties
  evaluation of church-sponsored higher
    education by 155-176
  inbreeding of 110
  number of members of 27
  Roman Catholic colleges, in 80
  salaries of 81-82
  selection and retention of 85-88
  training 100, 205-206
  undergraduate backgrounds of 108-110
  see also graduate education
Fairfield University 235
  studies of graduates 106
Farmer, Paul 13
fellowship holders, undergraduate
  backgrounds of 114-120
financial aid to students 28-29
Fisk University 217, 235
  studies of graduates 106
Flexner, Abraham 94
Florida Christian College 235
  personnel selection at 50
Florida Presbyterian College
  campus of 83
  innovation at 183-184
Florida, University of
  studies of graduates 118
Ford Foundation 203
Fordham University 235
  graduate education at 98
  studies of graduates 118, 120
Fortune 125
Franklin and Marshall College 235
  studies of graduates 106
"free Christian (or free Jewish) college"
  model 194-195
Free Methodist Church of North
  America 272
  see also Methodist institutions
freedom 60, 70
  Christian view of 67-68
  experiment, to 200
  faculty evaluation of 167-170
  models 192, 193, 194, 195
  reconciliation of, with responsibility
    and institutional purpose 73-75, 88,
    204-205
  record of church institutions 96
Freeman, Thomas 144
Friends institutions
  faculty evaluation of 162, 164,
    167, 169-170, 172
  innovation at 186-187, 190

Fund for the Advancement of
    Education 103, 203
Furman University 217, 235
    campus of 83
    studies of graduates 111, 113

geographical distribution of church-
    sponsored institutions 22-23
George Peabody College for Teachers
    studies of graduates 109
Georgetown College 236
    studies of graduates 112
Georgetown University 236
    control of 38
    founding of 4
    graduate education at 98
    studies of graduates 116, 119
Georgia, University of
    studies of graduates 119
German university influence 9-10,
    13-14, 16, 199
Gettysburg College 236
    studies of graduates 112
Gilkey, Langdon 124n, 128n, 136
Godard, James M. vi, 275
Gonzaga University 236
    studies of graduates 110
Gordon College 248
    studies of graduates 113
Goshen College 190, 236
Goucher College
    studies of graduates 109, 119
governmental relationships 1, 3-4, 5, 207
graduate education 9-11, 12-14,
    97-99, 205-206
    see also faculties
graduate schools of church-related
    universities 97-99
graduates, record of 68, 96-97, 102-123
Grand Canyon College 236
    studies of graduates 113
Great Lakes College Association 208
Greek Orthodox Church 22
Greenbaum, Joseph J. 102-104
Greenville College 236
    studies of graduates 109
Grinnell College 236
    studies of graduates 103, 109,
    116, 119, 120
Gustafson, James M. 124n, 129n,
    131n, 135

Hallowell, John H. 14

Hamilton College
    studies of graduates 104, 106,
    109, 116, 122
Hamline University 217, 236
    studies of graduates 116
Hampden-Sydney College 236
    studies of graduates 105
Hancher, Virgil M. vi
Hanover College 236
    church relationship of 47
Hardin-Simmons University 236
    studies of graduates 111, 113
Harvard University
    development into university 9
    founding of 2
    report on general education 17
    studies of graduates 103, 107, 109,
    115, 117, 122
    teaching apprenticeships at 205
Haverford College 217, 236
    Arts and Service Program at 190
    studies of graduates 103, 106,
    109, 115, 118, 120
Hawaii, University of
    studies of graduates 118
Hebrew Union College, Jewish Institute
    of Religion 47, 236
Hendrix College 236
    studies of graduates 106
Henrico, Virginia 1, 2
Hocking, William E. 14-15
Hofstadter, Richard 5, 9n, 72n, 131n
Hope College 236
    studies of graduates 104, 106, 110
Howard College 237
    studies of graduates 111, 113
Howard Payne College 237
    studies of graduates 112, 113
Howard University
    studies of graduates 106
human virtues 72
humanities 146, 210
Hunter College
    studies of graduates 118
Hutchins, Robert Maynard 94

Illinois Wesleyan University 47, 237
    studies of graduates 110
Illinois, University of
    studies of graduates 118
income of institutions 28, 58,
    80-83, 203
Idaho, College of 233
    studies of graduates 107

indebtedness of church-sponsored institutions 82-83
Indiana University
studies of graduates 107, 118
indoctrination 73
innovation and experimentation 191, 198
curricular 182-186, 190
evaluative 189
faculty training 205-206
instructional 186-187
organizational 178-182, 190
recommendation on 200-202
religious 187-189, 190
residential life 67
Inter American University
studies of graduates 106
institutional character see models
intellectual virtues 72
Iowa, University of
studies of graduates 110, 118

Jesuit Educational Association 268-269
see also Society of Jesus
Jewish institutions v, 18, 22, 30, 47, 194-195, 198, 214
see also College of Jewish Studies; Yeshiva University
John Carroll University 237
studies of graduates 107
Johns Hopkins University
founding of 9
studies of graduates 103, 106, 109, 118
Johnson Bible College
studies of graduates 113
Juniata College 237
studies of graduates 104
junior colleges 24, 25, 26

Kalamazoo College 217, 237
innovation at 186
studies of graduates 104, 116, 119
Kansas State Teachers College, Emporia
studies of graduates 110
Kansas, University of
studies of graduates 115, 117
Kelly, Frederick J. 55
Kentucky, University of
studies of graduates 119
Kenyon College 237
song quoted 79
studies of graduates 103, 107, 118, 120
Kerr, Clark 78-79
King College 237
studies of graduates 113

King's College see Columbia University
Klapper, Paul 11-12
Klein, Arthur J. 55
Knapp, Robert H. 102-104
Knox College
studies of graduates 103, 109, 119

Lafayette College 237
studies of graduates 119
land-grant colleges 8-9, 10, 22
LaSierra College 237
studies of graduates 105
Lawrence University 238
studies of graduates 109, 119
lay renewal in the church 134, 187
leadership
churches, of 212-213
colleges, of 58, 77-80, 158-163, 202-203
liberal education
design of 65, 92
history of 1-2, 5-9, 11
innovation in 182-186
recommendations on 210-212
relationship to sense of community 163
weaknesses in 11-13, 16-17, 92-94
see also British collegiate tradition
libraries 28, 55, 83, 96, 162
Lichtenberger, Arthur C. vi
Lilge, Frederic 14
Lilly Endowment 111, 219
Lincoln Memorial University
studies of graduates 107
Lincoln University (Pennsylvania)
studies of graduates 106
liturgical revival 133-134
Livingston, Sir Richard 73
Look 125
Loras College 238
studies of graduates 107
Louisiana College 238
studies of graduates 112
Louisiana State University
studies of graduates 118
Louisville, University of
studies of graduates 106
Lowell, A. Lawrence 94
Lowry, Howard F. vi, 8n
Loyola University (Illinois) 238
graduate education at 98
studies of graduates 107
Loyola University of Los Angeles 47, 238
Loyola University (Louisiana) 238
studies of graduates 106
Luther College 47, 238

studies of graduates 112, 116
Lutheran Church in America 21,
    131, 258
    Board of College Education and
        Church Vocation 258
    see also Lutheran institutions
Lutheran Church-Missouri Synod 21,
    45, 82, 251, 258-259
    Board for Higher Education 249, 259
    see also Lutheran institutions
Lutheran churches 128, 129, 133,
    139, 145, 147, 256
Lutheran institutions 15, 145
    description of 21, 24-26
    faculty evaluation of 157, 164,
        167, 173-174
    forms of relationships 32-37, 39-47, 51
    innovation at 179-180
    national agencies for 257-260
Lutherans
    association with colonial colleges 3
    establishment of institutions by 15

major fields selected by students 94
Manchester College 238
    studies of graduates 107
Mannheim, Karl 127
Manuel, William A. 105-108
Marillac College 178, 206, 238
Marquette University 217, 239
    graduate education at 98
    theology program at 142, 190
Massachusetts Institute of Technology
    studies of graduates 103, 116, 118
McGrath, Earl J. 12
Meiklejohn, Alexander 94
Memphis State University
    studies of graduates 106
Mennonites 181, 208, 272
    see also Bethel College (Kansas);
        Goshen College
men's colleges 21-22, 25
Mercer University 239
    studies of graduates 107, 111, 113, 114
Methodist Church 21, 40, 55, 97,
    126, 128, 133, 134, 145, 194,
    196, 260-262
    Division of Higher Education of
        251, 260-262
    Methodist University Senate 262
    see also Methodist institutions
Methodist institutions 15, 55,
    97, 145, 194
    description of 21, 24-26

faculty evaluation of 158, 161-162,
    165, 166, 168, 169, 170, 171, 173,
    174, 175, 176
forms of relationships 32-33, 35,
    37, 39-42, 44, 46-48, 51
innovation at 179
national agencies for 260-262
Methodists
    establishment of institutions by 15
    religious knowledge of students 147
Metzger, Walter 5
Miami, University of
    studies of graduates 119
Michigan State University 144
    studies of graduates 118
Michigan, University of 12n
    founding of 4
    development as a university 9
    studies of graduates 116, 117
    teaching apprenticeships at 205
Middle States Association of Colleges
    and Secondary Schools 23, 25
middle western colleges, productivity of
    104, 108, 112
Mill, John Stuart 7
Millsaps College 239
    studies of graduates 106, 119
ministers, undergraduate backgrounds of
    111-114
ministry 2, 129
Minnesota, University of
    research on creativity at 64
    studies of graduates 112, 116, 117
Mississippi College 240
    studies of graduates 107, 111, 113
Mississippi, University of
    studies of graduates 106
Missouri, University of
    studies of graduates 118
models, institutional 191-197, 213-214
Monmouth College 240
    studies of graduates 104
Montana State University
    studies of graduates 119
Moravian Church in America 272
Morehouse College 240
    studies of graduates 106
Morison, Samuel Eliot 2n, 5-6
Mormons see Church of Jesus Christ of
    Latter-day Saints
Morrill Act 8, 22
    see also land-grant colleges
Mount Holyoke College
    studies of graduates 110, 119

Mt. St. Mary's College (Maryland) 240
  founding of 4
  studies of graduates 107
Muhlenberg College 240
  studies of graduates 106
Mundelein College 240
  self-study 189

National Association of Biblical
  Instructors 111
National Catholic Educational Association
  206-207, 266, 267, 275-276
National Council of Churches 126n,
  127, 134, 252
  Commission on Higher Education 274
National Federation of Catholic College
  Students 151, 153
National Lutheran Educational
  Conference 256, 260
Nebraska, University of
  studies of graduates 119
Negro colleges 162, 205
New England Association of Colleges
  and Secondary Schools 23, 25
New York, City College of
  studies of graduates 118, 122
New York University
  studies of graduates 118
New Yorker, The 125
"newer groups," institutions of 24
  description of institutions 25-26
  forms of relationships 32-33, 35,
  37, 39, 41, 43, 44, 46, 51
Newman, John Henry 6-7
Newsweek 125
"non-affirming college" model
  193-194, 214
North Carolina, University of
  studies of graduates 117
North Carolina, University of, College
  for Women
  studies of graduates 119
North Central Association of Colleges
  and Secondary Schools 23, 25, 26,
  55-56, 219
North Dakota, University of
  studies of graduates 107
Northwest Association of Secondary and
  Higher Schools 23, 25
Northwest Christian College 241
  studies of graduates 113
Northwest Ordinance of 1787 4
Northwestern University 241
  board of trustees 40
  graduate education at 98

studies of graduates 117, 120
Notre Dame of Maryland, College of 233
  founding of 5
Notre Dame, University of 246
  graduate education at 98
  ownership of 42
  studies of graduates 115, 116, 117, 120

Obenhaus, Victor 130, 142n
Oberlin College
  studies of graduates 103, 106, 109, 115,
  117, 122
Occidental College 217, 241
  studies of graduates 118, 120
Ohio State University
  studies of graduates 118
Ohio Wesleyan University 241
  studies of graduates 110, 116
Oklahoma Baptist University 47, 241
  studies of graduates 111, 113
Oklahoma State University
  studies of graduates 116
Oklahoma, University of
  studies of graduates 116, 118
Olivet Nazarene College 47, 241
Oregon, University of
  studies of graduates 119
organization of institutions 179-180, 191-
  197, 202-203, 213-214
  see also administrative officers; boards
  of trustees
Orthodox Church 18, 126
  see also Greek Orthodox Church
Ouachita Baptist College 241
  studies of graduates 112
ownership of institutions 31, 34, 35, 42-
  43, 52
Oxford University 2, 6, 13

Pacific Lutheran University 47, 241
Pacific Union College 241
  studies of graduates 105
papal encyclicals 134-135
Parsons College 217, 241
  financial management at 190
Pennsylvania, University of
  curriculum of 8
  development into university 9
  non-denominational character of 3
  studies of graduates 104, 116, 117
Pentecostal Holiness Church 24
  see also Pentecostal sects; "newer
  groups," institutions of
Pentecostal sects 16
Pfnister, Allan O. 108-110

Phillips University 242
  studies of graduates 112
physicians, undergraduate backgrounds of
    105-108
Pittsburgh, University of
  studies of graduates 119
plant and equipment 58, 83-84
Pomona College
  studies of graduates 104, 110, 115, 117
positivism 13-15
Presbyterian Church in the U.S. 21, 22,
    24, 34, 145, 183, 262-264
  Division of Higher Education 263-264
  see also Presbyterian institutions
Presbyterian Educational Association of
    the South 263
Presbyterian institutions 15, 83, 145, 194,
    206
  description of 21, 24-26
  faculty evaluations of 158, 160, 162,
    169, 170, 174
  forms of relationships 32-37, 39, 41,
    43-44, 46-48, 51
  innovations at 179, 182-184, 190
  national agencies for 262-266
Presbyterians
  association with colonial colleges 3
  establishment of institutions by 15
  religious knowledge of students 147
  role in higher education 262
Princeton University 117
  founding of 3
  studies of graduates 103, 107, 109, 115,
    117, 122
Principia College 217, 242
  personnel of 50
private higher education 1, 3-4, 5, 16, 17,
    26-29, 200
Protestant institutions 18
  comparison of groups 32-39, 41-44, 46-
    47, 48, 51
  groupings 24-25
  quality of 97, 98, 141
  religion in 144-145, 147-148, 150, 166,
    172, 192-193
  see also institutions of various Protes-
    tant churches
public affairs 67, 97, 210
public higher education 4, 8-9, 16, 17, 22,
    26-29, 200-201
Purdue University
  studies of graduates 104
purpose, lack of in undergraduate educa-
    tion 11-12, 93-94

Pusey, Nathan M. 130

Quakers see Society of Friends
Queens College (New York)
  studies of graduates 103, 119, 122

Radcliffe College
  studies of graduates 118
Randolph-Macon College 242
  studies of graduates 106
Reader's Digest 125
Redlands, University of 246
  studies of graduates 115
Reed College
  studies of graduates 103, 106, 109, 117,
    122
Reeves, Floyd W. 55
Reformed Church in America 273
  faculty evaluation of colleges of 162-
    163
Reformed Presbyterian Church of North
    America, Synod of 24, 273
  see also Presbyterian institutions
Reinert, Paul C., S.J. vi
relationships with churches see church
    relationships
religion in higher education
  courses 140-142, 192, 194
  experimentation and innovation in 182-
    185, 201
  evaluation of, in church-sponsored insti-
    tutions 137-154, 163-166
  history of 1-4, 5-8
  problems concerning 17, 176
  recommendation on 211-212
  social concern and 151-153
  student knowledge 142-147
  student organizations 151, 187-189
  worship 147-151, 160, 172-173, 192,
    193, 194, 201
  see also faculty-student relationships
religion, literature, and the arts 135
religion, semantic problems in 125-126
religious bodies sponsoring colleges 20-21
religious education in local churches 129-
    130
religious orientation of non-church-related
    colleges 19-20, 248
Renison College 180
  see also Waterloo, University of
Reorganized Church of Jesus Christ of
    Latter Day Saints 272

responsibility and institutional purpose 70-75, 204-205

Rice Institute *see* Rice University

Rice University
studies of graduates 107, 118

Richmond, University of 246
studies of graduates 106, 112

Roanoke College 217, 242
studies of graduates 106

Rochester, University of
studies of graduates 104, 109, 118

Roman Catholic Church 21, 38, 126, 127, 128, 129, 131, 133, 134, 139, 147, 266
see also Roman Catholic institutions

Roman Catholic institutions 4-5, 15, 16, 18, 80, 82, 92, 97-98, 110, 111, 139, 147, 148-149, 151, 153, 192, 196, 198, 203, 206
description of 18, 21-24
faculty evaluations of 157, 158, 159, 163-164, 168, 169, 175-176
forms of relationships 31, 32-39, 41-48, 51, 52, 77-78, 82
innovations at 178, 180, 184-185, 189, 190, 208
national agencies for 266-270, 275, 276
religious knowledge of students at 140-142, 143, 144-146

Rosary College 217, 242
personnel of 51

Rudolph, Frederick 3-4

Russell, John Dale 55

Rutgers University
founding of 3
studies of graduates 117

St. Andrews Presbyterian College 47, 218, 242
campus of 83
Christianity and Culture Program at 182-183, 184

St. Augustine's College 47-48, 242

St. Jerome's College 180
see also Waterloo, University of

St. John's College (Maryland) 48

St. John's University (Minnesota) 218, 243
Church of 148-149, 150, 190
liturgical leadership of 133, 190

St. John's University (New York) 243
studies of graduates 119

St. Louis University 243
founding of 5
graduate education at 98
studies of graduates 118, 120

St. Mary's College (Indiana) 244
Christian Culture Program at 184-185

St. Olaf College 244
studies of graduates 110, 111, 115

St. Paul's College 180
see also Waterloo, University of

St. Thomas, College of 234
studies of graduates 107

St. Vincent College 244
studies of graduates 107

Samford University
see Howard College

Saturday Evening Post, The 125

scholars, undergraduate backgrounds of 102-105

Scranton, University of 246
studies of graduates 107

Second Vatican Council 127, 133, 139

secularity and secularism 7-9, 15, 17, 72-73, 135-136, 153-154, 193-194, 207, 213

self-surveys of institutions 57

Seventh-day Adventist institutions 21, 145, 270-271

Seventh-day Adventists, General Conference of 21, 145
Department of Education 270-271
see also Seventh-day Adventist institutions

Seventh Day Baptist General Conference 272
see also Baptist institutions

Shimer College 245
curriculum and instruction at 185

Smith College
studies of graduates 118

Smith, Huston 71-72

Society of Catholic College Teachers of Sacred Doctrine 142

Society of Friends 21, 48, 134, 145, 273
association with colonial colleges 3
see also Friends institutions; Swarthmore College

Society of Jesus 38
see also Georgetown University; Jesuit Educational Association

Sophie Newcomb College
studies of graduates 118

South Dakota, University of
studies of graduates 107

Southern Association of Colleges and Schools 23, 25, 26
Southern Baptist Convention 21, 126, 145, 253-254
  Education Commission 254
  see also Baptist institutions
Southern California, University of
  studies of graduates 119
Southern Methodist University 47, 245
  graduate education at 98
Southwestern at Memphis 245
  studies of graduates 105
Southwestern Louisiana Institute
  studies of graduates 119
Southwestern University 245
  studies of graduates 109
Spengler, Oswald 14
Springfield College
  studies of graduates 110
Spring Hill College 245
  studies of graduates 107
Stanford University
  founding of 9
  studies of graduates 107, 116, 117
state universities 4, 168-169
Stetson University 245
  studies of graduates 116
student life 58-59, 67, 84, 227-228
students in church-sponsored institutions 21-22, 25-26, 88-92, 212
Swarthmore College 245
  educational aims of 49
  history of 64
  studies of graduates 103, 106, 109, 116, 117, 120, 122
Syracuse University 245
  graduate education at 98

Talladega College 245
  studies of graduates 106
Tarkio College 245
  Academy of Christian Thought and Service 190
teaching, improvement of 186-187, 208-209
Temple, William 67-68
Texas Agricultural and Mechanical University
  studies of graduates 116
Texas Christian University 218, 245
  graduate education at 98
  studies of graduates 112, 116
Texas, University of
  studies of graduates 117

theological schools 18, 19, 32n, 111-114, 130-132
Time 125
Toronto, University of 190, 208
Transylvania College 246
  studies of graduates 109
Trinity College (Connecticut) 246
  church relationship of 47
  studies of graduates 104, 119
Tufts University
  studies of graduates 106
Tulane University
  studies of graduates 106, 119
Union University (Tennessee) 246
  studies of graduates 113
United Church of Christ 21, 134, 145, 194, 271
  Division of Higher Education 271-272
United Church of Christ institutions 194, 271-272
  Council for Higher Education 271-272
  faculty evaluation of 162, 173
  innovation at 179
United Presbyterian Church in the U.S.A. 21, 24, 47, 148, 179, 183, 194, 206
  Board of National Missions 264
  General Division of Higher Education of 264-266
  see also Hanover College; Presbyterian institutions
United States Office of Education 19n, 27n, 28n, 29n, 54, 249n
University of the Pacific 246
  studies of graduates 109
University of the South 246
  ownership of 42
  studies of graduates 103, 107, 116, 119, 120
Union College (Nebraska) 246
  studies of graduates 106
Union College (New York)
  studies of graduates 107
Upton, Miller 64
Ursinus College 246
  studies of graduates 106
Utah, University of
  studies of graduates 116, 119, 122

Valparaiso University 246
  campus of 83
  studies of graduates 116, 119
values 57, 69, 72-75, 99-100, 211-212
Van Buren, Paul M. 136

Vanderbilt University
  studies of graduates 106, 118
Vassar College
  studies of graduates 119
Vermont, University of
  studies of graduates 107
Virginia Military Institute
  studies of graduates 106
Virginia, University of
  studies of graduates 106, 118
  teaching apprenticeships at 205

Wabash College
  studies of graduates 104, 107, 116, 119, 122
Wake Forest College see Wake Forest University
Wake Forest University 247
  medical school of 99
  studies of graduates 106, 111
Walla Walla College 247
  studies of graduates 105
Wartburg College 247
  studies of graduates 112, 113
Washington and Jefferson College
  studies of graduates 106
Washington and Lee University
  founding of 3
  studies of graduates 107, 119
Washington Missionary College see Columbia Union College
Washington, University of
  studies of graduates 117
Washington University (St. Louis)
  studies of graduates 117
  teaching apprenticeships at 205
Waterloo, University of 180-182, 208
Wayland Baptist College 247
  studies of graduates 113
Wayne State University
  studies of graduates 119
Wellesley College 20, 248
  studies of graduates 118
Wesleyan Methodist Church of America 272
  see also Methodist institutions

Wesleyan University 48, 102, 103n
  studies of graduates 103, 106, 109, 116, 118, 122
Western Association of Schools and Colleges 23, 25
Westminster College (Missouri) 247
  studies of graduates 106
Westminster College (Utah) 218, 247
  interdenominational sponsorship of 179, 206
Wheaton College 218, 248
  purpose of 19
  studies of graduates 107, 111, 112, 114
Willamette University 247
  studies of graduates 107
William and Mary, College of
  founding and charter of 2, 3
  studies of graduates 104, 118
William Penn College 48, 247
Williams, Robin 133
Williams College
  studies of graduates 104, 107, 109, 115, 118, 122
Wilson, Woodrow 94
Wisconsin, University of
  development into university 9
  studies of graduates 104, 117
women's colleges 21-22, 25
Woodrow Wilson National Fellowship Foundation
  fellowships of 117-120
  internship program of 20
Woodstock College
  studies of graduates 109
Wooster, College of 234
  studies of graduates 104, 107, 109, 115, 116
Works, George A. 55

Yale University
  founding of 3
  studies of graduates 103, 110, 115, 117
  teaching apprenticeships at 205
Yeshiva University 218, 247
  graduate education at 98
  purpose of 48-49
  studies of graduates 122